TO THE FLAG

Richard J. Ellis

TO THE
FLAG

The Unlikely History
of the Pledge of Allegiance

University Press of Kansas

© 2005 by the University Press of Kansas

All rights reserved

Published by the University Press of Kansas (Lawrence, Kansas 66049),
which was organized by the Kansas Board of Regents and is operated
and funded by Emporia State University, Fort Hays State University,
Kansas State University, Pittsburg State University, the University of
Kansas, and Wichita State University

Library of Congress Cataloging-in-Publication Data

Ellis, Richard (Richard J.)
   To the flag : the unlikely history of the Pledge of Allegiance /
Richard J. Ellis.
      p.   cm.
   Includes bibliographical references and index.
   ISBN 0-7006-1372-2 (cloth : alk. paper)
   1. Bellamy, Francis. Pledge of Allegiance to the Flag—History.
2. Allegiance—United States—History.   3. Patriotism—United States—
History.   4. United States—Social conditions.   I. Title.

JK1759.E37 2004
323.6′5′0973—dc22   2004023110

British Library Cataloguing in Publication Data is available.

10 9 8 7 6 5 4 3 2 1

The paper used in this publication meets the minimum requirements
of the American National Standard for Permanence of Paper for
Printed Library Materials Z39.48-1984.

In memory of

MICHAEL P. ROGIN

Contents

Preface   ix

Acknowledgments   xv

1. Creating the Pledge   1

2. The Meaning of the Pledge   24

3. Spreading the Pledge   50

4. Making the Pledge Safe for Democracy   81

5. A Nation under God   121

6. Protesting the Pledge   153

7. One Nation . . . Indivisible?   174

Conclusion: Pledging Allegiance in a Liberal Society   209

Notes   223

Index   281

Preface

Most decisions made by federal courts of appeals barely get noticed by the media or the general public. The justices are largely anonymous—they never stand for election and their names are rarely mentioned in news stories. Until June 26, 2002, that had been the case with the distinguished career of the seventy-eight-year-old justice Alfred Goodwin. Friends knew him as "Tex," and Oregon political junkies and insiders knew him as a former state supreme court justice, appointed in 1960 by Governor Mark Hatfield. Elevated by President Richard Nixon to the Ninth Circuit Court of Appeals in 1971, the Republican Goodwin had served as a federal judge for over three decades, including a period as the circuit's chief judge. During all this time he had never made headlines. But on the morning of June 26 Goodwin announced a decision that stunned the nation. The "under God" clause of the Pledge of Allegiance, said every morning by schoolchildren across the country, was unconstitutional because it violated the separation of church and state.[1]

The public reaction was swift and overwhelmingly negative, particularly in the nation's capitol. When news of the ruling reached the U.S. Senate, debate on a defense authorization bill was promptly halted so that the senators could draw up a resolution condemning the decision. The resolution was passed unanimously—indeed every senator was listed as a cosponsor—though few if any could have had time to read Goodwin's opinion. In the House of Representatives all but three members approved a resolution drawn up the following day that declared: "The Pledge of Allegiance, including the phrase 'One Nation, under God,' reflects the historical fact that a belief in God permeated the Founding and development of our Nation." Senate majority leader Tom Daschle, who derided the ruling as "just nuts," requested that each of his colleagues be on hand the morning of the 27th so that the entire body could recite the Pledge in a public show of bipartisan protest against the decision. The House did the same, though many members were not content to wait until the following morning to demonstrate their patriotism and so gathered on the steps of the Capitol the evening of the 26th to recite the Pledge in front of a gaggle of television cameras.[2]

The House member who led the recitation of the Pledge on the Capitol steps was Pennsylvania Republican Joe Pitts. The ruling "by these loony, left-type guys," Pitts declared, had made a "mockery of the U.S. Constitution." The decision represented "a Stalinist purge of all that is not ideologically correct"—and if not overturned "the Constitution is gone and we are now being governed only by unelected despots in robes." Pitts's apocalyptic rhetoric may have been extreme, but the outrage coupled with disbelief was widespread. The dean of the Senate, Democrat Robert Byrd, who had been a member of the House when the "under God" clause was added to the Pledge in 1954, spluttered with indignation on the floor of the Senate chamber, deriding Goodwin as a "stupid judge" and an "atheist lawyer" and promising to "blackball" him. "I, for one," Byrd continued, "am not going to stand for this country's being ruled by a bunch of atheists. If they do not like it, let them leave." Senator Byron Dorgan, a Democrat from North Dakota, said that the judges responsible "need their collective heads examined." Republican senator Charles Grassley of Illinois agreed the decision was "crazy," and a Republican congressman from Peoria, Illinois, Ray LaHood, thought Goodwin "must have landed here from another planet." There was hardly a senator or House member in Washington who didn't rush to issue a press release to record his or her outrage at a decision characterized as either ridiculous or dangerous or both.[3]

But it wasn't only the politicians who rushed to condemn the decision. The public, too, was clearly roiled by the ruling. Michael Newdow, the man who initiated the lawsuit challenging the "under God" clause, received numerous death threats and was offered police protection. On his answering machine were scores of abusive messages calling him everything from un-American to a "freakin' commie bastard." Pollsters gauged the national mood and found that nine in ten Americans supported keeping "under God" in the Pledge. Irate letters to the editor poured into newspapers across the nation. In my local paper, roughly half the letters appearing in the paper in the weeks after the decision were reactions to the Pledge ruling. Some were supportive, but most were bitterly angry at what the writers perceived as an assault on America—like the man who saw "red" at this flagrant insult to the "thousands of young men and women who have been disabled or died to protect our Constitution" or the woman who believed the judges "should be dismissed" for violating the nation's beliefs. As for Newdow, he was "truly not an American at heart."[4]

Amid the expressions of outrage was a devout concern that the decision, in the words of President George W. Bush, was "out of step with the traditions and history of America." For the president, the decision underscored the need to appoint "common-sense judges who understand that our rights were derived from God." Attorney General John Ashcroft made the same point, insisting that "the decision is directly contrary to two centuries of American tradition." Timothy Johnson, a Democratic representative from Illinois, agreed that the ruling "goes against everything that this great country was founded upon and continues to be based upon today." Republican senator Kit Bond of Missouri was confident that "our Founding Fathers must be spinning in their graves" at this "political correctness gone amok." "Despite the ruling," declared Congressman Jerry Moran of Kansas, "we have always been 'one nation, under God.'"[5]

Over and over, members of Congress spoke of the Pledge as if it were an immutable part of an unchanging tradition that dated back to the nation's founding. In the congressional telling, there was no breach between yesterday and today; past and present were seamlessly woven together by an unbroken history and timeless traditions. Moreover, those traditions were remembered only as noble and heroic—soldiers dying selflessly for love of country, proud pioneers settling an uncharted wilderness, and great visionaries articulating immortal words. In short, the Pledge was pried loose from the disjunctions, ambiguities, and ironies that characterize real history and placed instead in the realm of ahistorical myth.

The true history of the Pledge of Allegiance is far more interesting and complex than the version peddled by our politicians. It is also darker and more unsettling. To encounter the history of the Pledge is to confront American history, warts and all. The words of the Pledge have inspired millions, but they have also been used to coerce and intimidate, to compel conformity, and to silence dissent. Their daily recitation in schools and legislatures across the nation tells us as much about our anxieties as a nation as they do about our highest ideals.

In this book, I argue that five anxieties loom particularly large in the creation, propagation, and amending of the Pledge of Allegiance. First, and most important, is the anxiety about immigrants. America, it is often said, is a nation of immigrants. And so it is. We rightly celebrate that fact. But celebration exists side-by-side with fear and sometimes loathing. That people from across the globe choose to come to the United States stokes feelings of national greatness and even superiority, but that same mass migration also fuels fears about the nation's future and identity. While acknowledging that past immigrants have strengthened the nation, Americans have often worried that the newest immigrants will undermine the American experiment. The story of the origins of the Pledge of Allegiance, as we will see in the opening chapters, is closely tied to the native-born American fear of new immigrants: fear of their strange customs and traditions, fear of their race and ethnicity, fear of their divided loyalties, and fear of their religion. To adapt a formula from Louis Hartz, no immigration, no Pledge of Allegiance.[6]

Second is an anxiety about materialism. Hartz famously argued that because the United States lacked feudalism and socialism, bourgeois capitalism developed virtually unchallenged. Although not without elements of truth, Hartz's observation obscures the tremendous anxieties about materialism that have periodically arisen alongside the culture of competitive capitalism. Those anxieties have roots in at least two traditions: the first a republican concern with maintaining public virtue amid growing luxury and corruption, and the second a Protestant preoccupation with serving God and resisting the demon sway of Mammon. Neither republicanism nor religion figure in Hartz's narrative, but the latter omission is arguably the more serious one for the history of the Pledge of Allegiance, steeped as it is in religion. Religious belief in the United States has only infrequently delivered a frontal assault on capitalism, but it has regularly produced jeremiads warning of the dire consequences of excessive individualism and self-seeking—Josiah Strong's *Our Country* is the classic nineteenth-century statement of this perspective. A society of individuals devoted to the pursuit of money and the acquisition of things risks neglecting not only its neighbors but also its nation. Or so the two devoutly religious men most responsible for the creation of the Pledge believed.

Third, and closely related, is what might be called, to borrow a phrase from Uday Singh Mehta, "the anxiety of freedom."[7] If the anxiety of materialism entails misgivings about the effects of capitalism, the anxiety of freedom is an apprehension directed at the deleterious effects of unrestricted individual liberties. Both anxieties share a common concern that liberalism is incapable of summoning the self-sacrifice necessary to sustain a nation under threat. Warren Barry, a Virginia state legislator and former Marine officer who sponsored a mandatory Pledge law in 2001, expressed the worry this way: "We cannot afford the luxury of being a nation of individuals divided by personal liberties, but we must be united under one flag and purpose." For Barry, the model was the Marine Corps, where success was due to "unity and dedication to responsible actions." "If the Marines were comprised of individuality, all self-serving," Barry explained, "it would have been destroyed years ago and this country along with it."[8]

The military's hierarchical culture and its ideal of heroic self-sacrifice have played a central role in the history of the Pledge, from its inception down through the present day. The Pledge of Allegiance was originally accompanied by a military-style hand salute, a practice that lasted in many places into the early 1940s. And the words of the Pledge itself ("one nation, indivisible") cast a self-conscious and wistful eye back to the heroic sacrifices of the Civil War. Moreover, war veterans were perhaps the primary political force behind the spread of the Pledge of Allegiance. The Grand Army of the Republic spearheaded the flag over the schoolhouse movement out of which the Pledge emerged, and in the twentieth century the American Legion and the Veterans of Foreign Wars led efforts to require that states mandate the Pledge of Allegiance in schools.

Fourth is an anxiety about radicals, an anxiety not fully separable from the anxiety about immigrants since aliens were very often feared precisely because they were perceived to be radicals. Radicalism, whether in the form of Bolshevism, socialism, or anarchism, was an un-American virus immigrants brought with them from their native countries. Or, if aliens were not yet radicals, they were peculiarly prone to the radical's subversive appeal since they did not yet appreciate the genius of American institutions. Fears of radicalism and labor unrest helped shape the creation of the Pledge but were even more instrumental in contributing to the spread of the Pledge in the first several decades of the twentieth century, as chapter three documents. Fear of aliens and radicals, coupled with the anxiety that neither America's political freedoms nor its economic successes were sufficient to gain the loyalty of newcomers, fueled an aggressive "Americanization" campaign, in which the Pledge of Allegiance played an increasingly important part.

Fifth is an anxiety about Communism. Although perhaps more properly subsumed under the anxiety about radicals, it deserves special mention because it played such a direct role in the 1954 decision to amend the Pledge of Allegiance by adding the words "under God." Fear of Communism in the 1950s was different from the early-twentieth-century anxiety about European "isms" in that radical subversion was no longer linked to immigration. The problem of radicalism instead became defined as a problem of foreign powers and native-born, privileged Americans. Anti-radicalism in the early twentieth century involved native-born Protestants demonizing newcomers, generally Catholics and Jews. But anti-Communism in the late 1940s and 1950s enabled the demonized—particularly Catholics—to become the demonizers. Un-American activities were still the problem, but old-style Americanization was no longer the easy answer. The old declarations of loyalty to a republic and the teaching of citizenship were no longer sufficient. The Pledge needed to be changed to reflect what truly set the United States apart from atheistic Communists: belief in God. To those who worried that Communism would convert or conquer the world, it was reassuring to know that God was on our side and that He guaranteed the eventual triumph of liberal democracy and free market capitalism.

In emphasizing the anxieties that lurk behind the Pledge of Allegiance, my aim is not to replace an ahistorical hagiography with a historical hatchet job. Rather, I have tried to draw attention to the paradoxes of the Pledge of Allegiance and to focus on aspects of the story that are either not well known or are insufficiently emphasized in most discussions of the Pledge of Allegiance. My hope is that this book will enable the reader to see the Pledge with new eyes, through which the Pledge will seem both more familiar and more strange— more familiar in that a reader of this history will hopefully become more aware of the origins and functions of the Pledge, more strange in that I hope to prompt the reader to reflect on the paradox of this most individualistic of nations requiring children to declare daily their allegiance to the state. But most of all, I have tried to tell the history of the Pledge of Allegiance, from its inception in 1892 through the Supreme Court's 2004 verdict in *Elk Grove Unified School District v. Michael A. Newdow,* as accurately and completely as I could. It is a fascinating American story, worth telling for its own sake as well as for what it reveals about our nation's politics and culture.

Acknowledgments

As a first-year graduate student at the University of California, Berkeley, in 1983, I took a seminar on countersubversion in America. I remember having little idea what that term meant when I enrolled in the course. The reading in the class was certainly not the sort of thing one customarily expects from a graduate course in American political science. How many political scientists assign Josiah Strong's *Our Country*? More than a few, I suspect, have never heard of the book let alone read it, though it was perhaps the most influential tract of its time. But Michael Rogin was no ordinary political scientist—indeed when I entered his class he had long since ceased to identify himself as a political scientist. He was also no ordinary teacher. Mike Rogin was, by quite some distance, the best discussion leader I have ever witnessed. His ability to knit together seemingly disparate student comments was uncanny, his lightning-quick mind enabling him to see and make connections between ideas that the rest of us could only marvel at. In retrospect, however, I realize that his success as a teacher was due not only to a quick and creative mind but also to his intense concentration on, and respect for, what students were saying. His energetic, rapid-fire speaking caught the attention of many, but his skills as an empathetic listener were at least as important in making him the brilliant teacher he was.

Mike Rogin died, quite suddenly, in November 2001, at the age of 64. The news of his death came as a shock to me. I found my thoughts going back to that class on American political demonology almost two decades before, trying to conjure up images of the man and his inimitable style. I dug up and reread the creditable paper I had written for the course comparing anti-Catholic demonology of the nineteenth century with anti-Communist demonology of the twentieth century. I pulled off my shelf the 1987 book *Ronald Reagan: The Movie, and Other Episodes in Political Demonology*, which Rogin had been working on at the time I took his seminar. I was pleased to discover that Mike had actually cited my seminar paper in a footnote in one of the book's essays, "Political Repression in the United States." Reading through that essay and others in the book, especially "American Political Demonology: A Retrospective," memories of the course and the readings came flooding back. I also realized that as much as Rogin the teacher had made an impression on me, the readings, arguments, and themes of that course had figured hardly at all in the work I had done in the intervening years. I had never followed up on Rogin's suggestion to try to publish my paper, "Catholicism, Communism, and the Protestant Mind." There were, I suppose, faint echoes of Rogin's class in my 1997 book, *The Dark Side of the Left*. But whereas Rogin's project had been to illuminate the demonology in the mainstream center-to-right core of American politics, the *Dark Side of the Left* had been about demonology on the radical egalitarian left. My project had been closer to Richard Hofstadter's than to Rogin's, though in truth it had been shaped most directly by the work on radical egalitarianism by my mentor Aaron Wildavsky, whose death in 1993 had been a catalyst for writing *The Dark Side of the Left*.

Roughly six months after hearing of Rogin's death came the startling news that the Ninth Circuit Court of Appeals had invalidated the "under God" clause of the Pledge of Allegiance. At the time I was finding it difficult to gain traction on a book I was trying to write on presidential character. Perhaps the subject was too familiar. Perhaps the argument was lacking. Whatever the reason, the project was floundering. I read the appeals court's opinion out of curiosity, mostly as a distraction from the real work I needed to be doing on presidents. But the opinion and, even more, the heated reactions drew me in. Why did so many people get so worked up about schoolchildren reciting a Pledge of Allegiance? Adult reactions were particularly striking since most of the kids I knew regarded the Pledge as a tiresome and meaningless bore. When and how did we get the Pledge of Allegiance? My questions were elementary ones, not surprisingly, since I knew nothing about the Pledge's history. Because I knew so little, what I found was fresh, exciting, unexpected. I also quickly found that although there were some revealing accounts of aspects of the history of the Pledge of Allegiance, nobody had written an in-depth history of it. But I was conscious that something else was drawing me to this new project as well. For my preliminary reading suggested that the Pledge offered the chance to return to some of the themes and literature I had first encountered in Mike Rogin's class, themes I had been thinking about quite a bit over the previous six months without ever connecting them to a viable research project. The Pledge of Allegiance provided me that opportunity to explore the anxieties of American national identity, particularly the anxieties about radicals and aliens that had so absorbed Rogin. The book is dedicated to Mike because, quite simply, it would not have been written without him.

Others, too, played crucial roles in the making of this book. Chief among these was my talented and industrious research assistant, Alexis Walker. I have often employed undergraduates to help with research projects, but no student ever proved more indispensable. Most important were the countless reels of microfilm she read, a task that, as any experienced researcher will tell you, is laborious, tedious, and hard on the eyes. Her mark is evident throughout the book, but her assistance was particularly crucial in the making of chapters three and four, which take the story of the Pledge of Allegiance from the 1890s through World War II. Several other Willamette University students helped out on aspects of the project, including Dustin Buehler, Amanda Conradt, and Charli Hancock.

Librarians and archivists in a number of different institutions have helped me locate relevant materials. Mary Huth of the University of Rochester library aided me tremendously with Francis Bellamy's papers, which were a vital resource in the writing of chapters one and two. Joel Thiele of the Malden Public Library sent me articles from the *Malden Evening News* that proved to be key pieces of the puzzle. Whitney Smith of the Flag Research Center graciously sent me a variety of useful materials from the rich depositories of that institution. Joseph J. Hovish of the American Legion kindly mailed me the entire 323-page transcript of the 1923 National Flag Conference. Jennifer Piscatelli, researcher at the Education Commission of the States, helped me with contemporary state laws regarding the Pledge in schools. Among the others who helped me retrieve information were Maura Straussberg, data librarian at the Gallup Poll; Tom Branigar, archivist at the Eisenhower Library; Pat Hopkins, research archivist at the Washington State Archives; Mark Brown, curator of manuscripts at Brown University Library; Susan H. Brosnan, archivist at the Knights of Columbus Museum; Georgina Flannery, reference librarian at the Newton Free Library; and Paige Roberts of the Archives and Special Collections at Northeastern University. I am particularly indebted to Bill Kelm of Willamette University's Hatfield Library, who fielded hundreds of interlibrary loan requests with unfailing good cheer and competence. Ford Schmidt, head of reference services at the Hatfield Library, also helped in important ways at various stages in the research process.

I also want to thank the many legislative staff members (and some state legislators) across the nation who took the time to answer inquiries, via e-mail and phone, regarding the origins of the practice of reciting the Pledge of Allegiance in the state legislatures. My research on this topic was also helped by some preliminary inquiries carried out by Joan Barilla of the National Council of State Legislatures. Similar thanks are due to the many city administrators and city council members in Oregon who answered similar inquiries about the Pledge.

I was also helped by telephone conversations and e-mail communications with various individuals who told me what they knew about the history of the Pledge of Allegiance. John Baer helpfully answered several of my early inquiries about its history, and Paul J. Upham and Andrew Maninos helped to educate me about James Upham and Freemasonry. Al Meinhold and Deborah Lipp related to me their stories of protest against the Pledge, and Michael Dukakis took time from his busy schedule to answer an inquiry about his veto of a mandatory Pledge law in 1977. A number of colleagues at Willamette University and elsewhere went out of their way to provide me with information about flag salutes in other parts of the world, including Stas Stavrianeas, Linda Tamura, Pam Moro, and Carol Doolittle. I am also grateful to a number of scholars who responded graciously to my inquiries and took an interest in my work, including Scot Guenter, David Tyack, Fred Greenstein, Michael Birkner, Lynn Dumenil, and Tsianina Lomawaima. Conversations with Steve Green helped sharpen my understanding of the legal issues surrounding the "under God" clause, as did reading the compelling friend of the court brief he wrote for *Elk Grove Unified School District v. Michael A. Newdow.*

Acknowledging the help provided by others is one of the most pleasant chores of an academic book. Inevitably, of course, there are those who are less helpful. But authors, at book's end, are a notoriously forgiving and gracious lot. Generally, discretion or sugar-coating are the recommended ways of dealing with the less helpful encounters. But on rare occasions it is necessary to single out particularly unhelpful and strategically situated individuals who significantly obstruct research. And so at the risk of seeming ungracious and most unauthorlike, I must highlight the lack of help I received from Mr. Frank P. Di Berardino, the man to whom Margarette Miller unfortunately entrusted her papers when she died in 1984. Miller spent her life researching Bellamy and the Pledge of Allegiance, and I was understandably anxious to view relevant portions of her papers. Unfortunately, Mr. Di Berardino denied me access— Miller's papers, he explained, "have not been appropriately categorized and inventoried" and so "have not yet been made available for public review." I was especially disappointed to hear that "there is no set timetable on when that task will be completed." One can only hope the relevant portions of these papers are soon made available to scholars. One hopes that Mr. Di Berardino's reluctance to allow researchers to see Miller's papers is not related to the plagiarism evident in her 1946 book, *I Pledge Allegiance* (the interested reader can learn more about this in note 26 in chapter three).

Although Miller was not always the most careful scholar, I have benefited tremendously from the fruits of her life work on Bellamy and the Pledge. Similarly, while Louise Harris's work has massive problems if judged as serious scholarship, her careful combing through the *Youth's Companion* was a valuable aid to me. The work of both Miller and Harris, while problematic, is an essential starting point for students of the Pledge of Allegiance. I also found John Baer's brief, self-published study helpful, as well as two illuminating chapters on the Pledge of Allegiance in Cecilia Elizabeth O'Leary's excellent book *To Die For: The Paradoxes of American Patriotism*, probably the best scholarly account of the creation of the Pledge, even if it does get wrong the year the Pledge was written—O'Leary says 1891 (on pages 3 and 161) when in fact it was 1892. I also benefited greatly from reading Scot Guenter's comprehensive study, *The American Flag, 1777–1924*, and David Manwaring's important *Render unto Caesar: The Flag-Salute Controversy*.

I have been fortunate to have several opportunities to present my research in progress, and I learned so much from reactions to that work. At the invitation of Ted Lascher, I presented a talk in spring 2003, "The Dark Side of the Pledge of Allegiance," at Sacramento State University, where I had the opportunity to meet Mike Newdow, who proved extremely gracious, even if not all of what I had to say about Bellamy and the "under God" clause was likely to have been music to his ears. A short précis of my argument about the origins of the Pledge appeared in *Oregon Humanities* (summer 2003), the journal of the Oregon Council for the Humanities, and the appreciative reactions to that essay from OCH staff, particularly Christopher Zinn, Carol Hickman, and Kathleen Holt, as well as from various readers of the essay, have been an encouraging spur to complete the book. I also had the opportunity to present my work at a faculty colloquium at Willamette University where I benefited from penetrating questions from several colleagues. My colleagues Ellen Eisenberg, David Gutterman, and Steve Green also read portions of the manuscript and provided constructive suggestions for improvement.

I would like to especially thank the organizations that provided generous financial support for this project. Chief among these were the National Endowment for the Humanities, the Oregon Council for the Humanities, and the Earhart Foundation. Each of these organizations has supported earlier work I have done as well, which makes my gratitude all the more heartfelt. My work on the Pledge was also greatly helped by two Atkinson grants from my home institution, Willamette University. Also I owe thanks to the Meyer Memorial Trust, which provided the funding that endowed the Mark O. Hatfield Chair in Politics, which has supported my work on this book in innumerable ways.

Finally, I want to acknowledge all of those at the University Press of Kansas for their help in making this a better book. Press director Fred Woodward was the source of a stream of relevant newspaper cuttings, as well as an unfailing source of sage advice and helpful encouragement. He also secured two excellent readers, Scot Guenter and Bruce Miroff, both of whom helped improve the book in crucial ways. It is with great pride that I publish my fourth book with the University Press of Kansas, a press worthy of any author's allegiance.

1

CREATING THE PLEDGE

Most educated Americans could probably tell you that Thomas Jefferson drafted the Declaration of Independence, and a substantial number could also identify Francis Scott Key as the author of "The Star-Spangled Banner." Anybody wanting to become an American citizen needs to know this information, since for years these two questions have been among the one hundred questions the Immigration and Naturalization Service draws from in the Civics Exam it administers to prospective citizens.[1] But no INS officer has ever asked a prospective citizen about the author of the Pledge of Allegiance, even though every citizenship ceremony closes not by reading from the Declaration of Independence or by singing "The Star-Spangled Banner" but by repeating the Pledge of Allegiance: "I pledge allegiance to the flag of the United States of America and to the Republic for which it stands, one Nation under God, indivisible, with liberty and justice for all." Those thirty-one words rank among the nation's best-known and most frequently recited words, so it is more than a little ironic that the author of those words, Francis Bellamy, remains so obscure.

The Pledge has grown since Bellamy's day—his original version, written in 1892, was a spare twenty-three words: "I pledge allegiance to my Flag and

Francis Bellamy at his desk in a photograph thought to have been taken around 1900. Department of Rare Books and Special Collections, University of Rochester Library.

to the Republic for which it stands—one Nation indivisible—with Liberty and Justice for all." In later chapters we will follow the story behind the accretions to the Pledge of Allegiance, but our immediate aim is to explore the origins of the Pledge. Who was Francis Bellamy and how did he come to write the Pledge of Allegiance? Why 1892? And what can the origins of the Pledge tell us about American national identity and citizenship?

A Flag over Every Schoolhouse

Today we are accustomed to seeing a flag in every public school classroom, but throughout much of the nineteenth century the American flag was only sporadically displayed in public schools. A flag salute, of course, presupposes a flag to salute. And so it is hardly a surprise that the Pledge of Allegiance has its origins in a movement begun in the late 1880s to have the American flag "wave over every schoolhouse" in the nation.[2]

Originally the primary use of the Stars and Stripes was to identify American naval vessels at sea. In the early days of the republic, one would typically

a pledge of allegiance suggested for the
Columbus Day salute to the Flag — F.B.

I pledge allegiance to my flag and to the
Republic for which it stands — One Nation
indivisible — with liberty and justice for all

The original twenty-three-word Pledge of Allegiance copied in Francis Bellamy's handwriting. Department of Rare Books and Special Collections, University of Rochester Library.

encounter the American flag flying over ships, U.S. military forts, and federal buildings. The War of 1812 and the Mexican-American War contributed to the flag becoming a more popular symbol of nationhood, but it was during the Civil War that the flag became the preeminent and hallowed symbol it is today. Following the fall of Fort Sumter, the American flag became omnipresent in the North. "When the stars and stripes went down at Sumter," recorded an 1880 text, "they went up in every town and county in the loyal States. Every city, town, and village suddenly blossomed with banners. On forts and ships, from church-spires and flag-staffs, from colleges, hotels, storefronts and private balconies, from public edifices, everywhere the old flag was flung out." Public schools, too, sometimes responded to the call to arms by flying the flag. In New York City during the war, remembered George Balch, "every public school . . . was dominated by a flag-staff, and . . . the national colors were always displayed whenever any occasion arose demanding it."[3]

These displays of the U.S. flag in schools were spontaneous and generally short-lived, reflecting wartime patriotism and not deliberate public policy. "As time went on and the stirring events of the war passed into history," lamented Balch, "the exuberance of patriotic ardor became less and less, [and] the flag was more infrequently seen on the schools, until in 1887, but about twenty-five flag-staffs remained on the one hundred and thirty two public school houses in [New York City] . . . and most of these were in an unserviceable condition." The city's board of education estimated that the cost of supplying flagstaffs to schools that lacked one, fixing staffs that were unsafe, and outfitting each school with new flags and halyards would be $28,000. Faced with this cost, as well as the continued maintenance costs connected with replacing flags and fixing leaking roofs damaged by the "racking motion of the staff during . . . high winds," many of the remaining staffs were removed.[4]

Balch, who had served proudly in the Union army, looked back on "the war of rebellion" as a time of tremendous patriotism, self-sacrifice, and national unity. He feared, as many of his generation did, that the sterner patriotic virtues were being neglected in the postwar pursuit of wealth and individual advancement. And he worried even more that national unity was threatened by the huge influx of immigrants to whom the patriotic sacrifices of the Civil War meant little. Nowhere was the press of immigration felt more keenly than in New York City's overcrowded public schools.[5]

But Colonel Balch was also heartened to find signs of renewed interest in patriotism in some of New York City's schools. In a visit to one of the city's largest public schools in April 1888 he encountered a stirring patriotic exercise focused on an American flag that was solemnly paraded before the assembled school by a student flag bearer. The exercise had apparently been introduced only a few months before by a trustee of the schools, Colonel De Witt C. Ward, who had recently purchased a number of American flags and presented them in formal ceremonies to a handful of schools across New York City. In attendance at one of these ceremonies was Charles F. Homer, a member of the Grand Army of the Republic (GAR), a politically potent organization that in 1890 counted over four hundred thousand Union army veterans as members (up from a mere twenty-seven thousand in 1876). Homer was impressed by what he saw and reported back to his compatriots in Lafayette Post 140, which was among the most active local branches of the GAR in New York City. The post promptly decided to present the "dear old Flag" to the City College of New York, which they did in an elaborate ceremony in June 1888. "Whatever nation you belong to by birth," the students were told, "whatever tongue your mother taught you, whatever your color or your race, no matter, there is only one flag." They were asked to "come and gather under its blessed folds. Let us be tangled in the stars and covered with the stripes."[6]

The City College ceremony seems to have inspired other GAR posts to carry out similar flag presentation ceremonies. The GAR post in Rochester, New York, for instance, used the occasion of Washington's birthday in 1889 to host a "flag extravaganza" in which flags were presented to every public school in Rochester. At the same time the New York department of the GAR proposed that the state should require every school to display an American flag. The burgeoning interest in flag presentations received further encouragement at the August 1889 national meeting of the GAR, wherein Commander-in-Chief William Warner commended to each post "the patriotic practice" of veterans presenting the American flag to local public schools that lacked one. Schoolchildren, he explained, must be taught to "look upon the American flag . . . with as much reverence as did the Israelites look upon the ark of the covenant." Imbue the boys and girls with such a reverence, he promised, and "the future of the Republic is assured."[7]

Over the next decade the GAR zealously pursued the goal of placing a flag above every schoolhouse. At the state level, veterans pressed legislatures to enact laws requiring the American flag to be flown over schoolhouses, and at the local level they organized flag presentation ceremonies at schools across the nation.[8] But even for as formidable and geographically widespread an organization as the GAR, introducing flags into every neighborhood school was a daunting task. That task, however, was made much easier by the involvement of the *Youth's Companion*, a weekly family magazine that by 1888 reached over four hundred thousand households, the largest circulation of any weekly at the time. The circulation numbers and advertising acumen of the *Youth's Companion* enabled the schoolhouse flag movement to reach a national audience.[9]

James B. Upham and the *Youth's Companion*

The *Youth's Companion* was a Boston-based magazine owned and run by Daniel Sharp Ford (1822–1899), a remarkable man who built a publishing powerhouse. When Ford bought the *Youth's Companion* in the late 1850s, it had been a small magazine with a circulation of under five thousand. In 1867, Ford assumed sole ownership of the magazine, and over the next three decades, until his death in 1899, he made it into one of the country's best-known and most-loved periodicals of the late nineteenth century. Central to the magazine's unrivaled success was its innovative use of premiums to attract subscribers. Every

October, readers would eagerly await the end of the month arrival of the colorfully illustrated "Premium List Number," containing a veritable cornucopia of goods, from dolls and chemistry sets to books and Bibles, all of which could be obtained cheaply or for free by soliciting new subscriptions. A highly sought after "magic *Scroll Saw*" was estimated by one *Companion* staffer to have produced forty thousand new subscribers. Through the premium department, a virtual "mail order business," according to one account, the *Youth's Companion* ingeniously enlisted the youth and families of America in the service of its own profitability.[10]

In its October 1888 premium issue, the *Youth's Companion* for the first time offered American flags for purchase. Flags of various sizes were offered to readers at reduced prices, from thirty cents for a 12-by-18-inch decorative silk flag to fifteen dollars for a giant 10-by-20-foot bunting flag. A 3-by-5-foot bunting flag could be obtained for two dollars, or for two subscriptions and seventy-five cents, and a 2-by-3-foot silk flag could be had for one dollar, or for one new subscriber and forty cents. The hope, the advertisement announced, was "to encourage the idea of Flag decoration in home and school-room." The *Companion* lamented that while "we decorate our homes most profusely," we seldom use "that most beautiful and inspiring of objects, the American Flag." The magazine hoped that the "Stars and Stripes [might] be hung upon the walls of every home, and of every school room in the land" so that "patriotism and love of liberty [would] be unceasingly taught."[11]

The flag advertisement in the premium issue was a sign of the increased interest in displaying the American flag, but there was no indication at this time of a concerted effort on the magazine's part to place a flag over every schoolhouse. The flag advertisement was not particularly conspicuous, and the regular pages of the *Companion* made no mention of the American flag being offered as a premium nor did it promote efforts to introduce flags into schools. Indeed in the early fall of 1889 the paper ran an editorial comment, "Teaching Patriotism," which poured cold water on the idea of hoisting the American flag "over every school-house in the country, and [keeping it] afloat so long as the school is in session." Attributing the idea to Balch (identified in the article only as "a gentleman of New York"), the *Companion* said that while daily flag raising and flag lowering was appropriate to military installations and naval vessels, there were far more fitting and more effective ways to teach patriotism, beginning with improving instruction of American history. "Our boys and girls are already very patriotic," the *Companion* concluded. "What they now need is to be taught the duties we all owe to such a country as ours—to keep it pure and good."[12]

We do not know who penned this editorial; the magazine's records were destroyed and it was company policy not to include names on articles written by members of the *Youth's Companion* staff. We do know from several sources, however, that Ford "did nearly all the real [editorial] work himself, carefully watching over every paragraph that entered the paper."[13] So it is inconceivable that such an article did not express some of Ford's skepticism about the utility of flag waving and flag raising as a way of promoting patriotism. Indeed the language of the concluding sentence as well as the article's emphasis on the importance of history suggests that it may well have come from Ford's own pen.[14]

Although we do not know who wrote "Teaching Patriotism," we can be certain that it was not James B. Upham, head of the Premium Department. At the age of twenty-seven, in 1872, young Upham had come to work for his uncle Daniel Sharp Ford and was put in charge of the premium department. He quickly showed he had a remarkable knack for identifying and promoting premiums that would sell magazines. His motto was, "The more we can do for our subscribers, the faster the *Companion* will grow."[15] For Upham, the flag program had a special significance that transcended the usual premium promotions. Although Upham had not served in the Union army,[16] he believed, as many GAR veterans did also, that patriotism in the postwar years had become "enfeebled" by postwar materialism and selfishness. Upham recalled having been "brought up in the very atmosphere of patriotism." Every Friday, "in the little red school house" of his youth, "some boy declaimed [Daniel] Webster's speeches about the Union and the forefathers." In contrast, many immigrant children did not know who Webster was or who the nation's forefathers were. Upham's aim was to rekindle the patriotic flame by lifting the flag over every schoolhouse in the country.[17]

"Teaching Patriotism" had sounded a warning about fetishizing the flag, yet just a few months later Upham prevailed on his uncle to sponsor an essay contest in each state on the topic "The Patriotic Influence of the American Flag When Raised over the Public Schools." Announced in the January 9, 1890, issue of the *Youth's Companion,* the contest was accompanied by a handsome illustration of a schoolhouse adorned with a massive, two-story-high American flag. The article noted that "the idea [of placing the flag in the public schools] is becoming popular, and the American Flag can now be seen floating over many a patriotic school." The *Companion* pledged to add to the growing number of schoolhouse flags by donating a giant nine-by-fifteen-foot flag to the school of the student who produced the winning essay in each state. The flags, moreover, were to be dedicated on July 4.[18]

The essay competition raised the profile of the schoolhouse flag movement, but it was not until the close of 1890 that the movement became a central preoccupation of the magazine. On December 25, 1890, the magazine declared its ambition to see the nation commemorate the "Four Hundredth Anniversary of the Discovery of America by Columbus" by "raising the U.S. Flag over every Public School from the Atlantic to the Pacific." The idea of linking the schoolhouse flag movement to the celebration of Columbus's discovery of America was Upham's and it was a political masterstroke, for it married the schoolhouse flag movement to one of the most eagerly awaited extravaganzas of the late nineteenth century—the World's Columbian Exposition. In April 1890, President Benjamin Harrison had signed into law a bill authorizing Chicago to host the exposition. Dedication of the buildings was to take place on October 12, 1892, and the exposition was to open later the following year. The *Youth's Companion* called for the national flag-raising celebration to coincide with the date of the dedication ceremonies in Chicago. For Upham this was more than just a shrewd promotional move; it was also a profound statement of his values. From Upham's perspective, the Columbia Exposition, advertised as an "international exhibition of arts, industries, manufactures, and the products of the soil, mine, and sea," was biased toward display of the technological wonders and material advancements of the nineteenth century. As such, in Upham's eyes, the exposition was a symptom of the materialism of the time. The flag-raising movement was a way of using the exposition to teach Americans, young and old, "a lesson in patriotism" and remind them of the "high ideals" that made America great.[19]

The December 1890 announcement promised to send every "Flag School" in America a free special illustrated souvenir of "Raising the School House Flag." But as nice as the souvenir was, the offer was not enough to meet the magazine's ambitious goal of a flag over every schoolhouse. The October 1890 premium issue had again featured flags for subscriptions, and at cheaper prices and in a wider variety than in 1888. Along with the largest flag, the *Companion* also offered a canvas bag for storing the flag; on the bag would appear the name of the school and the name of the person responsible for presenting the flag to the school. But the *Companion* needed more, which Upham provided in the March 19, 1891, issue, wherein was announced the ingenious idea of school flag certificates. "School Boys! School Girls!" trumpeted the article:

> Do you wish to raise a Flag over your Schoolhouse? We can help your School to raise the money for its purchase. In the first place talk the matter over with your parents, your teacher and school-mates. Then write to us and tell us of your decision,

and ask us to send you 100 School Flag Certificates. Ask your teacher to sign the
order for the Certificates. On receipt of your order we will send you free 100 Certificates. Each pupil can easily dispose of one or more of these Certificates to interested friends and neighbors at 10 cts. each. Follow this plan, and any school can
raise $10.00 for a beautiful Flag sixteen feet long in a day's notice.

Each certificate read, "This Certificate entitles the holder to a Share in the
patriotic influences of the School Flag." Appealing directly to students to become patriotic shareholders, Upham's plan enlisted entrepreneurial spirit in the
service of patriotism.[20]

For the next year and a half, the pages of the *Youth's Companion* were replete
with articles promoting the Columbian Public School Celebration and reporting
enthusiastically on the progress being made in raising the flag over schools across
the country. As the date of the event grew closer, the sales pitch became ever more
urgent. In May 1892, the *Youth's Companion* asked sharply: "Is Your School to
Celebrate? Ask your Teacher to decide about the Celebration at once and drop
us a letter or postal next week. We wish to know." The issue told students that
thirteen million schoolchildren would be participating in the Columbian Public School Celebration on October 12, 1892. "Don't let your school be left out,"
urged the magazine. The magazine also prefaced the promotional pitch with
inspiring stories, like the one about the "patriotic and plucky schoolmistress" in
Crawfordsville, Indiana, who, the day after raising the flag over her schoolhouse, found the flagstaff cut down and the flag "spirited away." The following
week the determined schoolmistress raised a new flagstaff and flag and "got a
Winchester rifle, with which to defend it." The flag, the *Youth's Companion*
proudly announced, "still waves over the little schoolhouse of District No. 9."[21]

Francis Bellamy Joins the *Youth's Companion*

Shortly after the flag certificate scheme was launched in March 1891, Daniel
Sharp Ford took on a new employee, thirty-five-year-old Francis Bellamy. Bellamy had been the pastor of Boston's Bethany Baptist Church for six years but
had begun to run into difficulties with the church because of his increasingly
radical economic views and heterodox religious views. Working with the poor
in tenement housing was one thing, but speeches before audiences of work-
ingmen on "Jesus the Socialist" were quite a bit more alarming to many genteel
Bostonians and "rigid old deacons." Bellamy's Christian socialist convictions
did not alarm Ford, however, who was more than just another well-to-do

parishioner at Bethany. Ford had largely financed the construction of the church upon its move from a lower-income Catholic area to a more affluent Protestant area and continued to be its leading benefactor, including underwriting Bellamy's salary. Ford did not share all of Bellamy's ideological enthusiasms, but he fully shared Bellamy's "spirit of sympathy with the poor classes" and a concern that America suffered from a spiritual impoverishment resulting from an exclusive pursuit of material goods and commercial success. In Daniel Ford, Bellamy had an influential benefactor and vital ally, but by the spring of 1891 Bellamy was finding the strain of "the contest between churchly experience and inner convictions" to be unbearable. He was also perhaps coming to the realization that he was "a better writer than a minister."[22]

In April 1891, after much soul-searching, Bellamy announced his resignation, and Ford, who admired Bellamy's command of language, both written and spoken, agreed to hire Bellamy. Despite having no previous experience in publishing or business, Bellamy was assigned to work with Upham in the premium department. As Ford well knew, Upham's most pressing need in the spring of 1891 was help organizing and publicizing the National Public School Celebration, which was mushrooming into a vast undertaking. Bellamy was exactly what Upham needed: an intelligent and energetic person uncommitted by other duties at the magazine, a gifted writer, and a practiced and articulate speaker.[23]

Upham and Bellamy

Although Upham's and Bellamy's heirs would later fight fiercely over who should receive credit for writing the Pledge of Allegiance, James Upham and Francis Bellamy quickly forged a productive working partnership. Their talents were different, but the two men had much in common. Although Upham was about ten years older than Bellamy, their backgrounds and upbringings, social classes, educational attainments, and religious outlooks were strikingly similar.

Both men had been raised in devoutly religious families that had converted to the Baptist faith during the religious revival that swept through New York and New England in the early nineteenth century. As a young man, Bellamy's father had initially set himself up as a country merchant in western New York but had quickly decided to give up the world of business to spread the word of God. For over three decades, David Bellamy (1806–1864) ably preached the gospel in churches across New York, during which period he is said to have "baptized into fellowship" some seven hundred believers, including his second wife (and Francis Bellamy's mother), Lucy Ann, who was herself the adopted daughter of a deacon. Bellamy's mother was "profoundly religious," bringing her son up "in great piety"—her aim was that Francis should follow in the footsteps of the father to the ministry. And so Francis had dutifully enrolled, first at the Baptist-affiliated University of Rochester, where he pursued "the regular course in preparation for the Baptist ministry," and then at the Rochester Theological Seminary.[24]

Upham's father, the Reverend James Upham (1815–1893), was also a Baptist minister, though unlike Bellamy's father, Upham's was college-educated (at Colby College, then known as Waterville College), later becoming a professor of theology at the New Hampton Literary and Theological Institution, including five years as president during the Civil War (one of the pupils there was his son James).[25] The values that Reverend Upham attempted to inculcate in his son are perhaps most clearly expressed in a tribute he wrote for his own father, Joshua Upham (1784–1858), who had been born the son of a farmer and became a wealthy master stonemason and respected citizen of Salem, Massachusetts. He "combined in his character," Reverend Upham offered, "independence, self-reliance, energy, enterprise, practical sense, and an all-controlling religiousness." Although economically successful, he had been "a decidedly benevolent man, and never given to mere money making," as was evident by his long tenure as the deacon of the First Baptist Church of Salem, where for four decades he cared for the church's poor and tended to its sick. His "dominant qualities," Reverend Upham concluded, "were integrity and godliness; and his greatest wish in his children's behalf was for their spiritual prosperity, and their service in the cause of Christ."[26]

In short, both Bellamy and Upham were brought up in households in which religion mattered profoundly. For both men, religion was not just a private faith but a public outlook and a critical standard by which to judge the ethical standards of a commercial society. Not inner contemplation but active engagement and good works were the ends of faith. In the early 1880s, Bellamy's religious principles drew him into the crusade against the evils of alcohol, even taking the stump in 1884 for the Prohibition party presidential candidate John Pierce St. John. Toward the end of that decade, Bellamy had migrated toward Christian socialism, which, as he explained in 1889 in the pages of *The Dawn* (a magazine founded and owned by the newly formed Society of Christian Socialists), "is the application of the Bible to business." *The Dawn*'s motto—"He works with God who works for Man"—captures not only Bellamy's outlook but Upham's (and Ford's) as well.[27]

Although their work took them to the big city, Bellamy and Upham were both raised in bucolic small towns. The son of a respected college president and professor in a small remote village in the north of Vermont, Upham did not leave Fairfax until at the age of twenty-one he went to work for a publishing company in Detroit. Bellamy, meanwhile, grew up in a "spacious house" in Rome, New York, a small town of about six to seven thousand people at the time the Civil War began. Rome was the site of Fort Stanwix, which was believed to be the place where the Stars and Stripes were first flown in battle during the American Revolution, a fact in which the residents of Rome took great pride. Bellamy and Upham shared a strong and deeply personal connection to the American past, a past that they saw as under threat from an expanding, industrializing urban America with its machine politics and municipal corruption and its smokestacks, poverty, and wealthy industrialists. For them the nation's past was their own personal history.[28]

A fascination with family genealogy characterized both Bellamy and Upham. According to Margarette Miller, Bellamy's "will to record the Bellamy geneology [sic] bordered on fanaticism." She found "quantities of scribbled notes and reports on the Bellamy family tree written by Bellamy at the start of his college life and continuing to the closing years of his retirement." Upham, too, showed a keen interest in his ancestors. In 1880 he moved back to the ancestral home of Malden (the last to live there had been his great-grandfather), where the gravestones of generations of Uphams still stood in the town's old burial ground. Among the gravestones not to be found there, mysteriously, was that of Lieutenant Phineas Upham (1635–1676), son of the very first American Upham. James Upham took it upon himself to solve the mystery. By laboriously probing "with a long iron rod" the ground next to the marked grave of the lieutenant's wife, Upham was able to determine that the body of a tall person had been buried at the side of the wife's grave. Upham's surmise was that the site marked the last resting place of his great-great-great-great-great grandfather.[29]

Both Upham and Bellamy could trace their families back to the earliest colonial settlements. John Upham (1600–1681) had arrived in the New World in 1635, a part of the great Puritan migration to Massachusetts that occurred between 1629 and 1640, during the "eleven years' tyranny" of King Charles I. Bellamy's ancestors arrived in New England only a few years later, settling in what would become New Haven, Connecticut. Upon arrival in the newly incorporated town of Weymouth, Massachusetts, John Upham was selected as a deputy to the General Court of Boston. For the remainder of his long life, John Upham continued to be a leading citizen in Weymouth and then later in the town of Malden, where he held the office of deacon for a quarter century until his death in 1681. Generations of Uphams became Malden deacons, including James B. Upham, who, carrying on the family tradition, was made deacon of Malden's First Baptist Church in 1888.[30]

Bellamy knew less about the first American Bellamy, but that was more than made up for by the fame of his great-great-grandfather Joseph Bellamy (1719–1790), a celebrated Puritan divine of the eighteenth century whose imposing house still stands today in Bethlehem, Connecticut, a town he helped found and name. A disciple and associate of Jonathan Edwards, Joseph Bellamy wrote over twenty books and preached throughout New England, attracting theological students (including Aaron Burr) from across the region. Bellamy's millennial message was a call to Christian arms: true Christians must "exert themselves to the utmost, in the use of all proper means, to suppress error and vice of every kind, and promote the cause of truth and righteousness in the world, and so be workers together with God." Christian soldiers must act to redeem the world, always remaining wary of the corruption that stems from excessive concern with wealth or power.[31]

Bellamy had little sympathy with his ancestor's "rigidly Calvinistic" theology, but his pride in being a descendant of the great Joseph Bellamy was unmistakable—indeed one of his most prized possessions was the honorary doctorate of divinity granted to Joseph Bellamy by the University of Aberdeen in 1768. Genealogy was a source of tremendous pride for both Bellamy and Upham. They were proud of their Anglo-Saxon heritages and of their ancestors' parts in the building of a new nation. They knew they came, as Bellamy expressed it, "from a long line of men of responsibility: preachers, teachers, writers, merchants." In the National Columbian Public School Celebration, both men saw themselves not only continuing the work of their ancestors but, in important ways, rekindling their spirit, a spirit of selflessness, local civic involvement, and American patriotism that they felt was threatened by a rootless and restless modern America increasingly dominated by sprawling cities, huge corporations, corrupt political bosses, and hundreds of thousands of new immigrants with little or no understanding of the American past.[32]

Advertising the National Columbian Public School Celebration

Leadership of the National Columbian Public School Celebration was formally bestowed upon the *Youth's Companion* in January 1892 by Judge Charles

Bonney, president of the World's Congress Auxiliary, which had been established by the governing body of the World's Fair for the purpose of giving expression "to the subjective [conditions and relations of modern civilization], just as in the material display was expressed the objective conditions and relations of modern civilization." The American Youth's Association, which had been established to promote the Columbian Exposition among the world's youth and provide a "simultaneous and appropriate celebration of the discovery of America in every public school on the United States," asked the *Youth's Companion* to coordinate the nationwide day of celebration and to prepare a program for the celebration. Daniel Ford agreed to have the magazine spearhead the planning and promotion of the celebration and appointed the newcomer Bellamy to head the effort.[33]

Bellamy's first task was to obtain the backing of the education establishment. To that end, at Ford's instruction, he presented the idea of the celebration to a national meeting of school superintendents in February. The convention embraced the idea (it helped that the idea had the enthusiastic backing of William T. Harris, U.S. Commissioner of Education) and selected a committee of leading educators to implement the program, including the immediate past president of the National Education Association. Bellamy, as the representative of the *Youth's Companion,* was selected as the chair. Having received the official blessing of educators, Bellamy now had the task of spreading the word across the nation and of designing an official program for schools to follow on the day of national celebration.[34]

For the former task, the pages of the *Youth's Companion* were a formidable advertising weapon, and Upham and Bellamy took full advantage of it, launching a full-court promotional press. But Ford, Upham, and Bellamy all recognized that to have a national celebration in every school in the nation, involving thirteen-million children, they needed the help of other media, as well as of local and national leaders. Bellamy would subsequently have a long career in advertising, but at the time that Ford tagged him for this job he was still a novice in such matters, his only real experience having been the past nine months of working under Upham's direction in the premium department. But under the tutelage of some experienced advertising men (Upham most notably, but also Francis Pratt, the *Companion*'s business manager) and savvy reporters (especially Harold Roberts, a young *Companion* staffer, who by the early summer had become Bellamy's publicity director), Bellamy quickly learned how to generate publicity and propaganda. In March, for instance, Roberts did an "interview" with Bellamy that was then published in the *Boston Herald* under the headline, "For Thirteen Millions: A Columbian Celebration for the Public Schools." The *Companion* printed hundreds of thousands of copies of the carefully staged interview and distributed them across the nation. Bellamy also sent publicity material accompanied by personal letters to many thousands of newspapers, as well as to countless educational and religious periodicals. One of Bellamy's aims in communicating with the religious press was to encourage "every Minister in the country . . . to preach on the relation of Free Education to our American life." Bellamy also wrote letters to every state superintendent and every local superintendent of education in the country, urging them to ensure that their schools participated in the planned celebration. Also targeted by Bellamy were the "chief men" of the Grand Army of the Republic, who were asked to enlist every local GAR post in the organizing of the local flag ceremonies, thereby "handing down the traditions of their patriotism to the younger generation."[35]

Bellamy searched for ways to keep the project in the news and came up with the idea of traveling to the nation's capital to gain interviews with national leaders and procure their support for the celebration and to disseminate their statements of support to newspapers across the country. After securing Ford's permission, Bellamy set off for Washington, D.C., at the beginning of May. First, however, he stopped off in Albany and New York City to meet, respectively, with General John Palmer, Commander in Chief of the GAR, and ex-president (and soon to be president once again) Grover Cleveland. Palmer promised the GAR's full support for the celebration: "It is no namby-pamby sentiment of patriotism," Palmer observed. "It will impress all these pupils that they've got a country. . . . The School is . . . the only thing that represents the nation to millions. It ought always to fly the flag!" Cleveland, who only a few years before had had the honor of dedicating the Statue of Liberty, also enthusiastically endorsed the celebration and permitted Bellamy to release his words of praise to the press across the country.[36]

Upon arriving in Washington, D.C., Bellamy immediately fixed his sights on the White House, and through the help of his congressional representative, Henry Cabot Lodge, he secured an audience with President Benjamin Harrison, who proved every bit as sympathetic to Bellamy's proposal as Cleveland. The president assured Bellamy that he "liked to see the Flag over the School" and warmly recalled the tremendous display of flags in the 1889 centennial in New York City, celebrating the one-hundredth anniversary of the establishment of the federal government (a celebration that, ironically, was organized and financed largely by private individuals and organizations). Harrison remembered remarking at the time, "What a wonderful thing this is—here are trade and commerce willing to be absolutely forgotten and hidden by the symbol of the Nation for one day." He recalled, too, that he had given a speech at a dinner that evening in which he suggested to the gathered businessmen that they present the flags purchased for the centennial celebration to the public schools as "a perpetual lesson in patriotism." Harrison was well aware of Balch's efforts in New York City to have "the children march around and wave flags," and he thought that had resulted in "very pretty and impressive exercises." The idea of making the public school a centerpiece of the celebration of Columbus's discovery of America particularly appealed to the president, who reminded Bellamy that the importance of America's "free educational system" had been a central theme of his recent nationwide speaking tour. Like many Americans of the late nineteenth century, Harrison believed that schools needed to do more than just "teach the '3 Rs,'" for schools were "the place for education in intelligent patriotism and citizenship."[37]

Encouraged by Harrison's enthusiasm, Bellamy asked the president if he would issue a proclamation declaring a national holiday on October 12, 1892. At this point, Bellamy received a typically frosty response from the man dubbed by some "the human iceberg" and by others the "refrigerator." Fixing Bellamy with an icy stare, the president sternly admonished Bellamy that the president lacked the authority to do such a thing without action by Congress. Bellamy's confident retort that he would just have "to get Congress to pass a bill authorizing [Harrison] to do this" could hardly have pleased the president, though Harrison did promise to give Bellamy "some words of warm commendation which you can use all over the country."[38] On their way out, Lodge scolded the political novice for his impertinence and for pressing the president too hard. Lodge thought it unlikely in an election year that Bellamy could secure congressional support, especially since the Senate was Republican and the House was controlled by Democrats. Bellamy, however, impervious to the calculations of the political insiders, remained confident he could get Congress to endorse the proposal. He could not imagine any patriotic American opposing the *Companion*'s plan.[39]

Lodge may have been skeptical of Bellamy's chances of securing congressional approval, but he nonetheless delivered a generous endorsement of the plan for Bellamy to use in his press campaign. A few members of Congress declined Bellamy's request for an interview or a statement of support, among them John Sherman, the influential Republican chairman of the Senate Committee on Foreign Relations, who had no time for such matters as flags and schoolhouses, as well as the wily senator from New York, David Hill, who was angling for the Democratic presidential nomination and instinctively opposed anything that his longtime party rival Grover Cleveland supported. But the great majority of members of Congress were highly receptive to Bellamy's plan. Bellamy lobbied aggressively, obtaining interviews with (at least by Bellamy's count) some "forty or fifty leading Congressmen" over the next few weeks, and soon had his congressional resolution.[40]

Bellamy returned to Boston elated over his success in obtaining Congress's approval of the celebration. After another carefully staged interview, written up by Harold Roberts and again published in the *Boston Herald,* Bellamy found himself "besieged by reporters and press associations" who wanted to know more about the big event. Having spent months laboring to drum up publicity, Bellamy now found he needed help responding to the demand for information that he had stirred up. He asked Ford to make Roberts his assistant, and the *Companion*'s owner obligingly appointed Roberts as publicity director for the Columbian school program. With Roberts handling most of the publicity, Bellamy could begin to devote more attention to the now pressing need to produce the official program for the day of celebration.[41]

Designing the Program

The general outline of the program had been sketched out before Bellamy had traveled to Washington. The plan was for a uniform morning celebration in every school in the nation. It was to be "simple but impressive," consisting of the raising of the flag and a flag salute, "a simple Religious exercise (probably)," as well as "an original Carol, an original Address, [and] an original Ode, prepared by the best American writers."[42] Local schools could then elaborate on the patriotic program as they saw fit. Recognizing the political influence and symbolic importance of the GAR, Bellamy also proposed that local posts of the GAR "send details of Veterans to every school-house to assist in the Salute to the Flag." GAR veterans would also serve as "an escort of honor to the Schools in the Afternoon Parade." The shape of this afternoon celebration was largely to be left up to local needs and preferences, but its focus was to be "the Public School idea."[43]

The *Companion* had promised to publish the official program for the morning celebration by the beginning of September. To meet that deadline they needed copy for each part of the program by early August. For Bellamy it was important that the song, ode, and address be written by famous individuals whose names would generate extensive press interest and public attention. Upham had already obtained a suitable ode ("Columbia's Banner") from the well-known poet Edna Dean Proctor (1829–1923), but the only original song they had was from the Reverend Theron Brown, a longtime *Companion* staff member who was responsible for the magazine's religious articles. Bellamy wanted better, but in the end he reluctantly settled for Brown's "Song of Columbus Day." Ford did not seem nearly as concerned as Bellamy about securing distinguished names for the program and suggested that Bellamy himself write the address. Bellamy demurred and instead suggested Kentucky congressman William Campbell Preston Breckenridge, a politician of national renown who was widely recognized as among Washington's most brilliant orators.[44]

Bellamy had interviewed Breckenridge when in Washington and had been deeply impressed by the Kentucky Democrat's eloquence and intelligence. The fact that Breckenridge was not only a Southern Democrat but the grandson of presidential candidate John Breckinridge and a former colonel in the Confederate army was an added bonus for Bellamy, who thought Breckenridge's involvement might stimulate interest in the program in the South, where so far the flag-raising movement had attracted the least enthusiasm. Ford consented, and Bellamy approached Breckenridge about writing an address on "the meaning of the four centuries." Breckenridge obliged, but Ford and others felt his submission was inadequate to the demands of the occasion, and so, with time desperately short, Ford directed Bellamy to write the address. Bellamy did so, though the address appears in the program without any attribution. Consistent with the company policy of anonymity, the program indicated only that the address had been "prepared for the occasion by *The Youth's Companion*."[45]

Still missing, however, was the salute. One option was to use the flag salute that had been written by Colonel Balch and was now used in a number of elementary schools in New York City: "We give our heads and our hearts to God and our country: one country, one language, one Flag." Upham and Bellamy were familiar with the salute but considered it lacking in the dignity and depth needed for this momentous occasion. So far Bellamy had paid scant attention to the flag salute—his efforts over the summer instead had focused on securing the presidential proclamation and a suitable ode, song, and address. It was Upham who was focused on the mechanics of the flag raising and the accompanying salute. According to Margarette Miller, Upham "talked of little else to his friends and family. Whether over the breakfast table or vacationing in New Hampshire, James B. Upham thought and talked 'Salute,' and daily scribbled off ideas, one after the other." Bellamy regarded the flag salute as properly Upham's business, since he was "the 'Father' of the schoolhouse flag movement."[46]

Upham, however, struggled to come up with a salute that expressed the spirit of true Americanism that he wished to capture. Increasingly frustrated, he pressed Bellamy to write it. Bellamy, meanwhile, insisted that Upham should have the honor. Upham continued to flounder, and at last, with the printing deadline looming, Bellamy relented. Over dinner the two men talked intently about what the salute should contain. They agreed that it should be a "vow of loyalty, or allegiance, to the flag, based on what the flag . . . stood for." The words of the salute must not only be an expression of loyalty to the nation but they should also express "the *reason* for loyalty." Upon returning to the offices of the *Companion,* Bellamy went to his room to try his hand at composing the salute. Two hours and many crumpled pages later, Bellamy emerged with twenty-three words: "I pledge allegiance to my Flag and to the Republic for which it stands—one Nation indivisible—with Liberty and Justice for all."[47]

Like a nervous father-to-be in the anteroom, Upham was anxiously pacing the hall. Bellamy called for his boss and read him the product of his hard labor. Upham, clearly excited, asked to look it over. After slowly reading the words to himself, Upham suddenly stood at attention in military salute, eyes fixed on an imaginary flag. He began to solemnly recite Bellamy's words aloud, and at the words "my flag" raised his outstretched arm, palm upward, in the direction of the imagined flag. Upham had a few questions about whether "the flag" might be preferable to "my flag" and whether "inseparable" was preferable to "indivisible," but finally he pronounced the newborn creation "right as it stands." The next morning, Daniel Ford rendered the same verdict, and the salute was done—the official program could now go to press.[48]

The Columbus Day Celebration

The Pledge of Allegiance appeared in print for the first time on September 8, 1892, when the *Youth's Companion* published the official program for the Columbus Day celebration. Every school in the nation was instructed to follow the program and to begin preparations for the celebration. It was to begin with the master of ceremonies reading the president's proclamation, "recommending to the people the observance in all their localities of the four hundredth anniversary of the discovery of America . . . by public demonstrations and by suitable exercises in their schools and other places of assembly." That reading was to be immediately followed by the raising of the American flag by Civil War veterans; as the flag reached the top of the staff the veterans were to lead a hearty shout of "Three Cheers for 'Old Glory.'" At the principal's direction, the students of the school, "in ordered ranks, hands to the side," were then to face the flag. In unison the students were then to give the military salute to the flag—"right hand lifted, palm downward, to a line with the forehead, and close to it." Still saluting, the students were then slowly to recite Bellamy's Pledge of Allegiance. And at the words "to my Flag," as Upham had planned, the students were to "gracefully" extend their right arm, "palm upward, towards the Flag." Upon completion of the "affirmation," all hands were to "immediately drop to the side," and the assembled were to sing "America—'My Country, 'tis of Thee.'" Following that was to be an "Acknowledgment of God" through a prayer or reading of scripture, the exact nature of which was left up to the local celebrants. The students and the audience next were to join in singing Reverend Brown's "Song of Columbus Day," which was to be followed by a reading of the address, "The Meaning of the Four Centuries," and the ode entitled "Columbia's Banner." Teachers were instructed to assign the reading of the ode and the address to "those who can render them most intelligently." A "simplified form" of the address was provided for primary schools. In addition, teachers were urged to have students "persistently rehearse" the flag salute and songs. Local schools were encouraged to amplify the ceremony through additional addresses, songs, and "historical exercises."[49]

The official program also envisioned a celebration in the afternoon so that the people of a town or city would have the opportunity collectively to celebrate their public schools. This might take the form of games or neighborhood picnics but probably would consist of a parade in most cities and villages. If there was to be a parade, Bellamy was anxious that it be dignified. "In all cases," the official program admonished, "the fantastic should be rigorously barred from the procession." The parade, moreover, should keep the focus on the public schools. The "Public School Review" should be the parade's "most honored feature." The program suggested that army veterans, "the Blue and the Gray alike," should accompany the students in the march as "special guards of honor." Upon passing the reviewing stand, each part of the column should offer a military salute to the flag. The parade might be followed by a citizens' mass meeting in the evening, in which some of the morning program could be repeated. At least one of the speeches at the mass meeting, the program urged, "should deal with the reasons for making the American educational system the centre of this Columbian celebration; for one of the aims of this movement is to impress the

American people with the significance of free education to American progress and citizenship."[50]

It is difficult to say precisely how many schools and students participated in the celebration and how exactly they followed the official program.[51] But it is clear from newspaper accounts that Columbus Day celebrations were widespread across the nation and that the morning celebration designed by Bellamy and Upham was faithfully followed in thousands and thousands of public schools as well as in some private schools.[52] Perhaps the greatest departure from the program was in New York City, where the celebrations revealed the divisions within the nation about the meaning of American patriotism and of the public schools' role in manufacturing American identity and patriotism.

The Columbus Day celebration was originally to have happened on October 12, but the final version of the congressional resolution changed the date to Friday, October 21, which some pedant in Congress had calculated was the true four-hundredth anniversary of Columbus's discovery of America, correcting for changes in calendars. One locale that chose to ignore the resolution and stick with the original date was New York City, which transformed the *Companion*'s one-day celebration into a three-day extravaganza of parades and pageants beginning on Monday, October 10. The opening day of the celebration featured a massive parade of nearly twenty-five thousand marching school boys (the only girls who participated were "a company of Indian girls"). Participating in the parade were not only the city's public schools but its many parochial and private schools as well; one Catholic school marched in the shape of a cross while the band played "The Star-Spangled Banner." The following day featured two more parades: a naval parade celebrating the advances in shipping since Columbus's day and an evening parade of the Catholic societies, as well as a Catholic historical celebration. On October 12, there was a huge, climactic military parade honoring Columbus, as well as an unveiling of a monument to Columbus in Central Park. The focus of the city's "Columbus Week" celebration was clearly not, as Bellamy and Upham had hoped, the importance of the public schools but rather the genius and daring of Columbus.[53]

The official script was much more carefully followed in Upham's hometown of Malden, Massachusetts. The morning school exercises, including the flag salute and Pledge of Allegiance, were carried out in the various city schools, followed by an afternoon parade of four thousand schoolchildren, boys as well as girls. Among the VIPs on the reviewing stand were not only Upham but special guest Francis Bellamy, who had been invited to deliver the main oration of the evening exercises. In his evening address, Bellamy reminded the citizens of Malden that, "while we honor the man Columbus," we are here to "celebrate America to-day." And America, Bellamy reminded them, "was built purely of Anglo-Saxon stuff. Those mighty men of the Lord that settled Massachusetts, the sturdy Dutchmen of New York, the clean Quakers of Pennsylvania, the cavalier stock that established itself on the James—these were the true makers of America." He asked the audience to imagine what would have been "the fate of this continent if the old thirteen colonies had been Spanish colonies or Portuguese colonies, instead of British colonies. Then all this continent would have wallowed on in the dirty ignorance and superstition and barbarism which have characterized all the colonies of Spain." Such speculation, he acknowledged, was idle, for the settlement of America was no historical accident. Americans had been specially chosen by God "to build a new commonwealth of liberty and justice." Lest the point be missed, Bellamy reiterated that "America is not due to the enterprise of Spain. If we have anything worth celebrating here, we are to remember it was in spite of Spain." Columbus, sailing under the patronage of the Spanish crown, may have discovered the New World, but the United States was a nation whose institutions and principles were founded and built by Anglo-Saxons.[54]

American Catholics, not surprisingly, often drew quite different lessons about the import and meaning of Columbus Day. For Catholics across the country, the day of celebration began not by gathering in the local public schools, as dictated by the *Youth's Companion* program, but by celebrating high mass "by order of his holiness, the pope." At St. John's Cathedral in Indianapolis, the bishop told the celebrants that Columbus Day was "a great occasion for our religion and for our country." For Columbus's discovery of America showed that "our religion presides over the fact of the discovery of America. . . . The catholic church has precedence over it all, for catholics settled and Christianized it." Columbus, he emphasized, was not only "a great genius," but he was also a great Catholic who "never lost sight of his confidence in God" and who "would have fought for the cross." Whereas Bellamy and Upham wanted the day to be a celebration of public schools, the bishop criticized "compulsory education," lamenting that "God is forgotten in the schools and in this country." The bishop, however, joined fully in the celebration of America. "We must thank God," he said, "for giving us this country in which the catholic church has liberty which is often denied us in the so-called catholic countries of the world." America was a haven for the "poor" and the "oppressed" who "have formed this glorious republic."[55]

Although not every city and school conducted the Columbus Day celebration in the way prescribed in the *Companion*'s official program, Upham and Bellamy justifiably felt a tremendous pride in the "abundant success" of the day of celebration.[56] Across the nation, boasted the *Companion* (the unsigned commentary was likely written by Bellamy), the Columbus Day celebration had witnessed "a patriotic and thoughtful uprising of the people, such as America had not seen since the Civil War." It was a day of celebration, the *Companion* marveled, "less attended with noise and mere display, and more marked by seriousness and unanimity, than any other single day in the last quarter of a century." Ignoring the millions of Catholics and thousands of parochial schools that participated in the day's celebration, the *Companion* suggested that the Columbus Day celebration affirmed Americans' belief that the public school system was "one of the principal sources, under God, of [America's] greatness" and that "the common education of the citizen in the common duties of citizenship is the function of the state." By placing the nation's flag over the public schools, the *Companion* concluded, "America seemed to utter her trust that the distinctive principles of true Americanism will not perish so long as free, public education endures." The flag over the schoolhouse, added the *Companion*, also "impressed powerfully upon the youth that we are a nation," while the words with which the youth of America pledged allegiance to the flag taught "a lesson of thoughtful patriotism . . . which will never be forgotten."[57]

2

THE MEANING OF THE PLEDGE

The story of how the Pledge of Allegiance was created is relatively straightforward, but its significance is less transparent and more open to dispute. What, if anything, can the circumstances of the Pledge's creation tell us about its meaning and about the nature of American patriotism and American society? What was the original intent behind the Pledge of Allegiance, and does it matter?

One interpretation of the Pledge is that it expresses America's enduring and foundational principles. It speaks to America's noblest aspirations and hopes. This is the meaning of the Pledge that we teach our children. So, for instance, the children's book *I Pledge Allegiance* (2002), by Bill Martin and Michael Sampson, instructs that the words of the Pledge mean that "we the people elect leaders who make our laws," that "no matter how much we might disagree about some things, we all agree on one thing: we are strongest when we stick together and help each other out," that "every person who lives in this country has a right to be free and to make his or her own choices," and that "all Americans have the right to be treated fairly by our laws."[1] The words of the Pledge express not just Americans' patriotic commitment to their nation but also Americans' adherence to universal ideals of democracy, freedom, and fairness. In a world afflicted with chauvinistic, ethnic nationalism, the Pledge embodies a nobler, civic patriotism, premised not on ethnic identity or racial bloodlines but rather on a shared set of allegiances to universal ideals. It represents a patriotism of which Americans can justly be proud.

There is much that is appealing in this interpretation, and in some respects it does illuminate a defining difference between national identity in the United States and national identity in much of the rest of the world. And certainly Bellamy's later (thirty years later) reconstruction of what was in his mind when he wrote the Pledge is consistent with this interpretation. He wanted, he recalled, to "tell something of the type of government which had been established by our fathers." And he wished for not just an affirmation of allegiance to that government but a statement of why the government warranted such allegiance. As he sat alone in his office turning words over in his mind, he "reviewed [the] country's history" and "recalled the great patriotic utterances of our statesmen." Those patriots who had died to keep the nation indivisible, he recalled thinking, had "lived to establish and hand down to us liberty and justice for all." In writing the Pledge, Bellamy was attempting not to innovate but to give "brief and memorable" expression to "the underlying spirit" of the American republic.[2]

The idea that Bellamy's inspired pen captured an unchanging American spirit is tempting but ultimately misleading. It collapses historical time and in so doing encourages us to ignore the historical chasm that separates us from Bellamy and Bellamy from the framers of the federal Constitution. When the words were composed ceases to matter. But it does matter if we are to understand why the Pledge of Allegiance was created and if we are to unlock the Pledge's significance for our own time. We must not assume that Bellamy was just like us, and that his concerns were our concerns. This ahistorical interpretation dims our historical curiosity in a second way by ironing out the late-nineteenth-century fabric so that we no longer can see the creases of contested values and interests. Ignoring the mixed motives and rival aims that contributed to the creation of the Pledge is bound to lead to oversimplified understandings of the American past. Fine perhaps for didactic children's books but not good enough for a history for adults.

A second, less common interpretation of the Pledge pays closer attention to the historical context, especially Bellamy's personal and political beliefs, most specifically his socialist sympathies. This alternative reading of the Pledge exposes its secret and even subversive history, a history that has been almost entirely obliterated from our historical memory, not to mention our children's books. The Pledge is a reminder, as Peter Dreier and Dick Flacks expressed it in the *Nation*, of how "much of our patriotic culture . . . was created by artists of decidedly left-wing and even socialist sympathies." According to Dreier and Flacks, "Bellamy intended the line 'One nation indivisible with liberty and justice for all' to express a more collective and egalitarian vision of America." It was meant, they continue, to "promote a moral vision to counter the individualism embodied in capitalism."[3] Dreier and Flacks's interpretation offers a useful corrective to the conventional narrative, particularly in an era when conservatives have often used the Pledge of Allegiance and the American flag to score political points against liberals, most notably in the 1988 presidential campaign when George Bush attacked Michael Dukakis for vetoing a bill that would have mandated the recitation of the Pledge of Allegiance in Massachusetts schools.

The children's books, of course, make no mention of Bellamy's politics; he is just a nice young man writing for a "children's magazine" with the reassuringly safe title of *Youth's Companion*. But Bellamy's politics were undeniably radical. He was the first cousin of Edward Bellamy, whose best-selling utopian novel *Looking Backward*, published in 1888, catalyzed reform sentiment in the United States. The novel imagines a well-to-do Bostonian, Julian West, who falls into a hypnotically induced sleep and awakens more than a century later, in the year 2000, to find that all of the social problems that had beset late-nineteenth-century America have been solved. Society has peacefully transformed itself from a selfish and anarchic capitalist order to a peaceful and orderly society based on cooperation. The conditions of work have been dramatically transformed. Rather than slaving away for long hours in abject conditions, workers now find there is ample time for leisure. Gone are the age-old concerns with unemployment, starvation, and poverty. Nobody begins work before they are twenty-one and no one works past the age of forty-five. Machines do most of the work, and thus everyone gets half a year off and many work four hours a day or less. The state is the only employer and rewards and protects each person equally regardless of their job or talents. Instead of concerning themselves with making ends meet, the men and women of 2000 can devote their lives to self-development and love of one's fellow human beings.[4]

Among the novel's chief appeals for middle-class readers was that this new world is achieved without violence or strife between employers and employees, capital and labor, and is achieved gradually and peacefully "in accordance with the principles of evolution." In the immediate wake of the widespread industrial violence of the late 1880s—in 1886 alone there had been over fifteen hundred strikes involving well over half a million workers and of course the infamous Haymarket Riot in Chicago to top it off—a world without labor strikes was particularly appealing to the middle class. Marxian socialists dismissed *Looking Backward* as a silly romance that retarded revolutionary action, but Francis Bellamy was one of many educated professionals who immediately became captivated by his cousin's vision of the future. Nationalist Clubs dedicated to promoting Edward Bellamy's vision sprang up across the country. The first of these was the First Nationalist Club of Boston, established in December 1888. Francis Bellamy was a charter member of the club, which included many of Boston's most prominent citizens, including the novelist William Dean Howells, the abolitionist orator and poet Thomas Wentworth Higginson, who had led the Civil War's first black regiment, and Edward Everett Hale, who, besides penning the famous patriotic short story "The Man without a Country" (1863), had been pastor of a Unitarian church in Boston since before the Civil War.[5]

Some of the club's chief organizers were retired military officers who seemed to be particularly attracted to Edward Bellamy's vision of an "industrial army" in which work would be organized along military lines. The military was the prototype for industrial organization, in Bellamy's view, because the military replaced wasteful competition with efficient hierarchy. Moreover, the new industrial army relied on "an arsenal of patriotic and national motives" rather than the self-interest and individualistic incentives on which capitalism depended. As Dr. Leete explained the transformation to a skeptical Julian West: "Now that industry . . . is no longer self-service, but service to the nation, patriotism, passion for humanity, impel the worker as in your day they did the soldier." What appealed to Francis Bellamy about the Nationalist movement, however, was less his cousin's military analogy than his insistence that "human brotherhood" and "fraternal co-operation" were the only principles on which a moral industrial society could be based.[6]

As if to underscore his commitment to the primacy of these principles, Francis Bellamy, together with the Congregational minister W. D. P. Bliss, used one of the earliest meetings of the newly created Nationalist Club to issue a call for a new and explicitly Christian organization dedicated to these principles. The new organization, which in February 1889 adopted the name Society of Christian Socialists, was to be "not hostile, but supplementary and auxiliary" to the Nationalist movement. The organization's objectives, as laid out in its Declaration of Principles, were "to show that the aim of Socialism is embraced in the aim of Christianity" and "to awaken members of Christian Churches to the fact that the teachings of Jesus Christ lead directly to some specific form or forms of Socialism."[7] Bellamy was made a vice president of the new society and the chairman of its Educational Committee, in which capacity he designed and promoted a course of study designed to promote the "study of the bearing of Social Christianity upon economics."

In lectures with titles like "What Is Christian Socialism?," "Jesus the Socialist," and "The Socialism of the Bible," Bellamy worked to spread the Christian socialist message that the current "every-one-for himself" economic system was inconsistent with the teachings and life of Jesus Christ and the Word of God. Christian socialism, for Bellamy, meant that the "law of love," not the heartless market, must be made to govern economic relations. Just as slavery and serfdom had disappeared, so now, Bellamy concluded, "Capitalism must pass into the kingdom of Organized Love." It was Bellamy's outspoken public advocacy of Christian socialist ideas in 1889 and 1890 that led directly to the growing tensions within his Baptist ministry and eventually his resignation from the pulpit in 1891.[8]

In short, there can be little question that at the time that Bellamy went to work for the *Youth's Companion* in April 1891 his economic views were radically subversive. Unlike his cousin Edward, Francis did not shrink from being identified as a "socialist," though he was at pains to point out that Christian socialists were "Christians first and Socialists afterwards." Or, more precisely, they were socialists because "they believe that their Lord was a Socialist."[9] Moreover, whereas Boston's stuffy and exclusive First Nationalist Club had as its objective, as Edward had in writing *Looking Backward*, "the conversion of the cultured and conservative classes," the Society of Christian Socialists established by Bliss and Francis Bellamy consciously reached out to the common people and tried to educate and engage the ordinary workingman. Many of Edward Bellamy's Nationalist admirers were fundamentally conservatives at heart, more fearful of strikes and union organizing than they were committed to equality. But this was not true of his cousin Francis, who strongly sympathized with the rights of labor. As he expressed it in one of the tracts he wrote for the society's educational program, "laborers need not benevolence, but justice."[10]

Yet if Dreier and Flacks are right about Francis Bellamy's socialist sympathies, the relevance of Bellamy's economic radicalism to our understanding of the meaning of the Pledge is less clear. To be sure, Bellamy later said that when writing the Pledge he had initially thought to borrow the "historic slogan of the French Revolution . . . 'Liberty, Equality, Fraternity'" but had decided that invoking equality and fraternity would be too controversial and too fanciful. The phrase "with liberty and justice for all" was preferable, he decided, because it would be "applicable to either an individualistic or a socialistic state, and could not be gainsaid by any party."[11] One can, moreover, detect distinct echoes of Bellamy's radical commitments in his Columbus Day address, most especially when he identifies "equal rights for every soul" as among the principles that define "the true Americanism," and perhaps also when he invokes the words of his famous cousin: "We look backward and we look forward."[12] And yet, when all is said and done, there is relatively little about the Pledge of Allegiance or the Columbus Day public school celebration that reflects the Christian socialist convictions that Bellamy articulated in the years leading up to his work at the *Youth's Companion*. In a country as phobic about socialism as the United States is, it is undoubtedly useful to remind ourselves that the Pledge of Allegiance was written by a socialist, but that shorthand obscures at least as much as it reveals. First, it oversimplifies Bellamy's own thought, particularly at the time he wrote the Pledge, which was almost two years after he had relinquished his active leadership role in the Society of Christian Socialists.[13] Second, and even more problematic, it focuses on Bellamy to the exclusion of the other individuals and organizations without whom there would have been no flag salute.

Bellamy's Hopes and Fears

From early 1889 into the early spring of 1891, Francis Bellamy tirelessly promoted Christian socialism, but almost immediately after resigning his ministry and beginning work at the *Youth's Companion,* this proselytizing activity ceased, soon to be replaced by proselytizing for the Columbus Day public school celebration. As spokesperson for the celebration, Bellamy lectured frequently. If we are to understand the meaning of the Pledge, it behooves us to pay close attention to what Bellamy said in these speeches, most of which were variations on the theme, "Americanism in the Public Schools." Among the most important audiences to which he delivered this address was the annual meeting of the National Education Association (NEA), in Saratoga Springs, New York, on July 15, 1892, less than a month before he wrote the Pledge.[14]

The former Baptist minister began by telling the NEA that the nation was "in the midst of a revival of Americanism," a revival that deserved to be "hailed with delight." After the Civil War, Bellamy observed, people were naturally concerned with returning to normalcy. "Material developments absorbed attention and our people had little mind for national ardors." Now, however,

Americans were awakening to a "new consciousness" of America's "true value and destiny." In defining Americanism, Bellamy cautioned, it was necessary to distinguish between "true Americanism and that which is inferior." True Americanism "cares for the highest destiny of the Republic," while the counterfeit variety "goes no further than markets for special industry and prerogatives on the seas":

> True Americanism is more than exultation over square miles and multitudes; it is a joyous sense that America must be another name for opportunity—opportunity for the realization of justice; opportunity for the free use of all native powers; opportunity for the rounded development of every individual. . . . And true Americanism, also, is more than solicitude for American wheat and iron and hogs; it is more than the fostering of wealth, more than the feeding and clothing of American bodies; the true Americanism is the putting steadily the thing that is fair, the thing that is just, into legislation.

The United States was not like other countries, "not narrow, grasping, selfish, like the old powers." Instead, America was "the generous benefactor, the moral guide, the strong example for the world."[15]

Bellamy issued a call for America to realize its higher self, not in the pursuit of material goods or foreign markets but in the pursuit of liberty and justice for all. Although the speech never really sounds remotely socialist, let alone Christian socialist, it certainly is a plea for an understanding of Americanism that goes beyond a celebration of capitalism. Moreover, Bellamy articulates an inclusive understanding of Americanism based on civic ideals, eschewing an exclusive nationalism premised on ethnicity or race. The speech, in short, offers support both to the civic patriotism interpretation of the Pledge and to the leftist interpretation of the Pledge.

But there is more to the speech, and much of this fits less comfortably within either of these interpretations. For the eloquent articulation of American ideals coexists with a more anxious note, particularly focused on the threat posed by immigration. "Americanism," Bellamy lectured, "brings a duty." For "it must be made a force strong enough to touch the immigrant population which is *pouring over* our country." Only the public schools had the capacity to inculcate the rapidly growing population of immigrants with the spirit of true Americanism. One certainly could not count on the "corrupt party machines," which were often, as in Bellamy's own Boston, controlled by immigrants. Teaching civics was essential to redeeming politics, but schools also needed to appeal to the "sentiment" of students, and this is where the school flag movement was so important. Bellamy dismissed those who "depreciate the use of the flag, call it a fetich, and claim that our generation has risen beyond the need of any symbol of textile fabric." Particularly for "children of foreign parentage," the daily practice of "raising and saluting [the flag] . . . is a daily object lesson in patriotism for the land of their adoption." The flag in the school "makes the nation a real thing to the very ones who are most in want of that lesson." As evidence, Bellamy pointed to the salutary effect that Colonel Balch's program of patriotic activities was having in New York City schools on "the children of Italy, and Germany, and Portugal, and Ireland." The "thrilling salutes" given to the flag by these immigrants were "evidence enough," Bellamy asserted, that "the flag has as great a potency to Americanize the alien child as it has to lead regiments to death." A flag salute was needed, in short, to Americanize the alien.[16]

Perhaps even more revealing of Bellamy's attitudes at this time was a speech he delivered six months later to the Women's Literary Union. As in the paper he read to the NEA, Bellamy began by lauding the revival of patriotic feeling. Before the predominantly female audience he delivered his indictment of the post–Civil War materialism in harsher terms, deploring the nation's worship of "the shameless, indecent almighty dollar." He was more explicit, too, about the importance of equality and fraternity, which he considered the defining attributes of "the new Americanism." The liberty characteristic of the old Americanism, he said, had "run into the ground":

> It had meant liberty for great corporations to oppress the people; liberty for gas companies to charge the American people ten per cent on 150 millions of fictitious gas stock; liberty for the West End railroad Company of Boston to stretch its death dealing wires so that in cases of great fires like that of the other day the burning flesh of the poor firemen sizzles and taints the atmosphere; liberty for the atoms on top of the sand heap to press down harder and harder the atoms below.

The nation, he concluded, had "had enough of that kind of liberty." What was needed instead was more fraternity, that is, a recognition that "we are not a sand heap, but a family," and more equality, which meant that "every man shall have the equal right to work and earn bread for his family; that every child shall be taken and given as good a chance as the government can afford." Here, then, were Bellamy's socialist sympathies laid squarely on the table. For Bellamy, the words "with liberty and justice for all" were meant not to affirm an allegiance to the individualistic America of old but to kindle the awakening spirit of the new Americanism.[17]

But if Bellamy's socialist commitments were more explicitly presented in his speech to the Women's Literary Union, so too were his anxieties about immigrants, particularly immigrants of a certain sort. The United States, Bellamy acknowledged, had "always been a nation of immigrants." Immigrants had "felled our forests and built up our institutions." But the immigrants who had done this "came from the northern and western nations of Europe, from peoples who were really Americans in spirit before they came." The problem America faced now with the "incoming waves of immigration" was that "a different class are coming now. They are coming from countries whose institutions are entirely at variance with our own—from Russia, Poland, Armenia, Bohemia, Italy." From Italy "we are receiving the vilest elements," and from Poland and Russia we are getting "expelled Jews who will not labor with their hands, but choose rather to be parasites of tenement houses and worthless vendors." America, Bellamy concluded ominously, "cannot live on what America cannot digest. We cannot be the dumping ground of Europe and bloom like a flower garden." It was this threat to American ideas and institutions that made it so essential that citizens nurture "a revival of [the] American spirit."[18]

Bellamy admitted that "it is hard to say what equality is," but it is clear from his speech what equality is not. It did not mean that all people were created equal. As Bellamy put it, "there are immigrants and immigrants." Bellamy made this point even more explicit in an editorial he wrote a few years later for the *Illustrated American*, where he served as editor for several years in the mid-1890s. "The hard, inescapable fact," Bellamy wrote, "is that men are not born equal":

> Neither are they born free, but all in bonds to their ancestors and their environments. . . . The success of government by the people will depend upon the stuff that people are made of. The people must . . . guard, more jealously even than their liberties, the quality of their blood. A democracy like ours cannot afford to throw itself open to the world. Where every man is a lawmaker, every dull-witted or fanatical immigrant admitted to our citizenship is a bane to the commonwealth. Where all classes of society merge insensibly into one another every alien immigrant of inferior race may bring corruption to the stock. There are races, more or less akin to our own, whom we may admit freely, and get nothing but advantage from the infusion of their wholesome blood. But there are other races which we cannot assimilate without a lowering of our racial standard, which should be as sacred to us as the sanctity of our homes.[19]

If it is useful to remind ourselves that the Pledge of Allegiance was written by a socialist, it is also instructive to remember that the Pledge was written by a race-conscious nativist. To see the Pledge of Allegiance as simply an affirmation of civic patriotism is to obscure the racial and ethnic anxieties that animated its creation.

The Anxiety about Immigrants

Of course, Bellamy was hardly unique in his racial anxieties. They were widespread in the 1880s and 1890s among Anglo-Saxon Protestants like Bellamy who, conscious of their pedigree, struggled to adjust to the "incoming waves" of strange and different immigrants. More people (over five million) emigrated to the United States between 1881 and 1890 than had come in the previous twenty years combined. In fact, more than one-third of the total number of U.S. immigrants between 1820 and 1890 arrived in the 1880s. But it was not the sheer numbers that alarmed people most—it was who was coming. In the 1860s and 1870s immigrants overwhelmingly came from northern Europe: Belgium, Britain and Ireland, France, Germany, the Netherlands, Scandinavia, and Switzerland. In 1882 still only about 10 percent of immigrants came from southern and eastern Europe. But by 1892 that number had jumped to closer to 44 percent. For every Italian, Slav, or Jew entering the United States in 1882 there had been four immigrants from Germany or Scandinavia; by 1892, however, the new immigrants from southern and eastern Europe easily surpassed the number coming from northern Europe.[20]

The sharp distinction Bellamy drew between the good immigrants of old and the newer undesirable immigrants had begun to gain widespread currency in the early 1890s. In 1890, Francis Walker, president of Massachusetts Institute of Technology, director of the 1870 and 1880 censuses, and the most distinguished American economist of the time, warned the American Economic Association (of which he was president) against the new tide of "races of . . . the very lowest stage of degradation." In 1892, the Grand Army of the Republic issued a report distinguishing sharply between those who come "with honest purpose to add to the brain or brawn of this free land" and "that portion of the tide of immigration sweeping upon our shores which represents only the poverty and the crime of other lands." Writing in the *North American Review* in 1891, Representative Henry Cabot Lodge, who would serve as Bellamy's calling card to the president, warned that the newest immigrants were "from races most alien to the body of the American people." This shift in the source of immigration, he warned, was "bringing to the country people whom it is very difficult to assimilate and who do not promise well for the standard of civilization in the United States." To shut off the increasing flow of Italians, Jews, Poles, Russians, and Slovaks, Lodge introduced into the House of Representatives a bill to prohibit illiterates from entering the country. Although race neutral on its face, the clear intent of the 1892 bill was to stem the tide of southern and eastern European immigrants, among whom illiteracy rates were generally very high.[21]

Lodge and Walker were conservative pillars of the New England establishment and strong critics of anything that smacked of socialism or radicalism.[22] But anti-immigrant attitudes were not limited to the conservative blue bloods of Boston. Indeed, as historian John Higham has pointed out, the discovery of an "immigration problem" probably occurred more quickly among the labor-oriented reformers than it did among more complacent conservatives. Lodge's idea of a literacy test as a way of restricting immigration had first been proposed in 1887 by a progressive economist, Edward Bemis, as a means of protecting American laborers. The American Protection Association, a virulently anti-Catholic organization founded in 1887, began life in Clinton, Iowa, after a slate of local candidates backed by the Knights of Labor were defeated, owing, the disgruntled losers said, to the Irish vote. After the economic downturn beginning in 1883, the Knights of Labor blamed their troubles on the cheap labor recruited by capitalists from countries like Hungary and Italy. Like "so many cattle, large numbers of degraded, ignorant, brutal . . . foreign serfs," they complained, were being lured to the country to replace American workers. In 1885, under intense pressure from labor, Congress enacted a ban on the practice of companies prepaying transportation in exchange for a promise of service.[23]

Probably the most influential early cry of alarm about immigration in the 1880s was sounded by the Congregationalist minister Josiah Strong in the book *Our Country,* published in 1885 by the American Home Missionary Society.[24] A seminal text in the burgeoning social gospel movement, *Our Country* assailed industrial capitalism both for the "gross materialism" and selfishness it engendered and for the vast disparities in wealth and power between rich and poor that it created. Strong pilloried the "conscienceless monopolies" and the arbitrary power placed in the hands of the capitalist, who "can arbitrarily raise the price of necessaries, can prevent men's working, but has no responsibility, meanwhile, as to their starving." The result was a "despotism vastly more oppressive" than that which had sparked the American Revolution a century earlier.[25]

Strong's passionate denunciations of the evils of industrial capitalism were accompanied by a searing indictment of the dangers posed to the United States by immigration. "During the last four years," Strong lamented, "we have suffered a peaceful invasion by an army more than twice as vast as the estimated number of Goths and Vandals that swept over Southern Europe and overwhelmed Rome." These new immigrants, "controlled largely by their appetites and prejudices," were degrading American morals and politics, "swelling our dangerous classes" and "[feeding] fat the liquor power." They were dangerously "building up states within a state," with different languages, loyalties, and religions. The question facing America was whether "this in-sweeping immigration is to foreignize us, or we are to Americanize it." The United States, Strong suggested, was like a lion and the immigrants like oxen. So long as the lion could dictate "what, when, and how much [oxen] he shall eat," then all is well— "the ox becomes lion." But if the lion, "without being consulted as to time, quantity or quality, is having the food thrust down his throat," then "the ignoble ox might slay the king of beasts." The country's only alternative, like the lion's, is to "digest or die." Slowing the pace of immigration was essential if the nation was to assimilate and Americanize "these strange populations."[26]

Among the most serious problems created by immigration was the increase in the number of Roman Catholics. Catholics were not fit to be American citizens because those who accept "absolutism in religion" also accept being "led to the polls like so many sheep." The Roman Catholic, Strong declaimed, is "suckled on authority" and "has been taught that he must not judge for himself, nor trust to his own convictions." Making matters worse, Catholics shunned the public schools, which Strong described as "the principal digestive organ of the body politic." Through the public school, "children of strange and dissimilar races" are typically "assimilated and made Americans" in a single generation, but Catholics, under orders from the Catholic hierarchy, were sending their children to parochial schools,[27] where they received "a training calculated to make them narrow and bigoted." "The object of the public school," Strong insisted, "is to make good citizens." In contrast, "the object of the parochial school is to make good Catholics. . . . The parochial school aims to lead, rather than to train the mind; to produce a spirit of submission rather than of independence. The one system is calculated to arouse, the other to repress, the spirit of inquiry. The one aims at self-control, the other at control by superiors." The American common school taught "intelligent obedience to rightful authority," whereas the Catholic parochial school taught "unquestioning obedience to rightful authority." Public schools prepared the young to become citizens in a democratic republic; Catholic schools trained the young to follow the dictates of Rome. Quoting Lafayette, Strong warned that "if the liberties of the American people are ever destroyed, they will fall by the hands of the Roman clergy."[28]

Perched uneasily alongside Strong's religious and racial anxieties and his dark forebodings of imminent danger are confident pronouncements of the divine mission destined to be fulfilled by the "mighty Anglo-Saxon race." Unless "devitalized by alcohol and tobacco," Strong asked rhetorically, "is there room for reasonable doubt that [the Anglo-Saxon] race . . . is destined to dispossess many weaker races, assimilate others, and mold the remainder until, in a very true and important sense, it has Anglo-Saxonized mankind?" He predicted that "this powerful race will move down upon Mexico, down upon Central and South America, out upon the islands of the sea, over upon Africa and beyond." The Anglo-Saxon race was being "schooled" by God for "the final competition of races" and the outcome was foreordained: "Nothing can save the inferior race but a ready and pliant assimilation." The United States would remake the world in its Anglo-Saxon and Protestant image.[29]

Strong warned against the perils facing the United States, but his was still ultimately an optimistic message, even regarding immigrants. The Anglo-Saxon race, Strong believed, owed its strength not to racial purity but to "its highly mixed origin," and America's superiority to England lay precisely in its greater mixture of races, making it hardier and more adaptable. So long as "the largest injections of foreign blood are substantially the same elements that constituted the original Anglo-Saxon admixture," the "general type will be preserved" and the racial "stock" strengthened. Strong was confident that if the "dangers of immigration . . . can be successfully met for the next few years, until it has passed its climax, [immigrants] may be expected to add value to the amalgam which will constitute the new Anglo-Saxon race of the New World." Strong echoed Herbert Spencer's judgment about America: "The eventual mixture of the allied varieties of the Aryan race . . . will produce a more powerful type of man than has hitherto existed . . . a civilization grander than any the world has known."[30]

Strong's book was widely read, and the *Youth's Companion* did its bit to boost its circulation. In the October 1891 premium issue, Upham launched his plans for reviving "the Lyceum League of America," which was to be a nationwide network of clubs in which the young men of America would debate important public questions, thereby promoting good citizenship. Accompanying this proposal, the *Companion* included a short list of books "for reference and study" to help prepare the youth of America for the topics likely to be debated. The second book on this select list was the newly revised edition of *Our Country* ("based on the census of 1890," the title page boasted), which the *Companion* offered to readers for free with one new subscription—or readers could purchase the book for sixty cents. The scope of this "important Book," read the *Companion*'s blurb, was "National Resources and National Perils: Immigration, Romanism, Public Schools, Mormonism, Intemperance, Socialism, Wealth, the City, The Exhaustion of Public Lands, The Anglo-Saxon and the World's Future."[31]

The influence of Josiah Strong on the thinking of those at the *Youth's Companion* is evident in an editorial published in the *Companion* on November 10, 1892, just weeks after the nationwide Columbus Day celebration. The article exhibited the same ambivalent mix of racial anxiety and racial pride that pervades *Our Country*. Citing the new census statistics, the *Companion* drew its readers' attention to the fact that "one-sixth of the whole country is of foreign birth" and about that same number were born of foreign parents (what the *Companion* didn't tell its readers was that this percentage had been unchanged since about 1860). More alarming still, in the eyes of the *Companion*, was that in Massachusetts the number of foreign born was over 40 percent, while in North Dakota the number was almost 80 percent. What did these numbers mean? The nearest parallel, in the *Companion*'s view, was the Argentine Republic, where comparable percentages of the population were foreign born, "chiefly the ignorant classes from Italy, France, and Spain." In Argentina the results had not been encouraging. But then again, the *Companion* noted, "native born Argentine citizens lack the instinct for civil order and good government which our native citizens inherit from centuries of Anglo-Saxon progress." "In our country," the *Companion* boasted, "the experiment which Europe watched with so great curiosity is resulting in the elevation of the new-comers to the moral and intellectual standards of the natives. But it needed a native-born race of high character and traditions to accomplish this." What began as a lament about the threat to American identity becomes in the end an affirmation of Anglo-Saxon superiority and American greatness. As in *Our Country*, racial anxieties are suppressed or sublimated by a belief in racial superiority.[32]

One cannot understand the timing of the schoolhouse flag movement and the creation of the Pledge of Allegiance without understanding the intense anxiety about immigrants that began to grip many native-born Americans in the 1880s. From the Civil War into the early 1880s Americans had generally shown great confidence in their nation's ability to assimilate new immigrants, at least those from Europe and Canada. Immigration remained almost completely unrestricted—with the notable and ignoble exception of the Chinese, who in 1882 were forbidden from coming to the United States. State governments actively promoted immigration and businesses welcomed new labor. Germans continued to pour into the Midwest, as they had since the 1850s, immigration from

Britain and Ireland remained high, and the nation continued to receive many immigrants from Scandinavia and French Canada. There was plenty of ethnic, religious, and racial prejudice, especially against German Jews and the Irish, but until the mid-1880s few seriously believed American institutions were imperiled by immigrants. The primary threat to national unity came not from strange newcomers but from disloyal Southern Confederates. While particular groups might be seen as backward economically or morally, America's distinctive strength lay in its ability to create a "new man" from the mixture of different nationalities. It was this that made American national character superior to that of the European.[33]

Our Country echoed this familiar national conceit about American superiority, but Strong's alarm about the perils of immigration signaled a shift that was taking place in the 1880s in American attitudes toward the immigrant. The postwar confidence that assimilation would happen almost effortlessly was shaken. Increasingly, Americanization was seen as something that had to be consciously manufactured. Left to themselves, these new immigrants would create, as Strong put it, "states within a state." The bomb thrown in Chicago's Haymarket Square in 1886 triggered nativist hysteria because it seemed to underscore the perils to the nation's existence posed by insular communities of lawless foreigners, the "scum and offal of Europe."

It might not be possible to Americanize foreign adults, but their young were more malleable. Public schools increasingly became seen as the front lines in the battle to Americanize the immigrant. The schoolhouse must become, as President Benjamin Harrison told Bellamy, "the place for education in intelligent patriotism and citizenship." Raising and saluting the flag was a central part of this education in patriotism and civics aimed at Americanizing alien children.[34]

Balch's Flag Salute

Evidence of the close connection between native anxiety about immigration and the adoption of the flag salute can be seen in the creation of the first flag salute in New York City by Colonel George Balch. Then, as now, New York City was an immensely diverse city. By 1880, immigrants and their children already constituted four-fifths of the city's population. A decade later about three-fifths of those in the city eligible to vote were born beyond the borders of the United States. Between 1884 and 1892 the population of the Lower East Side of Manhattan tripled as a result of immigration, much of it from Southern Italians and Russian Jews. During the 1860s and 1870s few seemed to care that the schools were woefully inadequate or that thousands of immigrant children did not attend schools because their families needed the income they could provide. This was true even after passage of the Compulsory Education Act in 1874. But coincident with the arrival of large numbers of Southern Italians and Russian Jews in the 1880s, pressure began to build for compulsory and improved schooling so that "little aliens" could be made into "little citizens."[35]

By 1888, anxieties about immigrants had reached a fever pitch. A request from an alderman that on St. Patrick's Day the city fly the Irish flag along with the national, state, and municipal flags brought an outraged rebuke from the city's mayor, who said that while he was "in favor of flying the American flag . . . under any pretext," he would fly "foreign flags under no pretext." A large rally was held at Cooper Institute to demonstrate support for the mayor's policy. Just a few months earlier, in January 1888, the Reverend Charles H. Parkhurst preached to his Madison Square Presbyterian Church that while it was "a nice idea" to "open our doors to everybody," America needed to attend to the dangers of unrestricted immigration. The nation was like a family, and like any family, the lines between members and nonmembers must be "sharply drawn" in order for the household to do its work. While wisely having "closed the back door to the Chinese," the nation at the same time had rashly "broken the bell, thrown away the locks, opened the windows, and demolished the whole Eastern front." The foreigners who had come pouring in, moreover, "treated America like a tenement house," and so great were their numbers that it was no longer clear "whether they are boarding with us or we with them." Immigrants could be tolerated only

> if they cease to be foreigners and become Americans. . . . We welcome the foreigner if his foreign ideas are left at home with foreign whims and prejudices, [but] we do not want an Irish Catholic . . . if he is going to put the Roman Vatican before our Government. . . . [W]e do not want Germans retaining their views on temperance, Scotchmen on religious observances, and Irishmen clinging to the notion that liberty means license. Having come here to get membership in a family they did nothing to found and little to preserve in its days of peril, it is but a matter of decency for them to leave our institutions as they find them.

America, he concluded, should be "for the Americans" and only for the rest when they consent to relinquish their old-world habits and customs. Patriotism had no place for diversity.[36]

It was against this backdrop of heightened ethnic tensions and anxieties that Balch began work on his program of patriotic activities for schools, which included the first-known flag salute. Balch had become interested in the city's schools after studying the appalling living conditions of immigrants in the tenement houses. Here he found what he described as "human scum, cast on our shores by the tidal wave of a vast immigration." In January 1889 Balch was commissioned to undertake a study of the industrial day schools run by the Children's Aid Society, schools that served about five thousand of the city's poorest immigrants. Balch, who had extensive experience as an auditor in the private and public sectors, investigated, among other things, the sanitary conditions of the schools, the kind of furniture used, the demographics of the student body, the training and experience of the teachers, the content of the curriculum, the provisions being made for students who came to school inadequately fed or clothed, the obedience and cleanliness of students, and the relations between teachers and parents. But what particularly interested Balch were the methods that teachers had begun to adopt to cultivate a "spirit of patriotism" among their students. For it was through instilling patriotism that the schools could most effectively combat the two greatest (and closely connected) threats to the nation's social, moral, and political character: immigration and crime.

In a speech before the teachers of the Children's Aid Society in June 1889 (by which time he had been appointed auditor of the city's board of education) he praised the Society for the excellent job it was doing in "rais[ing] the character and promot[ing] the well-being" of impoverished immigrants, many of whom were "the descendants of a long line of ignorant, stolid or debased progenitors." But schools, not only in New York City but across the nation, needed to do more and better to teach young people "those great political and moral axioms and principles upon which this government was founded." To that end, Balch proposed "a practicable plan" by which public elementary schools could be made into "a mighty engine for the inculcation of patriotism." Balch's plan was published the following year as *Methods of Teaching Patriotism in the Public Schools.*[37]

The American flag provided the symbolic center of the various patriotic exercises proposed by Balch. The flag was to be both reward and symbol. Balch proposed a daily ceremony in which the student in a class who had exhibited the most exemplary conduct would be presented with an American flag and a badge of citizenship by the school's principal. The flag and badge were not to be awarded for academic achievement, as this would be "inconsistent with democratic principles, quite as un-American as to make a particular nationality or religious creed, or the possession of a certain amount of property by the child's parents a sine qua non." Rather they were to be awarded for the kinds of behavior that were essential ingredients of good citizenship, such as punctuality, attendance, cleanliness, cheerfulness, truthfulness, "obedience to rules and instruction," and "respectful bearing toward superiors." The "Scholar's Flag" would be displayed on the student's desk until it was formally relinquished at the daily or weekly flag ceremony, which was to be "graceful and dignified" so as to impress upon the children "a profound sense of the nobility and dignity of American citizenship." Balch also envisioned a comparable weekly competition between classes that would result in the award of "the Class Flag" to the classroom with the best record of punctuality and attendance. Competition for the flag would induce the sort of self-restraint and orderly, responsible behavior that was necessary to becoming "a good American citizen."[38]

The flag was to be used not only as an incentive for good behavior but as a symbol to which students could pledge their loyalty to the nation and its ideals. At the daily morning exercise, the Class Flag was to be solemnly paraded into the assembly room by a deserving student and escorted by a color-guard. With "the color-bearer and guard" on the right and (hopefully) a drummer or fife player on the left, the principal would issue a signal for the entire school to stand and then, "after a brief pause, until the utmost stillness reigns," command the students to "*Salute the flag!*" At the command, each student was to raise "the extended right hand to the forehead (palm down), in unison . . . [and] salute the flag in military fashion." Simultaneously, the flag bearer was to "slowly and gracefully dip the colors, while the drummer beats three long rolls or the wind-instrument performs a flourish." After the music was finished, the hand was to be slowly and gracefully lowered to the side. The aim of the salute was to have the school show "its loyal allegiance to . . . [and] profound respect for the American Nation, of which the star spangled banner is the visible emblem and symbol." Shortly thereafter Balch devised his spoken salute—which he called "The American Patriotic Salute": "We give our heads and our hearts to God and our country; one country, one language, one Flag."[39]

Balch hoped his patriotic activities and flag salute would be taken up across the nation, by immigrants as well as natives, but there can be little doubt that immigrants were the motivating spur and the immediate audience. If Balch hoped his methods would spread beyond New York City's industrial schools, it is because he saw immigration as a national problem, not a local one. Over the previous seventy years, Balch observed, the nation had witnessed the arrival of

Schoolchildren give the "Balch salute" at New York City's Mott Street Industrial School. This photograph was taken sometime between 1890 and 1892. Prints and Photographs Division, Library of Congress.

fifteen millions of aliens, speaking more than forty distinct languages and dialects other than the English; a vast number of whom bear in their physical and mental features the indelible impress of centuries of monarchical or aristocratic rule and oppression, and who have been trained to an implicit belief in and reverence for ecclesiastical institutions which find no place in our form of government.

Immigration had "in many instances, so diluted our civilization, and so radically modified many of the social and political conditions, which in the past have characterized our national life, [including] the administration of our municipal affairs as to lead us to-day to the serious consideration . . . of adopting such heroic remedies as will in future protect us from the evils and dangers" of unrestricted immigration. The problem had been made worse by "our own questionable generosity in investing large numbers of the more ignorant and untrained of these accessions to our population with all the rights of American citizenship."[40] For Balch, as for Bellamy and Upham, saluting the flag in public schools was a central part of the effort to Americanize the alien. Teaching patriotism was a way of preserving the America of old in the face of a foreign invasion.

Balch, like so many late-nineteenth-century, middle-class Americans, was a bundle of racial conceits and ethnic prejudices, and yet, also like them, his attitude toward immigrants was powerfully shaped by a celebratory view of America. For the distinctive greatness of the United States lay in its ability to uplift and redeem the degraded people of the Old World. The immigrant children in the industrial schools came from the very lowest "social grade"; their parents were "the peasant laborers, the shepherds and the vine-dressers of the Italian provinces . . . a peasantry, who . . . for centuries have been practically never else than serfs; a people, whose social and political condition is to-day, practically no better than was that of their ancestors one thousand years ago." But American institutions brought about an almost "magical change" in the lives of these immigrant children, transforming lives of "dull despair" into lives of opportunity and promise. Like Josiah Strong, Balch combined warnings of imminent danger—"we should lose no time in adopting such measures," Balch urged—with a hopeful message of America's redemptive power. Balch's patriotic school program, like the Columbus Day celebration, was born of both a foreboding about the perils of immigration and a hopefulness about the power of America to remake and redeem the immigrant young. These elaborate patriotic rituals, in short, married the darkest ethnocultural anxieties with the brightest American ideals.[41]

The Call for Sacrifice

The adoption of the flag salute in public schools cannot be explained without understanding the growing anxiety about immigrants in the late 1880s, but it cannot be reduced to immigration alone. Immigrants, with their strange languages, customs, and religion, were seen in the late nineteenth century as a leading threat to the national character, but they were far from the only one. Another perceived threat to America's values and traditions came from the materialism, commercialism, and self-seeking of a rapidly industrializing society. This concern was not limited to those on the left but rather was widely diffused among America's educated and professional classes.

It was this anxiety about the prevalence of materialism and selfishness that helps to explain why the military proved such an attractive model for so many of those involved with the creation of a flag salute and related patriotic rituals.

Balch's original flag salute was taken directly from the military's flag salute. Moreover, Balch drew a direct analogy between the role of the flag in the school and in the military. The flag, Balch wrote, "represents the whole body of children under instruction—the school as a unit, as an entity; so employed, it bears the same relation to the school as an organized body, that a regimental flag in the United States Army bears to the entire regiment, having no regard to the nature of its component parts." For Balch, the military provided a model of self-sacrificing behavior, the sort of behavior that was not sufficiently cultivated in "this aggressively commercial metropolis." Daily life in industrial America too often fostered the "selfish and materialistic element in [one's] character," and neglected "the nobler emotions." When Balch designed his plan for having a flag over every schoolhouse, a key aspect was that schools not just be given flags but that students work to get the flag for their school. "The flag so secured," wrote Balch, "will have a depth of meaning, and will represent to these children what it represents to every man who has fought for it, and to every woman whose heart has been wrung for it: a supreme effort; a great trial; a costly sacrifice."[42]

Upham's views were similar to Balch's. In designing a fitting salute to the flag, Upham, like Balch, had used the military salute as a model. Students were directed first to give the military salute before extending their arm toward the flag at the words "my flag."[43] For Upham no less than for Colonel Balch, the military provided a model for the discipline and self-sacrifice sadly lacking in American society. And Upham also shared Balch's view that it was important that the flags not just be given to schools by rich benefactors but that the schoolchildren themselves work to obtain the flag for their school. Flying the flag over the schoolhouse, Upham explained, gives "children a new idea of the significance of law and order with freedom, so that they themselves become orderly and subject to a wholesome discipline." It helped boys and girls become "brave men and good women." As evidence, Upham cited representative letters the *Companion* had received from teachers across the country. A Connecticut teacher, for instance, reported that "it is easier to govern the children since the flag was raised," while another from Massachusetts testified that the presence of the flag in the school had been "a grand step . . . toward making brave, manly boys and womanly girls." Upham detested "those pale-blooded editors" who objected to the "worship of a textile fabric." The American flag, he insisted, represented not only loyalty to country but also "religion, liberty, law, self-sacrifice, mutual help and forbearance for a common good."[44]

War as a model of patriotic self-sacrifice explains the prominence of the GAR in the schoolhouse flag movement and the flag salute rituals. Veterans who had fought in the Civil War were widely viewed as the embodiment of the heroic ideal of sacrifice, a living indictment of the mundane materialism of every-day industrial life. In presenting flags to the schoolhouse and in leading the young in flag salutes, the veterans were to remind students of loyalties and self-sacrifice that extended beyond one's immediate family or work. As Balch explained,

> I can conceive of no public act more appropriate and timely than that of the veter-ans of the war, as the surviving representatives of that grand army of more tha[n] a million . . . men, by whose fortitude, courage, and valor the union of these States was preserved as a precious heritage for their children, thus coming forward in their declining years, bearing gifts of national flags to the children of the public schools— the wards of the State, to remind them not only of what they owe to that grand army of 1861–1865, but what an inestimable legacy of freedom and liberty this flag rep-resents, and under what weighty obligations these gifts place these youths.

The decision made by Bellamy and Upham to involve local GAR posts in the Columbus Day celebration reflected the same belief that the participation of the heroic generation of "war-worn and scarred veterans" would teach the young a never-to-be-forgotten lesson in the true meaning of patriotism.[45]

In the late 1880s and early 1890s the Civil War increasingly assumed a ro-mantic aura. War itself might be hell, but the accompanying self-sacrifice, unity, and cohesiveness all seemed attractive to Americans concerned with the tremendous social and economic dislocation of the late nineteenth century. The nostalgia for the Civil War was evident in the pages of the *Youth's Companion*, as, for instance, when it published an article by the historian James Parton, who wrote glowingly in 1891 of the contributions of the GAR and nostalgically about the bonds of war. "In an army," Parton wrote, "this strong feeling of com-radeship [binds] a million men into such coherency that they can move and feel and act as one man. It was wonderful to notice, in our late war, how strong and how universal this army feeling was. The common object, common perils, com-mon sufferings, common triumphs, knitted close together the hearts and minds of that vast multitude of diverse men." In 1889, the year after publishing *Look-ing Backward*, Edward Bellamy wrote a short story, "An Echo of Antietam," in which he described a Union regiment heading off to war: "The imposing mass, with its rhythmic movement, gives the impression of a single organism. One forgets to look for the individuals in it, forgets that there are individuals. Even those who have brothers, sons, lovers there, for a moment forget them in the impression of a mighty whole." Later in the story, the night before the lead character, Philip, is to die in battle, Bellamy offers the following observation: "What a pity it truly is that the tonic air of the battlefields—the air that Philip breathed that night before Antietam—cannot be gathered up and preserved as a precious elixir to reinvigorate the atmosphere in times of peace when men grow faint and cowardly and quake at the thought of death."[46]

The military as model for the schools was evident not only in the morning flag-raising ceremony itself—after all, at this time flags were routinely raised mostly over military installations and naval vessels—but in the afternoon parades of schoolchildren as well. Writing after the celebration, the *Youth's Companion* glowingly described "the marching of the army of eager children with drilled precision of step." In New York the young marchers—all boys—were divided into "regiments" under the "command" of their school principals. "The Army of Our Schools on a Grand March" read the headline in *The World.* The *Times* observed that "there was a spirit of intent to behave like soldiers among the [young marchers] that promised that they would." The *Malden Evening News* reported on the Malden parade of schoolchildren in much the same way: "They showed the effects of thorough drill, and their marching, everything considered, was perfection. . . . Perfect rank and file, heads erect, shoulders back, and eyes front, they presented a sight that even old veterans respected." Bellamy's evening address in Malden also celebrated "this army of the future, these 13,000,000 of our public school pupils" who were "the hope of America." Becoming grandiloquent, Bellamy continued: "This morning as the sun again lit the mountain tops and valleys of this continent, the glorious banner of our new world rose to greet it. His rays kissed the starry folds from ocean to ocean, as from the North to the South, from East to West, marched forth the willing feet of millions to raise their country's banner: not over forts and camps and battlefields, but over the bulwark of the nation's strength—the public school." The public schools would protect the nation from disorder and fragmentation, just as the Union army had unified and preserved the nation in the Civil War. Flying and saluting the flag in the schools would help instill the same spirit of altruism and sacrifice that a generation earlier had been created by war.[47]

The Search for Order

Bellamy's fervent defense of the public school can readily be accommodated within the storybook version of the Pledge of Allegiance, at least so long as one shuts one's eyes to the anti-Catholicism that sometimes lurked behind the aggressive promotion of what Upham and Bellamy called "the public school idea." But much of the rest of the story fits awkwardly or not at all within the confines of this sunny narrative. The final six words of the Pledge eloquently express the nation's commitment to enduring liberal ideals, but requiring schoolchildren to recite these words in unison to display their allegiance to the nation also paradoxically reflects a commitment to the decidedly unliberal ideals of order, discipline, and the subordination of one's self to a larger collective or cause.

The view that the Pledge of Allegiance was a creation of the radical left and only later co-opted by conservatives is untenable. From the outset, in critical ways, the Pledge reflected conservative currents in American society; the schoolhouse flag movement and flag salute were part and parcel of the "search for order" that the historian Robert Wiebe has seen as characteristic of this period.[48] Focusing on Bellamy's radicalism helps us understand something about the author's original understanding of the phrase "with liberty and justice for all," but it tells us nothing about why students all across the nation were asked to salute the flag and pledge allegiance to it. If we wish to understand why there is a flag in every public school and why children pledge allegiance to that flag, it is probably more appropriate to focus on Upham's beliefs than on Bellamy's.

It was Upham, as we discovered in the previous chapter, who was the prime mover behind the *Companion*'s schoolhouse flag movement and who insisted on the need for a flag salute. Prior to working for Upham, Bellamy had exhibited no particular interest in the place of public schools, nor did he express concerns about flagging patriotism. These were, by all accounts, Upham's particular passions. When he joined the *Companion*, Bellamy enthusiastically enlisted in the cause, but it remained Upham who provided both the animating vision and the practical direction.[49]

Because Upham preferred to work quietly behind the scenes and because his papers have not been preserved, we know far less about Upham's views than we do about Bellamy's. But one thing that stands out about Upham's thought is the way in which it is focused on recovering a simpler, more altruistic and patriotic past. For Upham, the solution to the ills of contemporary America was to revive or recapture older American values and ways of life. Upham talked nostalgically of "the days of the little, red school house" and bemoaned the disappearance of "the simple patriotic idealism of the former generations." Upham was a prototypical representative of the late-nineteenth-century American who responded to social change and dislocation by "trying to hold fast to an older image of [the nation]." Upham's attempt to recapture "the old patriotism" was a conservative impulse in the most basic and elemental meaning of that word.[50]

In understanding Upham's nostalgia for the past, it is instructive to recall that Upham was a Knight Templar,[51] the most prestigious and selective of the

Masonic orders, and the only Masonic order from which non-Christians (Jews and Muslims, as well as atheists) were (and are) excluded. The Knights Templar were named after Christian crusaders who had protected Christians en route to Jerusalem. The crusaders took vows of "poverty, chastity and obedience, and were renowned for their fierceness and courage in battle." The late-nineteenth-century romance with the chivalric age was not unique to the Knights Templar, but it is hardly surprising that it would be more central to the self-image of those who, like Upham, had entered a select band of brothers who fancied that their order was descended from its medieval namesake. On special occasions, the Knights would don their expensive regalia, including "glittering swords," "snowy plumes," and sashes, gloves, and belts bedecked with crosses.[52]

Among the most characteristic attitudes of the Knights Templar and of Masons more generally was a disdain for the rampant materialism and commercialism of modern society. Lynn Dumenil's fine study shows that late-nineteenth-century Masons were preoccupied with "the greed and commercialism that they felt permeated contemporary society. Rarely was a speech or article complete without reference to the 'growing greed for worldly goods . . . [that makes] money the God to be worshipped.'" As one Mason expressed it in 1892, "Money rules everything, and no one can escape its yoke; and money scorns the quiet habits of the old world; it pulls the old social machine to pieces, [and] puts what was below above." Masonry was conceived by its partisans "as an asylum where the commercialism and discord of the external world were excluded and morality, equality, and brotherly love prevailed."[53]

By situating Upham in his historical context, we can better understand what he meant when he criticized the rampant commercialism and materialism of his time. The temptation is to subsume his ideas within categories familiar to us, and so we may be quick to assume that his critique of materialism is in spirit similar to a leftist critique of individualism or capitalism. But Upham was not a leftist in any sense that Dreier or Flacks or any reader of the *Nation* would recognize. Upham was a pillar of a race-conscious and class-conscious Anglo-Saxon elite in Malden: the proud descendant of Puritan ancestors, deacon of the First Baptist church, and a Knight Templar (called "Sir Knight" as well as "brother" by his fellow Masons) in the Masonic "Converse Lodge." His criticisms of the economic order were aimed less at the hardships or inequities created by capitalism than at the enervating effects of prosperity, the softening of the nation's moral fiber produced by the pursuit of mere money. Upham's criticisms of "the current materialism" are better understood in terms of conservative nostalgia than radical economics.[54]

Upham's attitudes toward immigrants were no more liberal or enlightened than those of Bellamy or Balch or most others of his social class. For Upham, the schoolhouse flag movement was vital in large part because the flag provided a symbol of the American nation for "the children of the millions from abroad who inherit no love for our country." Through patriotic ceremonies like the flag salute, foreign-born children and the children of the foreign born would "begin to feel for America the same patriotic devotion which their fathers were taught from the cradle to manhood, in song and in story, to feel toward the lands from which they came." Flying the United States flag over public schools and having students salute that flag, Upham believed, would help create patriotic Americans out of suspect aliens.[55]

The Anxieties behind the Pledge

The creation of the Pledge of Allegiance, in sum, reflected two widespread anxieties among educated native-born Americans in the late nineteenth century, anxieties that are abundantly evident in the thought of both Upham and Bellamy, as well as Balch. Chief among these was the fear of new immigrants. It is no coincidence that the Pledge and the Balch salute had their origins in large eastern cities (Boston and New York) that teemed with recent immigrants. Absent large-scale immigration, it is difficult to imagine adults bothering to write a pledge of allegiance for schoolchildren.

But immigration was not the only anxiety that motivated the writing of the Pledge of Allegiance. Balch, Bellamy, and Upham were also preoccupied with the selfish materialism and excessive individualism of what historians have come to call "the Gilded Age." All three drew an invidious contrast between a disjointed, selfish present and a more stable, harmonious past. Whereas those of the Civil War generation had been characterized by patriotic duty and heroic self-sacrifice, the present native-born generation was self-absorbed and oblivious to the challenges and dangers facing the United States of America. The Pledge of Allegiance was part of an effort to rekindle the patriotic flame of the Civil War. It was aimed not only at Americanizing the alien but also at awakening the native born to their patriotic duties and obligations. Such a patriotic awakening was necessary for the United States to "fulfill her divine mission."[56]

3

SPREADING THE PLEDGE

The Pledge of Allegiance was written for a single, admittedly grand occasion. When Francis Bellamy penned the Pledge he did not know he was writing anything more lasting than the advertising copy he would later make his vocation. James Upham apparently had a different reaction, instantly judging that Bellamy's handiwork would "live after you and I are dead." At the time, Bellamy had no such premonitions. Initially he was proudest not of his twenty-three-word Pledge of Allegiance but of the address he had written, "The Meaning of the Four Centuries," and his role in securing (and drafting) the presidential proclamation regarding the Columbus Day celebration. Upon completing the Pledge, Bellamy felt relieved to have at last finished the final piece of the official program and "glad to have pleased [Upham,] the exacting idealist whose mastering enthusiasm had for months been a daily urge which left him [Bellamy] tired o'nights." For Bellamy, at the time, the significance of his evening's work was that the official program, a week behind schedule, could at last go to press.[1]

Bellamy's address, the presidential proclamation, the official program for Columbus Day, even the day of celebration itself, have long since slipped into the forgotten recesses of historical memory. Yet the Pledge has endured—indeed it has become among the most familiar words in American culture. How did this happen? How and when did the Pledge become an omnipresent and defining ritual of American life, not just in the schools but in private organizations and governmental bodies? The story of the spread of the Pledge of Allegiance is the subject of this chapter.

Codifying Patriotism

The Pledge of Allegiance was composed for a nationwide celebration of public schools that was, ironically, dreamed up and organized largely by *private* individuals and organizations. To be sure, the congressional authorization and presidential proclamation, as well as proclamations by most of the states' governors, were instrumental in the success of the operation. And the public school superintendents also played an important organizing and legitimizing role. But, at bottom, the national Columbus Day celebration was due to the work of private individuals and groups: chiefly Upham, Bellamy, and the staff of the *Youth's Companion*, but also the national leadership and local posts of the Grand Army of the Republic. Participation on the part of public schools was enlisted through relentless exhortation and persuasion, not compelled by the force of law.

Exhortation could work for a single grand occasion but was ill-suited to the day-to-day work of inculcating patriotism. The official program designed by Upham and Bellamy might teach a patriotic lesson, but a lesson not repeated was unlikely to be remembered. What was needed to instill patriotic sentiments in the youth of America was a regular regimen of patriotic activities. Indeed the premise of the schoolhouse flag movement was that the presence of the flag would be a perpetual reminder and reaffirmation of national loyalty. Some patriotic groups worried though that the flags would soon become worn or neglected, and that the presence of the flags would once again diminish, as they had in the years after the Civil War. For these groups the answer lay with the law. Teaching patriotism, they believed, required legislation.

In truth, almost as soon as the "flag over the schoolhouse" movement was launched there were efforts to get state government to lend a helping hand. In the spring of 1889 Wisconsin passed a law authorizing school boards to acquire flags at public expense. At the same time there was a concerted push in the Pennsylvania legislature to require school boards to purchase flags, though the bill was defeated. The following year, North Dakota and New Jersey passed laws that made it mandatory for schools to fly the American flag.[2] By 1895, according to the Woman's Relief Corps, seven more state legislatures had enacted such laws.[3] A decade later, at least eighteen states and territories had secured laws that required the American flag to be flown in schools.[4] And on the eve of World War I, twenty-nine states—still none of them from the old Confederacy—required public schools to display the flag.[5]

The first flag salute statute was passed in New York in 1898, the day after the United States declared war on Spain. The law required display of the United States flag in the state's public schools and encouraged patriotic exercises in the schools. The State Superintendent of Public Instruction was instructed "to prepare, for the use of the public schools of the state, a program providing for a salute to the flag at the opening of each day of school and such other patriotic exercises as may be deemed by him to be expedient, under such regulations and instructions as may best meet the varied requirements of the different grades in such schools."[6] New York's State Superintendent of Public Instruction complied with the new law by issuing a detailed *Manual of Patriotism* to be used by the state's public schools. The more-than-four-hundred-page manual included all manner of patriotic poems, verse, salutes, and songs to be used by teachers throughout the year. Patriotic activities were designed to celebrate everything from the home and hospital to the shield and sword as well as the New England poets Longfellow and Lowell and the Revolutionary Minute Men. The banal tenor of much of the manual is well captured by the prefatory remarks on the subject of "The School":

> Let us all praise and thank the Legislature of our great Empire State for that law which compels every schoolhouse to keep the flag flying during school time. . . . Faces of the sunniest teachers will sometimes be overcast with clouds; pleasantest voices sometimes be edged with sharpness; sweetest tempers sometimes grow sour, like the richest cream after a thunderstorm; but the flag, ah, the flag! As it floats over the proudest or poorest schoolhouse in the State, it always greets you in the morning with a smile of welcome on its pleasant face, and when you start for home, waves its benediction over you, and shakes out from its folds this cheery voice: " Come again! I'll be here to greet you."

The American flag was made the centerpiece of each of the patriotic holidays: it "blesses the Birthday of Abraham Lincoln," "consecrates the Birthday of George Washington," "hallows Memorial Day," and "makes sacred June 14th," Flag Day.[7]

The manual brought scorn from the editors of the *Nation*, who derided the exercises as "idiotic flag-fetishism." "The whole raison d'etre of the book," they wrote, lies in the belief that the sight of the flag is a signal for emotional hysterics. . . . What solemn nonsense it all is! Men loved the flag before they called it "Old Glory"; men died willingly for their country without special instruction in color symbolism; statesmen gave their lives to the public service without repeating a flag pledge every day. . . . Reading drivel to children and making them sing doggerel can hardly have any effect except to vulgarize them.

The *Nation* conceded that the idea of displaying the flag had "something to be said for it," but preferred that any ceremony accompanying the flag raising be "as brief and formal as possible." "Any haranguing of the young on the general matter of patriotism," the editors concluded, was "as inappropriate as introducing revivalistic appeals at the daily morning prayers would be."[8]

That New York was the first state to enact a law requiring patriotic exercises, including a flag salute, is ironic in view of Balch's warnings against mandating patriotic activities. For Balch, voluntarism was essential to prevent the flag salute and other patriotic activities from becoming rote or mechanical. "It is idle," Balch wrote,

to enact compulsory measures. . . . Neither patriots nor saints can be created by statute; there is no royal road to true patriotism through legislative enactments. . . . The animating force which imparts vigor to patriotic ardor must proceed from within, rather than act from without; it must be innate rather than extrinsic. In short, patriotism, to be real and enduring, must be the voluntary offering of a soul filled with the noblest and most generous impulses, and not a half-hearted, reluctant and perfunctory service rendered in obedience to arbitrary law.

Indeed, Balch went further to suggest that "the instant it is discovered that in either Principal or pupil there is a sense of weariness or ennui, or a disposition to execute the details of an exercise in a perfunctory manner, it is time to invest it with new and more attractive features, or to abolish it altogether. In such exercises as these, which are intended to excite the emotional nature mainly, it were worse than useless to continue to do that which carries with it neither heartiness nor sincerity." Balch even went so far as to insist that students should vote on whether they want to say the pledge, and so long as there was one dissenter they should forswear the patriotic activity.[9]

Balch died in 1894, and the patriotic groups that promoted his flag salute and published and adapted his *Patriotic Primer for the Little Citizen* had a quite different understanding of how best to foster patriotism. The New York state statute and the resulting manual represented the wave of the future. Under pressure from patriotic and veterans groups, other state legislatures also began to require patriotic activities in schools, including saluting the flag. Flag salute statutes similar to New York's were passed in Rhode Island in 1901, Arizona in 1903, and Kansas in 1907.[10] Laws requiring school exercises to mark certain holidays, such as Flag Day, Patriots' Day, Memorial Day, Lincoln's Birthday, Washington's Birthday, and Columbus Day, became increasingly common in the late nineteenth and early twentieth centuries. The Daughters of the American Revolution, Wallace Davies reports, "voted to petition state legislatures to require the reading of the Declaration and the Constitution at least once each term in all public schools." By directing their energies to lobbying the state legislature, patriotic and veterans groups could more effectively and efficiently achieve their aim of ensuring that "the Lessons of Loyalty" were taught in the public schools.[11]

The Early Years of the Flag Salute

Still, statutes mandating flag exercises remained the exception rather than the rule prior to World War I. Moreover, none of the four states with flag salute statutes included penalties for noncompliance or mandated the precise form that the salute should take. Indeed, when New York's state superintendent came to draw up the required *Manual of Patriotism,* he included not one but five possible "patriotic pledges" that teachers might use in their classes. One of these was Bellamy's (identified in the manual as "*The Youth's Companion* 'Pledge of Allegiance'"), but it was not given pride of place; in fact it was fifth on the list of five pledges. The other four appear to have been created by those who compiled the manual. They were:

1. Flag of Freedom! True to thee, / All our Thoughts, Words, Deeds shall be,— / Pledging steadfast Loyalty!
2. The toil of our Hands, / The thoughts of our Heads, / The love of our Hearts, / We pledge to our Flag!
3. By the Memories of the Past, / By the Present, flying fast, / By the Future, long to last, / Let the dear Flag wave!
4. I pledge myself to stand by the flag that stands for Loyalty, Liberty and Law!

Notably absent from the list is the Balch salute, though the second pledge appears to be loosely based on Balch's original salute. Also notable is that none of the five pledges included any reference to God.[12]

A diversity of flag salutes was also in evidence in San Francisco, California. According to one press report from 1895, each of the city's sixty public schools held patriotic exercises on the last Friday of every month. A salute to the flag was a universal part of these exercises and was generally rendered in the schoolyard with the right hand raised in military salute. But the words of the salute varied tremendously across schools. In one school the students recited, "Our country's flag, flag of the free; We pledge our loyal hearts to thee." Another school used an expanded version of the Balch salute: "I give my hand and my heart to my country. One country, one language, one flag; Bring forth the banner and let it rise; Cheer, O cheer, as it spreads to the skies; Hurrah, hurrah, for our flag's dear cause; Hurrah for our school and our country's laws!" Other students shouted in unison: "We turn to our flag as the sunflower turns to the sun. We give our heads and our hearts to our country. One country, one language, one flag." Among the other versions of the salute used were: "To my flag I pledge allegiance and [to] our Republic of Equal Rights; and to our God: one nation, and one flag forever"; and "To our country our allegiance we pledge; and to our Father in Heaven: one nation, with equal rights for all; one flag"; and "I pledge allegiance to our country's flag and to our God: one nation, indivisible, with liberty and justice for all." Most of these salutes were creative variations on either the Balch or Bellamy model, but there apparently was little effort made to standardize the words of the salute.[13]

Among the groups most actively involved in promoting the flag salute was the Woman's Relief Corps (WRC). In 1895, the WRC officially endorsed the use of Balch's flag salute, though to placate others who favored Bellamy's pledge its Committee on Flag Salutes encouraged use of all patriotic salutes, including Bellamy's.[14] When the American Flag Manufacturing Company produced a short booklet around the same time entitled "Ritual for Teaching Patriotism in the Public Schools," it included ceremonies using both the Bellamy and Balch salutes. One hundred thousand copies were given to the WRC Committee on Patriotic Teaching for distribution in the public schools, though the schools apparently refused to use the pamphlet because it included a commercial pitch to buy flags from the American Flag Manufacturing Company, which advertised itself as "the largest flag manufacturers in the United States."[15]

In 1899, the Grand Army of the Republic (GAR) also officially endorsed the flag salute, and circulated their recommended program to schools across the country. The GAR recommended two different flag salute ceremonies, one for the primary grades and the other for the upper grades. Elementary schools were to use the Balch salute, "I give my hand, my head, my heart to my country. One country, one people, one flag," whereas the older students were to use the Bellamy pledge. Many schools apparently followed the GAR's recommendations and had elementary students reciting the Balch oath and the upper grades reciting the Bellamy pledge. A pamphlet prepared by the *Youth's Companion* around 1918, for instance, reported that the Balch salute "is often used in the primary grade of schools." The widespread currency that the Balch salute had in the early twentieth century is evident, too, in its influence on the motto adopted in 1913 by the newly formed Veterans of Foreign Wars: "One flag, one language, one country." In 1919, a member of the Knights of Columbus could identify "one country, one language, one flag" as "one of our best advertised American mottoes."[16]

Unlike the Bellamy pledge, which assumed a standardized form relatively early on,[17] the Balch salute continued to survive in several different wordings. In Canonsburg, Pennsylvania, where the school district required "a salute of allegiance to the Flag" at least once a week, teachers were given a choice of three different salutes. The first was Bellamy's pledge, and the second and third were two common variations on the Balch salute. One version read: "I give my head, my heart and my hands to God and my country. One country, one people, one language, one flag." The other was sans God: "I give my hands and my heart and my head to my country; one country, one language, and one flag."[18]

In the beginning, the propagation and standardization of the Balch and Bellamy salutes owed a great deal to the proselytizing work of the GAR and especially the WRC and, ironically, very little to those who actually created the salutes. Balch's patriotic efforts were cut short by his death in 1894, but more puzzling is that neither Bellamy nor the *Youth's Companion* expended significant energy in popularizing the Pledge. In 1894 Upham did accede to a request from a WRC representative and printed ten thousand copies of the Pledge of Allegiance to be distributed by the WRC to the public schools.[19] But apart from that intervention, the *Companion* showed relatively little interest in the Pledge before World War I. The *Companion* did continue to press the virtues of raising a flag over every schoolhouse (and home), but rarely mentioned the Pledge in its pages.[20] Instead the magazine launched an ambitious new patriotic program—modeled closely on the schoolhouse flag movement—to secure a portrait of George Washington in every public school, and then spearheaded an effort to beautify rural school grounds, a cause long dear to Upham's heart.[21] When, in 1904, the *Companion* penned a retrospective on the magazine's role in the schoolhouse flag movement it made no mention at all of the Pledge of Allegiance.[22]

When Bellamy sat down in the early 1920s to write a history of his Pledge, he constructed a distinctly Whiggish history of its immediate and rapid diffusion throughout American society. But the truth is that a Martian landing in 1900 would have been hard-pressed to pick out the Pledge from the crowd of other patriotic activities that pressed upon the nation's public schools. Initially its words were not particularly well known. When in 1893 the Pledge was used at a flag-raising ceremony at the Sandy Hook Navesink Lighthouse in New Jersey—picked because it was the first spot that incoming immigrants could see upon their approach to the New York harbor—the *New York Herald Tribune* misreported the Pledge as: "I vow myself to my flag and the Republic for which it stands, and liberty and justice for all."[23] A few years later, a nineteen-year-old Kansas high school student easily passed off the Pledge of Allegiance as his own work, and it was not until several decades later that the fraud was recognized. Among the many duped by the boy's composition was Lillian Hendricks, "Patriotic Instructor" from the local chapter of the WRC.[24]

Even in Boston, birthplace of the Pledge of Allegiance, the ceremony was anything but universal in the prewar years. Not until the 1930s would Boston schools require all public school students to recite the Pledge. The popular historian and author Francis Russell remembered being a third grader in Boston in September 1918, just two months before the armistice would bring World War I to a close. The Pledge, he recalled, was "new to Boston that September, as was the silk flag that hung to the right of Miss Syke's desk." The school, "in a burst of patriotism," required teachers to have a flag in every classroom and to lead the class in the Pledge of Allegiance. At least in Miss Syke's class, however, the Pledge did not open the school day; that honor belonged to a reading from the Bible.[25]

That for almost thirty years Bellamy made few if any serious efforts to establish his authorship or to explain how it came to be written provides a clue to the Pledge's position in the early twentieth century. Prior to World War I there was apparently little interest in who wrote the Pledge, in large part because it did not yet occupy a special place in the patriotic pantheon. Not until 1918 did the *Companion* bother to set down its version of how the Pledge came to be written—the magazine wrongly credited Upham with drafting the pledge, thus setting off an acrimonious dispute about authorship that would rage for decades.[26] The schoolhouse flag movement had placed flags in thousands of schools, and in many and perhaps most of these there was a salute to the flag of some form. But prior to the war, the form and wording of the flag salute varied markedly across school districts and schools, and there were few sustained efforts to standardize the salute.

The 1923 and 1924 National Flag Conferences

The diversity of flag salutes is hardly surprising given the decentralized character of American education. Even in the handful of states that had enacted laws requiring a flag salute, there was no effort by the legislature to prescribe how the flag should be saluted nor even what words should be said. School boards and even individual schools and teachers were left a great deal of freedom in determining how they would salute the flag. Contemporary photographs of students saluting the flag, even up through the early 1940s, reveal some of that diversity: sometimes the hand is at the head in a military salute, sometimes next to the heart, sometimes raised up to the flag. Prior to World War I, this diversity of flag salutes did not seem to bother most people; what mattered to patriotic groups was the presence of the flag in schools and that schools inculcated patriotism. With the entry of the United States into the First World War, however, the attention given to the flag salute and the pressure to standardize it increased dramatically.

Patriotic and veterans groups agreed on the importance of promoting respect for the flag, but different groups often had quite different ideas about how this respect was to be displayed. Activities that were respectful in the eyes of some were viewed as improper in the eyes of others. Placing a bust of President Washington upon a draped flag was the height of patriotism for some and a terrible sacrilege in the opinion of others. One patriotic group might pay its respect to the flag by hanging it against the wall, only to find another group chastising them for failing to have the blue field of stars occupy the place of honor on the left hand side. If a woman left her hat on as a flag passed in a parade did she dishonor the flag? The military had clear rules about how men in uniform should handle and salute the flag, but for civilians there was not a universally agreed-upon flag etiquette.

At the end of the war, the National Americanism Commission of the newly formed American Legion resolved that one of its primary objectives would be to press for a uniform national flag code. The American Legion's aim was to replace "the maze of conflicting customs" governing flag usage with a single "code of rules so that every man, woman and child in the country may know how to honor and revere the American flag." To achieve this goal, the Legion turned not to federal lawmakers but instead called for a national flag conference at which the major patriotic, fraternal, and civic organizations could hammer out "a code for the correct use of the flag." The conference convened in 1923, in the Washington, D.C., meeting hall of the Daughters of the American

Students in Washington, D.C., in 1899 pledge allegiance to the flag. The salute offered seems to be a hybrid of the military salute and a hand-over-the-heart salute. Prints and Photographs Division, Library of Congress.

Forty-three years later, in May 1942, fifth-graders in Hollywood, California, offer the same hybrid salute during a recital of the Pledge. Prints and Photographs Division, Library of Congress.

The Pledge is recited in New York City's Central Park to commemorate "I am an American Day," May 16, 1943. Some render the salute with hand over heart and others render the salute in military fashion. Photo appears by permission of the *New York Times*.

Schoolchildren in a New York City school in March 1943 use Upham's raised arm salute as they recite the Pledge. Prints and Photographs Division, Library of Congress.

Schoolchildren in a New York City school recite the Pledge in January 1943 using a military-style salute and a huge American flag. Prints and Photographs Division, Library of Congress.

Schoolchildren in Norfolk, Virginia, in March 1941 employ the same military-style salute but with a rather smaller flag. Prints and Photographs Division, Library of Congress.

Students at the Raphael Weill School in San Francisco's "Little Tokyo" district render the now familiar hand-over-the-heart salute. This 1942 photograph was taken just weeks before the Japanese American students at the school were removed to internment camps. Prints and Photographs Division, Library of Congress.

Revolution, and brought together representatives from scores of patriotic and civic organizations.[27]

Although primarily a meeting of private organizations, government officials were conspicuously present at the conference. The assistant secretaries of the army and navy as well as the U.S. Commissioner of Education spoke to the delegates in fulsome praise of the convention's work. None other than President Warren Harding opened the conference. The president commended the delegates for their important work in promoting proper respect for the flag. Citizens, he opined, should show no less respect for the flag than do those in military uniform. "Every salutation," proclaimed the president, "makes my consecration to my country and the flag a little more secure." The president hoped the delegates would also devote time and thought to addressing the problem of people "mumbling" their way through "The Star-Spangled Banner." Maybe only 2 percent of Americans, he lamented, knew the words to the nation's greatest patriotic song.[28]

Most of the speakers at the conference framed the problem as one of remedying citizen ignorance or confusion, but not everyone took such a benign view. Assistant Secretary of War Dwight Davis agreed with the president that there was "a general lack of respect for the flag," but pinned the blame not only on popular ignorance but on "a deliberate desire to affront" on the part of a few radicals:

> Those who wish to destroy all defenses against their unbridled action and substitute the red for the red, white and blue, do not want our people to respect the flag. . . . Disrespect for the flag, reduction in our military defenses, discontent with our form of government and its institutions are the first steps in what is communistically termed the peaceful phase of the revolution.

Fear of subversive radicals pervaded the conference. Mrs. Reuben Ross Holloway, national chairperson of the U.S. Daughters of 1812 and chair of Maryland's Correct Use of the Flag Committee, succinctly expressed that fear: "They are invading our homes, our schools, our churches, and our very camps, our patriotic organizations, attacking our flag and our institutions." The U.S. Commissioner of Education John Tigert echoed these fears, warning the assembled delegates against "an enemy more insidious than armed battalions, a foe more fearful because unseen or held in light regard." The nation's new enemies were "preachers of communism and anarchism" who "take shelter beneath [the flag's] folds in order to bring it down." One of the Americanism Commission's chief aims in bringing together representatives of the major patriotic, civic, and fraternal organizations to forge a flag code was to unite the disparate, often competing forces of Americanism against what was seen to be a single-minded and cohesive minority of radicals.[29]

The delegates were treated to two days of stirring patriotic speeches from a variety of dignitaries, but the real work of the conference was entrusted to a select committee that was charged with creating a flag code that would instruct civilians in how to display, raise ("briskly"), lower ("slowly and ceremoniously"), salute, and dispose of flags. The seven-person committee was composed of representatives from leading patriotic groups such as the American Legion, Sons of the American Revolution, Daughters of the American Revolution, and Daughters of the Confederacy, as well as representatives from the PTA and the Boy Scouts. Military officers from the army and navy were also asked to assist the committee in its task. Appointed on the afternoon of the conference's first day, the committee was instructed to present a flag code to the convention delegates the following morning. In order to meet the impossibly tight deadline, the committee borrowed extensively from a "Flag Circular" issued earlier in the year by the War Department. Many if not most of the rules about handling and displaying a flag were adapted or taken wholesale from the army pamphlet, as was much of the language of the new flag code. When the new code declared that the United States flag "represents the living country and is itself considered as a living thing" that was language taken verbatim from the army circular. So, too, was the flag code's declaration that "the right arm is the sword arm and therefore the point of danger and hence the point of honor."[30]

Although much of the code could be lifted directly from army guidelines, there were a few areas where military practice was less obviously applicable. Chief among these were the Pledge of Allegiance and flag salute. The military, to be sure, did have regulations about how military men should behave toward the flag when in civilian dress. Army regulations called for those "in civilian dress and covered" to "uncover, holding the headdress opposite the left shoulder with the right hand." Those men without hats were to use the regular right-hand military salute. The army representative thought that since this custom was followed by those who had left the military it was proper that all citizens might follow this "simple rule." But this suggestion ran into two obstacles. First, it was felt that respectable women could not possibly remove their hats. Second, it was thought that the "honor" of giving the right-hand military salute should be reserved for those who had fought for their country. To accommodate these concerns, the committee drafted guidelines calling for a right-handed salute only by those men in uniform. Those men not in uniform "should remove the headdress with the right hand and hold it at the left shoulder." No provision at all was made for men who might have gone out without a hat. And women were instructed to "salute by placing the right hand over the heart." Such salutes were to be rendered whenever a flag was being lowered or raised, or when it passed in a parade, or during the playing of the National Anthem.[31]

Some of the female delegates were not at all happy about this suggestion. As soon as this portion of the code was read to the delegates, Mrs. J. W. Frizzell, representing the General Federation of Women's Clubs, wanted to know why there should be a different salute for men and women. "Why not let the men and women of America all salute the same way?" she asked. The surprised committee chair jokingly offered that the men on the committee were "perfectly willing" for the women to salute the same way as men so long as women were willing to remove their hats. His attempt at humor evidently fell flat, for he then hurriedly explained that the men on the committee had deferred to the two women on the committee on this point. Isabel Ball, representing the WRC, was not willing to let the committee off the hook so easily, however. She told the convention: "I do not like that idea. To me, at least, a woman is a rational creature. She is not a fool. Why can't a woman salute [using the right-handed military salute]?" The convention's chairman, Garland Powell of the American Legion, thought that having women render the military salute would be "very unusual," and reminded Mrs. Ball that "we are not trying to usurp the soldier's honor to his Flag. . . . We are civilians and let us stick by the civilian code." Powell's comments brought applause from the convention, but Mrs. Ball was unfazed. The four hundred thousand women of the WRC, she retorted, "cannot be controlled as to their method of saluting," and currently "everywhere, every time the flag goes by," they salute in the same way a soldier does. Powell conceded that the convention could not control these women, but he again emphasized (to further applause) that he did not care to see "the honor that I had [as a soldier] and the pleasure that I had, which was given to the soldier, in saluting the flag, used by everyone. I would like to see them keep that for themselves." Another delegate pointed out that the salute for civilian men and women was essentially identical except that women were not asked to remove their hats, an observation that was again met with applause. And with that, further consideration of the question was dropped and the provision approved.[32]

The committee also elevated Bellamy's Pledge of Allegiance to the status of the nation's "Pledge to the Flag," though it did not attempt to specify how the flag salute should be rendered during the recital of the Pledge. It did, however, propose a change in the wording. Instead of "my flag," the committee recommended the wording be altered to read "the flag of the United States." When the committee brought this alteration to the floor it did so expecting that the change might "provoke some discussion." But after the indomitable Mrs. Ball rose to declare that "there cannot be any material discussion of that," the convention promptly moved on without any further discussion.[33]

A proposal to modify the Pledge had first been made at the convention by a Mrs. Weyman, who, on the opening day of the convention, rose to request that a resolution be drafted to change "my flag" to "the United States Flag." Anyone, she said, no matter what their loyalties, could salute "my flag."[34] The individual who claims to have been most responsible for inserting the new wording into the Pledge was a member of the flag code committee: Gridley Adams. Some years later, Adams explained why he had pushed for the change:

"I did not like those words 'my flag,' believing that any alien or Hottentot could, and with all sincerity, pledge allegiance to whatever National emblem he held in his mind's eye. I wanted the Pledge of Allegiance to be *specifically American*." Adams felt that the ambiguity of "my flag" allowed devious or disloyal immigrants to avoid pledging their allegiance to the United States.[35] (In later years, some would try to obscure the ethnic anxieties behind the change in wording. The *New York Times,* for instance, writing at the close of World War II, interpreted the alteration as "a proper change from the slight suggestion of egotism in 'my' flag to the promise of unselfish devotion to the flag of the United States."[36])

The fifty-six-year-old Adams had come to public attention the preceding year after he persuaded Clare Briggs, a neighbor and nationally syndicated cartoonist, to devote his Flag Day cartoon to sketches Adams had drawn up promoting proper flag usage. The sketches created a minor tempest—the *New York Herald Tribune,* according to Adams, received some four hundred letters of protest, each of which the newspaper apparently gave to Adams to answer. Among those objecting to Adams's rules—which included such directives as not applauding at the singing of the national anthem and always placing the stars on the upper left-hand side of a hanging flag—were the Boy Scouts and representatives of several major patriotic organizations. Adams would later claim that the controversy sparked by his sketches had been the catalyst for the calling of the 1923 flag conference, but there seems little evidence to support this claim. What does appear to be true is that the sketches caught the attention of Garland Powell, chairman of the Americanization Commission of the American Legion, and brought Adams an invitation to attend the conference.[37]

Adams, although a member of the Sons of Veterans, attended the conference unaffiliated with any group and traveled to Washington, D.C., on his own nickel. Adams's inclusion on the committee charged with drawing up the code was thus something of an anomaly since the other committee members served as representatives of major patriotic and civic groups. Evidently Adams was chosen not because of the group he represented but for his fascination with and formidable knowledge of flag heraldry. Adams was never shy with his opinions. Over his long life he wrote many hundreds of letters to the editor, confidently offering up his opinions on everything from why helium should not be used ("we're too speedy a world as it is") to why the United States should withdraw from the United Nations—among other things, the UN would "annul our present immigration laws and open our doors to whoever landed on our shores, the poverty-stricken and saboteurs alike."[38] Adams was particularly uninhibited when it came to protecting the flag from desecration. During the 1923 conference he claims to have publicly chided one of the conference's keynote speakers, AFL chief Samuel Gompers, for having delivered an address in Los Angeles while standing on a table draped with an American flag. In later years he would chastise scores of public officials, including presidents Harry Truman, Franklin Roosevelt, and Dwight Eisenhower, for their inadvertent desecration of the flag.[39]

The flag conference convened again the following Flag Day to perfect the flag code that had been hammered out in under twenty-four hours the year before. Very few changes were made in flag etiquette, but quite a bit of attention was given to the flag salute. Most important, the convention rectified the failure of the first flag conference to provide for a salute that would be used during the saying of the Pledge of Allegiance. The revised code stipulated that "civilian adults"—no distinction was made between men and women—should follow what it claimed was "the approved practice in schools." All civilians should stand with "the right hand over the heart," and then at the words "to the Flag" the right hand should be "extended, palm upward, toward the Flag." At the close of the Pledge the hand was to be dropped to the side. Perhaps concerned that some adults might regard this ritual as childlike, the code allowed that "civilian adults will always show full respect to the Flag, when the pledge is being given, by merely standing at attention, men removing the headdress." Those in military uniform were still to use the right-hand salute. At Adams's urging, the convention also amended the Pledge again by adding the words "of America" after "the United States."[40] The change was important, Adams believed, because "people ought to be sure which united states they're talking about."[41]

With its work completed, the flag conference disbanded, never to meet again. The work of promoting the code was left to the individual patriotic organizations, which sent thousands upon thousands of copies of the new code to individual members as well as to businesses, schools, churches, and government officials. The convention also specified that a permanent National Flag Code Committee be entrusted with the task of propagating the code. Gridley Adams was selected as chair, though in truth he was never the chair of a functioning committee but rather a one-man organization. The committee did not meet again, but the voluble Adams used his impressive sounding post as chairman of the National Flag Code Committee—"representing over 100 patriotic and fraternal societies," Adams's letterhead declared—to launch a nearly thirty-five-year crusade in defense of the flag code, flag etiquette, and the Pledge of Allegiance.[42]

Bellamy's "Plan for Counterattack"

One person unhappy with the work of the flag conference was Francis Bellamy. No patriotic organizations consulted with Bellamy about the changes, which is hardly surprising since at the time the *Companion* was attributing authorship to the deceased James Upham. Precious few people at this time connected the words of the Pledge with Bellamy's name. Bellamy considered the changes "needless" and fretted that they only "interrupt the rhythm and make the pledge harder to say and remember,"[43] but he never objected to the anti-immigrant rationale for the change or to the anxiety about subversives that animated the patriotic groups. Far from it. In fact only six weeks prior to the 1923 flag conference, Bellamy had set down his own views on the matter in a never-published essay entitled "A New Plan for Counter-Attack on the Nation's Internal Foes: How to Mobilize the Masses to Support Primary American Doctrines."

In this remarkable document, Bellamy spelled out his vision of how the Pledge of Allegiance could be used to promote patriotism and ward off un-Americanism. The essay begins by presupposing that the reader recognizes "the dangerous mess into which our country has drifted" and knows of "the multifarious assaults being made upon the essential institutions of the Republic by foes which are of our own household." The internal foes that needed to be combated were

1. The red radicals of the I.W.W. type, including direct action communists and revolutionary socialists who are boring into the labor unions and are inciting revolt among all classes of working people.
2. The academic radicals of the colleges and lower schools, both teachers and students.
3. The radical newspapers both in our own and foreign tongues.
4. The large radical sections of Russian and Polish Jews.
5. The "pink" radicals of older American stock among whom are many clergymen, club women, society people and even men of wealth, who are giving aid and comfort to the active extremists.
6. The pacifists who are undermining national security.
7. The several "blocs" which are imposing their special aims upon political leaders of both parties.

These "sinister attacks," if left unchecked, were leading to "an impending cataclysm." The question then for loyal Americans was "what is to be done?"[44]

The problem, as Bellamy saw it, was exacerbated by the lack of a "great national leader of dominating personality and voice." Harding was no Teddy Roosevelt. Moreover, there was "no great Magazine of universal circulation whose eyes are open to the danger." All the nation had were "a small band of patriotic men and women" who "preach the truth." These dedicated individuals had formed themselves into patriotic organizations, but these groups had proved inadequate to the job of "moving the mass." The lack of coordination among these diverse groups was part of the problem, but the larger issue was their failure to speak "in the popular key." The "indifferent masses" cannot be stirred by sound arguments alone. To catch the imagination of the masses requires "an aggressive fight in which they clearly see they all belong. They require the simplest and most obvious slogans *which do their thinking for them* before they will stir a peg."[45]

Bellamy offered his Pledge of Allegiance as a model for the sort of patriotic education that the nation needed. In schools across the nation, Bellamy noted, "this little formula has been pounding away on the impressionable minds of children for a generation, awakening a daily enthusiasm for the flag, driving in the idea of loyalty, giving them a notion of the great republic, reminding them of a liberty and justice for all,—*thinking those thoughts for them*." Bellamy conceded that "the little school children" cannot have "much sense of what this Pledge means when they say it," but through repetition it "becomes a memory that sticks by as they grow older, and which in later years they begin to understand." The Pledge, he suggested, operates in much the same way as the catechism, or the Lord's Prayer, or the Ten Commandments: "Children can't comprehend those ideas, but the words instill, by repetition, a religious feeling which in after years becomes a basis of belief." The "inescapable" power of these early impressions, Bellamy noted without a hint of irony, was the reason "the Soviets prohibit any religious instruction to children under 18 years of age."[46]

Bellamy argued that by expanding the scope of the Pledge beyond the schoolhouse the nation could more effectively combat its internal enemies: the subversives and the cynics, the radicals, the reds and the pinks, and the pacifists. His ambition was to extend the Pledge not only to private schools and universities but also to fraternal orders, societies of war veterans, farmers' groups, churches, political conventions, and community gatherings. To some extent, he noted, this extension of the Pledge beyond the schools had already begun. The Boy Scouts and Girl Scouts had adopted the Pledge, and more recently the Elks had done the same. Moreover, the Pledge was used at "very many patriotic rallies of the people on National holidays." But to extend the Pledge still further required "a well-directed campaign," an advertising campaign of the sort that the *Youth's Companion* had engineered three decades earlier at a time of comparable national peril.[47]

Of primary importance was securing endorsements from high government officials, for that would provide the publicity necessary to "call the people's attention to the fact that our country possesses in briefest words a creed of unquestionable Americanism." What had worked when he was at the *Companion*, he believed, could work again. Bellamy freely admitted that "as this is a Plan to sell the Masses, it is essentially an advertising proposition." And after several decades in the advertising business, Bellamy felt he was particularly suited to drawing up such a plan. Key to the program was establishing a Press Bureau, which could then produce booklets, posters, cards, news copy, and films that would publicize the Pledge. The agency should be composed of "a small and self-assembled body of men who are experienced in mass enterprises and who look upon the task as chiefly executive." The bureau "must lean towards the inconspicuous methods of the Publicity Agency rather than follow the drum and trumpet methods of the ordinary patriotic propaganda."[48]

Critical to the success of the enterprise was identifying and reaching out to groups sympathetic to the patriotic agenda. Patriotic groups like the American Legion were an obvious target. But Bellamy also suggested that the bureau reach out to farmers through farm newspapers. Even if farmers were "disgruntled" and "clamor for special legislation, they are not subversive radicals." For at heart, "they are all capitalists." Another important constituency was "manufacturers, business executives and merchants," for they are the "most interested of all classes in balking the invasion of radicalism." Small-town newspapers were also "an ideal channel for a National propaganda based frankly on the doctrines of the Pledge." For the small-town paper had "a sound-hearted American audience" and was therefore "not haunted by the timidity of the Metropolitan Dailies or the General Magazines which have to look out for the protests of Red, Pink or Yellow readers and advertisers." By supplying the small newspaper with a "variety of interesting matter, —cartoons, serious pictures, stories about the Pledge and where it has been adopted, together with a steady pounding on the National truths it preaches," the bureau would be able to inoculate the "as yet untainted . . . Masses" against the subversive ideas and agitators that thrived in the cities.[49]

Bellamy was also interested in enlisting the churches in the cause. Noting that during the war many churches displayed the American flag inside and outside the church, Bellamy saw the churches as natural allies in the patriotic battle against subversion and division. "Most ministers," he noted, "love to preach patriotic sermons." Given this "sympathetic atmosphere," the Pledge of Allegiance might become a "congregational 'Amen' whenever the sacred hymn 'My Country' is sung."[50]

What was needed, however, was not only to extend the Pledge into other domains but also to teach its deepest meanings. For instance, the word "indivisible" formed "the text for showing up the absurdity of 'class consciousness'" and "the wrongness" of dividing the nation into special interest groups: "the farm bloc, the railroad bloc, the mining bloc, the labor union blocs":

> When the idea of indivisibility is driven in, the occasion for revolution is driven out. If the 'pinks' could be made to grasp our essential indivisibility, they would see the foolishness of the 'reds.' If the loose-thinking pacifists could be made to realize the need of maintaining our national indivisibility, they would have a second thought about national defense.

Liberty and justice for all, according to Bellamy, meant the withering away of special interest groups and an end to divisiveness. "All the sinister attacks upon our national security," Bellamy concluded, "are primarily attacks upon the two doctrines of the indivisibility of interests and the 'for all' application of liberty and justice." Bellamy believed that, properly taught, the Pledge had an almost mystical power to dissolve social divisions, harmonize social classes, and neutralize radicals. Its truths were "unanswerable." In its words Bellamy glimpsed the hand of Providence. How else to explain the Pledge's "providential comprehensiveness of doctrines, and [its] providential survival for a generation until it is known and loved by more than half of our population."[51]

Mandating the Pledge in Washington State

Bellamy's grandiose ideas about the Pledge may have been extraordinary, but his preoccupation with subversives and radicals was commonplace. Wartime hysteria about the loyalties of hyphenated Americans, especially German-Americans, had been quickly followed up by panic about alien Communists, "Bolshevists," and anarchists infiltrating the nation and subverting its institutions. Although a coordinated national propaganda plan of the sort that Bellamy envisioned never materialized, widespread anxieties about subversive aliens and radicals did spur efforts to require children to pledge allegiance to the American flag.

In Washington state, heightened vigilance and fear of subversives resulted in the adoption of a flag salute statute in the winter of 1919 that was quite unlike the flag salute statutes that had been enacted elsewhere in the decades before World War I.[52] The state decreed that every school board "shall cause appropriate flag exercises to be held in every school at least once in each week at which exercises the pupils shall recite the following salute to the flag: 'I pledge allegiance to my flag and the republic for which it stands, one nation indivisible, with liberty and justice for all.'" Earlier flag salute statutes adopted in other states had given the state superintendent of education broad authority in designing appropriate flag salute ceremonies and did not include direct mandates requiring schools to conduct the flag salute. The Washington state law was not only the first state law unambiguously to require that a salute be recited in schools but also the first to specify that the salute must be the Pledge of Allegiance. Moreover, unlike previous statutes, the Washington law attached penalties to the failure of school officers to comply. Failure to carry out the flag salute, either by administrator or teacher, was deemed a criminal misdemeanor and sufficient grounds for dismissal.[53]

This amendment to the school code received its first reading in the state senate on the last day of January 1919. Only a week before, Woodrow Wilson had succeeded in getting the Paris Peace Conference to accept the principle of a League of Nations. However, the main topic of conversation in Seattle in late January was not the peace process in Europe but the imminent threat of a paralyzing general strike. On January 21, about thirty-five thousand Seattle shipyard workers had gone on strike and issued a call for the rest of the city's workers to join them. The following day the city's Central Labor Council endorsed the idea of a citywide walkout and directed each of some 110 affiliated unions to vote on whether to join the strike. As one after another union voted to join the strike, anxiety slowly spread throughout the city. Newspapers issued dire predictions of the consequences of a general strike—essential services would come to a halt, women and children would go hungry, and lawless violence and anarchy would break out across the city. Radical hopes that concerted industrial action would result not only in higher wages and better working conditions but in a fundamentally transformed social order ("we are starting on a road that leads—NO ONE KNOWS WHERE!" declared Anna Louise Strong in an infamous *Union Record* editorial) only fueled growing fears that this general strike was but an opening salvo in the radical agitators' effort to foment a homegrown socialist revolution.[54]

Of particular concern to many was the Industrial Workers of the World (IWW), known commonly as the Wobblies. The Pacific Northwest was a region in which the IWW had been relatively strong, but in the wake of the Russian Revolution the organization's calls for revolution took on a more sinister and threatening appearance. Seattle's mayor Ole Hansen saw the shipyard strike as part of "a Wobbly plan to establish a soviet and start the flame of revolution." The strike, Hansen declared, was the opening salvo in the IWW's attempt "to take possession of our American Government and try to duplicate the anarchy of Russia." The contest was one between Americanism and Bolshevism. The general strike, as one Seattle newspaper put it, posed an "acid test of American citizenship—an acid test of all those principles for which our soldiers have fought and died. It is to determine whether this is a country worth living in and a country worth dying for. The challenge is right up to you—men and women of Seattle." The question for each citizen was, "Under which flag do you stand?"[55]—the alien red flag of socialism and anarchy, or the beautiful American red, white, and blue?

On February 2, the decision was made to begin the general strike on the morning of Thursday, February 6. On February 5, the state senate passed its omnibus school bill, which included the provision making the Pledge of Allegiance mandatory. The following morning, at 10 a.m., sixty thousand men and women across the city went on strike. For the next few days, activity in the city virtually ceased. "Most newspapers ceased publication, streetcars stopped running, and industry ground to a halt." The establishment's predictions of violence and mayhem turned out to be wide of the mark, however. Not a single arrest or act of violence was recorded during the strike. But the strike's peacefulness did little to dim the hysteria. Although the great majority of strikers were native born, the work stoppage was seen as the handiwork of radicals and aliens. The peacefulness of the strike notwithstanding, labor leaders were seen by many to be sowing the foreign seeds of violent revolution. On the day the walkout began, the *Seattle Post-Intelligencer* ran a front-page cartoon that showed the red flag of revolution flying above the American flag. The caption read, "Not in a Thousand Years!" The mayor announced that "the time has come for the people . . . to show their Americanism. . . . The anarchists in this community shall not rule its affairs." At the mayor's request, federal troops entered the city, led personally by the mayor, whose car was draped with a large American flag.[56]

The strike did not last long. Public opinion, stoked by a strongly critical press, was hostile to the strike. Many union leaders, seeing that the strike was sparking a backlash that could set back the union cause, worked to get the strike called off. At noon on Tuesday, February 11, the strike officially ended and the city's workers returned to work. The *Seattle Star* crowed that "this Bolshevik-sired nightmare is at an end." But if the strike was over, the nightmare of the postwar Red Scare was only beginning. An anti-syndicalism law passed by the state legislature in early January was now used by authorities to raid the head-quarters of the IWW and the Socialist party and arrest radical leaders. Labor's organ, the *Union Record,* was shut down, and many of the staff were arrested and charged with sedition.[57]

Meanwhile, the Washington state legislature sought ever more creative ways to coerce aliens and radicals. On February 9, in the midst of the general strike, the *Seattle Times* reported that there was "a small avalanche of bills pending be-fore the Legislature" seeking to "minimize the effect of labor agitation by aliens or by members of radical organizations like the I.W.W., or even anarchists." Among the bills introduced at this time was one that forbade the granting of fishing licenses to anybody who was not an American citizen. Another bill sought to prevent any public official or public agency from hiring a noncitizen who had been exempted from serving in World War I. Still another bill, in-troduced as a "step toward the Americanization of all public schools," would have forbidden the teaching of foreign languages.[58]

On the day the strike ended, the senate approved a house bill that not only compelled public schools to teach "the principles of American citizenship" but also prohibited schools from hiring as teachers any persons who had previously been discharged for being unpatriotic. The latter part of the bill was aimed di-rectly at Socialists, two of whom had been discharged—with the help of the bill's chief sponsor—from their teaching positions for opposing American in-volvement in World War I. "Had we done something in this direction in the past," the bill's sponsor explained, "we would not be so near the shoals of an-archy as we have been during the last two years."[59] The original version of the house bill had also forbidden public schools from hiring noncitizens as teach-ers. The *Seattle Post-Intelligencer* defended this provision of the bill, explaining that "it is in the schools that the young and plastic mind is shaped to its future bent." In a democracy, "where every voter is a co-ruler," it was imperative that each American citizen be "given [a] patriotic outlook upon his duties and ob-ligations." Alien teachers not only posed a risk of injecting "foreign propaganda" into impressionable young minds, they also could not be expected to convey ad-equately an understanding of the rigorous demands of "stalwart" American cit-izenship. The *Post-Intelligencer* was unapologetic in its parochialism: "We are in need of no interpretation of or instruction in American citizenship by aliens, nor do we desire the facts of our history and literature and political principles to be set forth to our children by teachers whose allegiance belongs to other lands." Eventually the bill was amended so that the superintendent was granted the power to hire foreign-born teachers so long as they had declared their intent to become citizens.[60]

At the end of February, the state senate, by a 33 to 5 vote, passed the "one flag and one loyalty" bill, which made it a felony to display the red flag of the IWW or wear IWW buttons. Indeed, the sweeping bill prohibited the display of any "flag, banner, standard, insignia, badge, emblem, sign, or other device of, or suggestive of, any organized or unorganized group of persons who . . . advocate any theory, principle or form of government antagonistic to or subversive of the constitution of the United States or this state."[61] The law reflected the philosophy expressed by the *Seattle Post-Intelligencer* on the day after the general strike had come to an end. "Divided allegiance," the *Post-Intelligencer* explained, is "suicidal" and always "a preliminary to revolt."[62] From this point of view, the nation's survival as a democracy depended upon insisting that new immigrants become "Americans first, last and all the time."[63] Old-world attachments were to be wiped out, through patriotic ritual and citizenship training when possible, through coercion, exclusion, and deportation when persuasion and propaganda failed.

It was against the swirling backdrop of such beliefs and anxieties that the state senate had passed the mandatory pledge statute on February 5. The state house then approved the same on February 21.[64] No serious objections appear to have been raised by either political party to the mandatory salute. It attracted no comment in the press and does not seem to have been a focus of legislative debate.[65] There was some wrangling in the conference committee over whether a school official must "willfully" refuse or neglect to comply with the statutory requirement, or whether simple refusal or neglect would be sufficient grounds.[66] But there was apparently no disagreement that failure to fly the flag and pledge allegiance to it should be a misdemeanor and cause for the dismissal of a teacher or principal. The survival of American democracy seemingly required it.

Fear of Subversives and Faith in the Pledge

Fears of violent revolution in America seem laughable now, but they were widespread in the immediate aftermath of the Russian Revolution and World War

I. The nation's attorney general A. Mitchell Palmer told a House committee in October 1919 that "on a certain day, which we have been advised of," subversives plan "to rise up and destroy the Government at one fell swoop." Shortly thereafter a justice department informant wrote to Palmer that "there is hardly a respectable citizen of my acquaintance who does not believe that we are on the verge of armed conflict in this country." The widespread labor strikes of 1919—thirty-six hundred strikes involving four million workers—were widely attributed to the influence of Communists and the IWW and were thought to be portents of a social or political revolution. Even Joe Tumulty, President Wilson's staunchly liberal aide, worried that February's general strike in Seattle "was the first appearance of the soviet in this country." A U.S. senator from the state of Washington warned that "there is real danger that the government will fall."[67]

Something of the irrational hysteria of that time can be gleaned from a story carried by the *Washington Post* in May 1919. According to press reports, an American sailor shot a man who had failed to stand for the playing of "The Star-Spangled Banner." As the stricken man collapsed, with three gunshot wounds in his back, the crowd reportedly burst into applause. More commonly, those showing a lack of proper respect for the flag were roughed up and forced to kneel and kiss the flag. Perceived disloyalty was punished not only by vigilantes but by the law. In March 1918, for instance, a Montana man enraged a patriotic mob by not only refusing to kiss the flag but by ridiculing the flag as "nothing but a piece of cotton with a little paint on it and some other marks in the corner there [and probably] covered with microbes." His remarks earned him a conviction for sedition and a minimum sentence of ten years imprisonment and hard labor.[68]

Even after the worst excesses of the Red Scare had receded, patriotic groups and individuals continued to sound the alarm of the dangers of subversion posed by aliens and to press for "one hundred percent Americanism." Representative of the rhetoric of the day was a Flag Day speech given by the governor of Louisiana, John M. Parker, who delivered his address on the same day that the flag conference was convening in Washington, D.C., to create a national flag code. Speaking in a field next to Theodore Roosevelt's grave, at the invitation of a local Elks lodge, Parker warned the assembled crowd that "the Constitution is being attacked at its foundation by a long-haired, anarchistic, Bolshevistic horde." The American public, preoccupied with "riotous jazz celebrations," were "unheeding and unmindful of the undermining going on." He called for "eternal vigilance" against those who would subvert the American system.[69]

When in 1927 a prominent Columbia University professor derided the "cult of flag worship," including the practice of "baring the head whenever it passes" and obliging "all the school children to get out and stand in regular rows and lift their hands to pledge allegiance to this flag," there were immediate calls for his dismissal. Demanding that the professor be "kicked out of the university bodily," Captain George Darte of the National Flag Association said that the professor "belongs to that group that raises the red flag in time of peace and the white flag in time of war." Such a man was "much too dangerous . . . to be permitted to handle the education of the youth of today." The same message was preached by Rabbi Herbert Goldstein, president of the Union of Orthodox Jewish Congregations of America, who said that "the greatest menace to American life today is the college professor who is breeding a spirit of irreverence everywhere in the land." What was needed, the Rabbi declared, was "more of the ceremonial in civic, social and religious life of America," such as when "we raise our hands in pledge to the flag as a civic ceremony expressing the idea of loyalty."[70]

Groups like the American Legion prided themselves on the vigilant watch they maintained against the dangers of "revolutionary radicalism, anarchy, sovietism and extreme pacifism." In 1927, for instance, the American Legion Post of West Chester, Pennsylvania, succeeded in having two teachers dismissed after charging that the area's public schools were being used to spread "pernicious and subversive propaganda, destructive of American ideals." Freedom of speech, the Legion continued, did not extend to "the right to pour poison into immature minds." Of particular concern to the West Chester post was a group called the "Liberal Club," which had sponsored speakers critical of government policies and opposed military drilling in schools. The Legion's report noted ominously that there seemed to be "some connection" between the Liberal Club and the American Civil Liberties Union. And if the ACLU advocated something, the Legion suggested, "nine times out of ten it has a Communistic purpose and [is] against the public interest." Moreover, if an accused man is defended by the ACLU then "ninety-nine times out of a hundred he is a criminal who deserves to be in jail."[71]

The vigilance of groups like the American Legion often took the form of determined efforts to secure new laws requiring the teaching of American citizenship and the promotion of patriotism. At the American Legion's first national convention in 1919 it was resolved that "a course in citizenship [should] constitute a part of the curriculum in every school in this country." The "spirit" animating the resolution, the Legion explained, was "the Americanization of

America." Through the proper teaching of civics and Americanism, the Legion predicted that "the next generation will see this country rid of the undesirable element now present in its citizenship, foreign colonies a thing of the past, the spirit of true Americanism prevailing throughout the length and breadth of our country."[72]

Before World War I only Connecticut required the teaching of citizenship, but by 1923 thirty-nine states had instituted such a requirement. Only Maine required the teaching of patriotism in 1913, whereas a decade later twelve states did so. In 1923 alone seventeen states passed laws requiring the teaching of the Constitution, and many of these were taken virtually verbatim from legislation being pushed by the National Security League's Committee on Constitution Instruction. In some states lawmakers went further in specifying the sort of teaching they had in mind. An Oregon law, for instance, specified that no text "shall be used" that "speaks slightingly of the founders of the Republic or of the men who preserved the Union, or which belittles or undervalues their work." Similarly, Wisconsin forbade the use of a text that "defames our nation's founders . . . or which contains propaganda favorable to any foreign government." Also on the increase were loyalty oaths for teachers and requirements that all teachers—no matter what subject they taught—pass a test on the Constitution. By 1925, thirty-three states (virtually every state outside the South) required public schoolteachers to pass such a test. Another curricular requirement pushed by the American Legion and other veterans and patriotic groups was requiring all public schools to use only English for instruction. By 1923, thirty-five states required that English be the only language of instruction, double the number of states that had such a law a decade earlier.[73]

State laws requiring a flag salute and/or the Pledge of Allegiance spread more slowly. In 1925, Delaware enacted a law much like Washington's. In 1932 New Jersey enacted a law that required students to recite an oath of allegiance every day, though it exempted children of "accredited representatives of foreign governments to whom [the] United States extends diplomatic immunity." Massachusetts required the Pledge of Allegiance in 1935. By 1935, about ten states plus the District of Columbia had statutes that could be interpreted as requiring students to salute the flag and/or recite the Pledge of Allegiance. A few of these state laws, as in Kansas, Delaware, and New Jersey, required the flag salute to be carried out daily; a couple, in Washington and Massachusetts, required only a weekly flag salute; and most, as in Arizona, Maryland, Rhode Island, and New York, did not attempt to specify the frequency with which the salute would be conducted. In Nebraska the flag salute only needed to be conducted on special occasions, such as Lincoln's Birthday, Washington's Birthday, Memorial Day, and Flag Day.[74]

To focus only on state laws, however, is deceiving, for it underestimates the extent to which the Pledge of Allegiance had gradually become a mandatory part of the school day in districts across the nation in the 1920s and 1930s. In states where the flag salute and Pledge were not prescribed by state statute, they were often mandated through the rule-making power of state school boards and local school boards. In Georgia, for instance, training in citizenship was required by statute, and that statute empowered local education boards to prescribe a course of study for the teaching of citizenship and patriotism. And citizenship training was often interpreted to include saluting the flag and reciting the Pledge of Allegiance. (In 1935 Georgia's legislature did enact a flag salute statute, but it required reciting a pledge of allegiance to the *state* flag on appropriate occasions.) Often states required patriotic exercises or instruction in flag etiquette, and the local school boards met this general mandate by requiring the Pledge of Allegiance. In 1935, for instance, the Illinois state legislature enacted a bill calling for instruction in the "proper use and display of the American flag," and the Chicago school board promptly voted to require all students to salute and pledge allegiance to the flag as well as sing the national anthem every school day.[75]

One indication of the Pledge's increasing prominence as a symbol of patriotism in the years after World War I was an NBC radio broadcast, which featured the vice president of the United States, Charles Curtis, speaking on the meaning of the flag and leading millions of children in reciting the Pledge of Allegiance. Through the coordinated work of veterans organizations and school officials across the nation, "home parties" for children were arranged so that on February 4, 1930, children all across the country would be listening to the radio broadcast and could join the vice president in reciting the Pledge. According to press reports, it was "the first time in history that such a large audience had stood and taken the pledge together." Sponsored by the United States Flag Association—an organization whose goal was "to build up peace-time patriotism" as "an antidote against bolshevism, communism, and all others 'isms' except Americanism"— this carefully scripted event was precisely the sort of coordinated national propaganda campaign that Bellamy had envisioned back in 1923.[76]

At the time of Bellamy's death in 1931 the Pledge was fast becoming a defining symbol of national patriotism, not quite on a par with "The Star-Spangled Banner" but not far behind either. Pledging allegiance to the flag was seen by many not just as an expression of patriotism but, in the words of the U.S. Flag Association, as an "antidote" to radical and alien ideas. The Pledge helped to inoculate impressionable young minds against the appeals of foreign propaganda. To be sure, as Bellamy recognized, many children might not understand the meaning of the words they were being asked to recite. But, as Gridley Adams, chairman of the National Flag Code Committee, expressed it in a 1936 letter he wrote to the *New York Times,* "just as in advertising 'repetition makes reputation,' so does reiteration of any creed make it become a part of the subconscious."[77] Bellamy the advertising man had explained the power of the Pledge in much the same way. The Pledge was propaganda, but the good kind of propaganda, in the service of a righteous, God-fearing nation. Not everyone agreed, however, as we explore in the next chapter.

MAKING THE PLEDGE SAFE

FOR DEMOCRACY

As the Pledge of Allegiance became an increasingly prominent ritual of American life, so, too, did it become an increasingly important symbol of American patriotism. And as it became an emotionally freighted symbol of undivided allegiance, it increasingly became a target for dissent. The desire to coerce patriotism and undivided loyalty began to run headlong into the values of the symbol. Could a nation dedicated to liberty and justice for all coerce its citizens into saying the Pledge of Allegiance? Did mandating the Pledge teach patriotism and citizenship, or did this violate the nation's deepest principles? The debate over whether individuals had to say the Pledge would culminate, when it finally reached the U.S. Supreme Court, in a profound meditation on the meaning of American democracy.

Resisting the Pledge in the Early Twentieth Century

From the beginning there had been resistance to the Pledge of Allegiance, but the opposition was generally sporadic and handled at the local level. During the last decade of the nineteenth century and the first decade of the twentieth century a few skeptical voices raised questions about the growing "flag fetish." The doubters most frequently took aim at the growing push for flag desecration legislation, which in these early years was aimed primarily at preventing the flag from being used in the advertising of commercial products. A few complained of the "superstitious reverence" for the flag that was being fostered by "self-styled 'patriotic' societies." During the Spanish-American War, *Harper's Weekly*, a strong critic of the war, assailed the newly formed American Flag Association's relentless boosterism of Flag Day. "The American flag," commented *Harper's* editors, "is taking care of itself just now, and doesn't need booming half as much as the Flag Association needs a bromide." The *Nation*, also a strong critic of the nation's military adventures in Cuba and the Philippines, sounded a similarly skeptical tone. Writing in 1906, the editors of the *Nation* derided the new enthusiasms for flag raisings, patriotic songs, and declamations as "purely superficial." Attempts to stimulate patriotism through flag exercises and song or to legislate patriotism through compulsory lessons were misguided and pernicious:

> The Truth is, that love of country, in the high and proper sense, cannot be taught. It is commanded by the country which deserves it. Give men justice, freedom, and equal treatment before the law, and you do more than all possible schools and schoolmasters to intensify their national love for land and kin. Try to stimulate this by hothouse methods, and you make patriotism artificial and false, an idle name; you stifle the noblest kind of love of country. . . . It is not shouting for the old flag. . . . It is doing justice and loving mercy.

Others worried that "the flag-salute, the singing, the national self-glorification will result in a nation of swashbucklers, not of patriots." Even those less worried about an excess of patriotism wondered "whether 'these mysterious flag gesticulations' served any useful purpose."[1]

Whatever doubts people may have had about the wisdom of the flag salute, there were few reported cases of students refusing to salute the flag until the second decade of the twentieth century. One of the earliest recorded cases occurred at the beginning of the school year in 1911, in Perth Amboy, New Jersey, where a fourteen-year-old girl refused to salute the flag or recite the oath of allegiance, both of which were required by the state. The girl and her family were British subjects, though she had lived in Perth Amboy all her life and her father had worked there for almost two decades. The school authorities responded by sending the girl home and asked the state authorities for guidance, as this was evidently the first time the New Jersey regulation had been challenged. The state board of education decreed that "the rule must be obeyed by all children in public schools whenever a Board of Education in New Jersey adopts it as part of the school routine." The *New York Times* took notice of the controversy—"the first case of the kind in the history of New Jersey"—opining that it "is not quite understandable . . . why school children should take the oath of allegiance every day, when there is so much arithmetic and geography to be learned." On the other hand, they agreed that "it would be making a mountain out of a molehill to exempt [the child], by special law, from a part of the school ceremonial." After all "a routine ceremonial is not very important." The *Times* concluded that the case was much ado about nothing and was, in any event, "an exceptional case."[2]

The subsequent school year produced another New Jersey case that showed that the case was less exceptional than the *Times* had hoped. In the village of Cedar Grove, a teenaged Canadian boy refused to pledge allegiance to the flag because, as his father explained, he had already sworn allegiance to the British flag. The father instructed his son to take his hat off to the flag "just as he would to a lady to whom he was speaking, but as for pledging his allegiance to the American flag by repeating that sentence about pledging hand, heart, and head that shall not be done." The local school board was adamant, however, that the boy must say the oath of allegiance just like every other student who attended the school. One school board member expressed the feeling that, "if he is not an American, he should go to a private school and pay for his tuition or go back to Canada or England. But if we make an exception in his favor I suppose that any anarchist might refuse to salute the flag." The *Times* again weighed in, criticizing the father for being an obstinate and "unassimilated immigrant" who preferred to live in the United States without assuming the "responsibilities of citizenship" and scolding the school board for "the lack of tact so often characteristic of small officials exercising unaccustomed power." Looking for a bright spot in an otherwise "absurd episode," the *Times* suggested that "it may help the children of Cedar Grove—and elsewhere—to remember that salute of the flag is not a formal and perfunctory ceremony, but that it is or ought to be full of grave significance for all those who take part in it."[3]

The school's refusal to allow the boy to attend public high school if he would not say the oath of allegiance met with strong criticism. The *New York Times* interviewed a number of students about the school board's decision and found them largely supportive of the student. One female student recalled approvingly that she knew of an American girl who had moved to Canada who was permitted to stand but not sing "God Save the King." The student had explained to her teacher that since "she was an American she could not sing the British National air with sincerity," to which the Canadian teacher had responded: "That is the proper spirit. It is right for you to maintain your love for the land that you were born in." Another observed that while "forced oaths of allegiance might do in Russia, . . . nothing could be more out of place in a republic. The American flag was a good one to die under and to live under, but a pledge to it wasn't worth anything unless it was voluntary." The *Times* also published three letters to the editor relating to the boy's suspension, all of which were critical of the school board's decision. One month later, after a hearing at the Newark courthouse, the state's assistant commissioner of education ordered the Cedar Grove school board to reinstate the boy. The boy could not be made to pledge allegiance to the flag, nor could he be removed from the room while the other students said the pledge.[4]

The case of the Canadian teenager is notable both for the widespread sympathy shown for the plight of the boy and his father and for the sharp condemnation of the Cedar Grove board of education for "needlessly making a miserable little row about nothing in the name of patriotism." Reactions were far less favorable, however, to the case of Oscar Whiting, a ten-year-old in Camden, New Jersey, who was also suspended in the fall of 1912 for refusing to salute the flag. Whiting reportedly told the principal of the school that his parents were Socialists and that they had instructed him "to salute only the red flag." According to press reports, the incident was brought to the principal's attention not by the teacher, who allowed the boy not to join in the salute, but by the boy's classmates, "who were indignant at the disrespect shown to the flag."[5] To one observer, Oscar's refusal to pledge his allegiance was different in kind from the Canadian boy's refusal. The letter writer agreed with those who thought it would be "a strange new device to require a boy to pledge allegiance to a flag not his own." But Oscar's case was different. For here was a boy who had been taught at home "to look with horror and loathing" on his nation's flag.[6]

Ideological opposition to the pledge intensified during World War I as authorities sought more insistently to enforce patriotism. During the war, radicals frequently criticized what Emma Goldman termed "flag mania." Goldman recounted one incident in Brooklyn, New York, in which "a principal of a Public School found it in keeping with his honor to denounce two teachers, who were suspected that they did not salute the flag." An able pedagogue, Goldman continued, "would perhaps think that servility and hypocrisy were rampant enough far and wide in the country and that it really is not necessary to foster them and force them on people." Another wartime refusal occurred in Chicago in the spring of 1916 when an eleven-year-old black student, Hubert Eaves, refused to salute the flag. The flag, the boy said, was "dirty," for it stood for the oppression and lynching of black Americans. Eaves vowed "to salute the flag as the flag salutes me." For his protest, the student was not only suspended but was arrested and tried before juvenile court. However, since it was not a crime in Illinois to refuse to salute the flag, the judge ordered that Eaves be sent back to school.[7]

The most important and enduring sources of resistance to the flag salute and Pledge of Allegiance were religiously based. Ultimately, it would be the religious objections to the Pledge that would be by far the most consequential in shaping the evolution of the relevant case law. David Manwaring guesses that religiously based opposition to the flag salute "probably is as old as the ceremony itself." But, as Manwaring also indicates, such opposition did not produce any conflict with school or state officials until after the entry of the United States into World War I. Over the subsequent two decades the great majority of pledge refusals would stem from a handful of small religious groups.[8]

The pacifism of the Mennonites led to an early clash with the state over the flag salute ceremony. In 1918, a nine-year-old Mennonite girl in West Liberty, Ohio, refused to salute and pledge allegiance to the flag and was thus sent home by school officials. Each morning the girl would go to school and each day she would be sent home after her morning refusal. After some time, her father, a conscientious objector, was prosecuted and convicted for not keeping his child in school. The father appealed his conviction and twenty-five-day jail sentence, noting that it was the school authorities, not he, who had kept his child from attending school. The judge rejected his appeal and condemned the man for his disloyalty and for poisoning the mind of his daughter. Had the father not instructed her not to salute the flag, "every one knows that the result would have been cheerful compliance. There is no instinct in the heart of the native-born American child to show disrespect, disloyalty and rebellion against the beautiful banner which symbolizes American independence, its free institutions and the glory of this great nation." Warming to his subject, the judge continued:

> This instruction was given by the foster father in the time of war, at a time when the rich blood of the free men is being shed, that our nation may remain free and its institutions may be preserved. . . . Such conduct on the part of our citizens is not

conscionable, for conscience would lead to respect for government and to its defense, especially in time of war, but rather it is the forerunner of disloyalty and treason. All true Americans are conscientiously opposed to war, but when war is upon us, we will fight and fight until the victory over our enemy is won.[9]

Even after the war, Mennonites continued to clash with authorities over the flag salute and Pledge of Allegiance. In Delaware, for instance, where the state had enacted a mandatory flag salute statute in 1925, thirty-eight Mennonite children were expelled from school in the town of Greenwood in 1928. The Mennonites' position was that pledging allegiance to the flag "implies a pledge to defend it against all its enemies, which would mean to resort to arms and to take human life." And this they could not do consistent with their religious beliefs. To avoid being arrested by the truant officer, the Greenwood Mennonites started a private school in the church as they worked to get the school board to reinstate their children. The American Civil Liberties Union, which had become interested in challenging the compulsory flag salute, offered to represent the children, but the Mennonites' belief in nonresistance prevented them from bringing a legal suit.[10]

The ACLU, founded in 1920, first became involved in a flag salute case in 1926 as a result of a clash between the Denver, Colorado, school board and a small religious sect called the Jehovites—not to be confused with the Jehovah's Witnesses. The Jehovites believed that saluting the flag was a form of "idol worship" and publicly announced that they would not permit their children to participate in the flag salute ceremony. Although there was no state law requiring students to recite the Pledge of Allegiance or salute the flag, the city's school board responded to the Jehovites' refusal by not letting the children attend school. By April 1926, approximately fifty children were being kept out of school in Denver because of their refusal to salute the flag. Public reaction to the Jehovites was strongly negative. The *Denver Post* dismissed the notion that saluting the flag was idolatry as "the limit of absurdity." If the Jehovites or "members of any other sect can't salute the American flag," the *Post* concluded, "they ought to get out of the country." Under the threat of a legal challenge from the ACLU, the standoff was quietly defused over the summer; the children were allowed to return to school and were not compelled to salute the flag.[11]

At roughly the same time, the ACLU also tried to involve itself in the case of a nine-year-old boy, Russell Tremain, from Bellingham, Washington, who, in September 1925, refused to salute and pledge allegiance to the flag. Russell and his family were members of a tiny religious sect called the Elijiah Voice Society, which rejected the flag salute largely on the grounds that "national patriotism tends toward militarism and war." To teach children the spirit of "America First" or "Deuchland Uber Alles" [*sic*], the sect explained, was to teach them "the spirit that makes world wars and other wars possible." Because the school would not allow Russell to attend school unless he agreed to salute the flag, the boy's father withdrew him from school. The father was then arrested and jailed for "contributing to the delinquency of his son." Meanwhile the boy was placed in the State Children's Home where he would be compelled to salute the flag. Anybody who advised Russell against saluting the flag would be cited for contempt of court. In June 1926, seeing that the parents had not relented in their opposition to the flag salute, the judge went still further, granting the state permanent custody of Russell with the purpose of putting him up for adoption with "Christian, patriotic parents." Since the parents were no longer legally his parents they were now forbidden from visiting Russell in the Washington Children's Home.[12]

The judge justified his order to take the child away from the parents on the grounds that the parents' anti-salute teachings were "placing the child in danger of growing up to lead an idle, dissolute or immoral life." For by teaching their child not to salute the flag, they were also inculcating in the child "a feeling to disregard all law." If Russell Tremain's parents "are to be allowed to be willful lawbreakers—to set a law aside because it suits a real or fancied religious conviction, then others may claim religious convictions and set other laws at naught, and that would be the end of all law." If one person is permitted to refuse to follow the law requiring the flag salute, then "another may violate the motor laws; another may violate the liquor laws and another may violate the law which says Thou shalt not kill." Taking Russell from his parents was necessary to stop the nation from descending down the slippery slope into "chaos" and "tumult." Moreover, the Tremains' religious objections to the salute could hardly be taken seriously. For Judge W. P. Brown it was inconceivable that saluting the flag could be "a wrong against God." How could "the noble men of the GAR" or the Spanish War Veterans and American Legion be acting contrary to God or injuring society? "Can it be," the judge asked, "that the millions of fine men and women of America who salute the flag are violating a law of God." Merely to ask the question was to answer it. The Tremains' beliefs were either insincere or wrong, for the judge felt certain that "God would [not] punish parents for following the laws as enacted and as on the statute books."[13]

Judge Brown's ruling earned him the ACLU's "dumbbell prize for interference with the liberty of a citizen." One caustic observer suggested that for "ruthlessly enforcing an official religion, brutally imposing ritualism and cruelly tearing a family apart . . . the judge ought to be put up for adoption by sensible adults." The ACLU's efforts to provide the Tremains with legal assistance were stymied by the father's refusal to recognize the authority of the "earthly courts," defend himself in court, or bring suit against the school district. Russell's father explained to the ACLU that he was "expecting our deliverance . . . to come in another way, and that God will vindicate his cause, even though it be through a worldwide revolutionary outburst of anarchy and the destruction of the present evil order of society under the reign of Satan, sin and death." Efforts at finding a compromise were hindered both by the intransigence of the Tremains as well as the refusal of any public school in the area to admit Russell if he would not salute the flag. Not until November 1927—over two years after having been separated from his parents—was Russell finally returned to his home, after Judge Brown's successor in the juvenile court rescinded the order, with the understanding that the parents would enroll their son in a private school where no flag salute was required.[14]

Judge Brown had no sympathy for the Elijiah Voice Society's contention that requiring patriotic flag salutes in the classroom promoted militarism and war, but the sect's argument was less fanciful or exotic than it perhaps appears. The same patriotic and veterans groups who were pushing the Pledge of Allegiance and other patriotic observances in the curriculum were also spearheading the effort to inject military training into the school curriculum. College courses in military training had become increasingly widespread over the previous decade. According to one count, the number of colleges and universities with courses in military training had increased from 56 in 1912 to 225 in 1927. Moreover, such courses were mandatory in over 80 colleges, and as many as 7,000 high school boys were compelled to do military drilling in school. So intense was the pressure for compulsory military training that in 1926 President Calvin Coolidge felt it necessary to issue a statement opposing compulsory military training in schools because it stimulated "a military spirit in the youth of the land." There was even a "Committee on Militarism in Education" that had been formed in the mid-1920s to combat the spread of militarism in schools. The Elijiah Voice Society may have been unique in seeing the shadow of militarism lurking behind the mandatory Pledge, but theirs were hardly the only voices in the 1920s that expressed concern about the efforts by patriotic groups to spread the military spirit in schools.[15]

Other episodes of resistance to the flag salute occurred in the 1920s, and almost all of these were religiously based. In Oklahoma City, for instance, in 1928, a twelve-year-old boy refused to say the Pledge of Allegiance. The boy's mother, a member of the Church of God, explained the decision: "The pledge of allegiance means fight, and we will go to the prison walls before we do that." The refusal reverberated all the way to the governor, who sharply criticized the actions of the student and the family. The boy, said the governor, was "a pervert of citizenship." One school board member derided the boy and his parents as "un-American" and indicated that the boy should either go to a private school "or to some other country." Many others in the community, however, including the boy's teacher and principal, were supportive of the boy, who was recognized as "a model pupil in every other respect." Deeply divided over the appropriate course of action, the school board eventually relented and agreed to let the boy remain in school even if he would not salute the flag.[16]

Another religiously motivated refusal occurred in Kansas in 1923, and the act of defiance brought fierce denunciations from prominent citizens. An editor of a local newspaper fumed:

> It seems well nigh incredible that any parents could assume such an attitude which is obvious evidence of a most deplorable conception of the relation of the citizen to the state. The schools of all institutions are the cradles of patriotism and parents who have "conscientious scruples" against having their children taught to love their country and its flag are themselves menaces to the land of their adoption or citizenship.

Similar outrage met a refusal in 1921 in Solano County, California, involving several children of a single family. The father's objection to the flag salute was that it was contrary to his understanding of the Bible and that it was wrong to teach patriotism because patriotism led to militarism. This claim brought a stern rebuke from a Sacramento superior court judge:

> There is obviously no force to such objection. It is indeed repugnant to every idea and every consideration of the loyalty and love for our government and political institutions so essential to the maintenance thereof. No government could long survive in the absence of patriotism in the people living under it, and one of the first or primary duties not only of the public schools but of every other educational institution in this country is to inculcate in those who attend them the principles of patriotism. The flag of our country symbolizes the principles of our government, and we can conceive of no more appropriate act or practice which could be followed in our public schools, or which could go further in developing in the young a high order of citizenship, than the requirement that the pupils thereof shall at every session of said school salute our flag or otherwise give some demonstration of their love for the great principles which it represents. And we can conceive of no just or reasonable interpretation of the Bible, or any part thereof, which could, in the remotest way, inspire the thought that the teaching of patriotism or love of country is in anywise or in any degree or measure contrary to its teachings.[17]

Not all the flag salute refusals were religiously based, however. In 1927, a thirteen-year-old public school student in Coney Island, New York, refused to salute the flag and was suspended when she explained to her teacher and then the principal that "my flag is the workingman's flag." She reportedly indicated that she believed that the United States should recognize the Soviet Union and that the Soviet educational system was better than the American system. Her sympathy for the Soviet Union did not go down well with the principal, who explained that since she was attending a public school supported by taxpayer dollars she "should respect the ideals, institutions and flag of America." Although "inclined to argue at first," the girl apparently relented under pressure from her widowed mother and the principal. Pressing his advantage, the principal insisted that the girl should not only salute the flag every day, but that she should show her respect for the flag by carrying it to its "customary pole in the assembly hall" that very afternoon. The girl yielded to the principal's demand and was readmitted to school.[18]

The previous year in Chicago there were reports of an eleven-year-old student who was suspended from school for refusing to sign the Pledge of Allegiance, an action that was evidently required of all Chicago public school-children. The student, who was a member of the Communist Young Pioneers of America, pronounced that schools were "merely tools of the capitalist class" and pointed to the inaccuracies of the textbooks as evidence. The teacher responded to the student's challenge by insisting that the student write out the Pledge of Allegiance. But instead of writing Bellamy's pledge, he offered his own: "I pledge allegiance to my flag, and the cause for which it stands—one aim thruout my life, freedom for my working class." This brought him a trip to the principal's office and suspension until such time he as was ready to sign the Pledge of Allegiance.[19]

Although the 1920s did not lack for refusals, the conflicts were generally settled at the local level of the school board and the juvenile courts. Often conflict was averted altogether because the teacher agreed to look the other way or the principal chose to accommodate the student. For instance, schools would sometimes allow those with conscientious objections to absent themselves from the ceremony, especially if the flag salute took place at a weekly school assembly.[20] By 1926, however, the ACLU had signaled a clear interest in challenging the constitutionality of mandating individual students to salute the flag and utter the Pledge of Allegiance. So far, however, the ACLU had failed to find the sort of case or client—specifically one willing to bring suit in the courts—that would enable them to enter the judicial fray. Not until the mid-1930s would the ACLU finally find a willing and uncompromising client: the Jehovah's Witnesses.

The Jehovah's Witnesses Challenge the Pledge

The Jehovah's Witnesses did not enter the flag salute controversy until 1935, but their challenge was far more widespread and better coordinated than the episodic challenges of the early twentieth century. Like some of the earlier religious groups that had challenged the Pledge, the Jehovah's Witnesses had no interest in compromise, but unlike previous sects they had few hesitations about using the law to further their righteous struggle.

Jehovah's Witnesses proselytize for their faith by distributing (and selling) literature, often going door-to-door in neighborhoods. Every Witness is considered "an ordained minister, an ambassador of Jehovah." In 1928 the Witnesses initiated their practice of doing door-to-door canvassing on Sunday, which brought them into immediate conflict with local authorities. In many locales they were arrested and charged with selling without a license and conducting business on the Sabbath. The Witnesses, who did not recognize any worldly authority, refused to apply for permits to spread the Lord's Word. In response to the wave of arrests, the Witnesses turned to the law. They developed a sophisticated legal department, and by 1933 they had a policy to appeal all judicial decisions that went against them.[21]

The Witnesses' leader at this time was the combative and charismatic Joseph Rutherford. In the summer of 1935, Rutherford issued a stirring denunciation of Hitler's Germany where Jehovah's Witnesses were being persecuted for their refusal to give the "Heil Hitler" salute. Speaking at the Witnesses' national convention in Washington, D.C., Rutherford paid tribute to the personal courage evidenced by the German Witnesses who resisted the "exaltation of . . . Hitler." Asked at the convention about the relevance of the German Witnesses' example, Rutherford pointed to the parallel between the "Heil Hitler" salute and the United States flag salute. Both were idolatry and evidenced "unfaithfulness to God." The similarities were visually arresting since both statements of allegiance were delivered with a raised stiff arm salute.[22]

Rutherford's statement came on the heels of a new flag salute statute in Massachusetts, which had been signed into law by Governor James Curley on May 14, 1935, despite strong objections from the state's commissioner of education. The law required that "each teacher shall cause the pupils under his charge to salute the flag and recite in unison with him at said opening exercises at least once each week the 'Pledge of Allegiance to the Flag.' . . . Failure for a period of two consecutive weeks by a teacher to salute the flag and recite the pledge, or to cause pupils under his charge to do so, shall be punished for every such period by a fine of not more than five dollars." The law differed from Washington state's 1919 law in placing the onus of responsibility squarely upon the teacher, but it was otherwise similar, though the punishment for noncompliance was substantially lighter than with the Washington statute. Neither the Washington nor the Massachusetts statute imposed a punishment on the offending student, leaving that task instead to the local school or school board.[23]

The new law took effect at the beginning of the school year in September 1935 and immediately met with resistance.[24] In Lynn, Massachusetts, an eight-year-old student, Carleton Nicholls, refused to participate in the morning flag salute because the flag was "the Devil's emblem." He could not salute the flag, he explained, because his faith told him that "he could only adore and bow down to Jehovah." On September 30 the conflict escalated when the boy's father, together with the nephew of the philosopher William James, joined Carleton in his third-grade class. Edward James was no Jehovah's Witness but proclaimed that "like my American ancestors, I will not submit to tyranny." The boy and the two men were directed to stand and salute the flag but refused, whereupon an angry principal ordered the men to leave the school premises. "I will stand for no such insult to the American flag," he reportedly told them. The dissenters refused and were then arrested and forcibly removed from the school.[25]

The dramatic showdown in the classroom and the arrest of the two men brought the case national attention. Interest in Carleton's case intensified when Rutherford took up the boy's cause in an October 6th radio address. Rutherford affirmed that "Jehovah's Witnesses conscientiously object and refuse to salute the flag and pledge allegiance to it," and he commended the "lad" in "declaring himself for Jehovah God and his kingdom." "All who act wisely," Rutherford said, "will do the same thing." At the same time, the ACLU publicly praised Carleton's "courageous stand" and offered to provide the boy's family legal support to defend "the American right of freedom of conscience and religious belief." The ACLU urged the Lynn school authorities to allow the boy to opt out of a ceremony that violated his religious principles.[26]

These statements of support had no effect on the Lynn school board, however, which on October 8 unanimously decided to expel Carleton from school until he agreed to say the Pledge of Allegiance with the rest of his class. The city's lawyer insisted that "my religion and your religion does not enter into it"— instead it was about showing respect for a symbol of the nation. Rutherford's endorsement of Carleton's example could not prevent the third grader from being expelled from school—despite a longstanding state law that prohibited the state from excluding any child from a public school "on account of race, color or religion"—but it did help spark extensive resistance to the flag salute ceremony on the part of Jehovah's Witnesses across the nation.[27]

At the same time that Carleton was being dismissed from school, officials in the nearby town of Saugus were faced with the same problem on an even larger scale when four siblings between the ages of nine and twelve, as well as a brother and a sister of twelve and thirteen, refused to participate in the Pledge of Allegiance. All were Jehovah's Witnesses, and as one of the parents explained, "We cannot salute the flag because we cannot serve two masters. Jehovah comes first and nobody else." Such resistance quickly spread beyond the borders of the Bay State, even into states where there was no state law mandating a flag salute or the Pledge of Allegiance.[28]

Within a few months, young Jehovah's Witnesses were being expelled from schools across the country for failing to salute the flag. An issue that had been virtually dormant for a decade suddenly filled national newspapers. By the following fall, in 1936, the ACLU counted at least 134 children expelled in eleven states for refusing to salute the flag. In addition, three teachers had been fired for refusing to lead the flag salute, one in Lynn, Massachusetts (who had taught in the town for forty-one years), and the other two in Pennsylvania. Over 60 percent of the dismissal incidents, each of which involved Jehovah's Witnesses, occurred in the state of Pennsylvania, with another quarter of the total from the three states of Massachusetts, New Jersey, and Washington.[29]

Not only were dismissals more common in Pennsylvania, they also were more often accompanied by violence, particularly in southwestern Pennsylvania. In the mining town of Nemacolin, students were not only expelled from school but frequently whipped for their refusals. One ten-year-old boy, Louis Wieliewicz, "was so badly whipped that his thighs were black and blue for two weeks." The school board topped it off by fining parents for failing to keep their children in school. In Pittsburgh, the same pattern of whippings, expulsions, and fines was followed, except the school board also initiated "proceedings towards having children sent to the House of Correction." Twelve-year-old Stanley Brachna of Grindstone, Pennsylvania, was "knocked around by [the] teacher; thrown against a desk; hit; [and the] teacher tried to force him to salute by holding up his hand."[30]

In Canonsburg, a small community near Pittsburgh, the list of horrors was particularly long. Thirteen-year-old Anna Prinos of Canonsburg, Pennsylvania, was "whipped and choked by [the] principal [and] sent home with great welts on [her] back from [the] beatings." So hostile was the community to the stance taken by the Jehovah's Witnesses that no doctor would agree to testify in court as to Anna's condition, forcing the family to bring in a doctor from Pittsburgh. Her twelve-year-old sister Pauline was also whipped, though evidently spared the choking. The principal, however, threatened to have her sent to reform school. Ruth George, another thirteen-year-old Canonsburg schoolgirl, needed medical treatment after being "beaten and taunted" by the principal. Adding insult to injury, the teacher accused Ruth of being an "anarchist." Ruth's eleven-year-old brother was "beaten by [his] teacher [and] carried marks of the beating for a week." He was also "threatened with incarceration in reform school."[31]

Things were little better in the town of Monessen, Pennsylvania, where the Witnesses had set up their own private school so that the expelled children could be educated and the parents could avoid being brought up on charges of making truants of their children. The mayor of the town, however, pronounced the school Communist and ordered it closed down. Finally the Witnesses managed to get an injunction against the mayor and the chief of police to prevent them from padlocking the school. However, after the injunction was issued, the community took matters into its own hands by throwing bricks through the school windows. When some townsfolk circulated a petition protesting the actions of the mayor and the police, the petitioners were arrested, relieved of their petitions, tossed in jail, and found guilty of disorderly conduct.[32]

The dismissals and violence were less pervasive in the rest of the nation, but the episodes were equally revealing of public hysteria and intolerance. In Atlanta, Georgia, a student who refused to salute the flag was not only expelled from school but the father's business was boycotted and picketed by the Ku Klux Klan. The family was "hounded by newspapers and various organizations until his business was ruined." In the small town of New Weston, Ohio, refusal led juvenile authorities to threaten the children with incarceration and the townspeople to boycott the family's business. The family was forced to move to another community.[33] In a great many of these cases the Jehovah's Witnesses fought their antagonists in the courtroom, but initially at least they met with little success in contesting their children's expulsions from schools.

The Legal Fight

The first case to make it to court was that of Carleton Nicholls. The boy had his day in court in December 1935, less than three months after being expelled from school. Although the case reached the Massachusetts Supreme Court with astonishing speed, the court took nearly sixteen months to deliver its verdict. The court's verdict was unanimous: The school board was within its rights to expel from school students who refused to salute the flag or say the Pledge of Allegiance. Writing for the court, the chief justice dismissed the claim that being compelled to say the Pledge violated religious freedom:

> The flag salute and pledge of allegiance here in question do not in any just sense relate to religion. They are not observances which are religious in nature. They do not concern the views of any one as to his Creator. They do not touch upon his relations with his Maker. They impose no obligations as to religious worship. They are wholly patriotic in design and purpose. . . . The pledge of allegiance to the flag . . . is an acknowledgment of sovereignty, a promise of obedience, a recognition of authority above the will of the individual, to be respected and obeyed. It has nothing to do with religion.

The chief justice did not deny that the student's religious beliefs were genuinely felt and that they were the grounds for his refusal to salute and pledge allegiance to the flag. But the court essentially decreed that the Witnesses' belief that the Pledge was a form of idolatry was ridiculous. No reasonable person, the court insisted, could believe that saluting a national flag was an affront to God. The flag salute and Pledge of Allegiance thus posed no conflict between loyalty to God and loyalty to the state.[34]

Because the Massachusetts court was so slow in announcing its decision, the first state supreme court to announce a decision on the constitutionality of the flag salute was the high court in New Jersey, which heard the case in January 1937 and announced its decision within two weeks. The case involved the plight of two young sisters who had been expelled from school in the fall of 1935. A unanimous court apparently had no difficulty in rejecting the schoolgirls' appeal. To the justices, the case was open and shut—the opinion was barely three hundred and fifty words long. New Jersey state law, as in Massachusetts, required every public school student to salute the flag and say the oath of allegiance. "Those who resort to educational institutions maintained with the state's money," the court opined, "are subject to the commands of the state." Moreover, religious freedom was not involved because "the performance of the command of the statute in question could, in no sense, interfere with religious freedom." The Pledge of Allegiance, the court concluded, was "by no stretch of the imagination, a religious rite." Instead it was clearly "a patriotic ceremony which the legislature has the power to require of those attending schools established at public expense." If the students didn't like saying the Pledge, they could find alternative, private schools in which the Pledge was not a required part of the curriculum.[35]

Several months after the New Jersey and Massachusetts court rulings, the Georgia Supreme Court rendered the same verdict in the case of a sixth-grade girl who had been expelled from an Atlanta school for refusing to salute the flag. As in Massachusetts and New Jersey, the high court unanimously refused to countenance the idea that the flag salute conflicted with any reasonable understanding of religious conscience. Since the state was providing students with the benefits of a "free education," the state could, in turn, reasonably command students to show respect for the American flag. Although the United States was "a land of freedom," the chief justice wrote, "those who reside within its limits and receive the protection and benefits afforded to them must obey its laws and show due respect to the government, its institutions and ideals. The flag of the United States is a symbol thereof, and disrespect to the flag is disrespect to the government, its institutions and ideals, and is directly opposed to the policy of this State." Moreover, the chief justice continued, in words that directly echoed the New Jersey court, "the act of saluting the flag of the United States is by no stretch of reasonable imagination 'a religious rite.' . . . [F]or a pupil to salute the flag of this country is just a part of a patriotic ceremony, an act of respect to the institutions and ideals of the land that is affording them a free education and a safe and bountiful place to live, and is not a bowing down in worship of an image in the place of God." The chief justice's long years at the bar had evidently made him an expert on the true nature of religion.[36]

In other cases the Witnesses confronted even more dismissive reactions from the courts. In 1939 the Florida Supreme Court heard the case of Fred Bleich's six children, who had been suspended from school in November 1937 for refusing to participate in the flag salute ceremony. The chief justice penned the opinion for a unanimous court. The court, the chief justice said, could not see that the verses of Exodus forbidding the children of Israel to worship graven images had "any relation whatever to the present situation. It would be as pertinent to rely on some requirement of the Assyrian, the Hittite, or the Code of Hammurabi." Saluting the flag, the judge continued,

> is nothing more than a symbolic expression or a restatement of one's loyalty and fervor for his country and its political institutions. It is patriotism in action. It has no

reference to or connection whatever with one's religious belief. Saluting the flag connotes a love and patriotic devotion to country while religious practice connotes a way of life, the brand of one's theology or his relation to God. They are as clearly distinguished as Communism is from Democracy, [or] as Calvanism [*sic*] is from Shintoism. . . . One is in no sense inconsistent with the other and saluting the flag does not approach religious rite. . . . To symbolize the flag as a graven image and ascribe to the act of saluting it a species of idolatry is too vague and far fetched to be even tinctured with the flavor of reason.

Having dismissed the Witnesses as crazy people and their religious beliefs as irrational, Florida's highest court upheld the school board's power to expel students refusing to take part in the flag salute ceremony.[37]

And so it went as court after court decided against the Jehovah's Witnesses. Justices seemed supremely confident that their legal experience outfitted them well for divining the difference between reasonable and silly religious beliefs. A number of court rulings, including the ones in Georgia and New Jersey, were appealed to the U.S. Supreme Court, but the highest court in the land rejected the appeals on the grounds that the dismissals raised no federal constitutional questions.

There were a few rays of hope in what otherwise was an ocean of judicial darkness. In California, a superior court judge in Sacramento agreed that the expulsion of a nine-year-old girl had unconstitutionally infringed upon her religious liberty. On August 31, 1938, however, the California Supreme Court unanimously reversed the lower court ruling, putting California back in line with the national judicial consensus. And there was a partial victory in New York, where in January 1939 the state's high court reversed the conviction of Mr. and Mrs. Sandstrom for allegedly failing to keep their thirteen-year-old daughter, Grace, in school. But on the question of whether school authorities were within their rights to expel the student, the New York court sided with other high courts: "Saluting the flag," wrote the court's chief justice, "in no sense is an act of worship or a species of idolatry. . . . The flag has nothing to do with religion." Moreover, the state was not required to tolerate every religious belief. It needed to be free to restrict those "actions which are in violation of social duties or subversive of good order." To avoid "a breakdown of the morale of its people," the government was justified in requiring a flag salute or other such measures it believed would "engender and maintain patriotism in the young." Unlike the other high courts, however, the New York court did express sympathy for Grace's plight and frustration at the school officials' rigidity. While allowing that school officials were within their rights and that Grace "must be obedient" if she was to stay in school, the court also expressed the view that there surely must be "a better way for accomplishing the purposes of this law than immediate resort to disciplinary measures." Had the school officials exhibited "a little more patience and some tact," the court was confident that the child would over time develop "a reverence for our flag" and that she would then "be glad that it is still here to salute."[38]

Even better from the Witnesses' point of view was the strong dissent of Justice Irving Lehman. Virtually all the important flag salute decisions up to this point had been unanimous verdicts, giving the Witnesses and the ACLU little hope for success. Lehman, who would be elevated to chief justice the following year, was the first state judge to press the Witnesses' case. Lehman noted that "Episcopalians and Methodists and Presbyterians and Baptists, Catholics and Jews, may all agree that a salute to the flag cannot be disobedience to the will of the Creator" and "all the judges of the State may agree that no well-intentioned person could reasonably object to such a salute." Yet the fact was that Grace Sandstrom, her parents, and her religious leaders believed otherwise, forcing the girl to "choose between obedience to the command of the principal of the school, and obedience to what she has been taught and believes is the command of God." Grace sincerely believed that should she submit to the principal's command she would be slain "when the battle of Armageddon comes," and the state lacked a compelling reason to force Grace to make such a terrible choice. To compel Grace Sandstrom to join in an act that she believed to be morally wrong and forbidden by her religion, the state must show that performance of the act was reasonably related "to the peace or safety" of the state or was necessary for "the orderly conduct of the school." But this, Lehman argued, the state had not shown. Even at the original trial, the principal who had expelled Grace readily conceded that there was no chance that Grace's refusal would influence other children to show disrespect for the flag. Lehman conceded that the school could punish acts of disrespect toward the flag, but he could not agree that Grace's refusal was disrespectful:

> There is no disrespect to the flag in refusal to salute the flag by a child who has been taught that it is a moral wrong to show respect in the form of a salute. . . . She does not refuse to show love and respect for the flag. She refuses only to show her love and respect in a manner which she believes her God has forbidden. She asks only that she be not compelled to incur the wrath of her God by disobedience to His commands. The flag salute would lose no dignity or worth if she were permitted to refrain from joining in it. On the contrary, that would be an impressive lesson for her and the other children that the flag stands for absolute freedom of conscience except where freedom of conscience is asserted "to justify practices inconsistent with the peace or safety of this State." . . . The flag is dishonored by a salute by a child in

reluctant and terrified obedience to a command of secular authority which clashes with the dictates of conscience. The flag "cherished by all our hearts" should not be soiled by the tears of a little child. The Constitution does not permit, and the Legislature never intended, that the flag should be so soiled and dishonored.[39]

The *Gobitis* Case

The most important legal ray of hope, however, emanated from Pennsylvania. State courts had proved decidedly unsympathetic, and so the Witnesses' national legal counsel, Olin Moyle, looked to bring suit in federal court instead. Expulsions were plentiful in Pennsylvania so Moyle did not lack for potential plaintiffs. Moyle decided to take the case of two siblings who had been expelled from school in the small coal-mining town of Minersville, Pennsylvania. In May 1937 he filed suit on behalf of the Gobitas children in the United States District Court for the Eastern District of Pennsylvania at Philadelphia. Walter Gobitas, the children's father, had been a lifelong resident of the town. A hard-working and successful grocer, he was well liked in the town, perhaps in part because he had helped many of the miners who had lost their jobs during the depression that had devastated the town's coal industry. Until 1931, when he converted, Gobitas had been a Catholic, just like 80 percent of the other townsfolk of Minersville. His and his family's new faith was seen as eccentric but was by and large tolerated.[40]

Refusals in eastern Pennsylvania had usually been met with greater lenience than in the western part of the state. There was generally little or no violence, and school officials often sought out some form of compromise that might prevent expulsion. When, in October 1935, Lilian Gobitas, a month shy of her twelfth birthday, told her teacher that she could no longer salute the flag because of her reading of Exodus, the teacher reportedly "hugged her and praised her valor." The superintendent of schools, Charles E. Roudabush, was much less supportive, however. Roudabush, who had a reputation as a strict disciplinarian, was enraged by the girl's conduct as well as that of her younger brother. Pennsylvania, however, had no state law requiring the flag salute and Pledge of Allegiance, and the Minersville school district had no regulation requiring it, although the ceremony had been a well-established custom in the Minersville schools for about two decades. Roudabush promptly sought an opinion from the state as to whether he had the authority to punish students for their refusal to salute the flag. He was informed that he could punish the students for insubordination if the school district had a formal flag salute requirement. On

October 26, the state's attorney general issued a legal opinion explaining that, "regardless of one's religious views, there can be no justification for any refusal to respect the standard of our nation. . . . When disloyalty to our country is part of any creed, it constitutes a defiance to the Constitution which guarantees that creed's existence." Not only could school officials require the Pledge of Allegiance but, in the attorney general's view, it was their "duty" to do so. The Minersville school board promptly met and passed a resolution requiring a daily flag salute and specifying that refusal to salute the flag would be treated as "an act of insubordination and . . . dealt with accordingly." Immediately, Roudabush declared that he was expelling the Gobitas children for insubordination.[41]

It is easy to see why Moyle and the ACLU were attracted to championing the Gobitas children's case. Among its virtues were the absence of any state statute requiring a flag salute, the superintendent's unseemly haste in expelling the children for conduct that occurred prior to the passage of the board's resolution, and the unimpeachable, good character of William Gobitas and his family. Moreover, they could pursue the legal case in the relatively tolerant and cosmopolitan environment of the Quaker city of Philadelphia. When the Minersville school board attempted to have the suit dismissed from federal court on substantive as well as jurisdictional grounds, the case was heard by a Philadelphia Quaker and FDR appointee, federal judge Albert Maris. Maris refused to decide on whether there was federal jurisdiction in the case but made clear his total lack of sympathy for the school board's position. The school board, he said, had used "our beloved flag, the emblem of religious liberty, to impose a religious test as a condition of receiving the benefits of public education. And this has been done without any compelling necessity of public safety or welfare." Maris rejected the idea that the school board could decide whether refusing to salute the flag was a religious act. In Maris's view, that judgment must be left to the Witnesses. "Liberty of conscience," wrote Maris, "means liberty for each individual to decide for himself what is to him religious." Allowing public officials "to determine whether the views of individuals sincerely held and their acts sincerely undertaken on religious grounds are in fact based on convictions religious in character would be to sound the death knell of religious liberty."[42]

Maris's ruling, issued on December 1, 1937, was favorably received in many quarters, especially among professional educators. The state superintendent of schools welcomed the ruling and characterized the compulsory flag salute as "fine for Hitler and Mussolini, but not for the American public." "Forcing children to salute the flag," he argued, "doesn't get at the fundamental attitude of respect. . . . It ought to come from the heart." The superintendents of several eastern Pennsylvania counties also endorsed the ruling and criticized the compulsory salute. Lining up on the other side were local patriotic and veterans organizations that vowed to support the Minersville school district, with financial aid if necessary.[43]

On February 15, 1938, the trial finally began in the courtroom of Judge Maris. The defense summoned only a single witness: Superintendent Roudabush, who was to provide expert testimony on the deleterious effects that would result if schools could not require citizens to salute the flag. Roudabush testified that a few children refusing to salute the flag would have a "demoralizing" effect on all the children. When queried as to why, Roudabush explained:

> The tendency would be to spread. In our mixed population where we have foreigners of every variety, it would be no time until they would form a dislike, a disregard for our flag and country. May I say that the thing that goes hard with us when some one refuses to salute the flag is to refuse to pledge allegiance to the country for which it stands. Now, I believe when we make a citizen out of an alien the first thing that we require is they have to denounce their allegiance, to the foreign country, and it would seem reasonable to suppose that they would be required to pledge allegiance to the country in which they want to become citizens.

Nearly a half century after the Pledge's creation, Roudabush's testimony showed that anxiety about immigrants and aliens remained a powerful motivating force in the ritual of the Pledge of Allegiance.

Maris was unpersuaded by Roudabush, and on June 18, 1938, he delivered his opinion explaining why the refusal to salute the flag on the part of "two earnest Christian children" did not "even remotely prejudice or imperil the safety, health, morals, property or personal rights of their fellows." Whereas Roudabush looked at the nation's diverse religions and ethnicities and saw the need to mandate conformity and obedience to keep America strong, Maris surveyed the "current world scene" and concluded that upholding individual liberty was more important than ever:

> The safety of our nation largely depends upon the extent to which we foster in each individual citizen that sturdy independence of thought and action which is essential in a democracy. . . . Our country's safety surely does not depend upon the totalitarian idea of forcing all citizens into one common mold of thinking and acting or requiring them to render a lip service of loyalty in a manner which conflicts with their sincere religious convictions. Such a doctrine seems to me utterly alien to the

genius and spirit of our nation and destructive of that personal liberty of which our flag itself is the symbol.[44]

Maris's ruling in favor of the Gobitas children was a great victory for the Witnesses, but the Minersville school district was unmoved. Roudabush publicly condemned the decision: "Boys and girls who do not acknowledge allegiance to their country of birth are aliens, and do not belong in the public schools which are tax supported." Period. The judge, the superintendent argued, had embarked on a slippery slope that would result in anarchy and licentiousness. "Some years ago in Pennsylvania," Roudabush recalled, "a hex-murder was justified by the murderer because he felt that he was doing what his religion required of him to do. Would the Court say that this murderer was entitled to his belief?" The school board refused Gobitas's request to have his children readmitted to school and opted to appeal the decision to the Third Circuit Court of Appeals. The costs of the appeal were paid for entirely by several patriotic groups, with by far the largest sum coming from the Patriotic Order of the Sons of America.[45]

Meanwhile the ACLU was continuing to aid the Gobitas family. Among the ACLU's contributions was a friend of the court brief urging the court of appeals to uphold Maris's ruling. Even more insistently than Maris, the ACLU pointed to the world situation to shore up its position. Compelling Witnesses to violate their deeply held religious beliefs by saluting and pledging allegiance to the flag was, the ACLU said, part of a "rising tide of political dictatorship and religious intolerance" in the world. The brief likened the compulsory flag salute to the "outstretched arm of fascism and nazism where one stands in fear of his life or the concentration camp if he does not comply with the dictator's wish and whim." The compulsory salute was fitting in Nazi Germany or fascist Italy but not in a free democracy.[46]

In November 1939, two months after the Nazi blitzkrieg in Poland had set off World War II, the three-member appeals court unanimously upheld Maris's ruling. Included in the rambling opinion was a footnote quoting Adolf Hitler's judgment of the Jehovah's Witnesses: "I consider them quacks. I dissolve the 'earnest Bible Students' in Germany; their property I dedicate to the people's welfare; I will have all their literature confiscated." Roudabush dismissed the opinion as a "hodge-podge of perverted quotations," and again the school board appealed, this time to the United States Supreme Court. The Supreme Court, which had on multiple occasions in the past several years refused to overturn state supreme court judgments against the Witnesses, accepted the school board's appeal. Oral arguments were heard on April 25, 1940, only weeks after the Germans invaded Denmark and Norway, and on June 3, 1940, with the war now having spread to France, Belgium, and the Netherlands, the Court issued its 8-1 ruling overturning the appeals court's decision and coming down emphatically on the side of state power and judicial restraint.[47]

Events in Europe were clearly on the minds of the justices, and they preyed particularly on the mind of Felix Frankfurter, who had been chosen by the chief justice to write the Court's opinion. A Jewish émigré from Vienna, Frankfurter confessed, in a May 26 letter to President Roosevelt, that "hardly anything else has been on my mind" than the spreading war in Europe. The well-connected Frankfurter spent much of the spring trying to prepare the nation for a war that he felt would inevitably require America's involvement. Two days before issuing his *Gobitis* opinion, for instance, Frankfurter was descending on the White House to press the president to replace his isolationist secretary of war with Henry Stimson (a switch the president did in fact make several weeks later). National unity and attachment to democratic ideas, Frankfurter believed, would be essential to defeat the evils of Nazism. National unity was, he wrote in *Gobitis*, "an interest inferior to none in the hierarchy of legal values." For "national unity is the basis of national security." Without that "unifying sentiment" among the people of a nation, "there ultimately can be no liberties, civil or religious."[48]

The case was a difficult one for Frankfurter—"nothing," he told another justice, "has weighed as much on my conscience, since I have come to this Court." Frankfurter was a committed civil libertarian and one of the original founders of the ACLU. Privately he described the course pursued by the Minersville school authorities as "foolish and perhaps worse." He believed that it was not for the courts to correct the illiberalism of officialdom, but rather that it was the task of the people acting through their elected representatives to decide what was wise and what was foolish. To the sole dissenting justice, Frankfurter explained that he wanted to use his opinion "as a vehicle for preaching the true democratic faith of not relying on the Court for the impossible task of assuring a vigorous, mature, self-respecting and tolerant democracy by bringing the responsibility . . . directly home where it belongs—to the people and their representatives themselves." Frankfurter also reminded his fellow justice that the ominous events in Europe made it more important than ever that legislatures be empowered to take the steps they deemed necessary to advance national security. The "time and circumstances are surely not irrelevant considerations in resolving the conflicts that we do have to resolve in this particular case." Specifically, Frankfurter feared that a decision in favor of the Gobitas family could have "a tail of implications" that would handicap democratically elected legislatures from promoting "a common feeling for the common country" and "securing effective loyalty to the traditional ideals of democracy." The Court could inadvertently cripple national unity at the very time that it was so vital to national security and the cause of democracy and liberty. For those who, like the Witnesses, compared the compulsory flag salute with the Heil Hitler salute, Frankfurter had only scorn. "It mocks reason," he said, "and denies our whole history to find in the allowance of a requirement to salute our flag on fitting occasions the seeds of sanction for obeisance to a leader."⁴⁹

A different perspective was tentatively offered up by the Court's newest member, Justice Frank Murphy, who only a few months earlier had been the country's attorney general. Murphy drafted a dissent in which he challenged Frankfurter on what the war meant for America. The rise of fascism, Murphy countered, meant that it was more imperative than ever that the Court defend civil liberties and ensure that the nation remain a beacon of freedom:

> Especially at this time when the freedom of individual conscience is being placed in jeopordy [sic] by world shaking events, it is of vital importance that freedom of conscience and opinion be protected against all considered regulations that have no practical efficacy and bear no necessary or substantial relation to the maintenance of order and safety of our institutions.

Murphy was persuaded, however, by his more senior colleagues, probably especially the domineering Chief Justice Charles Evans Hughes, to abandon his dissent. Murphy dutifully shelved the dissent and joined Frankfurter's opinion.⁵⁰

One member of the Supreme Court, however, remained unpersuaded and unbowed: Harlan Stone, who had been appointed to the Court by President Coolidge in 1925. Reading his opinion in full from the bench, an emotional Stone condemned the mandatory salute law as "unique in the history of Anglo-American legislation." Through it, "the state seeks to coerce these children to express a sentiment which . . . violates their deepest religious convictions." Stone conceded that government had "a right to survive," but he reminded his fellow justices that "the Constitution expresses more than the conviction of the people that democratic processes must be preserved at all costs. It is also an expression of faith and a command that freedom of mind and spirit must be preserved, which government must obey, if it is to adhere to that justice and moderation without which no free government can exist." The Supreme Court need not become "the school board for the country," as Frankfurter warned, but it must protect individuals from government compelling them to express views that violate their religious convictions. Responding directly to Frankfurter, Stone observed that "while such expressions of loyalty, when voluntarily given, may promote national unity, it is quite another matter to say that their compulsory expression by children in violation of their own and their parents' religious convictions can be regarded as playing so important a part in our national unity as to leave school boards free to exact it despite the constitutional guarantee of freedom of religion." Moreover, Stone continued, "even if we believe that such compulsions will contribute to national unity, there are other ways to teach loyalty and patriotism which are the sources of national unity, than by compelling the pupil to affirm that which he does not believe and by commanding a form of affirmance which violates his religious convictions."[51]

The Aftermath of *Gobitis*

Stone's dissent drew strong praise in many quarters. According to one count, at least 170 newspapers sided with Stone against the majority. "Dead wrong" was how the *St. Louis Dispatch* characterized the Court's decision:

> We think its decision is a violation of American principle. We think it is a surren-
> der to popular hysteria. If patriotism depends upon such things as this—upon vio-
> lation of a fundamental right of religious freedom—then it becomes not a noble
> emotion of love for country, but something to be rammed down our throats by
> the law.

Similarly, the *Des Moines Register* saw in Frankfurter's opinion not the application of American principles but "a by-product of the new circumstances that have developed in the world in the last month or two." The *New Republic*, which Frankfurter had helped found several decades earlier, was even more direct. The nation, the editors opined, was "in the grip of war hysteria" and seemed "in great danger of adopting Hitler's philosophy in the effort to oppose Hitler's legions." The *Gobitis* decision showed that the Supreme Court had veered "dangerously close to being a victim of that hysteria." A little over a month later, the magazine went further still, directly comparing the Supreme Court's decision with a recent decree by a Nazi court punishing Jehovah's Witnesses for refusing to offer the Heil Hitler salute.[52]

    If Frankfurter had to endure criticism from many longtime friends, that was nothing compared to what Jehovah's Witnesses were subjected to in the wake of the *Gobitis* ruling. Violence against Witnesses certainly preceded the Supreme

Court's ruling, but after the ruling, as Lilian Gobitas later recalled, it was "open season" on the Witnesses. Across the nation, Witnesses were subjected to brutal attacks by vigilante mobs, often with the assistance of local law enforcement officers. Wild rumors spread that Witnesses were Nazi agents, a particularly perverse accusation in view of the systematic persecution and murder of Witnesses being carried out by the Nazi regime in Germany. People capable of believing such patent absurdities were not surprisingly also capable of interpreting the Supreme Court's ruling as a license to coerce, intimidate, and humiliate Witnesses who refused to salute the flag.[53]

Toward the end of June, in Richmond, West Virginia, Witnesses were rounded up and roped like cattle by the sheriff's deputy. Those who resisted had castor oil poured down their throats by members of the American Legion aiding the sheriff's deputy, who by this time had removed his badge. One of the more defiant Witnesses was forced to consume so much castor oil that he later urinated blood. All of this took place in the mayor's office, with the chief of police guarding the door. The sheriff's deputy marched the roped line of prisoners out into the main street, where before a crowd of townspeople he recited the preamble to the American Legion's constitution—which included the admonition "to make right master of might [and] to promote peace and good will on earth"—and led them in reciting the Pledge of Allegiance. When the Witnesses refused to join in the flag salute, they were marched to the outskirts of town in military drill and instructed to get out of town. Their cars were waiting for them, "doused with castor oil and defaced with crudely painted swastikas and epithets—'Hitler's spies,' 'Fifth Column,' 'Heil Hitler,' and 'Beware.'"[54]

In Litchfield, Illinois, just south of Springfield, virtually "the whole adult population" of the town reportedly spent most of June 16, 1940, attacking sixty Witnesses who had come to the town to proselytize. One Litchfield man "draped an American flag over the hood of [a Witness] car," and, "when the Witness stubbornly refused to salute, vigilantes grabbed his head and repeatedly slammed it against the flag-covered hood." According to one eyewitness, the crowd beat his head against the car for nearly half an hour. "The chief of police sat in his car while all this was going on." Asked to explain why they were savagely attacking defenseless Witnesses, one responded: "Why, they wouldn't even salute the flag! We almost beat one guy to death to make him kiss the flag." Unlike in Richmond, West Virginia, the Witnesses had to leave the county by bus because their cars had all been "overturned . . . and pounded . . . with curbstones, paving material, and baseball bats."[55]

Many of the wartime vigilante attacks on Jehovah's Witnesses were led by members of the American Legion. By one count, 176 of 843 vigilante incidents against Jehovah's Witnesses between 1940 and 1943 involved individuals who were known to be Legionnaires. Their prominence was noticeable enough that when a U.S. attorney in Texas took to the radio in February 1942 to urge respect for the civil liberties of Witnesses, he singled out the Legion:

> You American Legion boys have been presenting the Jehovah's Witnesses with the American flag, and have asked them to salute it, and they have refused to do it. This starts trouble. You should not do that. . . . You gentlemen are acting too hasty, you let your patriotism get the best of your judgment. . . . Please leave your flag at your Legion Post. . . . If you do not want to hear the Jehovah's Witnesses, do not listen to them. No man should want to fight religion because he does not agree with it.

The Legion was only minimally responsive to such appeals. The head of the Legion's National Americanism Commission, the organization that had spearheaded the establishment of a flag code two decades earlier, referred to the Witnesses as a "supposed" religious group who were "unamerican" and spread a dangerous "doctrine of disloyalty." He encouraged Legionnaires to "keep up the good work" of confronting and verbally abusing Witnesses. When the Japanese attacked Pearl Harbor, a representative of the ACLU contacted the national commander of the American Legion to propose they meet to discuss how to prevent violence against Witnesses. The Legion commander declined to meet, adding that he thought "this is not the time for Jehovah's Witnesses or any other organization to be engaged in a nationwide program teaching disloyalty to our Flag, disloyalty to the defense of the United States when our supreme effort is needed for the unification of all elements toward our national safety." Many within the Legion would have agreed with the sheriff in a southern town who, when asked why a mob was attacking and abusing a small group of Witnesses, replied, "They're running them out of here. They're traitors—the Supreme Court says so. Ain't you heard?"[56]

The acts of violence perpetrated against Jehovah's Witnesses in the early years of World War II, including the sadistic castration of a Witness in Nebraska at the close of the summer of 1940, generated its own outraged response. Federal officials and newspaper editors urged tolerance and condemned the mob violence, and many pointed an accusing finger at the Supreme Court. After widespread rioting in the normally peaceful town of Kennebunk, Maine, resulted in the burning of the Witnesses' Kingdom Hall, the *New York Herald*

Tribune editorialized that "the Supreme Court's recent decision that the Jehovah's Witnesses must salute the flag seems to have convinced several hundred Maine rustics that it is their personal responsibility to see this decree carried out." The Court's decision seemed to legitimize the patriotic vigilantes who now took the law into their own hands, convinced in their own minds at least that they were carrying out the will of the Supreme Court.[57]

Some Americans began to worry that the violence visited on the Witnesses undercut the nation's claim to be a land of liberty and justice for all. The United States seemed to be behaving toward the Witnesses in ways that were disturbingly similar to the ways that Nazi Germany treated them. Solicitor General Francis Biddle sounded insistent warnings against meting out "mob punishment." He deplored the "Nazi methods" of "self-constituted bands of mob patrioteers . . . roaming about the country, setting upon these people, beating them, driving them out of their homes." Biddle warned that the government "shall not tolerate such Nazi methods." He complained bitterly that local law enforcement officials were not only allowing this "cruel persecution" to continue, but in some instances "have been the leaders of the mob." "We shall not defeat Nazi evil," Biddle insisted, "by emulating its methods. . . . Hitler's methods cannot preserve our democracy, which demands justice for all alike." The nation must combat the Nazis not by becoming like them but by demonstrating to the world the profound difference between democracy and dictatorship.[58]

By 1942 the number of Jehovah's Witnesses expelled from school had climbed into the thousands. The increase in expulsions was largely due to more stringent enforcement of existing rules, but it was also due to the proliferation of new flag salute regulations in the wake of court rulings, particularly the Supreme Court's ruling in *Gobitis*. In Raymond, New Hampshire, for instance, a week after the *Gobitis* ruling, the school board "resolved that every pupil, regardless of religious persuasion . . . shall salute the Flag, whenever the salute is called for. . . . Failure to comply . . . shall immediately exclude any pupil." Old rules were often reinterpreted in light of the Supreme Court's pronouncement. So in Washington state, for instance, the attorney general's response to *Gobitis* was to reverse an earlier advisory opinion that had instructed schools not to expel those who had conscientious objections to saluting the flag.[59] In Oklahoma, where anti-Witness violence was widespread, the state superintendent of schools reinterpreted a 1921 flag-exercise statute as a mandate that the flag salute and Pledge of Allegiance must be performed in all public and private schools. The brutal violence against Witnesses that flared up in the summer of 1940 after *Gobitis* was never quite equaled in the subsequent years, but incidents of violence and intimidation remained a pervasive problem for the next two years, particularly in small towns. In the immediate aftermath of the bombing of Pearl Harbor in December 1941, there was a virulent new wave of anti-Witness violence that demonstrated once again the Witnesses' extreme vulnerability to the violent and unholy alliance of "mob patrioteers" and local law enforcement officials.[60]

The persistent pattern of expulsions, arbitrary arrests, and violent intimidation led to a rethinking among the Supreme Court justices of the wisdom of the *Gobitis* decision. In June 1942, the Court, in *Jones v. Opelika*, decided that localities could require proselytizing Witnesses to pay a solicitation fee because their activities had a commercial character—they accepted donations for the literature they distributed. Harlan Stone, who was now chief justice, again strongly dissented, but this time he was joined by three other justices: Frank Murphy, Hugo Black, and William Douglas. Each of the three had sided with the majority in *Gobitis*, but remarkably now announced their change of heart. *Gobitis*, they flatly declared, had been "wrongly decided" and was inconsistent with the protection of the free exercise clause of the First Amendment. Black later explained that they had initially been "mesmerized" by Frankfurter. "Felix was an immigrant, passionate about the flag and what it meant to him. We were so moved by his appeal that we went for it." Frankfurter was enraged by the defection of his three colleagues, which he disparagingly referred to as "the Axis." Meanwhile some clerks derided the *Gobitis* opinion as "Felix's Fall-of-France Opinion."[61]

The repudiation of *Gobitis* by three of the justices who had joined in the opinion emboldened lower courts to ignore the ruling. In Washington for instance, the state supreme court was asked to rule on whether local authorities could declare the parents unfit and the children wards of the court merely because the children refused to salute the flag. The trial court, relying on *Gobitis*, had affirmed the juvenile court's decree, but the state of Washington Supreme Court would have none of it. The *Gobitis* opinion, the court wrote, "can scarcely be deemed to have become authoritative" in view of its rejection by three of its authors. Instead, the court endorsed the reasoning of Harlan Stone's *Gobitis* dissent. Moreover, whatever the federal Constitution might allow, the Washington justices insisted that such actions violated the state constitution's guarantee of "freedom of conscience in all matters of religious sentiment, belief and worship." The Kansas Supreme Court showed a similar lack of deference to *Gobitis*, holding in July 1942 that the state could not compel Jehovah's Witnesses to salute the flag or utter the Pledge of Allegiance. In expelling students in the fall of 1941, several Kansas school districts in Cherokee County had relied on *Gobitis*, but the Kansas court was unimpressed, noting first the recent public change of heart of three of the Supreme Court justices and then building their case upon the state constitution's declaration that "the right to worship God according to the dictates of conscience shall never be infringed."[62]

State courts could justify their departures from the U.S. Supreme Court's ruling by arguing that freedom of religion was more stringently protected in the state constitution than in the federal Constitution. But federal courts had no such recourse. So the decision of a federal district court in West Virginia to forbid the state board of education from requiring that public schoolchildren salute the American flag was a particularly bold repudiation of the Supreme Court's holding in *Gobitis*. West Virginia was a state with a relatively large number of Jehovah's Witnesses, and on January 9, 1942, a month after the bombing of Pearl Harbor and America's formal entry into the war, the state board of education passed a resolution requiring all teachers and all students in public schools to participate in the flag salute and directed that refusals be treated as insubordination. Over the course of the next year, Witnesses were expelled in every county in the state. The resolution was preceded by five "whereas" clauses, which were largely a pastiche taken from Frankfurter's *Gobitis* opinion, including his dicta that "national unity is the basis of national security," that the flag "is the symbol of our National Unity transcending all internal differences," and that public schools are "dealing with the formative period in the development in citizenship." The district court, knowing that four of the seven justices who participated in *Gobitis* and who were still on the Supreme Court now objected to the decision, curtly brushed aside Frankfurter's reasoning in *Gobitis*. "The salute to the flag," the district court held, "is an expression of the homage of the soul. To force it upon one who has conscientious scruples against giving it, is petty tyranny unworthy of the spirit of this Republic and forbidden, we think, by the fundamental law." The court's ruling was appealed by the state of West Virginia, giving the Supreme Court the chance to reconsider its much criticized ruling less than three years after it was announced.[63]

Barnette: The Court Reconsiders

By the time the case was argued before the Supreme Court in March 1943 it was clear that the Court would reverse itself.[64] Four justices were on record as wanting to reverse *Gobitis*, which meant that the four only needed to gain the backing of one of the two newest members of the Court, neither of whom had taken part in *Gobitis*. One of the new justices was Wiley Rutledge, who as a federal district court judge had dissented from a 1942 decision to convict two Jehovah's Witnesses of selling religious materials without a license. A disapproving Rutledge wrote:

> Jehovah's Witnesses have had to choose between their consciences and public education for their children. In my judgment, they should not have to give up also the right to disseminate their religious views in an orderly manner on the public streets, exercise it at the whim of public officials, or be taxed for doing so without a license.

The other recently elevated justice was Robert Jackson, who had been FDR's attorney general at the time the *Gobitis* opinion had been handed down. As the nation's chief law enforcement officer, he was well aware of the violence and injustice that had been perpetrated against the Witnesses by state and local authorities in the wake of the Court's ruling. Even before joining the Court in 1941, Jackson had made public his view that the *Gobitis* opinion was an unfortunate deviation from the Court's customary and admirable vigilance "in stamping out attempts by local authorities to suppress the free dissemination of ideas, upon which the system of responsible government rests."[65]

Although the outcome of *West Virginia v. Barnette* was never in doubt, the ruling was dramatic nonetheless. The Court carefully chose to announce its decision on June 14, 1943, Flag Day, a day that had long been used by veterans and patriotic groups as well as educators to promote respect for the American flag. The 6–3 opinion was decisive, and the opinion, written surprisingly not by Chief Justice Stone but by the novice Jackson, included what would become some of the most famous and most quoted language in Supreme Court history. But the greatest surprise was the expansive ground upon which Jackson erected his argument. Jackson insisted that what was at stake here was more than religious liberty. The reason the state could not compel Jehovah's Witnesses to salute the flag was not just that Jehovah's Witnesses had conscientious, religious objections to saluting and pledging allegiance to the flag. Rather, the reason was that the state lacked the power under the federal Constitution to compel anyone to salute and pledge allegiance to the flag, for in doing so it "invades the sphere of intellect and spirit" that the First Amendment was designed to protect. Jackson's language was stirring and is widely quoted to this day:

> If there is any fixed star in our constitutional constellation, it is that no official, high or petty, can prescribe what shall be orthodox in politics, nationalism, religion, or

other matters of opinion or force citizens to confess by word or act their faith therein. If there are any circumstances which permit an exception, they do not now occur to us.

Jackson eviscerated Frankfurter's effort to ground the constitutionality of a coerced salute in the importance of national unity. That public officials may foster "national unity by persuasion and example" Jackson did not deny. But the problem arises when compulsion is used to secure uniformity:

> Struggles to coerce uniformity of sentiment in support of some end thought essential to their time and country have been waged by many good as well as by evil men. . . . Those who begin coercive elimination of dissent soon find themselves exterminating dissenters. Compulsory unification of opinion achieves only the unanimity of the graveyard. It seems trite but necessary to say that the First Amendment to our Constitution was designed to avoid these ends by avoiding these beginnings. There is no mysticism in the American concept of the State or of the nature or origin of its authority. We set up government by consent of the governed, and the Bill of Rights denies those in power any legal opportunity to coerce that consent. Authority here is to be controlled by public opinion, not public opinion by authority. The case is made difficult not because the principles of its decision are obscure but because the flag involved is our own. Nevertheless, we apply the limitations of the Constitution with no fear that freedom to be intellectually and spiritually diverse or even contrary will disintegrate the social organization. To believe that patriotism will not flourish if patriotic ceremonies are voluntary and spontaneous instead of a compulsory routine is to make an unflattering estimate of the appeal of our institutions to free minds. We can have intellectual individualism and the rich cultural diversities that we owe to exceptional minds only at the price of occasional eccentricity and abnormal attitudes. When they are so harmless to others or to the State as those we deal with here, the price is not too great. But freedom to differ is not limited to things that do not matter much. That would be a mere shadow of freedom. The test of its substance is the right to differ as to things that touch the heart of the existing order.[66]

Jackson's sweeping opinion and the defection of a number of fellow justices infuriated Frankfurter, who responded with a scathing and starkly personal dissent. He began by calling attention to his Jewishness: "One who belongs to the most vilified and persecuted minority in history is not likely to be insensible to the freedoms guaranteed by our Constitution." Were his own personal feelings at issue, he would "wholeheartedly associate [him]self with the general libertarian views in the Court's opinion, representing as they do the thought and action of a lifetime." But, Frankfurter insisted, his own personal views were irrelevant. How wise or evil he thought a law was immaterial. The only thing that mattered was "whether legislators could in reason have enacted such a law." And while a compulsory flag salute may be unwise or counterproductive or even evil, it was reasonably related to the state's goal of "the promotion of good citizenship." The only proper constitutional course therefore was to defer to the judgment of the democratically elected representatives of the people.[67]

The public and press reaction to the Court's ruling was overwhelmingly favorable, and few paid any attention to Frankfurter's grousing. *Time* magazine celebrated the "Blot Removed," and the *Christian Century* congratulated the Court for having "set right a legal blunder." No longer compulsory, the flag salute and Pledge of Allegiance could become affirmations of the nation's commitment to democracy and liberty. Now there was a clear difference between the way the Americans conducted their flag salute and the way the Germans saluted their Führer. The Supreme Court's decision was an occasion to celebrate the tolerant democracy of the United States. "That a democracy, in time of war, and a time of intense patriotic emotions could excuse any resident from saluting its flag," David Lawrence wrote in the *New York Times*, "is impressive evidence of the high regard in which the Bill of Rights is held in this country."[68]

Amending the Salute

In *Barnette*, the Supreme Court acted to distinguish clearly the American practice from that of Nazi Germany. Six months prior to the Court's decision, in December 1942, Congress, too, had acted to address the embarrassing resemblance between the "Heil Hitler" salute and the salute that accompanied the Pledge of Allegiance. Both salutes were performed with the arm stiffly extended and raised at about eye level. The only substantial difference was that the Nazis performed the salute with the palm facing down, whereas the Pledge of Allegiance was performed with the palm facing upward.

The similarities in the salute had begun to attract comment as early as the mid-1930s. At first, it was mainly Jehovah's Witnesses and the American Civil Liberties Union that pointed to this uncomfortable fact. But others too increasingly began to draw attention to the disturbing resemblance. An early preview of the struggle to come occurred in New York City after the state department of education issued a recommendation for a revised pledge to the flag in which students would place the right hand over the heart before extending (at the words "to the flag") the arm forward with the palm turned skyward. The state directive—issued in the fall of 1936—was based on new recommendations by the National Flag Association. The recommended new salute was met

Students and faculty at Lincoln High School in Milwaukee, Wisconsin, give the raised arm salute as they recite the Pledge on Flag Day in 1939. Although Upham's salute was supposed to be delivered with the palm facing upward, in practice the salute was often rendered in ways that wcrc difficult to distinguish from the "IIeil Hitler" salute used in Nazi Germany. Staff photo of the *Milwaukee Journal*.

with a firestorm of criticism and resistance. Headlines in the *New York Times* referred to the new salute as a "Nazi-type" salute. Frank Whalen, the president of the Principals Association of New York City, reported that the recommended new salute had been immediately met by "a wave of protests" from teachers and principals. Some objected to the confusion that stemmed from the change, but "the greatest objection . . . rested in the close similarity of this salute to the Nazi one." The "new-fangled" salute, according to Whalen, was "un-American." A clearly mystified state commissioner of education could not understand what all the fuss was about: "Some people," he explained to the press, "have construed the National Flag Association as following the newer Fascist salute in Europe. Nobody ever had that in mind." Moreover, he insisted, schools were free to use the older salute if they preferred that. All that mattered was that the flag was saluted.[69]

The state commissioner's consternation was understandable since the National Flag Association's recommended change had only been to substitute the hand-over-the-heart civilian salute for the military salute; there had been no change in the Nazi-like outstretched arm, which had been part of the original salute as it was conceived by James Upham back in 1892. In countering the charges that the new flag salute was "Nazi-like," state school officials pointed out that the outstretched arm had been part of the state's traditional salute since its official adoption in 1917. So why the outrage and charges of Nazism? The answer, it turns out, is that many New York City schools had in fact not been following the prescribed traditional salute but had long since simplified the salute so that students rendered the military salute but dispensed with the raised arm part of the salute.[70]

With the onset of war, such concerns about the resemblance between the flag salute and the Nazi salute intensified. The Supreme Court in *Barnette* noted that concerns that the salute was "too much like Hitler's" had been voiced by the Parent and Teachers Association, the Boy Scouts and Girl Scouts, the Red Cross, and the Federation of Women's Clubs. Many schools revised the salute in order to avoid the uncomfortable parallel. For instance, on September 19, 1939, just about two weeks after England and France declared war on Germany, Roosevelt Elementary School in River Edge, New Jersey, decided to eliminate the raising of the arm, instead requiring the children to leave the hand on the heart throughout the ceremony. In October 1941, the Washington, D.C., board of education elected to modify the pledge by abandoning the "arm-extended salute" in favor of the "regulation Army salute." In February 1942, West Virginia's state board of education, responding to widespread complaints, decided to have all schools abandon the raised arm salute in favor of the hand over the heart salute.[71]

The reaction on the part of the national headquarters of the United States Flag Association, a self-appointed arbiter of flag etiquette, was to dismiss such concerns. The association conceded that the salutes appeared to be "quite similar" but insisted that should not matter:

Americans used the present method of saluting in rendering the Pledge to the Flag years before Naziism and Fascism were ever heard of. . . . [I]t would be unwise to attempt to make a change because [the American salute] is well established, and [it] would take several years and much educational work to change. It would, indeed, be illogical and nonsensical for us Americans to change a well-established practice every time some foreign country adopted something similar. In times like the present the emotions are easily aroused and stirred into frenzy, or hysteria, passing all bounds of reason. Let us Americans who are normally sensible and reasonable guard against war-hysteria in this as well as in all other matters. If the Nazis, in the pagan-like religion they are instituting, should invent a religious symbol similar to the Star of David, would it be logical for the Jews to discard that symbol? Or should the Nazis adopt a gesture similar to the sign of the Cross, would that give the Christians cause to discontinue making the sign of the Cross? Let the Nazis and Fascists go on with their salute—that is their affair. Let us Americans continue using our salute to the Flag which is prescribed by the Flag Code and which we were using before anyone had ever heard of Naziism or Fascism.

The Daughters of the American Revolution echoed this position. A spokeswoman from the DAR's National Defense through Patriotic Education Committee lamented that "propaganda as to alien foes can make us change our own accepted ways for fear of misinterpretation." She advocated that instead "we should stick to our own with more and more tenacity."[72]

But the Pledge had become far too important a national patriotic symbol to allow it to become tarnished by the brush of Nazism. An indicator of its national importance could be gleaned from a radio address delivered by Franklin Roosevelt on July 4, 1941, in which the president warned that the United States could not survive as an "oasis of liberty" in "a desert of tyranny." The address closed with the admonition: "And so it is that when we repeat the great pledge to our country and to our flag, it must be our deep conviction that we pledge as well our work, our will and, if it be necessary, our very lives." Immediately after FDR had signed off with those words, Chief Justice Harlan Stone came on the radio and led an audience of millions in a recital of the Pledge of Allegiance. The Office of Civil Defense arranged that all across the nation Americans should "cease whatever they were doing" to recite the Pledge along with Chief Justice Stone. According to an AP report, "pleasure-bound motorists stopped their cars, soldiers in cantonments snapped to attention, children turned their thoughts, momentarily, from their games, and housewives dropped their chores to renew the spirit of 1776." It was, wrote the *New York Times*, "a pulse-quickening moment" as "a vast unseen audience repeated the words pledging fealty to their flag."[73]

In June 1942, at the urging of the American Legion and the Veterans of Foreign Wars, Congress had officially codified flag rules and etiquette, including how to salute the flag during the Pledge of Allegiance. The congressional codification closely followed the flag code that emerged out of the 1923 and 1924 flag conferences, including the raised arm salute that had been prescribed in 1924. The content of the flag code received virtually no scrutiny from mem-

Chief Justice Harlan Stone, flanked by a color guard from a local American Legion post, leads the citizens of the nation in reciting the Pledge on July 4, 1941. The photograph appeared in the *Denver Post*, July 5, 1941.

bers of Congress, and there was no discussion in Congress of the appropriateness of a raised arm salute, despite the controversy it had generated in a number of school districts across the country.[74]

However, Congress's endorsement of the flag code in June 1942, including the raised arm salute, stirred a number of flag devotees into action. Chief among these was Gridley Adams, who found fault with several aspects of the code adopted by Congress. It was "as full of holes as Swiss Cheese," he would later write with typical hyperbole—his natural contrariness perhaps exacerbated by the fact that Congress had not consulted him before approving the flag code. Adams was particularly upset that the code adopted by Congress, like the 1923 code, stipulated that "when not on a staff the Flag should be hung flat against the wall." This rule proved an impediment to the work of Adams's newly founded "Flag in Every Home Committee," which had determined that one of the primary obstacles to getting an American flag in every home was that many

Citizens of Denver, Colorado, gathering at a free picnic hosted
by the *Denver Post,* enthusiastically recite the Pledge along
with Chief Justice Stone, whose voice was heard across the
nation over radio. The photograph appeared in the *Denver Post,*
July 5, 1941.

households lacked the wall space to lay a flag flat against the wall and lacked
the money to buy a flagstaff, which was several times more expensive than a
flag. The committee managed to persuade several New York department stores
to sell a staffless flag that could be conveniently draped from a hook, and the
sales of these flags were "fairly brisk" until a vigilant American Legionnaire informed the stores that the staffless flag was illegal under the recently adopted
law. Adams rushed off to Washington to persuade the law's original sponsor
that the law should allow for the staffless flag. This change, along with a half
dozen other changes, including the amended salute to the flag, was incorporated into Public Law 829, which passed in December 1942.[75]

Citizens of Vale, Oregon, listen attentively as the Chief Justice recites the Pledge on the Fourth of July, 1941. Prints and Photographs Division, Library of Congress.

The available records do not allow us to specify precisely whose idea it was to amend the hand salute. Writing a decade later, Adams indicated that while calling the House Judiciary Committee's attention "to the errors in their first draft" (that is, the law Congress passed in June, Public Law 623), he and perhaps others told the committee that in fact the straight arm salute had been dropped at the original 1923 flag conference in favor of the "Lincoln hand-over-the-heart" salute. According to Adams,

> a young woman was once standing beside President Lincoln when a parade was passing. Seeing a Flag approaching she turned to Mr. Lincoln and said: "Whenever I see the Flag I have such a feeling of exultation here (placing her hand over her heart); how can I best show that feeling?" To this Mr. Lincoln replied: "By standing just as you are, with your hand over your heart." How much more lasting upon the minds of little children is this story than the calisthenics of extending their hand, and missing all thought of the words they were repeating.

According to Adams, when chairman Sam Hobbs heard this story he said, "Why in the 'deuce' didn't that story ever get to this Committee before."[76]

It is difficult to know how much of this to believe. Adams is clearly wrong about what was adopted by the two flag conferences in the 1920s. The code adopted by the 1924 flag conference prescribed that at the beginning of the Pledge of Allegiance the right hand should be placed over the heart, but at the words "to the flag" the right arm should be "extended, palm upward, towards the Flag" and remain there until the final words. Nowhere in the over three-hundred-page transcript of the 1923 conference is the hand-over-the-heart salute connected with Lincoln. Nor was Representative Sam Hobbs the chairman of the Judiciary committee or the subcommittee that reported out the resolutions. Hobbs, an Alabama Democrat, did sponsor the relevant resolutions, however, and Adams certainly did communicate to him his misgivings about the June law. Those conversations may very well have extended to the manner of the salute, but if the conversation happened the way Adams relates then it would appear that he seriously misled the Alabama Democrat.

It appears to be true that Adams was no fan of the "meaningless" raised arm salute.[77] It was, after all, the rival United States Flag Association (Adams headed up the United States Flag Foundation) that was the most vocal champion of the raised arm salute. Adams's preference was instead for what he now described as the "Lincoln salute."[78] But Adams's views about the proper way to salute a flag were less important than the concerns about the raised arm salute that various school districts and organizations had been expressing with increasing frequency. Since the code was already being amended to fix errors or inconsistencies in the original resolution, it was a simple enough task for Congress to remove the raised arm portion of the salute. Together with the Supreme Court's ruling that students with conscientious objections could not be compelled to say the Pledge, the federal government had finally made the Pledge of Allegiance safe for democracy. Now nobody, it was hoped, could mistake the American Pledge of Allegiance with the coercive conformity of the "Heil Hitler" salute mandated in Nazi Germany. But when the enemy shifted from Nazi Germany to Soviet Communism after World War II, politicians in Washington as well as patriotic groups in the country would again turn their attention to the Pledge of Allegiance to find ways to shape it to serve in the fight against the nation's newest and most formidable enemy, the Godless Communists.[79]

5

A NATION UNDER GOD

We are, says the Pledge, "one nation under God." Polls show that Americans overwhelmingly favor leaving the Pledge as it is. But, of course, the words "under God" have not always been a part of it. They were added over sixty years after Bellamy penned the original. Some who have challenged the constitutionality of the "under God" provision point to this fact as evidence that the words "under God" are alien to the original spirit of the Pledge. Bellamy's great-grandson and great-granddaughter have bolstered this by suggesting that Bellamy would have opposed adding the words "under God." Perhaps he would have opposed the addition of these two words—during his life he opposed every effort to amend the Pledge—but the claim that the words "under God" are at odds with the original spirit of the Pledge is more difficult to sustain.[1]

Why No God in the Original Pledge?

To begin with, it is helpful to recall that Bellamy had been a Baptist minister for over a decade before quitting the ministry the year before he wrote the

Pledge. Moreover, both Daniel Sharp Ford and James Upham were deeply religious and actively involved with their church—Upham as a deacon of the First Baptist Church in Malden and Ford as one of the chief benefactors of Bellamy's church. Upham, moreover, belonged to an exclusive Masonic order into which only Christians were admitted. Religious belief colored the political outlook and activity of each of these three men, most obviously in the case of Bellamy's Christian socialism.

The absence of any reference to God in Bellamy's spare twenty-three-word pledge had little if anything to do with a desire to keep religion out of the public schools. Indeed God suffused the school program crafted by Bellamy and Upham. The program was to open with a reading of the presidential proclamation declaring October 21 a national day of celebration. The proclamation, drafted by Bellamy, closed with the following admonition: "In the churches and in the other places of assembly of the people let there be expressions of gratitude to Divine Providence for the devout faith of the discoverer and for the divine care and guidance which has directed our history and so abundantly blessed our people." Immediately following the raising of the American flag and the saying of the Pledge of Allegiance, all were to sing "America—My Country 'Tis of Thee," a song that at the time (at least in New England) had the status almost of a "national hymn." Today most Americans know only the opening stanza, but the assembled sang through to the last stanza: "Our fathers' God, to thee, / author of liberty, / to thee we sing; / long may our land be bright / with freedom's holy light; / protect us by thy might, / great God, our King." After completion of this last verse, Bellamy's program called for an "Acknowledgment of God" either through "Prayer or Scripture." So even if God were absent in the actual words of the Pledge, Bellamy made sure it was sandwiched between explicit appeals to the Almighty.[2]

Nor was Bellamy averse to invoking God in his own speeches. In the Columbus Day address he wrote for the official school program, "The Meaning of Four Centuries," Bellamy spoke of "faith in the underlying principles of Americanism and in God's destiny for the Republic." And in the speech he delivered at Malden on the evening of the day of celebration, Bellamy declared that America "lifts up the school system as *under God* her most trusted support for the future." America, in Bellamy's mind, was not just one nation under God, it was God's chosen nation. As he explained to the citizens of Malden: "The settlement of America was not a matter of chance but of design. God had a will in the matter. A chosen people had been prepared to possess this land and to build a new commonwealth of liberty and justice. So when the times were ready, Spain's Armadas were swept from the seas, and the chosen of God passed under a mighty hand and outstretched arm."[3]

Moreover, it should be recalled that Bellamy's pledge was not the only game in town. Colonel Balch's salute, used widely in grade schools in New York, explicitly invoked God, even before country: "We give our heads and our hearts to God and our country: one country, one language, one Flag." The widely used *Patriotic Primer* that Balch wrote for New York's schoolchildren explained that God was the source of "our dearest possessions," our head, "the seat of intellect," and our hearts, "the fountain of our affections and our love." Therefore, "it is right that we shall recognize first of all the Ruler of the universe, the Almighty God." For those who might mistake the message, Balch underscored that "we give our heads and our hearts to God first, and our country afterwards." For a nation that possessed supreme confidence that America was God's chosen nation, putting God first entailed no conflict of loyalties between the sacred and the secular.[4]

We know that Bellamy and Upham considered Balch's pledge "weak and childish" and lacking in the dignity required for the occasion, but there is no evidence that either Bellamy or Upham ever objected to Balch's inclusion of God in the salute. The problem with Balch's "American Patriotic Salute," in Bellamy's view, was not that it mentioned God but that it did not articulate the ideas for which the flag stood.[5]

Moreover, Bellamy did not seem particularly averse to mixing religion in with the Pledge. He often likened the Pledge to the Lord's Prayer. And in 1923, when he outlined a plan for extending the Pledge beyond the schoolhouse, he specifically targeted the churches as a domain in which the Pledge should be recited. "In its sheer ethics," Bellamy explained, "the Pledge has a home in the Churches, and its doctrines should be urged by the clergy."[6]

The liberal use of God in the official school program and in Balch's salute is not particularly surprising when one recalls that Bible readings and prayer were commonplace in late-nineteenth-century public schools. The Balch salute was intended to be performed "immediately after the reading from the Scriptures, in the usual order of morning exercises, as prescribed in the public schools of this city." Many Protestants attacked the religious indoctrination of Catholic parochial schools, but that did not mean they wanted religion removed from public schools. Josiah Strong was typical. The "evil results" stemming from parochial schools, Strong insisted, could "certainly not [be solved] by secularizing the public schools." Our government, he continued, "is, and has always been, religious . . . in every part—legislative, judicial, and executive—Christian in nature, form, and purpose." Indeed, American civilization itself was dependent upon Christianity—or, as Strong put it, "the Anglo-Saxon race would speedily decay but for the salt of Christianity."[7]

It was not until 1948, more than a half century after the writing of the Pledge of Allegiance, that the United States Supreme Court for the first time used the establishment clause to invalidate a state law relating to religious instruction in public schools. Prior to the 1940s the nation's highest court showed little concern about the mixing of religion and public life. In the same year that Bellamy wrote the Pledge, a unanimous Supreme Court declared confidently that the nation's laws and mores clearly demonstrated that the United States "is a Christian nation." In support of this proposition the Court pointed to

> the form of oath universally prevailing, concluding with an appeal to the Almighty; the custom of opening sessions of all deliberative bodies and most conventions with prayer; the prefatory words of all wills, "In the name of God, amen;" the laws respecting the observance of the Sabbath, with the general cessation of all secular business, and the closing of courts, legislatures, and other similar public assemblies on that day; the churches and church organizations which abound in every city, town and hamlet; the multitude of charitable organizations existing every where under Christian auspices; the gigantic missionary associations, with general support, and aiming to establish Christian missions in every quarter of the globe.

And even as late as 1931, the highest court in the land could still insist that "we are a Christian people." Not until the early 1960s would the Supreme Court outlaw the use of the Lord's Prayer or Bible verses in public schools.[8]

Becoming a Nation "under God"

The phrase "under God" has a distinguished history in America. The most famous and influential usage is, of course, from the Gettysburg Address, in which Lincoln declared "that this nation, under God, shall have a new birth of freedom and that government of the people, by the people, for the people, shall not perish from the earth." Where he got the phrase is unclear; some speculate that he improvised it on the spot or that it occurred to him after listening to the opening prayer or to the speech by Massachusetts senator Edward Everett. Perhaps the preface to the King James Bible, a paean to King James, had lodged in his fertile brain: "You, that Your very name is precious among them: their eye doth behold You with comfort, and they bless You in their hearts, as that sanctified Person, who, under God, is the immediate Author of their true happiness."[9]

Despite the fame of the Gettysburg Address, the phrase "under God" was not commonly used in the ensuing years. The *Messages and Papers of the Presidents*, which spans the presidencies from George Washington through William Howard Taft, contains no usage of that term in the half century after Lincoln's address.[10] President Herbert Hoover used the phrase at the opening of his inaugural address but then never used it again during his presidency. Moreover, he used the words not to describe the nation, as Lincoln had, but to describe the oath he had just taken, which he said was "a dedication and consecration under God to the highest office in service of our people."[11] Prior to the bombing of Pearl Harbor, FDR used the phrase only once, in a 1937 letter on the importance of religious tolerance. After Pearl Harbor, Roosevelt used the phrase more often, employing it six times, including in two fireside chats, in his 1944 State of the Union Address, and in his last speech to Congress in March 1945.[12]

The first president to rely heavily on the phrase was Harry Truman, particularly after 1948 as the Cold War heated up. In a St. Patrick's Day address in New York City in 1948, Truman denounced Communism for denying "the very existence of God." Under Communism, he continued, "religion is persecuted because it stands for freedom under God." In remarks broadcast across the nation on the day before the historic 1948 election, Truman told voters to "go to the polls tomorrow and vote your convictions, your hopes, and your faith—your faith in the future of a nation that under God can lead the world to freedom and to peace." Speaking in Casper, Wyoming, in the spring of 1950, Truman assured his listeners that "in the tremendous conflict that exists in the world today, our fundamental strength is our belief in the worth of the individual, under God." After the outbreak of war in Korea, he told a national television and radio audience that America "stands before the world as an example of how free men, under God, can build a community of neighbors, working together for the good of all." And dedicating a chapel in Philadelphia a few months later, he declared that "the unity of our country is a unity under God. It is a unity in freedom, for the service of God is perfect freedom." All told, President Truman used the expression "under God" on at least seventeen occasions in public speeches.[13]

Eisenhower continued where Truman left off. In his acceptance speech at the Republican National Convention in the summer of 1952, Eisenhower declared that "we are now at a moment in history when, under God, this nation of ours has become the mightiest temporal power and the mightiest spiritual force on earth." He used the phrase "under God" several more times in 1953. Then on February 7, 1954, Eisenhower went on the radio to lend support to the American Legion's "Back to God" program, which was designed "to increase our awareness of God in our daily lives." In his address, Eisenhower recalled the power of Lincoln's address "on the battle-torn field of Gettysburg" and his recognition "that only under God could this Nation win a new birth of freedom." For Eisenhower, "whatever our individual church, whatever our personal creed, our common faith in God is a common bond among us. In our fundamental faith, we are all one."[14]

"A New Spirit Has Fallen upon Our People"

Truman's and Eisenhower's rhetoric reflected a revival of interest in religion in the early years of the Cold War. The Methodist Council of Bishops, meeting in the spring of 1954, opined that the nation was witnessing a "great upsurge in church life." Noting the increased number of churches built and the increase in church attendance and giving, the bishops declared that "a new spirit has fallen upon our people." Will Herberg, in his 1955 best seller, *Protestant-Catholic-Jew*, concluded that it "can hardly be doubted [that] there has in recent years been an upswing of religion in the United States. . . . [T]he evidence is diverse, converging, and unequivocal beyond all possibilities of error." One United States senator even introduced an amendment to the U.S. Constitution that declared: "This nation devoutly recognizes the authority and law of Jesus Christ, Saviour and Ruler of Nations, through whom are bestowed the blessings of Almighty God."[15]

This particular amendment never got far, but other efforts to promote religion and recognize God fared much better. In 1952 Congress mandated an annual National Day of Prayer. At the suggestion of Ezra Taft Benson, Eisenhower's secretary of agriculture and a leading Mormon, Eisenhower began each cabinet meeting with a prayer, albeit a silent one. Eisenhower also inaugurated the practice of the presidential prayer breakfast (today called the National Prayer Breakfast), and Congress followed suit by creating a prayer room in the Capitol building. In 1955 Congress added the words "In God We Trust" to paper money—coins had carried those words since Lincoln's presidency. The following year, the same four words became the nation's official motto, replacing "E Pluribus Unum." The post office even got into the act, introducing a stamp adorned with the "In God We Trust" motto; the stamp was unveiled on national television by Eisenhower, many of his cabinet, and prominent religious leaders of the Protestant, Catholic, and Jewish faiths. Inserting the words "under God" into the Pledge of Allegiance, then, must be understood as only one of many actions taken in the early years of the Eisenhower presidency that were designed to inject religious faith into public life.[16]

Sociologists in the 1950s debated whether the nation was experiencing a revival in church attendance and religiosity, but there is no question that in the early years of the Cold War religious language infused political rhetoric and defined national identity in new and significant ways. The strength of the United States, in the view of many, was its religious faith. And it was faith in God that distinguished the United States from the godless Communists. One of the clearest expressions of this view was proffered by Senator Joseph McCarthy in a speech at Wheeling, West Virginia, in which he famously claimed to have had in his hand a list of the names of 205 Communists who worked in the U.S. State Department. Speaking in February 1950, McCarthy explained that "we are engaged in a final, all-out battle between Communistic atheism and Christianity." The "real, basic difference," continued McCarthy, "between our western Christian world and the atheistic Communist world is not political, . . . it is moral." The Communist threat to mankind stemmed primarily not from the Communist economic or political system but rather from its "religion of immoralism."[17]

Not everyone, of course, shared McCarthy's judgment that the government was infested with treacherous Communists, but his conception of the Cold War as an epochal clash between atheism and religious belief was commonplace in the late 1940s and early 1950s. Speaking in 1950, ex-president (and Quaker) Herbert Hoover issued a call for a "spiritual mobilization of the nations who believe in God against this tide of Red agnosticism." At the 1951 annual meeting of the Jewish National Federation of Temple Brotherhoods, the federation's honorary president painted a picture of a "world-wide clash of two divergent beliefs: the Judeo-Christian philosophy" on the one hand and the "crass materialism" of atheistic Communism on the other. Truman, too, though he despised McCarthy and his tactics, would not have disagreed with the Wisconsin senator that belief in God was a defining difference between the American way of life and the Communist way of life. Publicly declaring the United States to be a nation "under God" was a direct expression of the contemporary anxiety about the threat of Communism.[18]

Eisenhower assiduously avoided the equating of the United States with Christianity, preferring instead the more inclusive language of "Judeo-Christian" or nonsectarian references to God.[19] But no less than McCarthy, Eisenhower placed belief in God at the center of what it meant to be American. "Our form of government," President-elect Eisenhower declared in December 1952, "is founded in religion." "Without God," President Eisenhower told a national television and radio audience in 1955, "there could be no American form of Government, nor an American way of life. Recognition of the Supreme Being is the first—the most basic—expression of Americanism." Churches, Eisenhower declared in 1953, were "citadels of our faith in individual freedom and human dignity. This faith is the living source of all our spiritual strength. And this strength is our matchless armor in our world-wide struggle against the forces of Godless tyranny and oppression."[20]

It was this understanding of the necessary relationship between religious belief and American national identity that enabled federal judge (and devout Roman Catholic) Frank McLaughlin to deny American citizenship to twenty-four-year-old Wladyslaw Plywacki for refusing to repeat the phrase "so help me God" that closes the official oath of allegiance. Plywacki had been imprisoned by the Nazis for five years and, after escaping, served in the U.S. Air Force, including a tour of duty in Japan. He was also an atheist and told the judge that he could not in good conscience repeat the four words that referred to God. Rather than offer Corporal Plywacki the option of an affirmation of allegiance instead of reciting the oath, the judge lectured Plywacki on the centrality of God in the American governmental system. "Our Government," he explained to Plywacki, "is founded on a belief in God." Plywacki appealed (and prevailed), but McLaughlin was unbowed. "I appreciate the right of a person to be an atheist," the judge explained, "but if you join an organization that has principles based on the existence of a Supreme Being—from the Declaration of Independence on down to the latest pronouncements by President Eisenhower on the importance of religion—you must abide by the rules of that organization." And Plywacki's "atheist philosophy," McLaughlin insisted, "demonstrates a lack of attachment to the United States Government's first principle: a belief in a Creator, from whom the Founders proclaimed come man's unalienable rights subsequently guaranteed by the Constitution."[21]

Plywacki's case was admittedly an oddity, more an indicator of where a religious revival would take the country if taken to its logical extreme than a reliable sign of where the nation was heading. But the insistence that belief in God defined what it meant to be American was no oddity. It was what political and religious leaders of almost all stripes told the American people in the late 1940s and early 1950s. True, America may no longer have been best described as a Christian nation, but Americans were still, as the Supreme Court declared in 1952, a "religious people whose institutions presuppose a Supreme Being."[22] It was the near-consensus on this proposition combined with fear of the threat posed by Communism that made possible the amendment to the Pledge of Allegiance.

In the closing years of the Cold War, Communists posed only a military threat to the United States. But in the Cold War's early years, Communism was seen to be a dangerous rival for the allegiance of men and women in the United States and across the globe. Communism seemed capable of instilling a devotion and loyalty that some feared the West could not match. Only religious faith, many Americans believed, could counter the appeal of totalitarianism. The attraction of Communism, ex-Communists like Whitaker Chambers testified, was that it offered a reason for living and for dying. The West, having allowed its spiritual core to become corroded by materialism, was fast losing the power to instill such commitment. Only a religious revival, many felt, could provide effective protection from the Communist threat. "At every point," Chambers wrote in his 1952 book *Witness,* "religion and politics interlace, and must do so more acutely as the conflict between the two great camps of men— those who reject and those who worship God—becomes irrepressible." God, in Chambers's view, was the "incitor and guarantor" of freedom. Writing in the same year, Herberg agreed that democracy alone "cannot serve as our saving faith." What the United States needed was to be anchored in "something more ultimate, in some really total commitment that will protect it from inner corruption as well as from external attack." Declaring the United States to be a nation under God was not a casual or symbolic addition, but an integral part of a life-and-death struggle between two rival ways of life: atheistic and totalitarian Communism on the one hand, and God-fearing and freedom-loving Americanism on the other.[23]

Amending the Pledge

Amending the Pledge, however, required more than heightened anxiety coupled with a revival of religion. It required the mobilization of political interests and political pressure. In the first half of the twentieth century, the groups that had spearheaded efforts to legislate patriotism and Americanize the alien had been predominantly Protestant. The promotion of the flag salute and Pledge of Allegiance had largely been the handiwork of a familiar cast of veterans groups and patriotic organizations, like the Grand Army of the Republic, the American Legion, and the Daughters of the American Revolution. The pressure to enact the "under God" clause, however, came, at least initially, from a very different source, from a Catholic fraternal organization called the Knights of Columbus.

Founded in the early 1880s, the Knights of Columbus, like many other associations of the late nineteenth century, originated as a means of pooling resources to pay for funerals and care for the sick or disabled. The organization's founders also hoped that by offering a Catholic fraternal alternative they would prevent "our people" from entering Protestant-dominated secret societies. The all-male organization was dedicated to "consolidating Catholic manhood into a social force," and by the mid-twentieth century it had become by far the largest Catholic voluntary organization in the United States.[24]

In its early history the Knights played an important role in both celebrating Catholic contributions to American history and resisting anti-Catholic nativism. But by the middle of the twentieth century, the group had entered the fraternal mainstream and, under the leadership of Supreme Knight Luke Hart, was focused less on championing a beleaguered minority than on policing the boundaries of Americanism against the perils of Communism. The Catholic Church had long opposed Communism, even if, as in the Spanish Civil War, it meant supporting fascists. But after the Iron Curtain descended across Europe at the close of World War II and the Soviets began to suppress the Catholic Church throughout Poland and the rest of eastern Europe, Catholics became more vociferous in their opposition to Communism, often outdoing even the most vigorous Protestant-American patriots. The Cold War enabled Catholics and Protestants to bury many of their religious animosities in the fight against a common enemy: atheistic Communism.[25]

The organized movement for adding "under God" to the Pledge of Allegiance can be traced to a resolution adopted by the Knights' national board of directors in April 1951, at the height of the Korean War. The resolution called on all Knights to add the words "under God" to the Pledge customarily recited at the openings of local meetings. The following year, in August 1952, the national leadership enacted a resolution that called on the U.S. Congress to modify the Pledge of Allegiance to include the words "under God." Copies of the resolution were dispatched to the president of the United States, as well as to the vice president and the Speaker of the House. The following month, Supreme Knight Luke Hart, who also was president of the National Fraternal Congress, persuaded that organization to join in the call for congressional action.[26] The Knights of Columbus, together with other groups belonging to the National Fraternal Congress, urged individual members to write their representatives in Congress.[27]

One such letter, from a Mr. H. Joseph Mahoney of Brooklyn, New York, landed on the desk of veteran Democratic congressman Louis Rabaut of Michigan in early April 1953. According to Rabaut, a devout Catholic, the letter from Mr. Mahoney moved him, on April 20, 1953, to introduce the first congressional resolution calling for the words "under God" to be added to the Pledge of Allegiance. Rabaut was eagerly looking for ways to affirm the importance of God in American life and thereby strike at "the philosophical roots of communism, atheism, and materialism." Only days before receiving the letter from Mahoney, Rabaut had introduced a bill to make the motto "In God We Trust" a cancellation mark on U.S. mail. Adding the words "under God" to the Pledge, like adding "In God We Trust" to U.S. mail, expressed Rabaut's "deep-seated conviction" that "the religious origins and traditions of our country" were "our real bulwark against communism." The United States of America, Rabaut explained, "was born under God, and only under God will it live as a citadel of freedom." For the American system of government was founded on a belief in "the worthwhileness of the individual human being," which in turn rested on the conviction that "the human person is important because he has been created in the image and likeness of God and that he has been endowed by God with certain inalienable rights." Remove the belief in God, and the justification for America's democratic institutions collapses, opening the way for the triumph of tyranny. Adding "under God" to the Pledge would alert Americans to "the true meaning of our country and its form of government" and thereby help to "preserve our precious heritage."[28]

Already by the end of March 1953 the issue had become prominent enough that Gallup pollsters included a question about the "under God" clause in a survey of sixteen hundred Americans. The result was overwhelming: Almost 70 percent of the respondents favored adding "under God" to the Pledge of Allegiance, while only a little over 20 percent opposed the change. Support for the Pledge crossed party lines and the Catholic-Protestant divide. Jews were substantially less likely to support the change, but even among Jews a clear majority favored the change. About the only demographic group to oppose the change were those few Americans (about 1 percent in the Gallup survey) who said they had no religious affiliation or who described themselves as atheists.[29]

Meanwhile the Knights of Columbus continued to press the idea. At their annual meeting toward the end of the summer of 1953, the Knights again passed a resolution to add "under God" to the Pledge of Allegiance. This time copies went not only to the president, vice president, and Speaker of the House, but also to every member of both the House and Senate. According to Hart, "many favorable replies" were received from members of Congress. But despite the best efforts of the Knights of Columbus and other groups that had joined in the crusade, most notably the American Legion,[30] the movement to have the "under God" clause added to the Pledge languished throughout 1953. Apart from Rabaut, nobody in Congress appeared to show much enthusiasm for the idea, and the Eisenhower administration was preoccupied with enacting its domestic agenda and ending the war in Korea. The political momentum shifted dramatically, however, when, on February 7, 1954, in a sermon commemorating Lincoln's Birthday, the Reverend George Macpherson Docherty chose to make Lincoln's phrase "under God" the subject of his weekly sermon at Washington's New York Avenue Presbyterian Church. In attendance, seated at the front in the Lincoln pew, were the country's most famous Presbyterians, the president of the United States and the First Lady.[31]

There was something missing from the Pledge of Allegiance, Docherty told his parishioners. Apart from the words "the United States of America," Docherty noted, the Pledge of Allegiance "could be the pledge of any republic." The minister imagined that "little Moscovites" might easily "repeat a similar pledge to their hammer-and-sickle flag in Moscow with equal solemnity." Russia after all claimed to be an indivisible republic dedicated to freedom and justice. By adding "under God" to the Pledge the nation would affirm the distinctive and defining characteristic of the American way of life: belief in God. "An atheistic American," Docherty insisted, was "a contradiction in terms." Indeed atheists were worse than that—they were "parasites" who were living off of the nation's "accumulation of spiritual capital."[32]

Like so many other public figures of the day, Docherty defined the battle between Communism and the West as "a theological war." "It is not basically a conflict between two political philosophies—Thomas Jefferson's political democracy over against Lenin's communistic state. Nor is it a conflict fundamentally between two economic systems between, shall we say, Adam Smith's Wealth of Nations and Karl Marx's Das Capital." Rather it was "a fight for the freedom of the human personality. . . . It is the view of man as it comes down to us from Judaio-Christian civilization in mortal combat against modern, secularized, godless society."[33]

To those who might object that adding "under God" would violate the First Amendment of the United States Constitution, Docherty was ready with a response. The First Amendment, Docherty instructed, said only that "Congress shall make no law respecting the establishment of religion." This, the minister explained, "is separation of church and state; it is not, and never was meant to be, a separation of religion and life." Those who would object to adding "under God" to the Pledge were guilty of "a confusion of the first amendment with the First Commandment": Thou shalt have no other gods before me. He conceded that adding the phrase "under the church" would be "dangerous," but the recent émigré from Scotland assured his congregation that a nation "under God" carried no such dangers.[34]

Docherty's sermon hit a responsive chord. Eisenhower reportedly told Docherty he agreed with it "entirely." The minister's sermon was covered widely in the nation's newspapers, and Docherty recalls receiving "hundreds of letters" commending his idea. One of Docherty's Presbyterian parishioners, a freshman congressman from Michigan by the name of Charles Oakman, was moved to introduce a resolution in the House the following day that would codify Docherty's idea. Oakman, apparently unaware of the similar resolution that had been offered by Rabaut nearly a year before, prevailed on his fellow Republican, Michigan senator Homer Ferguson, also a Presbyterian, to introduce an identical resolution, which he did two days later. In introducing SJR 126, Ferguson told his Senate colleagues that the amended pledge would highlight "one of the real fundamental differences between the free world and the Communist world." The United States, he continued, was "founded on a fundamental belief in God." Communism, in contrast, "rejects the very existence of God." Over the next three months, another thirteen members of Congress would introduce joint resolutions that proposed to add "under God" to the Pledge of Allegiance.[35]

The effort to change the Pledge was bipartisan. Of the eighteen "under God" resolutions introduced between April 20, 1953, and May 20, 1954, eight were put forward by Democrats, nine by Republicans, and one by an Independent. Each of the eight Democrats who proposed "under God" resolutions was Roman Catholic. The Republicans were more religiously diverse: several were New York Catholics, four were Presbyterians, and the remainder were Protestants of various denominations. All told, ten of the eighteen resolutions stemmed from Catholics, at a time when the percentage of Catholics in Congress was only about 15 percent. Clearly, while Catholics did not have a corner on the "under God" clause, it was an issue in which they took a particularly strong interest.[36]

Rabaut, picking up on the publicity generated by Docherty's sermon, promptly took to the floor of the House to praise Docherty for having "seized the opportunity" to urge that Lincoln's famous phrase be added to the Pledge. Acknowledging that Docherty and he were "not of the same Christian denomination," he proclaimed that the minister had "hit the nail right on the head." Rabaut quoted extensively from Docherty's sermon, enthusiastically endorsing Docherty's contention that an atheistic American was a "contradiction in terms." "From the root of atheism," Rabaut maintained, "stems the evil weed of communism and its branches of materialism and political dictatorship." One could, he said, "argue from dawn to dusk" about the differences between the two nation's political and economic systems, but the "unbridgeable gap between America and Communist Russia is a belief in Almighty God." And "unless we are willing to affirm our belief in the existence of God . . . we . . . open the floodgates to tyranny and oppression."[37]

The following week, Republican congressman (and Episcopalian) Oliver Bolton chimed in with his own "under God" resolution. He had first heard the idea proposed, he told his House colleagues, at the 1953 annual dinner of the Washington Pilgrimage of American Churchmen. Ever since then he had been "studying it and discussing it" with his constituents and found that it had the support of "Protestants, Catholics, and Jews alike." Bolton called his colleagues' attention to the words of President Eisenhower who, he reminded them, had "repeatedly in his public utterances expressed the conviction" that only by recognizing "the spiritual foundations of our democratic institutions and the divine God-given dignity of man" could the nation "preserve these free institutions against the forces of atheist materialism which surround us." Without "a recognition of our basic faith," Bolton concluded, the Pledge of Allegiance was radically incomplete. Affirmation of loyalty to the nation must be accompanied by affirmation of a belief in the "sovereignty of God in the affairs of men."[38]

Docherty's sermon—combined with the media coverage that accompanied the president's presence at the church—had clearly helped to focus attention on the "under God" issue,[39] but it was by no means clear that the resolution would be enacted. Ferguson's resolution had been referred to the Senate Judiciary Committee, but on April 5 the committee opted to postpone indefinitely any action on the resolution. Perhaps the Senate was preoccupied at the time with more important matters, like the Army-McCarthy hearings, or perhaps senators had concerns about the resolution's implications for the separation of church and state.[40] Whatever the reasons, the resolution seemed dead, just another symbolic gesture buried in the legislative labyrinth of Congress's committees. But through the determined efforts of various civic, veterans, and fraternal organizations, as well as the Hearst newspapers, House and Senate members found themselves deluged by letters urging support for adding the words "under God" to the Pledge. One House member, a Democrat from Illinois and a Catholic, reported that he had received between two thousand and three thousand letters from his constituents in support of the change, which was "by far" the largest amount of constituent mail he had received on any subject during the 83d Congress. A Senate Republican, speaking on May 4, indicated that in the "past few days" he had received "literally hundreds of messages" from constituents. Many of these letters, the senator noted, "included clippings from an editorial in the *Milwaukee Sentinel*," a Hearst newspaper, which urged its readers to cut out the editorial and send it to their senator. The letter-writing campaign paid immediate dividends.[41]

On May 5, a subcommittee of the House Judiciary Committee unanimously approved the change to the Pledge. The action in the House spurred the Senate Judiciary Committee to reconsider, and on May 10, the Senate Judiciary Committee reversed course and sent SJR 126 to the floor with only a single amendment. Instead of Ferguson's original "one Nation indivisible under God," the Judiciary Committee, after consulting with the Library of Congress's Legislative Reference Service, proposed instead "one Nation under God, indivisible." The following day the Senate, after hearing a short explanation of the resolution's rationale from Ferguson, unanimously passed the amended resolution without debate.[42]

The House of Representatives took up the resolution on June 7. The closest the House heard to a substantive objection came from Republican representative Kenneth Keating, who counted among his constituents the son of Francis Bellamy, who had contacted the congressman to register his objections to having Congress rewrite an American classic.[43] Keating assured the House that he "strongly supported" the resolution and that he offered not objections but only observations. At a time when "the forces of anti-God and antireligion" have spread so widely, it was "wholesome" for the nation to be reminded of "the spiritual values which alone have permanence and which have played so prominent a part in the life, history, and traditions of this Republic." However, Keating wished to offer a warning about the perils of having Congress tread too heavily in "the field of American literature." The Pledge of Allegiance was "a priceless gem of American prose, comparable in many respects to Lincoln's Gettysburg Address." Although Keating felt certain that the "under God" resolution "will and should receive unanimous favor" from Congress, he cautioned his fellow members to "move with extreme caution" in this domain in the future.[44]

The only remaining obstacle to the passage of the bill concerned who would get credit for changing the Pledge. Since the Senate had approved the measure first, protocol and expediency suggested that the House substitute Ferguson's SJR 126 for the nearly identical HJR 243. Proponents of the measure were anxious to have a bill ready to be signed by the president on Flag Day, June 14, only one week away. When Iowa congressman and Legionnaire Paul Cunningham rose on the floor of the House to ask unanimous consent that the Senate resolution be substituted for the House resolution, few could have expected an objection. But Congressman Rabaut did object. He conceded that there were no important differences between the two resolutions but said he wished for the House to receive the credit, since seventeen resolutions had been introduced on the House side and only one on the Senate side. And, of course, the first resolution (his) had been introduced in the House. In insisting on a vote on HJR 243 rather than on SJR 126, he explained, he was only "championing the action of the House."[45]

The Republican majority leader Charlie Halleck expressed surprise and frustration that Rabaut would endanger the timely passage of the bill for so minor a cause. If the House refused to act on SJR 126 and instead passed HJR 243, then the House resolution would have to go back over to the Senate for another vote. Halleck testily intimated that Rabaut's actions had less to do with championing the House than with championing himself and warned the Michigan Democrat that if his opposition led to no bill being enacted then "he will have to take the responsibility for that." Rabaut was unfazed and replied that he was willing to assume that responsibility. Other members rose to plead with Rabaut "to waive the pride of authorship" on this "grave and universal subject." But there was more than personal pride at stake—partisanship was involved, as well as a little religion. Each of the members who asked Rabaut to make the substitution were Republicans and all were Protestants. Those who defended Rabaut's stand were all Democrats, and his two most vigorous backers—the freshman Illinois congressman Barratt O'Hara and the veteran Pennsylvania representative Herman P. Eberharter—were both Catholic.[46]

After a lengthy, unedifying squabble over the rectitude of Rabaut's stance, the House relented and passed HJR 243 instead of SJR 126. Fortunately for the "under God" clause, Senator Ferguson did not stand on ceremony and graciously agreed to ask the Senate to pass the House measure "without regard to the question of who is its author."[47] There was never any doubt that the president would sign the resolution, but the sponsors hoped for more than just the president's signature. They also hoped for a public signing ceremony. Rabaut wrote to Eisenhower, requesting that the president invite the eighteen members of Congress who had sponsored "under God" resolutions to the presidential signing. Meanwhile Congressman Bolton called the White House to ask that the presidential signing be covered by television, "with the President perhaps giving a short prayer." If television was not a possibility, he hoped, at a minimum, to "have pictures with five or six principal sponsors in attendance." Bolton also recommended that "a Protestant, a Catholic, and a Jew be in the group."[48]

The appeals by Bolton and Rabaut met with no success. Gerald Morgan, administrative assistant to the president, informed the congressmen that there would be no public signing ceremony for the resolution. Instead Morgan recommended that the president issue a signing statement through the president's press secretary, James Hagerty. The White House did agree to have the president sign the bill early Monday morning, June 14, so that the new Pledge of Allegiance could be used in Flag Day celebrations across the nation. Unable to secure a public signing ceremony by the president, the legislative sponsors, with the assistance of the American Legion, organized a televised Flag Day celebration of their own on the steps of the Capitol.[49]

In attendance were most of the congressional leadership, including the Senate majority leader, William Knowland, the Senate minority leader, Lyndon Johnson, and the House majority and minority whips. A new flag (donated by the American Legion) was raised over the Capitol, while Rabaut and Ferguson together led the assembled dignitaries in reciting the new Pledge of Allegiance. Then "a bugle rang out with the familiar strains of 'Onward, Christian Soldiers!'" The "stirring event," in the words of Walter Cronkite, was televised live by CBS and broadcast nationwide on the network's morning show.[50]

On the same day, the White House issued a brief presidential statement announcing the president's signing of the bill. "From this day forward," the president declared, "millions of our school children will daily proclaim . . . the dedication of our nation and our people to the Almighty." Such an avowal was particularly meaningful at a time when millions across the globe were being "deadened in mind and soul by a materialistic philosophy of life." By adding the words "under God" to the Pledge, Americans were strengthening "those spiritual weapons which forever will be our country's most powerful resource, in peace or in war."[51]

Reactions to the new Pledge of Allegiance, at least in Washington, D.C., were overwhelmingly positive. Rabaut was so pleased with the new Pledge that he persuaded a composer of popular songs to set the Pledge to music and then had the Singing Sergeants of the Air Force perform the musical Pledge the following year on the floor of the House.[52] Not everybody welcomed the change, however.

In May 1954 the Unitarian Ministers Association adopted a resolution opposing the addition of the words "under God" to the Pledge of Allegiance. In
their view it was as much "an invasion of religious liberty" as was the practice
of issuing coins with the words "In God We Trust" on them. The Unitarian
ministers heard from Mrs. Agnes Meyer, who warned against "the frenzy which
has seized America to legislate Christianity into people's consciousness." Such
attempts, she predicted, would "harm the Christian religion more than the persecution it is now suffering under the tyranny of Communists." Religion, she
feared, had become a fad. "If you don't bring God into every Cabinet meeting,
political convention or other assembly it is bad public relations." Adding "under
God" to the Pledge, she declared, was "contrary to the principle of separation
of church and state."[53]

Another who opposed the change was the crotchety old Gridley Adams,
who wrote to Congressman Abraham J. Multer, a Jewish Democrat representing Brooklyn, imploring him to "get up in the House and yell to high heaven
against this monkeying with the first amendment." Adams believed that adding
"under God" to the Pledge was a clear violation of "the long-observed basic law
of the separation of church versus state." Declaring himself "vehemently opposed to any and all attempts to write religious dogmas into the law of the
land," he warned, with typical Adams hyperbole, that such acts risked eventually inducing "a war of religions that will outrun the St. Bartholomew massacre
and Bloody Mary's regime in London."[54]

One letter writer to the *New York Times* wanted to know how the new
Pledge of Allegiance, in requiring everyone to believe in God, was consistent
with the last clause of the Pledge, "with liberty and justice for *all*." The letter
set off a minor flurry of other letters debating the merits of the Pledge. Those
defending the new Pledge as consistent with the American tradition pointed
to the references to God that could be found on the nation's coins and in the
Declaration of Independence. Those defending the original letter writer argued
that such points were "diversions" that failed to answer the question posed.
Moreover, they pointed out that "In God We Trust" was not put there by the
Founding Fathers, who preferred instead to inscribe only the word "liberty"
on their coins.[55]

The argument presaged an argument that would continue off and on in the
courts, down to the present day. Probably more interesting at the time, however, was the debate about what it meant to describe the United States as a nation "under God." To many it meant that the United States was the chosen nation, selected by God to carry the torch of freedom and battle the evil forces

of Communism. But others offered a more humble understanding of its meaning. In August 1956, Republicans gathered in San Francisco to nominate President Eisenhower to be the standard bearer of the Republican party once again. Many of the Republican convention leaders, including Eisenhower's chief of staff Sherman Adams, attended a special service at Grace Cathedral where they listened to Episcopalian minister Julian Bartlett warn political leaders against the "dangerous business" of assuming or intimating that God was on America's side. The phrase "under God," the dean of the Cathedral declared, should be understood instead as meaning that America in all its actions was "under the judgment" of God. The same message had been delivered in the Episcopalian magazine *Living Church* shortly after the president had signed the bill into law. "Let us not understand 'under God' as a declaration of national righteousness," the writer in *Living Church* intoned. "Let us rather understand it as an admission of national imperfection and incompleteness." It was a statement not of national parochialism but "a declaration of internationalism because we know that God loves all men impartially."[56] Eisenhower showed a similar sensibility in a letter he wrote to Luke Hart commending the Knights of Columbus for its role in initiating the idea of adding "under God" to the Pledge. The words, Eisenhower said, would "remind Americans that despite our great physical strength we must remain humble."[57]

Even among those who approved of the Pledge, adjusting to the new wording was not always easy. In front of television cameras at the 1956 Democratic National Convention, the Pledge of Allegiance was recited and the phrase "under God" was inadvertently left out. The following year, President Eisenhower, speaking before a national television and radio audience about his decision to send federal troops to Little Rock, Arkansas, to enforce the Supreme Court's desegregation order, closed with the hope that "thus will be restored the image of America and of all its parts as one nation, indivisible, with liberty and justice for all." In both cases the omission of the "under God" clause created a small ripple of comment in the press, but, apart from a little embarrassment, these verbal slipups were of scant importance.[58]

The Road to *Newdow*

Although objections to the "under God" clause from politicians were generally muted, the new phrase did meet with objections from public school teachers and students. A few complained that the change destroyed the cadence of the original Pledge, and a number of students found getting accustomed to the two new words a challenge. More serious was the objection mounted by the Freethinkers of America, who requested that the New York State Commissioner of Education delete the phrase from the Pledge.

The case went to court in 1957, and the trial judge rejected the claim of the Freethinkers. The First Amendment, Judge Isadore Bookstein explained, was "to prevent and prohibit the establishment of a State Religion," but it "was not intended to prevent or prohibit the growth and development of a Religious State." As evidence, Bookstein pointed to the Supreme Court's pronouncement in 1952 that "we are a religious people whose institutions presuppose a Supreme Being" and referenced the invocations of the divine in the Declaration of Independence, the Gettysburg Address, the New York State Constitution, the presidential oath of office, and the nation's money. If the court were to accept the contention that the "under God" clause was unconstitutional, then one might have to accept that neither the Declaration of Independence nor the Gettysburg Address could be read in school. Perhaps even the singing of "America" would need to be forbidden in public schools. And would not even the presidential oath be of "questionable constitutional status"? Since such outcomes were clearly absurd, the "under God" clause must be constitutional.[59]

Moreover, the judge pointed out that nonbelievers could readily omit the words "under God" during the recitation without bringing attention to themselves, thereby avoiding the coercion that can result from the pressure to conform. But even if a nonbelieving student did feel pressure to go along with the crowd, the judge denied that the right to dissent could be turned into a right not to be embarrassed. Bookstein strongly affirmed the petitioners' right not to recite the words "under God" but concluded that to strike the words "under God" would be to favor the nonreligious over the religious. The First Amendment, he concluded, affords the nonbeliever "no preference over those who do believe in God and who, in pledging their allegiance, choose to express that belief."[60]

The Freethinkers appealed but met with defeat at every turn. In two courts of appeals, including the state's highest court, the Freethinkers failed to get even a single justice to take their side. In November 1964, the U.S. Supreme Court ended the interminable appeals by declining to review the case, much to the relief of the thirty state governments that had asked the Court—which had banned school prayer in 1962 in *Engel v. Vitale* and Bible readings in school in 1963 in *Abington School District v. Schempp*—not to review the case. The *New York Times* hailed the Supreme Court's decision not to hear the case as "sensible."[61]

But the Supreme Court's rulings in *Engel* and especially *Abington* had encouraged many to think that the "under God" clause of the Pledge could be challenged. Immediately after the *Abington* ruling, the American Civil Liberties Union, on behalf of a high school teacher, filed suit in Los Angeles Superior Court to remove "under God" from the Pledge on the grounds that the phrase constituted "a requirement of adherence to the Judaeo-Christian religion, in contradistinction to the religious or ethical beliefs of Buddhism, Taoism, Ethical Culture and Secular Humanism and other faiths" that did not posit a single deity. The infamous atheist Madalyn Murray, who had been a party to the suit that resulted in the Court outlawing Bible reading in public schools, was also quick to initiate legal action against the Pledge. She threatened legal action against the Baltimore board of education if it did not delete "under God" from the Pledge of Allegiance. Shortly thereafter she moved to Hawaii, and in September 1964 she filed suit on behalf of her eleven-year-old son. The following February, just months after the U.S. Supreme Court's refusal to hear the Freethinkers' case, a federal judge dismissed her suit.[62]

The hope that the Supreme Court would smile favorably on a challenge to the Pledge overlooked judicial dicta in both *Abington* and *Engel*. Justice Hugo Black, who wrote the majority opinion in *Engel,* stressed in a footnote that there was "of course nothing in the decision reached here that is inconsistent with the fact that school children and others are officially encouraged to express love for our country by reciting historical documents such as the Declaration of Independence which contain references to the Deity or by singing officially espoused anthems which include the composer's professions of faith in a Supreme Being, or with the fact that there are many manifestations in our public life of belief in God. Such patriotic or ceremonial occasions bear no true resemblance to the unquestioned religious exercise that the State of New York has sponsored in this instance." The same statement was cited approvingly by Justice Arthur Goldberg in his concurring opinion in *Abington,* while Justice William Brennan, in a separate concurring opinion, laid down the principle that "activities which, though religious in origin, have ceased to have religious meaning" cannot be violations of the establishment clause. Such a principle, he suggested, would protect the "In God We Trust" motto on the currency and

> might also serve to insulate the various patriotic exercises and activities used in the public schools and elsewhere which, whatever may have been their origins, no longer have a religious purpose or meaning. The reference to divinity in the revised Pledge of Allegiance, for example, may merely recognize the historical fact that our Nation was believed to have been founded "under God." Thus reciting the pledge may be

no more of a religious exercise than the reading aloud of Lincoln's Gettysburg Address, which contains an allusion to the same historical fact.[63]

The string of legal defeats for these early legal challenges to the "under God" clause, combined with the relevant Supreme Court dicta in the school prayer decisions, tended to discourage further challenges to the "under God" clause. Periodically, cases did pop up, but the results were the same. In 1968, for instance, a federal judge, relying on the Supreme Court dicta in *Engel* and *Abington,* tossed out a challenge to the "under God" clause brought by some students in Redding, California. The appeal the following year was dismissed on the grounds that the students had now graduated and no longer had standing. Twenty years later the issue again surfaced in federal court, when atheist Rob Sherman challenged the "under God" clause on behalf of his son. Sherman's claim that "under God" violated the establishment clause was rejected first by a federal district court judge and then by a unanimous court of appeals. Once again, the Supreme Court refused to hear the appeal.[64]

Mike Newdow's Legal Challenge

In short, at the time Mike Newdow launched his challenge to the "under God" clause, his case had the distinct look of a no-hoper. In various challenges to the "under God" provision dating back to the 1950s, plaintiffs had not managed to get a single judge to agree with their position. When Newdow began his legal odyssey, nobody would have predicted that he would win in federal court and then end up arguing his case before the Supreme Court.

Newdow first challenged the "under God" clause in June 1998 in district court in Florida, where he lived at the time. His four-year-old daughter had not yet entered school—and in fact never lived in Florida or attended school there—and the district judge ruled that because the daughter was not enrolled in a Broward County school Newdow lacked standing to sue. Newdow appealed on the grounds that he was a taxpayer in Broward County, but the appeals court dismissed the appeal in January 2000 without comment. Unfazed, Newdow then filed suit in California in March 2000, where his daughter, then five, was in kindergarten. In May, Magistrate Judge Peter A. Nowinski, citing the Seventh Circuit's opinion in *Sherman v. Community Consolidated School District* as well as various Supreme Court dicta, recommended that Newdow's suit be dismissed. The opinion was barely a few hundred words, dismissing Newdow's establishment clause case without ever seriously engaging it. The magistrate's recommendation to dismiss Newdow's suit was accepted in July by federal district judge Milton Schwartz who felt no need to add anything to what little the magistrate judge had said. Newdow was not just losing, he was not even being taken seriously.[65]

Mainstream civil liberties and church and state organizations wanted nothing to do with Newdow's initial challenge. When he approached the American Civil Liberties Union during the Florida litigation, he was advised to "drop the case." Americans United for Separation of Church and State (AU) refused to read his brief, although the group wished him luck. AU spokesperson Steve Benen predicted to a reporter in 1999 that, although "it's a sound argument, . . . Mr. Newdow likely won't prevail." Benen observed that "the courts are just unwilling to consider the controversy," in part because "many judges . . . fear political consequences" that would ensue if "under God" were to be removed from the Pledge. Benen acknowledged that the AU's decision not to help Newdow in his Pledge fight was a pragmatic choice to reserve energies and resources for "more timely and winnable battles," such as school vouchers.[66]

Even after Newdow's surprising victory in the Ninth Circuit Court of Appeals in March 2002, mainstream civil liberties organizations remained wary. No longer dismissing Newdow's case as hopeless, their worries now focused on the political implications of the case. The ACLU's legal director Steven Shapiro admitted that Newdow was "clearly correct on the issue," but was terrified of the political effects the case could have. "There could be enormous political consequences from this being argued and decided in the midst of the presidential campaign," he fretted. Shapiro and the ACLU would end up joining the friend of the court brief submitted by AU, yet Shapiro continued to hope the Court would "avoid turning this case into a major battleground in the culture wars at the height of a presidential election campaign"—which, of course, the Court could only do by rejecting Newdow's position and the position taken in the friend of the court brief submitted by the ACLU. A lawyer for the American Jewish Congress (AJC), a group traditionally vigilant about a strict separation of church and state but which would write an amicus brief defending the constitutionality of the "under God" clause, admitted that although "Newdow might be right in a Platonic sense . . . [i]n the messy world in which we live, it's hard to see how any good can come of it." Even AU wrote to the Supreme Court in September 2003 suggesting that it "defer consideration" of the case until Newdow's custody battles over his daughter were sorted out.[67]

Lawyers for groups like the ACLU, AU, and AJC foresaw at least three possible outcomes from Newdow's challenge, each of them bad. First, if Newdow succeeded in persuading the Supreme Court to strike "under God" from the Pledge that would open the door for a constitutional amendment, an amendment that might not only permit "under God" in the Pledge of Allegiance but also prayer in public schools. Second, a constitutional victory for Newdow might produce a public backlash that would spell victory for Republicans in November 2004, which in turn would mean the appointment of more judges hostile to favorable interpretations of the establishment clause. Third, a Newdow defeat might provide the occasion for a rolling back of the establishment clause jurisprudence of the past forty years.

None of these pragmatic calculations entered into the ruling by the Ninth Circuit Court of Appeals, which rigorously applied Supreme Court precedents to Newdow's "under God" claim. Justice Alfred Goodwin, a lifelong Republican, found that whether the court used the three-prong *Lemon* test, the "endorsement" test, or the "coercion" test, the "under God" clause ran afoul of the establishment clause. The *Lemon* test (so called because it was first articulated in a 1971 case *Lemon v. Kurtzman*) requires that a government action must (1) have "a secular purpose," (2) have "a principal or primary effect that neither advances nor inhibits religion," and (3) not create "an excessive government entanglement with religion." If the government conduct fails any one of these three prongs it fails the *Lemon* test. The endorsement test, first articulated by Justice Sandra Day O'Connor in a 1984 case, demands that the government not endorse religion in such a way that it sends a message to nonadherents that they are "not full members of the political community" and a message to believers "that they are insiders, favored members of the political community." Finally, the coercion test, as formulated in the 1992 case *Lee v. Weisman,* held that "the government may not coerce anyone to support or participate in religion or its exercise." In the school setting, this prohibition against coercion includes not just formal compulsion but informal pressures that come from forcing students to choose between participation in a state-sponsored religious exercise or protest of that exercise.[68]

Goodwin looked to the legislative history of the 1954 act to argue that it failed the first prong of the *Lemon* test since "the Act's sole purpose was to advance religion, in order to differentiate the United States from nations under communist rule." He also maintained that the revised Pledge, codified in federal law, "impermissibly takes a position with respect to the purely religious question of the existence and identity of God," thereby marking nonbelievers who refused to take the government's Pledge as outsiders. Thus both the school board's policy and the 1954 federal law violated the endorsement test. Finally, the school board's policy failed the coercion test because it "imposes upon schoolchildren the constitutionally unacceptable choice between participating and protesting."[69]

Goodwin's opinion brought a sharp dissent from Justice Ferdinand Fernandez, but even the dissent seemed to concede that a literal reading of the Supreme Court's previous tests favored the result reached by Goodwin. Fernandez complained that judges could not "limit themselves to elements and tests, while failing to look at the good sense and principles that animated those tests in the first place." In Fernandez's view, the problem with the decision was its lack of common sense. Of course, reciting the Pledge of Allegiance with the words "under God" was not going to bring about an establishment of religion. "The danger that 'under God' in our Pledge of Allegiance will tend to bring about a theocracy or suppress somebody's beliefs is so minuscule as to be de minimis. The danger that phrase presents to our First Amendment freedoms is picayune at best."[70]

After Goodwin's decision was announced, the school district asked that the case be reheard by an eleven-judge panel of the Ninth Circuit. The request was narrowly turned down by the full court, but not before Goodwin's opinion was amended in two crucial ways. First, the amended opinion dropped all discussion of the constitutionality of the 1954 act, focusing instead only on the constitutionality of the school board policy. The opinion was thus purged of arguably its weakest link—Goodwin's claim that the purpose of the 1954 act was solely to advance religion. Religious motives there were aplenty, but clearly, too, the act had the secular purpose of combating Communism. Second, the amended opinion evaluated the constitutionality of the school board's policy solely in terms of the *Lee v. Weisman* coercion test, leaving out altogether whether the policy survived the *Lemon* test or endorsement test.[71]

Lee v. Weisman dealt with the use of nonsectarian prayer at a public school graduation, specifically an invocation at the opening and a benediction at the close of the ceremony. A sharply divided Supreme Court struck down the practice on the grounds that the prayer "bore the imprint of the State and thus put school-age children who objected in an untenable position." Students who objected to the prayer were forced into the position of either participating in a ceremony that violated their conscience or protesting the ceremony. Although no student was compelled by threat of force to participate, Justice Anthony Kennedy noted that "there are heightened concerns with protecting freedom of conscience from subtle coercive pressure in the elementary and secondary public schools." Goodwin had little difficulty showing that if a nonsectarian prayer at a graduation ceremony was unconstitutional then "under God" in the Pledge of Allegiance was suspect too. After all, students in a high school graduation are typically seventeen and eighteen years old, and the ceremony takes place once in a student's life, whereas the Pledge of Allegiance is recited by impressionable grade-school-age children on a daily basis. Moreover, attendance at school is legally compulsory, whereas attendance at one's graduation is not. Finally, the graduation prayer was led by a member of the clergy, not by school officials, whereas the Pledge was typically led by school authorities, whether the teacher or principal. Thus, if *Lee v. Weisman* was correctly decided, then surely the "under God" clause was unconstitutional.[72]

When the Elk Grove Unified School District appealed to the United States Supreme Court, the central challenge the district faced was to explain why the rationale advanced by the Court in *Lee* should not control the question now facing the Court. The howls of derision aimed at the Ninth Circuit's decision, particularly from conservative commentators, might lead one to expect that the High Court justices would have had little difficulty disposing of the issue. But while the Supreme Court did end up reversing the Ninth Circuit's ruling—on the technical grounds that Michael Newdow lacked legal standing to bring the suit—only two of the justices, William Rehnquist and Sandra Day O'Connor, were prepared to argue that the Ninth Circuit had misinterpreted recent Supreme Court rulings.

Support for the Ninth Circuit's interpretation of Supreme Court precedent came from a surprising quarter—the Court's most conservative justice, Clarence Thomas. In a concurring opinion, Thomas wrote that the Ninth Circuit's conclusion was "based on a persuasive reading of our precedent, particularly *Lee*." For Thomas, that suggested, however, not that the Ninth Circuit was right that the Pledge was unconstitutional but rather that previous Supreme Court cases had been wrongly decided. Thomas used the Pledge case, as the ACLU and others had feared, to invite the Court to rethink the establishment clause jurisprudence of the last forty years. In *Lee*, Thomas (along with Chief Justice Rehnquist and Justice Byron White) had signed Antonin Scalia's stinging dissent that excoriated Kennedy for inventing a "boundless, and boundlessly manipulable, test of psychological coercion" that "lays waste a tradition that is as old as public school graduation ceremonies." In *Elk Grove v. Newdow*, Thomas reiterated this criticism, claiming that Kennedy's expansive conception of coercion, even in school settings, had "no basis in law or reason." Only coercion that is achieved "by force of law and threat of penalty" was forbidden by the establishment clause.[73]

An alternative way to uphold the "under God" clause is to distinguish *Lee* from *Elk Grove* on the grounds that *Lee* involved an "explicit religious exercise," whereas *Elk Grove* did not. This was the route pursued by Chief Justice Rehnquist in his concurring opinion. Although Rehnquist had dissented in *Lee*, he saw no need to revisit that argument since the Court in *Lee* had been concerned "only with 'formal religious exercises,' which the Pledge is not." In Rehnquist's view, following the position adopted by the government in oral argument, the phrase "under God" is neither a prayer nor an endorsement of religion, but rather "a descriptive phrase," recognizing the fact that those who founded and built the United States of America believed that the United States was a nation under God.[74]

Even Newdow, in oral argument, seemed willing to concede that the "under God" phrase did not turn the Pledge of Allegiance into a prayer. But, as Newdow pointed out, the establishment clause is not limited to prayer. Schools can't post the Ten Commandments, even though those commandments are not prayers. So one returns to the question of whether having students pledge their allegiance to a nation "under God" establishes religion. And, as Newdow also pointed out in oral argument, it's hard to see how having a daily, state-sanctioned and promoted Pledge of Allegiance to "a nation under God" is not establishing religion. To be sure it is not endorsing Christianity over Judaism, or Protestantism over Catholicism, but from the perspective of an atheist like Newdow or a Buddhist, it's hard to see much difference between one nation under God and one nation under Jesus. In both cases individuals are being asked to pledge allegiance to a nation that is defined in such a way that it does not include them. To be sure, as Rehnquist points out, there may be others who disagree with the phrase "with liberty and justice for all." But, of course, the difference is that there is nothing in the Constitution that prevents the United States government from promoting liberty and justice, whereas the establishment clause, at least as interpreted by the United States Supreme Court over the last half century, does forbid the government from promoting religion.[75]

Justice O'Connor confronted this issue directly in her own concurring opinion. Like Rehnquist and Thomas, O'Connor believed that the "under God" clause should be upheld as constitutional, but unlike them she had sided with the majority in *Lee*. But O'Connor had never shown much enthusiasm for Kennedy's coercion test. Her own preference was the "endorsement test" she had first articulated two decades before, which had formed the framework for the Court's 1989 decision *Allegheney v. ACLU*, in which the Court ruled that placing a nativity scene and menorah outside the county courthouse violated the establishment clause. O'Connor used the Pledge case to reiterate her view that the endorsement test "captures the essential command of the Establishment Clause, namely, that government must not make a person's religious beliefs relevant to his or her standing in the political community by conveying a message 'that religion or a particular religious belief is favored or preferred.'" Unlike Goodwin, who in his first opinion had argued that the Pledge failed the endorsement test, O'Connor found that the Pledge of Allegiance did not constitute an impermissible government endorsement of religion.[76]

The key for O'Connor was that the test must be applied from the vantage point of "a reasonable observer." Otherwise the "dizzying religious heterogeneity" of the United States would "reduce the test to an absurdity." Just because an individual feels that a government action sends a message of exclusion is not enough to establish that the government action violates the establishment clause. Newdow and other sensitive souls like him cannot be granted a "heckler's veto." Moreover, a "reasonable observer" must take into account not only "rational judgment" but also must "embody a community ideal of social judgment." That is, the reasonable observer "must be deemed aware of the history of the conduct in question, and must understand its place in our Nation's cultural landscape." In other words, a judge must exercise the common sense and sense of perspective that Newdow lacked.[77]

A reasonable observer, according to O'Connor, would understand the "under God" clause of the Pledge of Allegiance not as an expression of religious belief but as a way of "solemnizing public occasions." Invoking God in the Pledge of Allegiance is less like a prayer than it is like the words that signal the opening of the Supreme Court ("God save the United States and this honorable Court") or the national motto ("In God We Trust"). Each are instances of what the Court has designated as "ceremonial deism," a category of government action, as Justice Brennan famously wrote, that is "protected from Establishment Clause scrutiny chiefly because [the words] have lost through rote repetition any significant religious content." O'Connor admitted that in the case of the Pledge of Allegiance this was "a close question" but insisted that on balance the "history and ubiquity" of the "under God" clause qualified it as an instance of ceremonial deism rather than an unconstitutional endorsement of religion.[78]

As evidence, O'Connor pointed to the fact that "the practice has been employed pervasively without engendering significant controversy." She reported that Newdow's suit was "only the third reported case of which I am aware to

challenge [the Pledge of Allegiance] as an impermissible establishment of religion." O'Connor's history is problematic at several levels. First, it understates
opposition to the "under God" clause, both by ignoring the unsuccessful legal
challenges to the clause launched in the 1950s and early 1960s and by over-
looking the many individuals who have refused to say the Pledge because of opposition to the "under God" clause. Second, and far more important, it over-
looks the fact that the paucity of legal challenges has been a product of courts'
hostility to legal challenges to the "under God" clause. As we have already seen,
the "under God" clause was challenged immediately after Congress added the
two words, but the courts repeatedly swept away such challenges. As important, the Supreme Court in judicial dicta dating back to the early 1960s has
repeatedly signaled that the "under God" clause in the Pledge of Allegiance was
a form of ceremonial deism and therefore immune from constitutional challenge. It is disingenuous, therefore, if not tautological, for O'Connor to cite a
paucity of legal challenges as evidence that the "under God" clause is an instance of ceremonial deism.[79]

Moreover, O'Connor's admission that it is "a close question" whether the
Pledge qualifies as an instance of "ceremonial deism" seems to undercut her reliance on the "reasonable observer" standard and her worries about granting
oddballs like Newdow a "heckler's veto." If it is a close question, one wonders
how one can sustain the proposition that Newdow's position is not that of a
reasonable observer. Moreover, Newdow's position was supported by twenty-
one amicus briefs, including a brief by organizations representing more than
three hundred thousand Buddhist Americans. A fair reading of the historical
record would suggest that there is nothing remotely unreasonable in Newdow's
position. The evidence for Newdow's position is at least as strong as the evidence against it. One may reasonably decide that on balance the "under God"
clause does not unconstitutionally endorse religion, but the "reasonable observer" standard helps one not at all in the case of the Pledge of Allegiance. The
opponents of the "under God" clause are certainly a minority—if they were a
majority they would not need the courts to remove the clause—but what they
ask is not at all unreasonable.[80]

O'Connor's chief contention is that whatever the intentions of those who
amended the Pledge in 1954, the addition of the words "under God" did not
change the meaning of the Pledge, which retained its secular character. "Whatever the sectarian ends its authors may have had in mind, our continued repetition of the reference to 'one Nation under God' in an exclusively patriotic context has shaped the cultural significance of that phrase to conform to that

context. Any religious freight the words may have been meant to carry originally has long since been lost." It is possible that O'Connor may be right about this, but she provides no evidence in support of this proposition. The claim is an empirical one that could be tested by close anthropological study of the meanings schoolchildren assign to the Pledge or by survey research. Do children understand the Pledge's reference to God as an endorsement of the existence of God, as a prayer, or as a historical description of the beliefs of the Founding Fathers? Or do they assign it no meaning at all? In the absence of systematic studies perhaps it is best for judges to stay their hand and let the Pledge alone, but O'Connor's confident declaration about the meanings attached to the Pledge of Allegiance is judicial arrogance masquerading as judicial self-restraint. O'Connor essentially consults her own feelings (and the feelings of past justices) about the meanings attached to the Pledge in deciding on its cultural significance, but why we should trust her feelings more than Newdow's is never explained.[81]

O'Connor, Rehnquist, and Thomas all offered different reasons for why the "under God" clause does not violate the establishment clause. The rest of the Court, however, dodged the thorny establishment clause question altogether, focusing instead on the question of standing. Newdow, the Court's majority decided, lacked standing to bring his suit in federal court. The majority opinion was written by Justice John Paul Stevens, who in the oral argument had shown great sympathy for the merits of Newdow's establishment clause argument. In his majority opinion Stevens zeroed in on the continuing custody disputes that were swirling around Newdow, his daughter, and his daughter's mother, Sandra Banning. "In our view," Stevens wrote, "it is improper for the federal courts to entertain a claim by a plaintiff whose standing to sue is founded on family law rights that are in dispute when prosecution of the lawsuit may have an adverse effect on the person who is the source of the plaintiff's claimed standing." Under these circumstances it was better for the Court to "stay its hand rather than reach out to resolve a weighty question of federal constitutional law."[82]

In the original deliberations of the Ninth Circuit Court of Appeals, Newdow's standing had not been an important issue. Even the dissenting judge accepted that Newdow had standing "as a parent to challenge a practice that interferes with his right to direct the religious education of his daughter." But after the Ninth Circuit's decision in June 2002, the standing issue became muddied by developments on the domestic front. Goodwin's opinion, and the ensuing uproar, prompted Banning to ask that the case be dismissed. Banning pointed out that while her daughter shared time between mother and father, the custody court in February 2002 had granted her "exclusive legal custody," including "the sole right to represent [the daughter's] legal interests and make all decision[s] about her education." Moreover, she maintained that her daughter was, like her, a Christian who believed in God, and that neither she nor her daughter had any objections to reciting the Pledge of Allegiance. Most important, Banning argued that the case should not be allowed to go forward because her daughter could be the target of scorn and hate if she was perceived as the atheist who wanted to remove the words "under God" from the Pledge. In September 2002, the California Superior Court agreed that the mother, as the sole legal custodian, had the right to decide what was in the best interests of the child. Newdow was thus compelled to withdraw his daughter from the suit.[83]

Even though Newdow no longer represented his daughter, the three judges of the Ninth Circuit Court, including the dissenting judge, affirmed that Newdow still had standing to sue because "the grant of sole legal custody to Banning" did not "deprive Newdow, as a noncustodial parent, of . . . standing to object to unconstitutional government action affecting his child." After the Ninth Circuit's ruling was appealed to the Supreme Court, the waters were muddied still further by a revised custody ruling in September 2003 that renamed the legal arrangement "joint legal custody" but still granted Banning the final say on matters regarding the education, health, and welfare of the daughter. To the Supreme Court's concurring justices, the majority's forbearance was misguided and its principles ad hoc. The implication was that the majority had not had the courage of its convictions and so punted. Politically wise perhaps, but judicially suspect.[84]

For many observers, the Court's decision was a huge anticlimax. Commentators across the country accused the Court of having "chickened out." Others breathed a big sigh of relief at having dodged a political bullet. Presidential candidate John Kerry and other Democrats could now look forward to a presidential campaign without the Pledge of Allegiance operating as the sort of Republican "wedge" issue it had been in the 1988 presidential campaign against another Massachusetts Democrat, Michael Dukakis. But if the Supreme Court had blinked, it had also for the first time taken seriously the constitutional problems posed by the "under God" clause. Of the three justices willing to consider the merits of the case, one justice (O'Connor) conceded the case was a close call and another (Thomas) conceded what many lawyers believe, namely that if Supreme Court precedents are taken seriously then Michael Newdow is right.

And it showed, too, that as a constitutional matter, Alfred Goodwin's opinion was not the misguided judgment that politicians who pilloried him after his decision had claimed. None of which necessarily means that Newdow or someone like him will eventually succeed. The chances of that remain slim. But that probably tells us less about the constitutionality of the "under God" clause than it does about the contemporary politics of the Pledge, which is the subject of the next two chapters.

6

PROTESTING THE PLEDGE

In the middle of May 1988, Gallup conducted a presidential preference survey and reported that the likely Democratic nominee, Michael Dukakis, was sixteen percentage points ahead of Vice President George H. W. Bush.[1] Dukakis, whose main Democratic opponent was Jesse Jackson, appeared to be succeeding in portraying himself as a mainstream man of the middle. Republican operatives were clearly worried. On May 19, the day that Dukakis handily defeated Jackson in Oregon to add another twenty-seven delegates to his insurmountable total, Georgia Republican Newt Gingrich called up a *New York Times* reporter to draw attention to a veto the Massachusetts governor had issued eleven years earlier. The bill, which was enacted over Dukakis's veto, required teachers to lead students in the Pledge at the beginning of each school day. Gingrich relished the prospect of Dukakis having to explain his veto to a national audience: "When the country realizes that the lawyers who advised him to veto that bill are the people he'd put on the Supreme Court, we've won the South."[2] Gingrich proved prophetic. Throughout the fall campaign, Vice President Bush and his fellow Republicans suggested that Dukakis was anti-

Pledge and used the governor's veto to portray him not as a competent moderate but as a closet liberal out of step with the patriotic mainstream.

Given the U.S. Supreme Court's 1943 *Barnette* ruling, one might wonder how Dukakis's veto of a mandatory Pledge bill could possibly have become a campaign issue. Hadn't the Supreme Court decided nearly a half century earlier that no student could be forced to participate in the Pledge? And if elementary school students could not be compelled to say the Pledge, how could adults be compelled to say it? Did teachers have fewer constitutional rights than children? Moreover, Dukakis had vetoed the bill only after receiving legal counsel not only from the state's attorney general but also from the state's highest court. Both entities agreed that the bill was an unconstitutional infringement of the First Amendment rights of teachers and that it could not be enforced. And while the law remains on the books today, it has never been enforced under Republican or Democratic administrations. How then did a law that was a dead letter from the moment of its passage become a major campaign issue in a presidential election a decade later? To answer that question, it helps first to understand why Dukakis was ever in the position of having to veto such a bill, which will help us understand why the Pledge became a partisan issue in the 1988 campaign and why for conservative Republicans it was a continuation of their fight against the liberal-left that began in earnest in the mid-1960s.

Prior to the 1960s, the Pledge of Allegiance was rarely used as a partisan weapon. It was not identified with a particular party or ideology, in large part because protests against the Pledge of Allegiance were either insignificant or not associated with a particular side of the political spectrum. One would have to go back to World War I to find politically motivated refusals of any national significance. The refusals in the 1930s and 1940s were almost entirely by Jehovah's Witnesses. And in the 1950s, flag salute refusals were most likely to emanate from the South. In 1957, for instance, the Kiwanis Club of Marshall, Texas, refused to recite the Pledge of Allegiance as a protest against Eisenhower's decision to send federal troops into Little Rock, Arkansas, to enforce the Supreme Court's school desegregation order. The club instead determined to pledge allegiance to the Texas flag, although after an intense public backlash, the group quickly retreated from its position.[3] Only with the flag salute refusals in the 1960s and 1970s did the Pledge of Allegiance become clearly aligned with the left side of the political spectrum and thus become a prominent symbol in the culture wars that have continued ever since.

With Liberty and Justice for All

The Supreme Court's 1943 decision in *Barnette* had settled the legal question of whether a public school student could be compelled to recite the Pledge of Allegiance if to do so violated a student's religious beliefs. But while the High Court's opinion helped to quell the persecution of Jehovah's Witnesses in the 1940s, it did not prevent school districts in the 1960s from trying to dismiss students who refused to pledge allegiance to the flag. The refusals in the 1930s and 1940s had been largely rooted in religious objections rather than in any specific protest against U.S. government policy, but the refusals in the 1960s were grounded in political protest, particularly against racial discrimination.

Justice Jackson's opinion in *Barnette* was cast as a defense not just of religious liberty but of individual conscience, whether "in politics, nationalism, religion, or other matters of opinion." But it was arguably unclear whether a majority of the Court's justices accepted Jackson's more sweeping defense of "the sphere of intellect and spirit." Justices Black and Douglas had signed a separate concurring opinion, emphasizing that the fundamental problem with a mandatory pledge was that it failed "to accord full scope to the freedom of religion" guaranteed by the Constitution. The ambiguity encouraged some school boards, when faced with student refusals, to ignore Jackson's soaring rhetoric and argue that the Supreme Court had carved out a narrow defense of religious conscience, not an open invitation to student disobedience and political protest.[4]

One of the earliest such cases occurred in 1963 in the community of Elizabeth, New Jersey, where five black elementary school students were suspended from school for failing to recite the Pledge of Allegiance. The reason given by the children's parents, all of whom were Black Muslims, was that the Pledge was contrary to the teachings of Islam. The local school board acknowledged that state law included an exemption for those with "conscientious scruples" but ruled that the exemption did not apply to these students because the Black Muslim movement was political and racial, not religious. The state commissioner disagreed and nine months later reversed the school board's ruling, insisting that whether the teachings of Islam were religious or political or both did not matter since the students' refusal clearly reflected "conscientious scruples." The school board appealed and met with a final setback from a unanimous state supreme court, which in January 1966 agreed with the commissioner that New Jersey's "conscientious scruples" exemption was not limited to religious scruples. The question of whether the conscientious objections were religious in nature was thus irrelevant.[5]

Nearly a year after the suspension of the Elizabeth students, several hundred high school students in the town of Scarsdale, New York, signed a petition protesting a new law requiring that all public school students recite the Pledge at the beginning of each day. The students objected that being forced to recite the Pledge violated their First Amendment rights of freedom of speech. Meanwhile as many as thirty students in East Williston High School on Long Island refused, for the same reasons, to recite the Pledge of Allegiance, prompting the local board of education to seek an opinion from the state. In April 1964 the state education department ruled that students could only be exempted from the ceremony if they had religious objections to the flag salute. *Barnette,* the state held, provided constitutional protection for religious refusals, but other objections, whether based on political or personal grounds, had no constitutional grounding. If a student could refuse to salute the flag, the board's legal counsel reasoned, then nothing could stop a student from refusing to take a required course in United States history. "No argument is needed," stated the board's legal opinion, "to prove that the constitutional provisions of freedom do not go so far as to grant 'license' to a pupil in attendance at the public schools to refuse to carry out statutory requirements."[6]

As the civil rights movement and the protests against the Vietnam War gained momentum, so too did protests against the Pledge of Allegiance. The refusals in the early 1960s generally did not stem from objections to particular words in the Pledge but instead from objections to being compelled by school authorities to recite the Pledge. But by the end of the 1960s Pledge refusals had become clear statements of political protest. If students in the early 1960s objected primarily to the compulsion, students by the end of the decade typically saw their refusal as a way to protest against particular government policies and national inequalities. By far the most common target of student criticism in the late 1960s and early 1970s was the final clause of the Pledge. America, many students claimed, was not a land of liberty and justice for all, and to state otherwise was hypocritical at best, a lie at worst. Moreover, by 1969 the legal focus had shifted from the much-litigated question of whether a student could be compelled to say the Pledge to the far murkier waters of whether a student who refused to say the Pledge could be compelled to stand or whether such a student had a right to remain seated.

New York witnessed a host of student refusals in the late 1960s by middle school and high school students. The first of these to attract statewide attention was a refusal by a Queens high school senior, who refused to pledge allegiance to the flag because she neither believed that there was a God nor that the United States was a land of liberty and justice for all Americans, particularly for "minority groups." The student wished either to sit or to leave the room during the daily flag salute, but the principal refused, insisting that she would be suspended if she did not stand at attention during the Pledge. Principal Louis Schuker was a veteran administrator, having been principal of the high school for nearly fifteen years and an employee in the New York City public schools for over four decades. Schuker eyed the rebellious youth of the sixties with great suspicion, worrying that they were undermining academic standards and discipline in New York City's schools. As he explained to a colleague on the board of education, "Jamaica High school . . . has all the well-known problems of a difficult urban high school. We have the usual percentage of sick kids. We also have a number of paranoid blacks (sporting Panther and Liberation buttons) who have been inspired to look for trouble. We have a handful of white New Leftists. Though I can name them on my fingers, they keep the pot boiling because they're constantly coached by the New York Civil Liberties Union." The principal was quickly overruled, however, by the superintendent of schools, who ruled that the student should be allowed to leave the room without punishment. "Our policy," explained a representative of the board of education, "is that the schools do not interfere with matters of conscience."[7]

But while the superintendent's directive acknowledged that court rulings indicated that students had "a right, as a matter of conscience, to refuse to salute the flag and recite the Pledge of Allegiance," he also believed that "no pupil should be permitted to sit during such a ceremony, since to do so might create disorder." Although the Queens senior was content to leave the room, it was only a matter of time before a student would insist on the right to sit. And that is precisely what happened the following school year, when another student from the same Queens high school insisted on sitting during the ceremony and was promptly suspended. The New York Civil Liberties Union entered the case, contending that the suspension violated the board of education's policies since the student had neither been disruptive nor endangered others. The board, however, insisted that its policy was that students who objected to the Pledge had either to stand at attention or leave the room. The policy, in the eyes of the board, was reasonable and respected the rights of both the dissenters and those who wished to recite the Pledge of Allegiance.[8]

The issue made it into the courtroom of Federal Judge Orin Judd, who was asked to decide whether the student had a right to remain seated during the Pledge. The case was combined with the case of two seventh-grade girls at a Queens junior high school who had also been suspended for refusing to stand or leave the room during the recitation. All three students said their reason for not taking part was that they did not believe the United States was a nation in which there was "liberty and justice for all." Poor people, explained one, "have to live in cold, miserable places. And it's obvious that the blacks are oppressed." One of the middle school girls, an atheist, also objected to the words "under God." They refused to stand because that would have meant participating in a "lie," and they refused to be compelled to leave the room because that would be a form of punishment. The Jamaica high school principal countered that allowing a student not to rise during the Pledge of Allegiance would pose "a real and present threat to the maintenance of discipline" and would be "pedagogically foolhardy."[9]

Judd recognized that the Supreme Court's 1943 *Barnette* decision could not by itself dispose of the case. For not only had two of the six justices based their decision on the grounds of religious freedom, but the students in *Barnette* had been faced with the choice of participation or expulsion from school, while the students now were only being asked to wait outside the room for the duration of the Pledge ceremony. Still the judge seemed to have little difficulty deciding the case. Citing the reasoning in the recent Supreme Court case *Tinker v. Des Moines,* which upheld students' right to wear black armbands to school as a form of protest, Judd noted that in order to restrict student freedom of expression the school must be able to demonstrate that the act of remaining seated "materially infringed the rights of other students or caused disruption" of school activities. A fear that an action might produce a "disorderly reaction" was not sufficiently compelling grounds to justify restricting peaceful expressions of protest. The judge observed that the schools had provided no evidence that the actions of these students had disrupted school activities or caused disorder in the classroom.[10]

The state board of education elected not to appeal the decision, but that did not settle the issue. Indeed, it only seemed to add to the confusion. The High School Principals Association, upset that the board had not appealed the decision, recommended that the Pledge of Allegiance no longer be recited at high schools until the legal status of doing so was definitively settled.[11] The *New York Times* editorial page criticized the judge for his ruling and the board for not appealing but also wondered about "the wisdom or efficacy of a daily salute as opposed to one only at special occasions." The state superintendent of schools, while disturbed by the action of the principals' association, also wondered (on the front page of the *Times*) about the wisdom of a mandated patriotic ceremony, since "it might lead to more disrespect for the flag from dissenting students than any gain in loyalty." Meanwhile, a number of press reports indicated that in many classrooms the Pledge was frequently ignored, despite the state regulation requiring its daily recitation. The state department of education tried to quell the confusion by ordering all school administrators to continue the practice of the daily Pledge, while leaving it to the courts to decide how to handle dissenters who refused to comply with school regulations. The directive was implicitly an invitation to principals to suspend students who refused to stand for the Pledge, since the courts would only become involved after disciplinary action had been taken against a student.[12]

And that is exactly what some principals did. In Orange County, New York, for instance, a high school girl was suspended for refusing to stand. The words of the Pledge, the girl explained, were "not true" since "there is no liberty and justice for all" in America. Kristina Bielenberg's case was brought before the state commissioner of education, who ruled that the student did not have a constitutional right to remain seated. Conveniently ignoring Judge Judd's recent ruling to the contrary, Commissioner Ewald Nyquist insisted that the act of sitting during the Pledge was inherently disruptive to the work of the school and the rights of other students. Nyquist chastised the girl for her "callous disregard for the rights and interests of her classmates who wish to participate in a meaningful ceremony" and for lacking "the simple courtesy of standing or leaving the room" during the Pledge ceremony. The student not only lacked good manners but had "wholly misconstrued" the Pledge. It was, the commissioner instructed, not "a statement of prevailing conditions in the United States" but rather "a statement of our goals and our national aspirations."[13]

The continuing argument over the meaning of the Pledge's last clause led the principal and senior class president of one New York high school to launch what they promised would be a nationwide campaign to change the final clause of the Pledge to read "seeking liberty and justice for all." The principal urged New York senator Jacob Javits to introduce a bill to change the wording. Letters were also sent to student council presidents of all six hundred New York high schools. Such a change was necessary, the principal explained, because students earnestly believed that the last clause was "hypocritical as applied to blacks and other groups." The principal had tried arguing what he called "the Establishment position," namely that the words were meant to describe the nation's aspirations that guided reform efforts, but students, he said, "just wouldn't buy it." *Look* magazine got into the act as well by asking a former U.S. Commissioner of Education to suggest a new pledge of allegiance. The former commissioner complied, offering a forty-one-word pledge that would have appalled the proud wordsmith Bellamy: "I pledge allegiance to the Flag of the United States of America and dedicate myself to the principle that the Republic for which it stands shall be in truth one Nation, under God, indivisible, dedicated to liberty and justice for all." At the same time, the White House Conference on Children, after a five-day meeting of some four thousand delegates, forwarded to President Richard Nixon a list of twenty-four recommendations, among which was that the Pledge of Allegiance be modified so that it more clearly indicated that its words describe what the nation aspires to be rather than its current condition. The conference's proposed pledge read: "I pledge allegiance to the Flag of the United States of America and dedicate myself to the task of making it one nation under God, indivisible, with liberty and justice for all." None of these proposed changes to the Pledge went far.[14]

Meanwhile, there was the more pressing matter of clearing up the widespread confusion in New York over whether dissenting students could remain in their seats. Commissioner Nyquist's ruling meant that principals, teachers, and students in Judge Judd's jurisdiction—Brooklyn, Queens, Staten Island, and the counties of Nassau and Suffolk—had to choose between a federal judge's edict that students could remain seated during the Pledge ceremony and the conflicting directive of the state commissioner of education that forbade such action. Compounding the uncertainty was a ruling by a federal judge in Brooklyn who decided that fifteen-year-old Donald Richards did not have the right to remain seated while his classmates said the Pledge of Allegiance. In reaching his decision, the judge relied on testimony from the boy's teacher that on at least two occasions the student's refusal had resulted in "incipient disturbances." The boy's refusal to stand or leave the room during the ceremony, the judge ruled, created a distraction that intruded on "the educational experience" of other students.[15]

The state continued to act as if Judd's ruling had never been issued. In 1971 it issued guidelines on the rights and responsibilities of students that reiterated the state's position that students must either stand or leave the room. The guidelines cited the recent case involving Donald Richards to bolster its case but made no mention of the decision by Judge Judd that had enjoined New York City schools from enforcing the rule. Students, however, continued to resist.

Among the resisters was Theodore Goetz, honor student and senior class president at a high school in Latham, New York. He, too, felt the Pledge was a lie because there was not liberty and justice for all in the United States. His effort to get a preliminary injunction was rebuffed by a federal district judge, but the federal court of appeals overruled the lower court. "The act of standing," the court ruled, was "itself part of the pledge" and so could not be compelled any more than the words of the Pledge could. And if the state could not compel participation in the Pledge ceremony, then neither could it punish non-participation. Although the state did not construe leaving the classroom as a form of punishment, the court opined that "being required to leave the classroom during the pledge may reasonably be viewed by some as having that effect." Echoing Judge Judd, the court decreed that only if there was evidence "of disruption of classwork or disorder or invasion of the rights of others" could a student be prevented from remaining seated. The school district worried that if a student were allowed to remain seated then the student might also feel free to "kneel, lie down, stand on his hands" or "make derisive motions." The court assured the district that, were the students to engage in such "disruptive acts," it would have "no hesitancy in holding them unprotected." There was a clear difference, the court noted sensibly, between standing on one's hands and remaining seated and silent.[16]

The appeals court's unanimous ruling in favor of Goetz seemed to settle the question in New York's public schools. But in other states the battle continued. In neighboring New Jersey, state law still required that students with "conscientious scruples" against reciting the Pledge must stand at attention. Students were not allowed either to leave the room or to remain seated. In 1977 Deborah Lipp, a sixteen-year-old New Jersey high school student, enlisted the help of the American Civil Liberties Union in preventing the school from forcing her to stand during the flag salute. The Pledge's description of America as a land of liberty and justice for all, she explained, was a lie, particularly for women, homosexuals, minors, and minority groups. By compelling her to stand, the state was compelling her to endorse a lie. "Standing," as an ACLU spokesperson put it, "compels symbolic speech and . . . that violates the First Amendment." Or, as Lipp expressed it: "If I'm only free to stand and not sit during the pledge, then I'm not free at all."[17]

The federal judge had little difficulty disposing of the case. So long as students did not "whistle, drum, tap, dance, or otherwise be disruptive," they could remain seated during the Pledge. For Lipp, the judge's decision was a vindication of freedom. "Everybody," she explained, "has the right now to do what they want. There's no mandatory sitting or mandatory standing—you're free to do what you see fit." Lipp explained that her refusal was not so much a protest against the flag or the country as it was an "affirmation of her own right to choose to stand or sit." It was an affirmation of freedom more than it was a protest against the nation's failure to achieve justice for all. As she explained to a reporter: "I love the freedom to fight a law I don't like. In other countries I'd have to keep my mouth shut."[18]

Lipp's stance brought her the stern disapproval of her father as well as an "enormous amount" of hostile mail and dozens of critical phone calls "that maligned her patriotism and attacked her character." The New Jersey Veterans of Foreign Wars favored her with a letter, instructing her that standing for the Pledge was "a measure of paying respect to the nation's war dead." The judge's decision sparked a host of angry letters to the editor. One complained that patriotism is treated "as a cancer instead of a source of pride." State officials were among those upset by the decision. Republican state legislator Peter McDonagh drafted a bill that would require dissenting students to be removed from the classroom during the Pledge. If the Pledge ceremony was held outdoors, the bill called for the dissenters to be cordoned off from the participating group. "I resent the fact," McDonagh explained, "that one misguided student could essentially destroy the meaning of the pledge of allegiance ceremony for all students in the classroom." The state's attorney general showed his displeasure by appealing the ruling to a higher court. There the state met with yet another rebuff, as the Court of Appeals for the Third District unanimously sided with the student. The court swept aside the state's argument that remaining seated during the Pledge of Allegiance did not constitute symbolic speech. Pointing to several earlier decisions, including the appeals court's decision in the case of Theodore Goetz, the court insisted that requiring students to stand at attention did indeed violate students' First and Fourteenth Amendment rights to freedom of expression.[19]

The issue was posed and resolved in similar fashion in Dade County, Florida, where guidelines required that students who, out of "religious or other deep personal conviction," refuse to recite the Pledge of Allegiance to the flag must "stand quietly." In 1970, high school senior Andrew Banks, citing his religious beliefs as a Unitarian, refused to stand and was promptly suspended. Banks, who wished to become a Unitarian minister, believed that only by committing to a "Uni-world" government could there be world peace. In addition, he intended his refusal as a protest against "black repression" in the United States. The court agreed that standing "is an integral portion of the pledge ceremony and is no less a gesture of acceptance and respect than is the salute or the utterance of the words of allegiance." If, as the U.S. Supreme Court held in *Barnette,* schools could not compel students to recite the Pledge of Allegiance, then neither could they compel students to stand for the Pledge.[20]

By 1973, then, virtually every court that had considered the question had agreed that students could not be prevented from remaining seated during the Pledge of Allegiance so long as they did not disrupt the classroom. If students could wear black armbands as a form of protest, as the Supreme Court held in *Tinker*, then it was difficult to avoid the conclusion that students could register a silent protest by remaining seated during the Pledge. Both were forms of symbolic speech, and students did not, as the Supreme Court insisted in *Tinker*, "shed their constitutional rights to freedom of speech or expression at the schoolhouse gate."[21]

Teachers' Rights

While students fought for the right to remain seated during the Pledge of Allegiance, teachers were battling for the right not to have to recite or lead it. Although *Barnette* established that students could not be compelled to recite the Pledge if they had conscientious objections, school districts generally did not recognize this principle as applicable to teachers. Teachers were expected to lead their class in the Pledge of Allegiance. Where teachers refused, they risked dismissal for failure to carry out their pedagogical duties.

On February 2, 1966, a ninth-grade social studies teacher in Nevada, Al Meinhold, stood in silence, hands at his side, during the flag salute at a school assembly. The thirty-three-year-old schoolteacher had voted for Lyndon Johnson in 1964 but had become disillusioned by the administration's escalation of the war in Vietnam. Meinhold organized the Southern Nevada Committee for Peace in Vietnam, one of many local "end the war" committees that were established across the country in the wake of the sustained U.S. bombing of North Vietnam that began early in 1965. After almost a year of heavy bombing of North Vietnam, President Johnson made a dramatic Christmas Eve announcement that the United States would halt the bombing in favor of a "peace offensive." But the raised hopes were soon dashed, and on January 30 the president announced that the bombing would resume. There would be no quick diplomatic end to the war. It was at the school assembly only a few days later that Al Meinhold engaged in his silent protest against U.S. policy in Vietnam.

Meinhold was a newcomer to Nevada, having moved there from New York in 1963. His Brooklyn accent, combined with his antiwar politics, helped clearly mark him as an outsider, a person to be watched carefully. One of the school's students did just that and reported the teacher's actions to his parents, who in turn went to the principal to demand Meinhold's ouster. The press got hold of the story, and soon the young teacher was engulfed in a raging controversy. At the local university he was hung in effigy. Others vilified him as "the scumbag who won't salute the flag." Meinhold was kicked out of his union by the local branch of the American Federation of Teachers. Later, when the national AFT pressed the local chapter to reinstate Meinhold, the membership, after a raucous debate "marked by frequent boos, hisses and catcalls directed at Meinhold," voted to secede from the AFT rather than accept Meinhold back into the fold. Meanwhile, the local post of the American Legion took legal action to prevent Meinhold from teaching in the district. The school board threatened to dismiss him if he failed again to salute the flag, and then, even though Meinhold agreed to continue to salute the flag, dismissed him anyway. In late 1966, the dismissal was overturned—although a few years later the district would fire Meinhold for allegedly telling his daughters that it was okay if they did not go to school on any given day.[22]

Such outbreaks of intolerance were not limited to the untamed West. In 1967, a Queens high school teacher was dismissed for refusing to lead his class in the Pledge of Allegiance. The teacher objected to reciting the Pledge on a number of different grounds, saying that it was "contrary to his personal convictions," that "rote repetition" of the words was "meaningless," and that it was a coercive loyalty oath. Seymour Jacobs, a teacher of French, linked the Pledge of Allegiance with militaristic patriotism and the war in Vietnam. Patriotism, he opined, contributed little to making life better for people. Far more valuable, he told the trial examiner, was "a sense of the world, [a] sense of the earth and a love for it and its people and animals." The trial examiner, prominent New York attorney Bethuel Webster, sided with the dismissed teacher and urged the board of education to reinstate Jacobs. Webster, who had been appointed by the board of education to arbitrate the case, noted that neither state law nor school regulations specifically required a teacher to lead his class in reciting the Pledge of Allegiance. Moreover, Webster noted that Supreme Court precedents suggested that schools must find ways of promoting patriotism in the schools that "do not impair the personal liberties of teachers."[23]

Jacobs got his job back, but the following spring, the New York state assembly showed its displeasure with Jacobs and the ruling by passing a bill that would require the firing of any teacher who refused to salute or pledge allegiance to the flag. Although the bill did not become law, increased attention to the matter led a number of schools to emphasize that the Pledge must be recited daily, as required by a 1962 state law. Among these schools was James Sperry High School in Henrietta, New York, which at the outset of the

1969–1970 school year let it be known that "all students and staff members [are] expected to salute the flag." At this school the Pledge of Allegiance was rendered every morning over the school's public address system, and students and teachers in the classrooms would join in reciting the Pledge. Susan Russo, a newly hired art teacher, shared homeroom responsibilities with another, more senior, teacher. The senior teacher, Catherine Adams, participated in the flag salute and Pledge of Allegiance each morning, while Russo faced the flag and stood silently, hands at her sides, in "respectful attention." This went on without incident for virtually the entire school year, until in April several students and parents informed the principal of Russo's behavior. The principal told his new art teacher that if she would not salute the flag and recite the Pledge of Allegiance, her contract would not be renewed. Russo responded that she could not in good conscience repeat the words of the Pledge since the nation was not currently a land of "liberty and justice for all."[24]

Had Russo been a student, there would have been no action taken against her. In fact, at the beginning of February the local school board had sent a directive to the area's principals reminding them that students must stand in respectful attention if they did not recite the Pledge of Allegiance. In the middle of April, shortly before the principal had met with Russo, the local school board, responding to the recent federal court ruling by Judge Judd, had actually reversed its ruling and announced that students with conscientious objections to the Pledge of Allegiance could remain seated. So at the very moment that a principal was proceeding to dismiss a teacher for standing in silence during the Pledge, students in Russo's classroom were free not only to stand in silence but also to leave the room or even remain seated. Indeed, the civilian flag code, as formulated in 1924 and endorsed by Congress in 1942, explicitly declared that during the flag salute, "full respect to the flag will always be shown when the pledge is given by merely standing at attention."[25]

Upon her dismissal, Russo filed suit in federal court, but her case was dismissed by a district judge who was unsympathetic to her claims that her First Amendment rights had been violated. The judge accepted uncritically the school board's contention that Russo's refusal to participate in the Pledge of Allegiance constituted a failure to follow school regulations and to perform her duties as a teacher and was therefore grounds for dismissal. Russo then appealed to the federal court of appeals, where she received a far more sympathetic hearing. Were Russo a student, the court observed, the case would be easily settled by the Supreme Court's *Barnette* ruling of thirty years before. But teachers were not students. She had "voluntarily assumed" the responsibility "to shape and to direct the still impressionable minds of her students in accordance with the policies of the school board." Still the court could see no compelling reason why teachers should have fewer constitutional rights than their students. Indeed the court noted that *Tinker* itself, though a case about student protest, had explicitly declared that neither teachers nor students "shed their constitutional rights to freedom of speech or expression at the schoolhouse gate." Moreover, since Russo's homeroom class participated in the Pledge of Allegiance each morning under the supervision of the senior instructor, the "state's interest in maintaining a flag salute program was well-served in Mrs. Russo's classroom, even without her participation in the pledge ceremonies." Russo, the court added, "made no attempt to proselytize her students," and there was no evidence that the teacher's silent protest "had any effect [and] certainly [not] a destructive effect . . . on Mrs. Russo's students." The court then shifted abruptly from legal reasoning to political exhortation. Had Russo not been fired, the court declared, it would "clearly have been evidence to her students that the injustice and intolerance against which she was quietly protesting was not merely not well-founded but a demonstrable falsehood at least within the confines of one school's homeroom class." Even the most sympathetic observer of the court's decision could be excused for wondering how permitting a teacher the liberty not to say the Pledge of Allegiance would demonstrate that the teacher was wrong to think that the United States was a society riddled with racial and economic injustices.[26]

The school board appealed to the United States Supreme Court, convinced of the rectitude of its course. In April 1973, the High Court announced that it would not hear the case, leaving the appeals court's judgment in place. But court rulings are not self-enforcing, and as the summer of 1973 came to a close Russo was still without a job in the school district, three years after being dismissed. Only after a federal court order at the end of August did the district at last reinstate Russo.[27]

The same double standard that Russo faced was applied in nearby Connecticut. In December 1969, the Roxbury school board, acting on the recommendation of the superintendent of schools, adopted a new policy requiring a daily Pledge of Allegiance in elementary and junior high schools. Although, as originally proposed, the policy had no exceptions, after public hearings the board agreed to include an exemption for students who had "religious or conscientious" objections. A middle school teacher, Nancy Hanover, promptly notified her principal that she could not lead her class in the Pledge of Allegiance because its final phrase was untrue since liberty and justice did not exist for minority groups. She arranged for a student to lead the class in reciting the Pledge, while she remained seated at her desk "with her head bowed." The school superintendent informed Hanover that it was her responsibility to lead the class in reciting the Pledge of Allegiance. When she refused she was suspended for insubordination and subsequently fired by the school board.[28]

The suspension and dismissal created a local furor. The playwright Arthur Miller and novelist William Styron were among the several dozens of local Roxbury residents who rallied to Hanover's cause by setting up a fund to defray the teacher's legal fees and affixing their names to a statement declaring that to prevent a person from abstaining from the Pledge of Allegiance was contrary not only to the Constitution's First Amendment guarantees but also to the Pledge's promise of liberty for all. Hanover went to federal court to recover her job. The judge, citing the Supreme Court's rulings in *Tinker* and *Barnette*, as well as Judge Judd's ruling in *Frain v. Baron*, noted that the legal trend was toward affording "an increasing measure of protection for the exercise of first amendment rights in the schoolhouse." And there was no question in the judge's mind that Hanover's refusal to lead the class in reciting the Pledge of Allegiance was "a form of expression protected by the first amendment which may not be forbidden at the risk of losing her job." That the expression took the form of silent protest did not make it any less protected constitutionally. Nor, the judge continued, was it relevant "whether her expression is attributable to a doubtful grammatical construction of the Pledge of Allegiance or outright disagreement with it." Whether she was correct in her interpretation did not matter from a constitutional perspective. Although school officials testified that they feared that Hanover's behavior might undermine "the maintenance of discipline" at the school, the record showed no evidence that these fears had been realized. The judge allowed that some of Hanover's students followed the teacher's example in refraining from the Pledge but endorsed Judge Judd's view that "the First Amendment protects successful dissent as well as ineffective protests." The school board, the judge concluded, had clearly violated Hanover's constitutional rights in dismissing her and so must reinstate her.[29]

The same conflict was playing out across the country. In 1970, in Broward County, Florida, a junior high school social studies teacher, Leroy Bates, was suspended for "gross insubordination" after refusing to recite the Pledge. Bates, an African American, regarded the Pledge as hypocritical since the nation was neither indivisible nor a land of liberty and justice for all. In Bates's view, the nation was moving "toward two societies, one black and one white." Refusing to participate in a lie, Bates stood outside while his class said the pledge. The

principal ordered Bates to supervise his class during the flag salute, but he refused. The all-white school board unanimously voted to uphold the suspension,
a decision that inflamed race relations in Broward County. Bates also lost his
job as a part-time counselor with the city recreation department. Although
reciting the Pledge was not part of his daily responsibilities as a counselor, the
recreation department, believing that Bates's refusal to salute the flag made him
a poor role model for children, insisted that he take a job that would not involve working directly with children. Bates got his teaching job back after a federal judge ordered the school board to reinstate him. The judge noted that previous court cases clearly indicated that a teacher was well within his or her
constitutional rights to refuse to recite the Pledge of Allegiance. "The school
board," the judge noted, "has known for some time it cannot dismiss this fellow for not saluting the flag."[30]

Thus, the various cases from the late 1960s and early 1970s pointed to an
emerging consensus in the legal community that teachers had a constitutional
right to refuse to lead or recite the Pledge of Allegiance. But the judicial rulings did nothing to prevent state legislatures from passing bills that required
teachers to salute the flag and recite the Pledge. Indeed the judicial rulings of
1969 and 1970 seemed to spawn a legislative backlash. In the spring of 1970,
for instance, the Maryland legislature passed a bill making the Pledge of Allegiance mandatory for teachers as well as students unless the individual had "religious reasons" for not reciting it. The Maryland governor signed the bill into
law in May 1970 but at the same time recommended that there be a court test
of the bill. He justified signing the bill as a way to settle the legal questions
"once and for all" rather than have the bill "make the rounds in the legislature
again next year." The governor got his wish, as a teacher was waiting in the
wings with a challenge to the new law.[31]

August L. Lundquist was a Baltimore high school teacher and an ideal lit-
igant. He was a World War II veteran, a naval reservist who had volunteered to
be placed on active duty during the Korean War, and an active Boy Scout, first
as a youth and then as a father. He was articulate and politically sophisticated.
His aim as a social studies teacher, he explained to the court, was "to teach all
students about the democratic principles which make this country great." And
what made America a great and democratic country, in Lundquist's view, was
that love of country was a matter of individual choice, not something compelled
by the government. "To force patriotism . . . on anyone," he explained, was "extremely repulsive" and contrary to the principles of the nation he held so dear.
Ultimately, it was also "an act of futility[,] for patriotism is something you feel,

something you believe, something you do as you are a part of your country, but it is something that cannot be forced." After "much soul searching," the veteran teacher concluded that he could not in good conscience lead his students in a ceremony that he regarded as antithetical to his teaching and to America's democratic principles. His protest was not against particular words or even government policies but against prescribed, compelled patriotism, a patriotism not of the heart but of government edict.[32]

Lundquist's suit found a sympathetic audience in the courtroom. A circuit court judge quickly struck down the mandatory Pledge law as unconstitutional, and then, when the state appealed, the judge's ruling was upheld by the Maryland Court of Appeals. The state of Maryland argued that its new law, by allowing for religious exemptions, was crafted in a way consistent with the holding in *Barnette*. For, by the state's count, at least six of the justices in *Barnette* understood the "decisional issue" as freedom of religion. The appeals court, echoing the circuit judge, disagreed. While acknowledging the emphasis on religious liberty in the concurring opinions, the court maintained that the religious liberty was best understood as "supplementary" to Jackson's free speech rationale rather than as mutually exclusive. The court found no evidence in the concurring opinions that the concurring judges rejected the free speech rationale articulated in Jackson's majority opinion. And absent such direct evidence, the appeals court argued that the rationale of *Barnette* must control their decision. Therefore the new law mandating that teachers and students participate in the Pledge of Allegiance was unconstitutional.[33]

The five-member appeals court was not united on the ruling, however. One judge strongly dissented from the decision to invalidate the mandatory Pledge law. The holding in *Barnette*, the dissenting judge insisted, was limited to schoolchildren with religious objections. Maryland's 1970 statute, which allowed for religious exemptions, was thus perfectly consistent with the Supreme Court's narrow holding in *Barnette*, a holding that had been obscured for decades by the "high-flown and sometimes fanciful rhetoric" of Justice Jackson. The judge also suggested that *Barnette*'s "extraordinary departure" from precedent (specifically the 1940 Supreme Court ruling in *Gobitis*) was "close to judicial irresponsibility" and was "an added reason" why *Barnette*'s holding should not be extended. Moreover, contrary to assertions by the majority, *Barnette* had caused serious harm to the nation: "Not only has national unity been gravely impaired to an unprecedented extent during the 30-year period [since *Barnette*], but desecration, abuse and contempt for the flag and, indeed, for American institutions and ideals have substantially increased." As further evidence, he pointed to a recent attempt "to destroy the Nation's Capitol," as well as to the "more than 2,000,000 young men—otherwise qualified for the military service of their country—[who] have refused such service on grounds of supposed 'concientious [*sic*] scruples' not resulting from any religious belief or teaching." This "extraordinary lack of patriotism on the part of this many of the Republic's younger citizens" suggested to the judge that "a case might well be made for a finding of a 'clear and present danger' to the Nation resulting from the lack of proper patriotic training in the public schools of this state and the public schools of other states." If further reason for not extending *Barnette* was needed, the judge added that First Amendment freedoms were restrictions on the federal government, not on state governments. No matter that the Supreme Court had held otherwise decades ago. Judge Wilson Barnes's dissent was passionate, but his was a decidedly eccentric voice crying out in the judicial wilderness. No other federal or state justice during this period took the view that states had the power to compel teachers to recite the Pledge of Allegiance.[34]

Dukakis's Veto of the 1977 Flag Salute Law

When, in 1977, the Massachusetts legislature passed a law requiring teachers to recite the Pledge of Allegiance, the state of constitutional law on this question was reasonably clear: Teachers and students had a constitutional right not to participate in the Pledge of Allegiance.[35] So when Governor Michael Dukakis asked the Supreme Judicial Court of Massachusetts to render an advisory opinion on the constitutionality of the bill, the answer he received did not surprise those people familiar with the law. Certainly it did not surprise Dukakis, who had expressed "grave doubts" about the constitutionality of the bill, as had the state's attorney general.[36]

Since 1935, Massachusetts state law had required that a teacher "cause the pupils under his charge to salute the flag and recite [the Pledge of Allegiance] in unison with him" at least once a week. The 1977 bill changed the wording of that sentence to read that "each teacher at the commencement of the first class of each day in all grades in all public schools shall lead the class in a group recitation of the 'Pledge of Allegiance to the Flag.'" Massachusetts public school teachers and students, in other words, had been required by statute to salute the flag and pledge allegiance for more than forty years. All the statute really changed was to require a daily rather than a weekly pledge. Although the language about the teacher's role in directing the Pledge was more unambigu-

ous in the 1977 version, the 1935 version also required the teacher to participate in and lead the class in reciting the Pledge of Allegiance. The statutory
punishment for noncompliance by a teacher remained unchanged from the
1935 law: a fine of about fifty cents a day. The real compulsion, however, was
the threat of the loss of one's job for failing to follow school board rules.[37]

Although the change in law was minimal—and its effects even less so since
many Massachusetts public schools already recited the Pledge daily—that did
not mean the new law was any more constitutional than the old one. As the
Massachusetts high court pointed out, the question posed to it was an unusual
one since the "constitutional problems which are apparent in the proposed
amendment . . . are present in [the law] as it now exists." The Massachusetts
high court acknowledged that the U.S. Supreme Court had never ruled directly
on the question of whether a teacher could be compelled to recite the Pledge
of Allegiance, but, like every other court that had considered the question, the
Massachusetts justices concluded that there was no reason to doubt that "the
rationale of the *Barnette* opinion applies as well to teachers as it does to students." Since the statute clearly infringed on the First Amendment rights of
teachers, it was necessary for the state to show that it had "a countervailing interest which is sufficiently compelling to justify its action." Instilling "attitudes
of patriotism and loyalty" in young people was a commendable purpose, but
since there were alternative ways of achieving the same end without compro-
mising the constitutional rights of teachers, the court concluded that the bill
would fail to pass constitutional muster.[38]

However, two of the seven justices on the Massachusetts high court, Francis Quirico and Robert Braucher, disagreed with their colleagues. Quirico and
Braucher had both been appointed to the court by Dukakis's immediate predecessor, Republican governor Francis Sargent (whom Dukakis defeated in
1974). Both judges were World War II veterans and self-professed conservatives. Both felt that the court "must be ever mindful that judicial inquiry does
not extend to the expediency, wisdom, or necessity of the legislative judgment."
Justices Quirico and Braucher accepted the majority's premise that *Barnette*
stood for the proposition that those with moral objections to the flag salute,
whether teacher or student, could not be compelled to recite the Pledge. But
while accepting the controlling power of *Barnette,* Quirico and Braucher preferred to construe the bill as providing only "an opportunity for voluntary participation by students and teachers in a pledge of allegiance." Since this was essentially how the previous statute had been treated for the past thirty-plus years,
the two dissenters did not see any reason why the new statute should not be

understood in the same way. "The proposed amendment," they concluded, "introduces no constitutional difficulty not found in the present statute."[39]

In 1988, the Dukakis campaign tried to defend the governor's decision by emphasizing that he could not, in good conscience, have signed a bill he knew to be unconstitutional—he simply had no choice but to veto the bill. Bush responded by pointing to the example of Illinois Republican governor Jim Thompson who, the vice president said, had faced the same choice as Dukakis but had found a way to sign the bill. Bush was correct that in 1979 the Illinois state legislature had passed a bill requiring that the Pledge of Allegiance "be recited each school day by pupils in elementary educational institutions supported or maintained in whole or in part by public funds." But what Bush did not tell audiences at the campaign stops was that the Massachusetts and Illinois statutes were significantly different. The Illinois law said nothing about requiring teachers to participate in the Pledge of Allegiance, nor did it attach any penalties to noncompliance on the part of teachers, as the Massachusetts statute did. The Illinois statute was most sensibly construed not as an effort to make the Pledge of Allegiance compulsory for each public elementary school student, but rather as requiring each public elementary school classroom to conduct the Pledge of Allegiance ceremony daily. Unlike the Massachusetts law, the Illinois law did not seek to punish individuals who exercised their constitutional rights not to participate in the daily ceremony.[40]

Such distinctions, however, did not deter the Bush campaign from pressing its advantage on the Pledge of Allegiance. Dukakis tried to counter by alleging that Bush was not fit to be president if he would sign a bill he knew to be unconstitutional. The Massachusetts governor also attempted to tie Bush's position on the flag salute law—that he would have signed it and left it to the courts to decide on its constitutionality—to a larger pattern of illegalities and disregard for the Constitution in the Reagan administration, most notably Iran-Contra. But Dukakis's effort to redirect the attacks by redefining the problem fell flat. Bush immediately seized upon Dukakis's counterattack as an opportunity to intensify his own attacks and elevate the issue's prominence.

As Republican operatives had grasped early on, Bush had placed Dukakis in a no-win situation: Ignore the attacks and appear to cede the argument, or combat the attacks and keep the issue on the front pages. Symbolism, they knew, would trump legalism. Careful analysis of the legal precedents would lead an impartial observer to the conclusion that, absent a major change in direction by the United States Supreme Court, federal courts would vindicate Dukakis's contention that it was unconstitutional to require teachers to participate in the Pledge of Allegiance ceremony. This fact did not help Dukakis, however, because the overwhelming majority of Americans believed that not only teachers but students as well should be compelled to recite the Pledge.[41] Thus, Dukakis could win the legal argument and still lose the political fight. Indeed, by appealing to the law, Dukakis played right into Bush's hands since Bush's contention was not just that the governor's veto was a mistake but that liberal lawyers and soft judges had lost touch with the American people and American values. That the legal system would prevent states from mandating the Pledge of Allegiance was itself a mark of the poverty of contemporary liberalism.

"What is it about the Pledge of Allegiance that upsets him so much?" Bush asked to roars of approval at a partisan rally in late August. The following day, Bush suggested that Dukakis's "fervent opposition to the pledge is symbolic of an entire attitude best summed up in four little letters: ACLU." Dukakis's veto of the Pledge, Bush intimated throughout the campaign, was a symptom of the pathologies of the left—a left that was ashamed of patriotism and prayer, questioned authority, rejected discipline, was weak on national defense, and let murderers and rapists out of jail. For Democrats and much of the mainstream press, the Pledge of Allegiance was a cynical distraction from the real issues of the campaign—jobs, taxes, the economy, the environment, and so on—but for many Republicans the Pledge of Allegiance symbolized a fundamental cultural divide between liberals and conservatives. Although the Republicans had controlled the White House for the previous eight years and sixteen of the last twenty, Bush and his allies worked tirelessly (and successfully) to cast the election as a "referendum on liberalism," and Dukakis's veto of the Pledge was a perfect symbol for all that was wrong with the permissive, liberal mindset of the late 1960s and 1970s. The Pledge of Allegiance, the words of which proclaimed the United States to be "one nation, indivisible," had become a partisan wedge issue.[42]

ONE NATION . . . INDIVISIBLE?

The 1988 campaign was replete with irony. There was, to begin with, the irony that the Pledge was made a central campaign issue by a man who, as a child, had attended an exclusive private school where it was not recited. Meanwhile, Dukakis, the son of immigrants, had attended Massachusetts public schools where the Pledge was said regularly, if not daily. There was also the irony of a presidential candidate cloaking himself in a political tradition with which he sometimes seemed to have only the most passing acquaintance. So, for instance, on August 24 Bush told a partisan crowd that "it is very hard for me to imagine that the Founding Fathers—Samuel Adams and John Adams and John Hancock—would have objected to teachers leading students in the Pledge of Allegiance to the flag of the United States. I just don't believe that was their concept when they wrote the Constitution of our great country."[1] Of course, neither of the Adamses nor Hancock were among the Massachusetts delegates at the Constitutional convention who helped to write the Constitution. But these ironies are dwarfed by the central irony of the 1988 campaign—that a pledge that celebrates an "indivisible" nation was used as a partisan "wedge issue," designed to divide and conquer the Democratic coalition.

Ronald Reagan and the Pledge

Although Bush was the first presidential candidate to use the Pledge of Allegiance for blatantly partisan purposes, his predecessor, Ronald Reagan, had done much to inject the Pledge into national politics. Reagan invoked the Pledge of Allegiance more than any previous president. In April 1982, speaking before the National Catholic Education Association in Chicago, Reagan lamented that "the Pledge of Allegiance [was] now missing from too many of our classrooms." Reagan most commonly invoked the Pledge in the context of a broader argument about God's central role in the American political tradition. Typical were his remarks at a White House ceremony marking a national day of prayer on May 6, 1982, in which he observed that "prayer is still a powerful force in America, and our faith in God is a mighty source of strength. Our Pledge of Allegiance states that we are 'one nation under God.'" Two weeks later, in a message to Congress that accompanied a proposed constitutional amendment on prayer in school, Reagan pointed to the Pledge of Allegiance as an example of the way in which the nation had long "acknowledged God's guidance" in public affairs. In September of the same year, on the Jewish holiday of Rosh Hashanah, Reagan addressed the nation by radio on the power of prayer. People came to America, Reagan said, from many different parts of the world, but "all of them . . . came here with prayers on their lips and faith in their hearts. It's because of this shared faith that we've become, in the words of the Pledge of Allegiance, 'one Nation under God, indivisible, with liberty and justice for all.'"[2]

Reagan picked up this theme again in 1984. In February he addressed the nation by radio, focusing specifically on the need for prayer in schools. In building the case for a constitutional amendment allowing voluntary prayer, the president again pointed to the references to God in the Pledge of Allegiance as evidence of God's place in America's public life. He returned to the theme on August 23, the day he accepted the Republican nomination for president. Speaking at an ecumenical prayer breakfast in Dallas, he deplored the efforts to remove religion from public life, singling out legal suits that had been brought "to abolish the words 'under God' from the Pledge of Allegiance and to remove 'In God We Trust' from public documents and from our currency." The truth, Reagan concluded, is that

> politics and morality are inseparable. And as morality's foundation is religion, religion and politics are necessarily related. We need religion as a guide. We need it because we are imperfect, and our government needs the church, because only those humble enough to admit they're sinners can bring to democracy the tolerance it re-

quires in order to survive. . . . Without God, there is no virtue, because there's no prompting of the conscience. . . . Without God, there is a coarsening of the society. And without God, democracy will not and cannot long endure. If we ever forget that we're one nation under God, then we will be a nation gone under.

For Reagan, the Pledge of Allegiance's reference to the United States as a nation under God was no empty phrase but a fundamental statement about the importance of God and religion in the definition of the American nation.[3]

Reagan linked the Pledge of Allegiance not only to prayer in public school but also to education reform. In May 1987, Reagan highlighted success stories like Chambers Elementary School in Cleveland, where students were improving despite the poverty and economic hardship of the students. How did the school do it? Well, to begin with, the principal of the school began every morning by reciting the Pledge of Allegiance over the public address system. In fact, Reagan observed, "Secretary [of Education] William Bennett tells me that one of the most striking things that he's learned in his many visits to our nation's classrooms is that those schools which instill a sense of patriotism in their students by saying the Pledge of Allegiance or singing 'The Star-Spangled Banner' invariably are the most successful." Patriotism and moral virtue bred excellence and academic achievement. Four years earlier, when Reagan went to speak to the annual convention of the American Federation of Teachers, he again highlighted the special place of the Pledge in American schools. At this venue he did not claim it made better students, but he did insist it made better citizens, especially among the children of new immigrants. It was in schools, Reagan reminded the AFT, where "most Americans heard and spoke the Pledge of Allegiance for the first time [and] that transformed those heart-stirring words into a living ideal." And it was schools that "provided the social bond that gave meaning to the word 'America'—that made us, in the midst of our ethnic diversity, 'one nation under God, indivisible, with liberty and justice for all.'"[4]

The Pledge also was woven into Reagan's campaign appearances. In September 1982 he came to New Jersey to help Republican congresswoman and U.S. Senate candidate Millicent Fenwick in her ultimately unsuccessful battle against Frank Lautenberg. As part of his brief campaign swing, the president visited a swearing-in ceremony where he led seventy-seven new citizens in reciting the Pledge of Allegiance. In October 1984, a month before the general election, Reagan made a conspicuous appearance at a naturalization ceremony in Detroit, where fifteen hundred newly naturalized citizens recited the Pledge. Reagan told the new citizens that the Pledge contained "the best definition of our country, it contains our greatest hope: to always remain 'one nation under God, indivisible, with liberty and justice for all.'" The following day, at a campaign rally in Brownsville, Texas, to chants of "four more years," Reagan recalled the "very moving experience" he had witnessed the previous day in which "1,548 new citizens, . . . the oldest of them . . . 92 and the youngest . . . only two, took the Pledge of Allegiance for the first time." These new citizens, Reagan said, "spoke with such a belief, and [hearing them] I thought that this is still—and will . . . always [be]—'one nation, under God, with liberty and justice for all.'" As he sometimes did, Reagan inadvertently dropped "indivisible" from the last clause of the Pledge.[5]

Reagan was fond of reciting the Pledge of Allegiance in public. In 1983 the president used a White House ceremony celebrating Flag Day to lead the audience in reciting the Pledge of Allegiance. At a Flag Day ceremony in 1985 in Baltimore, Reagan remarked: "I always get a chill up and down my spine when I say that Pledge of Allegiance." The president, plugging the "Pause for the Pledge of Allegiance" program that had been dreamed up by the National Flag Day Foundation, asked that "everyone here will join us and Americans all across the country when we pause for that pledge tonight." On Flag Day in 1986, Reagan gave a radio address in which he again asked the country to "join Nancy and me and millions of other Americans at 7 o'clock this evening . . . when we pause a few minutes to say the Pledge of Allegiance." The following year he again used his weekly radio address to plug the "Pause for the Pledge" program and to ask that America join Nancy and him in saying the Pledge. "The 31 words of the Pledge of Allegiance to our flag," Reagan said, "takes only a moment to recite, yet their meaning reaches across the many decades of our history as a free people." And on the occasion of the Bicentennial of the Constitution, Reagan, flanked by four youths, including the national winner of the spelling bee, led a recitation of the Pledge of Allegiance on the steps of the U.S. Capitol that was broadcast across the nation. "Everybody watching and listening throughout the land" was invited to join the president in reciting "the words that we all know by heart." And in the final months of his presidency, in July 1988, he began a speech to the Student Congress on Evangelism by asking that they all stand and join him in reciting the Pledge of Allegiance.[6]

Reagan also had no qualms about using the Pledge of Allegiance against Dukakis as he stumped for Bush. In countless campaign rallies between August and November 1988, Reagan pounded away on the Pledge of Allegiance as a defining difference between Republicans and Democrats, Bush and Dukakis. The Republican party, Reagan declared in a campaign rally in Texas just days before the election, was "the party of working people; the family; the neighborhood; the defense of freedom; and, yes, the American flag and the Pledge of Allegiance to 'one nation under God.'" The Democrats, in contrast, were "the party of 'no'—'no' to holding a line on taxes, 'no' to spending cuts, 'no' to the line-item veto, 'no' to the balanced budget amendment, 'no' to the Pledge of Allegiance, 'no' to the death penalty, 'no' to tough-minded judges, 'no' to the school prayer amendment, 'no' to the right to life, and 'no' to adequate defense spending." One of Reagan's oft-used lines on the hustings was that while the nation had come a long way during the previous eight years, if the Democrats won the election, "everything could be lost faster than you can say the Pledge of Allegiance." Like Bush, Reagan framed the contest as a referendum on liberalism, and no issue more clearly laid bare the poverty of liberalism than liberals' lukewarm attitude toward the Pledge of Allegiance. [7]

The Partisan Pledge

It would be a mistake to assume that the Pledge was a political innocent before Bush and Reagan. In the mid-1960s in New Jersey, for instance, the Republican gubernatorial nominee Wayne Dumont promised that if elected he would push for legislation that would make the Pledge compulsory in public schools. Dumont's call placed his Democratic opponent, Governor Richard Hughes, on the defensive. Against the backdrop of escalating antiwar protests, including militant student teach-ins at Rutgers University,[8] the incumbent governor had to explain why he would veto a bill promoting the Pledge of Allegiance. Much as Dukakis did in 1988, Hughes counterattacked by scolding his Republican opponent for pushing legislation that was plainly unconstitutional. Hughes said his opponent's position "smacks of the McCarthy syndrome" and declared that he would not "abuse the religious freedom of small children and violate his constitutional oath in order to stir false patriotism." Like Bush more than twenty years later, Dumont was not interested in legal precedents but rather in dramatizing what he perceived as his opponent's pale patriotism. Dumont believed that Communists were behind the antiwar protests, and he saw the Pledge as a way of inculcating patriotism and thereby inoculating the young against Communist subversion. For Dumont, the Pledge was also a way to dramatize the defining difference between himself and his opponent, namely that unlike Dumont the "Governor doesn't understand the danger of Communism." Voters evidently disagreed, reelecting Hughes in a historic landslide.[9]

Prior to the 1980s, however, these sorts of partisan fights over the Pledge were rare. Student protests about race and about Vietnam did, as we saw in the previous chapter, sometimes focus on the Pledge, but the partisan implications were at first muted. Student refusals to recite the Pledge were perceived as part of a division between the youth and their elders, the Movement and the Establishment, but only slowly did attitudes toward the Pledge of Allegiance begin to take on the sharp partisan overtones that characterized the 1988 campaign.

Even when Dukakis vetoed the Pledge bill in 1977, his veto never became particularly controversial. The senate and assembly unanimously overrode the veto, and that was pretty much the end of it. To be sure, Dukakis was dealt a stunning setback the following year in the Democratic primary when he lost to Edward King, but the Pledge of Allegiance was never made an issue by King or by others. Nor did the veto surface as an issue in Dukakis's subsequent gubernatorial campaigns in 1982 and 1986.

But during the 1980s there were clear signs that the Pledge of Allegiance was becoming more politicized and that it could be successfully exploited for partisan gain. President Reagan stressed the importance of the Pledge of Allegiance in a way that no previous United States president had done and made patriotism a central motif of his partisan appeal, particularly in the 1984 campaign that was awash with American flags.[10] Other events across the country prefigured the polarized Pledge politics of the 1988 presidential campaign, including in Dukakis's liberal hometown of Brookline, where the Pledge became embroiled in controversy only a year after Dukakis had reclaimed the governorship by defeating King in a primary rematch in 1982.

Town meetings in Brookline had traditionally opened with a prayer, but in 1983 the prayer was dropped. A disappointed town meeting member (the town has 250 elected meeting members) asked if the Pledge of Allegiance could take the place of a prayer, but the request was rejected. The following year the town meeting members agreed to begin sessions by singing "The Star Spangled Banner" but refused to add the Pledge of Allegiance. Each year throughout the rest of the 1980s and into the early 1990s proponents of the Pledge pushed for town meetings to open with a recital of the Pledge of Allegiance, but each year they were defeated. Proponents of the Pledge argued that it demonstrated "the patriotic unity of Brookline residents" and warned that by refusing the Pledge "you may well bring down upon our townspeople the wrath, scorn and indignation of an outraged nation." Opponents, on the other hand, likened the Pledge to the loyalty oaths of Nazi Germany. They were concerned that by beginning town meetings with the Pledge, the town would "possibly [be] holding up to opprobrium people who don't stand and do it." There was no need, opponents of the Pledge argued, for "requiring anyone to prove their patriotism." The conflict became increasingly acrimonious—the leading proponent of the Pledge called those who opposed the Pledge a "perverted" minority—and candidates who opposed the Pledge found themselves the target of anonymously circulated negative campaign literature. The Pledge of Allegiance, as one town meeting member ruefully observed, has "been a bitter, nasty and divisive issue." The standoff persisted for a decade until a compromise was reached in 1992, whereby the meeting's moderator would lead a recitation of the Pledge of Allegiance fifteen minutes before the town meeting began, thereby allowing those who did not wish to recite the Pledge to opt out inconspicuously.[11]

On the other side of the country, in Berkeley, California, a similar drama was being played out. In 1971, at the height of the protests against the Vietnam War, a sharply divided Berkeley city council decided not to recite the Pledge of Allegiance at the beginning of its meetings. According to press reports, council members who tried to say the Pledge were drowned out by audience members yelling, "Power to the people." For the next thirteen years, the Pledge of Allegiance was absent from council meetings. In 1983, however, a flag-burning incident at a protest against the Reagan administration's invasion of Grenada sparked calls to reinstate the Pledge of Allegiance at council meetings. The city council ignored these pleas, leading the Alameda County board of supervisors to exclude Berkeley from a seat on a county board responsible for allocating federal dollars for job training. It took the intervention of a federal district judge in May 1984 to reverse the county's order. A week after the federal court ruling, however, the city council crafted a compromise measure that returned the Pledge of Allegiance to the council chambers. The Pledge of Allegiance would be recited annually at the beginning of the council's first meeting of the year. It could also be recited at other meetings if requested by a Council member "in order to commemorate an occasion of national significance."[12]

In the New York state legislature, the conflict was openly partisan. In February 1983, assembly Republicans proposed to have legislators recite the Pledge of Allegiance at the beginning of each day's session. The Democrats, who controlled the state assembly by a large margin, defeated the measure on a party-line vote: 88 Democrats opposed, 51 Republicans in favor. Democrats insisted that such a Pledge was "superfluous," since members already "take an oath of office to defend the United States and the State Constitution." The Democratic assembly leader acknowledged, however, that some Democrats had cast their votes with great trepidation, fearing that the votes would be used against them in future campaigns. Republicans strenuously denied any partisan motives, a claim met by "loud groans" from the Democratic side of the aisle. In 1987 Republicans were back again with the same proposal, and were met with the same result, though this time a number of Democrats ducked the vote rather than cast a potentially costly vote against the Pledge. As one Democrat explained, "I left and stood outside the door . . . because it would kill me back home" to be seen to be voting against the Pledge. Democrats who tried to explain the vote sounded a tad defensive. "And we don't sing 'God Bless America' or 'The Star Spangled Banner' either," explained one.[13]

Democrats were right to be nervous. In 1983 there had been little political fallout after the vote, but in 1987 the political temperature seemed considerably higher. Letters to the editor registered some of the intense displeasure with the assembly's action. Two representatives of the Knights of Columbus, for instance, expressed "incredulity" that the assembly would reject the Pledge of Allegiance. "The Pledge of Allegiance," the Knights wrote, "not only expresses our patriotism and love of our country; it reinforces that love." They urged the "citizenry to awaken our elected officials to their responsibilities and to realize how dastardly and perfidious it is to prefer party to country." Veterans groups heeded that call and communicated their displeasure to the assembly. Further increasing the pressure on assembly Democrats was the decision by the Republican-controlled state senate to begin reciting the Pledge at the beginning of each day. After several months, the Democrats relented and decided to make recitation of the Pledge of Allegiance a part of the assembly's daily business, though not before an acrimonious two-hour debate on the floor of the assembly. "We are not children," declared a Democratic representative from Manhattan who was one of only two legislators (the other was also a Democrat from Manhattan) to oppose the daily recitation of the Pledge. "Having us stand each day to recite the Pledge of Allegiance is not going to contribute one iota to our patriotism." Some opponents of the Pledge believed that requiring a daily display of loyalty was an act better befitting an authoritarian regime than a democracy, but to a Republican legislator from Schenectady the real threat to democracy stemmed from those who opposed reciting the Pledge: "People who keep quiet about their beliefs—those are Hitler's people." And on that edifying note the Pledge of Allegiance was made a permanent part of the New York state assembly's daily business.[14]

These conflicts over the Pledge of Allegiance during the 1980s in New York, Massachusetts, and California show that partisan feuding about the Pledge predated the 1988 campaign. But if George H. W. Bush was not the first to discover the partisan possibilities of the Pledge of Allegiance, his 1988 campaign provided the most dramatic demonstration of the political potency of the Pledge as a symbol and weapon in the culture wars. After 1988, the Pledge of Allegiance would be injected into national, state, and local politics in ways that would have been largely unimaginable before.

The Politics of the Pledge after 1988

Bush's focus on the Pledge of Allegiance resulted in the Pledge, for the first time in its history, becoming a plank in a party platform. The 1988 Republican platform committed the party to "protect[ing] the Pledge of Allegiance in all schools as a reminder of the values which must be at the core of learning for a free society." Four years later, the Pledge again made its way into the Republican platform, though now the party's backing of the Pledge of Allegiance emphasized the importance of religion. The party now advocated "recitation of the Pledge of Allegiance in schools as a reminder of the principles that sustain us as one Nation under God."[15]

In September 1988, Republicans in Congress took their cue from their party's presidential nominee by introducing a resolution requiring the Pledge of Allegiance to be said at the opening of each day's session. This was not the first time that this idea had been broached in Congress. Way back in 1954, on the day that Eisenhower signed the "under God" clause into law, Representative Lester Holtzman of New York had introduced a resolution to amend the rules of the House so that the Pledge of Allegiance would immediately follow the chaplain's prayer at the opening of each day's session.[16] But Holtzman's proposal was ignored—the Pledge of Allegiance was for kids, not for the highest elected officials in the land. In the heat of the 1988 presidential campaign, however, it was no longer possible for Congress to ignore the Pledge.

The 1988 proposal came from a thirty-one-year-old Connecticut Republican, John G. Rowland (he subsequently became a three-term governor of Connecticut, and his political career came to a spectacular close in 2004 when he resigned to avoid being impeached for lying about gifts he accepted from friends as well as from state contractors and employees), and the proposal clearly caught the unsuspecting Democrats off guard. At first the Democrats tried to rule it out of order (as indeed it was, since changes in House rules are reported out by the Rules Committee), but Republicans succeeded in forcing a vote on the ruling, thereby sticking Democrats with the unhappy choice of either appearing to vote against the Pledge or seeming to repudiate the position of their party's presidential nominee. Democratic leaders kept their troops in line, with only seven Democrats defecting, and sustained the procedural ruling. But many Democrats, particularly those from moderate and conservative districts, were reportedly "howling" at being maneuvered into an anti-Pledge vote. Republicans gloated at the political discomfort they were causing Democrats. One Republican leadership aide explained, "We wanted to put them on the hot seat, particularly southern Democrats who don't feel the same way as Dukakis." Anxious to minimize the partisan damage, Speaker of the House Jim Wright convened an emergency meeting with Democratic leaders to devise a strategic response. Wright defended the correctness of the procedural ruling on the House floor but announced that, starting the following week, he would appoint members to lead the House in reciting the Pledge until which time as the House rules could be formally changed. And to a standing ovation from House Democrats he scolded Republicans for using the Pledge for partisan advantage: "All of us embrace the Pledge of Allegiance," he told the House. "But it is important for all of us to recognize that the Pledge of Allegiance to the flag is something intended to unite us, it's not intended to divide us. . . . Patriotism knows no political party." However, Wright was not above partisanship himself. When, on the following Tuesday, Mississippi Democrat Sonny Montgomery led the Pledge on the House floor in front of some fifty representatives, the House television cameras, which the Democratic majority controlled, spotlighted only the Democrats reciting the Pledge.[17]

Although the House rules have yet to be changed, the Pledge of Allegiance continues to be recited daily, immediately after the chaplain's prayer. It is hard to imagine any House member challenging the Pledge of Allegiance, especially since few members are even present when it is recited in the morning. One brave or foolhardy Democrat did, and his comments brought down a hailstorm of criticism. The culprit was Texas Democrat Henry Gonzalez, who in 1993 compared the Pledge of Allegiance to the practice in Nazi Germany. The House, he said, was "like a good little herd, reminiscent of the Hitlerian period: 'Sieg Heil, Sieg Heil.'" Angry Republicans asked for the Democratic leadership to reprimand or censure Gonzalez, but Gonzalez was anything but contrite: "What they want to do is punish thought, not behavior. . . . It must have hit pretty close to those goose-steppers."[18]

That the Pledge of Allegiance would be established first in the highly polarized and partisan House of Representatives is not surprising. In the Senate, where there is, or at least was, some modicum of interparty collegiality, the

Pledge took longer to become an established practice. During the 1988 campaign there was no effort in the Senate to follow the House's lead. It was not until over a decade later, in June 1999, that the United States Senate initiated the practice of beginning the day by reciting the Pledge of Allegiance. Again the proposal emanated from a Republican, the Senate's most conservative member, New Hampshire's Bob Smith. At the time Smith introduced the Pledge resolution, he was in the midst of a quixotic run for the Republican presidential nomination. Democrats wisely put up no resistance, and the Senate, with little fanfare, unanimously adopted Smith's resolution.[19]

Democrats had evidently learned from the Dukakis debacle that the Pledge of Allegiance was a political third rail. Elected officials could not afford to be seen as anti-Pledge. The political damage that could result from being on the wrong side of the Pledge was evident in a nasty political spat in Wisconsin that contributed to the unseating of first-term state legislator Sarah Waukau in November 2000. Waukau had stunned the state's political establishment by winning a special election in April 1999, becoming the first Democrat to carry the solidly Republican 35th Assembly District since it was redrawn after the 1970 census. Democrats hailed Waukau's victory as "historic," auguring "the resurgence of the Democratic party in the Assembly." Republicans downplayed the significance of the loss—their first loss of a seat in a Wisconsin special election since 1993—but immediately targeted Waukau, who had prevailed by a mere 216 votes over her Republican opponent, as a vulnerable seat they could take back in 2000.[20]

Waukau had prevailed by using a populist campaign, promising to "fight for the north," while also carefully positioning herself as a social moderate, a posture designed to appeal to a district with little sympathy for Madison-style liberalism. One of her first staff appointments, however, was twenty-five-year-old Jamie Kuhn, who had been a staffer for the assembly's Democratic caucus. Kuhn was also a member of the Dane County Board of Supervisors, representing the left-leaning town of Madison. Although board elections were nonpartisan, the thirty-nine-member board was sharply polarized between conservatives, who were overwhelmingly Republican, and liberals or progressives, who were almost entirely Democrats. Relations were particularly testy between the newly elected, outspoken Kuhn and the cantankerous and no less outspoken retired Air Force colonel Don Heiliger, who had been a prisoner of war in North Vietnam for six years and a thorn in the side of liberals ever since his election to the board in the early 1990s. Heiliger was particularly angered by the refusal of Kuhn and another board member to recite the Pledge at the opening of board meetings. But despite considerable public badgering, Heiliger was unable to change the behavior of the two youngest board members, both of whom had strong ties to the Madison student community.[21]

Conservatives on the board sensed a political opportunity to embarrass what they saw as the "blame America first" crowd and strengthen the conservative slate that was being readied for the following spring's board elections. In July 1999, county supervisor Dave Wiganowsky, a politically ambitious Republican and a strong conservative, talked openly with a newspaper editorial board about plans to make a political issue of the fact that two liberal members stood silently when the Pledge was recited. Within a month the conservative supervisors had devised a plan. Heiliger would use his connections with veterans groups to obtain the names and addresses of veterans who lived in Waukau's district in northern Wisconsin and then write a letter to the veterans informing them that Waukau had on her staff a person who refused to say the Pledge of Allegiance. Heiliger wrote, "I am outraged by those who take their freedom for granted, so much so that even as elected officials they would openly defy our nation in this manner. . . . I find it very disturbing that Ms. Waukau would hire an individual who feels that hostility toward her own nation is a value worth promoting." Heiliger urged veterans to write to their local newspapers and contact local media to call attention to the outrage. Heiliger's outrage over Kuhn's behavior was deeply felt and genuine. But the method selected was carefully calculated to maximize partisan advantage. The aim was not only to embarrass and punish Kuhn but to tar Waukau with the same unpatriotic brush and thereby help Republicans regain her seat. The executive director of the state Republican party denied knowing anything about the letter but wasn't about to distance the party from it. "It certainly is a fair issue," he told reporters, "and one that the people of Waukau's district, particularly veterans who served their country, would be pretty juiced up about."[22]

Helping to lift the visibility of Heiliger's charges was the action of the Republican-controlled state assembly, which, on the day before Veterans Day, approved a bill to require a daily Pledge of Allegiance and the display of an American flag in every public school classroom in the state. (Wisconsin state law already mandated that the Pledge of Allegiance be recited in grades one through eight and that the flag be displayed at all public schools.) Only three legislators, all Democrats, were willing to vote against the measure. Within a week of the assembly vote, Heiliger's letter targeting Kuhn and Waukau had become front-page news. A few days later Kuhn announced that she was leaving Waukau's legislative staff. Kuhn also decided against seeking reelection to the county board of supervisors. The following spring Waukau lost her seat by a decisive margin to a Republican challenger, a loss that a number of Democrats attributed in part to the negative publicity generated by the Pledge of Allegiance letter-writing campaign.[23]

The divisiveness and bitterness created by Heiliger's actions were profound, but even his campaign opponents were afraid to criticize his behavior for fear of being labeled unpatriotic. Of his two opponents in a February 2000 primary, one refused to discuss the matter, and the other would only call it unfortunate, offering only the most gentle chiding. "I can understand why Don would feel the way he did," he offered. "But I think his reaction was excessive." And voters showed no inclination to punish Heiliger, reelecting him to a fifth term by a wide margin.[24]

Today the Pledge of Allegiance is a fixture in local government. It is difficult to say precisely how widespread is the practice of opening public meetings with the Pledge of Allegiance, but a survey conducted of the city councils in Oregon's fifty most populous cities documents the phenomenon in one state. More than three-quarters of these fifty city councils recite the Pledge before every public session, whereas prior to the 1988 election fewer than half of the city councils recited the Pledge. The change is most pronounced among the state's largest cities. Only two city councils in Oregon's ten most populous cities recited the Pledge of Allegiance prior to 1988. By 2004, seven of these ten city councils recited the Pledge daily. This suggests perhaps that in smaller towns, where partisanship is less pronounced, the politicization of the Pledge since the 1988 election has had less impact than in larger cities where councils tend to be more divided along de facto partisan lines.[25]

At the state level, too, the daily (or sometimes weekly) ritual of reciting the Pledge of Allegiance has become commonplace in recent decades. To be sure, a number of state legislatures have long recited the Pledge of Allegiance, though often initially only on a weekly or irregular basis. The California state assembly, for instance, unanimously adopted a weekly Pledge in 1941. The Arizona house, Nevada assembly, and Maine senate began saying the Pledge of Allegiance in 1955, immediately after Congress added "under God" to the Pledge. But by the end of the 1950s the Pledge of Allegiance in state legislatures was still very much the exception rather than the rule. A number of state legislatures, including the state senates in Arizona, Florida, Nevada, New Hampshire, and Tennessee, added the Pledge in the latter part of the 1960s, at the height of the Vietnam War, and a number more, including both houses in Alaska and Kentucky, added the Pledge between 1980 and 1981, apparently in reaction to the Iranian hostage crisis. In the intervening decades, state legislatures have continued to add the Pledge, sometimes in clear response to events (the adoption of the Pledge in the Georgia senate and Washington house, for instance, was in response to the first Gulf War, and the Massachusetts senate's adoption of the Pledge in 1989 was a direct product of the 1988 campaign) and sometimes just because an individual legislator thought it would be a good idea. By the end of 2003, all but thirteen of the ninety-nine state legislative bodies (Nebraska has a unicameral legislature) recited the Pledge on a daily or weekly basis. Only in Hawaii and, surprisingly, Texas is the Pledge of Allegiance not recited in the house or senate on either a daily or weekly basis. At least twenty-six of the eighty-seven state houses in which the Pledge is regularly recited added it sometime after the 1988 election, and a number of other legislatures (e.g., the state senates in Missouri and Mississippi) transformed what had been a weekly ritual to a daily one during this period. Eleven state legislatures added the Pledge of Allegiance in the two years after September 11, 2001.[26]

The Pledge of Allegiance after September 11

September 11, 2001, gave the Pledge of Allegiance renewed meaning and prominence. It appeared to be a reassuring, unifying ritual in the wake of terrible devastation and horrific loss of life. On September 14, at a memorial service for those who had died in the terrorist attacks, President George W. Bush joined with former presidents Clinton, Carter, Ford, and George H. W. Bush in reciting the Pledge at Washington's National Cathedral. And when President Bush came to New York City several weeks later, one of his stops was a first-grade classroom, where he recited the Pledge with the students, the teacher, Mayor Rudy Giuliani, and Governor George Pataki. The picture made newspapers across the country. But barely concealed beneath the conspicuous displays of patriotism were the same partisan motives and agendas that had fueled the politics of the Pledge in the 1980s and the 1990s.

My hometown city council, which had never recited the Pledge at its public meetings, adopted the Pledge immediately after September 11. The vote in favor of adopting the Pledge was unanimous, and from a distance its adoption might seem a symbol of unity and togetherness. But the public facade of unity disguised sharp political dissension. The Pledge proposal, which included a requirement that the recital of the Pledge be led by a local policeman or firefighter, was advanced by Glenn Wheeler, the council's most conservative

In Washington, D.C., at the National Cathedral, President George W. Bush and former presidents Bill Clinton and George H. W. Bush join in pledging allegiance to the flag at a service for those who died in the terrorist attacks of September 11, 2001. White House photo by Eric Draper.

member who had been soundly beaten in the previous mayoral election by incumbent Mike Swaim, a liberal Democrat. Wheeler and his few conservative allies were consistently outvoted by the left-liberal-progressive majority that had come to power in the preceding election. The Pledge enabled Wheeler to place the council majority on the defensive, forcing them to go along with Wheeler's plan (although the council did manage to remove the requirement that firefighters and policemen lead the Pledge after it was suggested that these city employees probably had more important things to do, like keeping the city safe) or hand conservatives a political bludgeon before the upcoming election. Before September 11, the city council members might have tried to ignore Wheeler's proposal, but in the wake of September 11 that was not a politically viable option.

Had the Salem council members had any doubts on that score, they needed only to look at events in Madison, Wisconsin. In 2001 the Wisconsin state legislature passed a law requiring that every classroom in every K–12 public and private school have an American flag and begin the day by either reciting the Pledge of Allegiance or singing the national anthem. The bill was the brain-

President George W. Bush, accompanied by New York governor George Pataki and New York City mayor Rudy Giuliani, leads a classroom of New York City elementary students in reciting the Pledge on October 3, 2001. White House photo by Paul Morse.

child of assembly speaker Scott Jensen, a conservative Republican from a Milwaukee suburb, who had been pushing the idea since 1995, initially with little success. Several times the bill had passed overwhelmingly in the Republican-controlled assembly, only to be quietly strangled by the state senate. Assembly Democrats would vote for it, knowing full well, as one explained, that it would "get killed somewhere else, and why put yourself through a tough vote?" But in 2001, Jensen tried a new tactic, attaching it as a rider to the state budget. When the legislature and the governor approved the budget they also approved Jensen's Pledge law.[27]

Jensen made no apologies for his tactics. At stake, he insisted, was nothing less than the survival of the nation. "We must teach our children to love their country when they are young," he explained, "so that they are willing to defend her when they are older." Jensen sharply criticized the liberal "cultural elite," among whom it was "trendy . . . to mock our patriotic traditions." The bill was a small but significant step in the struggle to take back the nation from the cultural relativists who were undermining the moral fiber of the young and their willingness to sacrifice for the nation and its values. Today, he lamented, "our schools and our society go to great lengths to preach diversity and to claim that all cultures and nations are morally equal. Patriotism is devalued and patriotic traditions are belittled. Elitists constantly tell our children that our society, our country, our ideals are not objectively superior to those of other cultures." Jensen, however, still believed "in the objective superiority of our nation and its values," just, he said, as the Founding Fathers had. The Pledge law, he hoped, would "start us on the long road back to a nation where patriotism is not mocked and where America's greatest generation is a generation yet to come."[28]

The new law was originally supposed to take effect on September 1, 2001, but an error by state officials, who initially reported that the new law would not take effect until 2005, meant that it was not until the latter part of September that most school officials found out that the new requirements were effective immediately. Schools that lacked the requisite flags scrambled to locate them, but in most of Wisconsin the new law was implemented with relatively little fuss, though generally also with little enthusiasm. In Madison, however, the law drew angry protests from parents and teachers who phoned school board members and principals to register their displeasure with the requirement. The school superintendent announced that the new requirement would go into effect immediately, but that each school in the district would be allowed to decide for itself whether to recite the Pledge or sing the anthem, when to conduct the ceremony during the day, and whether to use a public address system or let teachers lead the Pledge. The superintendent also emphasized that the law allowed any student to opt out of the ceremony if he or she chose to do so.[29]

But the right to opt out was not enough for some Madison parents, a handful of whom showed up at a school board meeting at the beginning of October to register their dissent. One parent, who was also an elementary school teacher in the district, opined that though students had the right not to participate, the reality of the classroom was that they would feel compelled to. "How can they not? It is like being a non-smoker in a room full of smokers." At home and in her classroom, she explained, she avoided overt displays of patriotism because patriotism was "a short step away from nationalism, jingoism, and yes, fascism." Another parent and teacher worried that the law was creating "little Stepford children" who mindlessly repeated what the adults wanted—a reference to the classic 1975 sci-fi thriller *The Stepford Wives*, in which wives are made into mindless robots who do the bidding of their husbands. Still another parent was concerned that her son, who was not a U.S. citizen, was so confused about whether he should say the Pledge that he found it difficult to sleep at night. "No child should have to endure this on a daily basis," she implored. Other parents complained that the "under God" clause violated the doctrine of the separation of church and state.[30]

After listening to the complaints, the board president decided to call a special meeting of the board to "discuss how the district is implementing the law." Another small collection of parents attended the special meeting, and again each parent who spoke did so in opposition to the new law. After discussing the matter for about an hour, the board voted 3 to 2 (two of the seven board members were absent) that each school in the district would comply with the law by offering an instrumental version of the national anthem over the public address system. The two who dissented from the decision did not support reciting the Pledge daily; rather they worried that the board's compromise proposal of a wordless anthem still did "not remove the coerciveness of the classroom."[31]

The decision brought on a ferocious reaction that caught the school board members by surprise. Prior to September 11, the decision, particularly the requirement that the national anthem be played without words (which was in response to concerns expressed by parents "opposed to the militaristic tone and phraseology" of the song), would likely have invited strong local criticism, but in the immediate wake of September 11 (and coming the day after commencement of the U.S. bombing campaign in Afghanistan, "Operation Enduring Freedom"), the decision became a magnet for statewide and national derision. Although the board ruling did not prevent a school from reciting the Pledge of Allegiance if the school chose to do so, the decision was immediately excoriated as an effort to "ban the Pledge" in schools. The state's Republican governor Scott McCallum dismissed the school board members as "oddballs" and wondered aloud "what country these people are from." While "most Wisconsinites are looking for ways to enhance our armed forces and support our country," McCallum continued, "some people are looking for ways to diminish our belief in God and country." Republican congressman Steve Nass joined in the chorus of criticism, expressing disbelief that "the Madison School Board would decide that political correctness outweighs patriotism at a time of war." Rush Limbaugh made Madison's ban on the Pledge a featured exhibit in the litany of liberal looniness and urged his listeners to communicate their outrage at the school board's un-American action. E-mail messages bombarded the school board at "the rate of a thousand per hour," according to one report. A few were supportive, a number were abusive—one expressed disappointment that terrorists had not flown planes into the Madison school board rather than the World Trade Center, while another suggested that "if anyone is ashamed of saying the Pledge of Allegiance, our flag, or any other symbol of being an American citizen, get the hell out of the country." The great majority were strongly critical. Some threatened to boycott Madison until the district lifted the ban, while one state legislator threatened to introduce legislation that would withhold state funding from schools that failed to comply with the law.[32]

The overwhelmingly negative reaction prompted the school board to quickly convene another meeting to reconsider its decision. This time it was standing room only as 1,200 people, many from outside Madison, packed into a school auditorium to express their views. The board sat through nearly ten hours of testimony from 166 individuals, and an additional 700 people submitted written statements. Before any individuals had begun to speak, a segment of the audience took to the stage and shouted the Pledge of Allegiance, followed by "fist-waving chants of U.S.A.! U.S.A.! U.S.A.!" At the end of the meeting, at 2:30 in the morning, having listened to impassioned pleas on both sides (and in about equal numbers), the board reversed its decision by a 6–1 vote. The decision about whether to comply with the law by reciting the Pledge or singing the national anthem would be left up to school principals. However, the school board did insist that the ceremony must be prefaced each day with a cautionary preamble: "We live in a nation of freedom. Participation in the Pledge or Anthem is voluntary. Those who wish to participate may stand; others may remain seated."[33]

The school board's reversal, however, did not bring the matter to a close. Sensing a historic opportunity to dent if not defeat the long-dominant progressive faction in Madison politics, conservatives announced—on the same evening and in the same building in which the council was about to reverse itself—that they would launch a recall campaign against the three board members who had voted for the silent anthem resolution. It turned out that two of these three board members were up for reelection in a few months, so the recall advocates decided to focus their efforts on recalling the third board member, Bill Keys, a veteran board member who had not only introduced the silent anthem proposal but was also the sole board member not to reverse his vote. The chairman of the Madison School Board Recall Committee was Scott Klug, a recently retired Republican congressman whose name was occasionally mentioned as a potential gubernatorial candidate for 2006. For Klug, a Madison native, the Pledge issue provided an ideal platform for distancing himself from what he ridiculed as Madison's "bead and sandal crowd." "This is Madison," he informed reporters. "Before this is over, there'll be somebody somewhere holding a bake sale for Osama bin Laden, saying he's been misunderstood and is the way he is because he didn't have any mittens as a child in Saudi Arabia."[34]

Klug and others predicted that the people would throw the rascals out. "Banning the Pledge," was going too far, even for a liberal-progressive stronghold like Madison. Keys, however, refused to be cowed or apologize for his position. "These are intemperate, rush-to-judgment times," he explained, "and some folks want to use it to reclaim power." Keys predicted that Madisonians would not be fooled by partisanship dressed up as patriotism. And as it turned out, Keys proved to be correct, for the expected electoral retribution never materialized. The recall campaign against Keys fizzled. The conservative challengers to the other two council members were handily beaten in February. In April the new council selected Keys to be council president. In six months the once white-hot controversy over the Pledge had become a distant memory. The following spring, Keys ran for reelection, unopposed.[35]

Elsewhere in the country there were other occasional profiles in courage. The most notable of these was in Minnesota, where Governor Jesse Ventura vetoed a 2002 bill mandating that the Pledge be recited in public schools at least once a week. Passed by overwhelming margins in both houses of the state legislature, the bill not only stipulated that students and teachers could not be compelled to participate in the ceremony but also permitted school districts to opt out so long as the school board put the matter to a vote every year. Ventura, a former Navy SEAL, was unimpressed by these concessions, condemning the bill as "political posturing by politicians who want to do something to say, 'Look how patriotic we are.'" In the message accompanying his veto, Ventura explained:

> I am vetoing this bill because I believe patriotism comes from the heart. Patriotism is voluntary. It is a feeling of loyalty and allegiance that is the result of knowledge and belief. A patriot shows their patriotism through their actions, by their choice. . . . There is much more to being a patriot and a citizen than reciting the pledge or raising a flag. Patriots serve. Patriots vote. Patriots attend meetings in their community. Patriots pay attention to the actions of government and speak out when needed. Patriots teach their children about our history, our precious democracy and about citizenship. Being an active, engaged citizen means being a patriotic American every day. No law will make a citizen a patriot. . . . Our government should not dictate actions. The United States of America exists because people wanted to be free to choose. All of us should have free choice when it comes to patriotic displays.

Because the legislature had already adjourned when Ventura issued his veto, the lawmakers had no chance to override Ventura's veto.[36]

Ventura's veto message won praise in many quarters, but the victory was short-lived. The following year, with Ventura no longer in the governor's office, the state legislature again overwhelmingly passed a virtually identical law. This time the bill was immediately signed into law by the newly elected Republican governor Tim Pawlenty, who as a state legislator had been one of the chief proponents of the Pledge bill. In his second State of the State address (delivered in January 2004) Pawlenty trumpeted the new Pledge law as one of the major achievements of his young administration. And the law, by all accounts, was certainly a popular one. According to a poll taken in May 2003, on the eve of the bill's passage, two-thirds of Minnesotans supported the idea of requiring schools to set aside time at least once a week to say the Pledge of Allegiance. Support for the weekly Pledge was markedly higher among the old (83 percent supported the idea among those sixty-five or older) than among the young (only 51 percent of those ages eighteen to twenty-four gave their support to the plan). There was also an ideological divide, with eight in ten of those who called themselves conservative embracing the proposed law, and only 47 percent of self-described liberals supporting it.[37]

As in the case of the Wisconsin law, the push for the Pledge in Minnesota predated September 11, but the terrorist attacks helped to change the politics surrounding the Pledge debate. The idea was first proposed by Republican state senator Bob Kierlin in January 2001. Much to the surprise of Kierlin, who appears to have earnestly hoped his measure would unite people, the proposal provoked strong partisan reactions. A puzzled Kierlin reported that at least a third of the many e-mails and phone calls he received were strongly critical of his proposal. Kierlin's proposal made no headway at all in the Democratic-controlled state senate, though a companion version of the bill did pass the Republican-controlled house. The chief proponents of the bill were the American Legion and the Veterans of Foreign Wars, whose members watched from the gallery as the house debated the bill. Playing to this audience, one Republican representative explained that "the bill is to remember soldiers who never returned home to marry their sweethearts . . . play with their children . . . pursue their dreams." The house voted 126 to 6 to approve the Pledge legislation, including an amendment that fifth graders should receive instruction in flag etiquette and patriotic exercises, a cause that has been dear to veterans groups for over a century. Since the senate showed no interest in adopting the legislation, however, the bill died when the legislature recessed in May.[38]

When the legislature convened again in January 2002, rookie Republican senator Mady Reiter, known in the legislature for her patriotic outfits, particularly her trademark American flag scarves, introduced a Pledge bill similar to the one passed by the house the previous year. Reiter, a member of the American Legion Auxiliary, cast her bill as a response to September 11. In fact, a week after September 11, she and three other Republican senators, as well as representatives from local veterans organizations, held a press conference calling for a Flag Appreciation Act, one part of which would require the Pledge of Allegiance in public schools. "Our children," Reiter believed, are "not learning all that they should . . . about our history. About what's gone before us and how important freedom is."[39]

Senate Democrats recognized that the post–September 11 political climate made it nearly impossible to bottle up the Pledge bill in committee this time and so instead attempted to amend the bill to soften its impact. First, one of the Democratic Whips proposed an amendment that would require that every classroom, at the beginning of each school year, have a class discussion about the Pledge of Allegiance, to be followed by a secret ballot among the students to decide whether and how often the Pledge should be recited. This proposal failed, garnering fourteen Democratic votes but not a single Republican vote. A few votes later, another Democratic Whip was back with a different amendment, this one requiring that "once every quarter," prior to reciting the Pledge, the person leading the Pledge read the following words: "For personal reasons, you may choose not to recite the pledge. For those who choose to recite the pledge, please understand that people who choose not to participate are not unpatriotic but may have personal or religious convictions that prevent them from reciting the pledge." This time the amendment passed, 34 to 29, on a strict party-line vote. Reiter and other Republicans were incensed by the Democratic "disclaimer." Reiter tabled the bill to prevent Democrats from approving the amended bill. Her Republican colleagues slammed the "bleeding-heart liberals" who had watered down the bill. The public, proclaimed Republican senator Dick Day, was "getting sick and tired of the politically correct whining" by Democrats. Another outraged Republican fumed: "What would the troops fighting in Afghanistan right now think of this debate? . . . It almost makes me ashamed to be a member of the Senate."[40]

Reiter and other Republicans were only partially mollified when the senate later relaxed the requirement so that the disclaimer only needed to be said once a year and did not need to precede the reciting of the Pledge of Allegiance. Nor did the amended version dictate the exact words to be spoken by the teacher or principal; rather the "person in charge" needed only to communicate, in the course of the yearly discussion, that a person choosing not to recite the Pledge should "not be considered unpatriotic." Reiter still did not like it, but it was the best she could do in the Democratic-controlled chamber. She fared much better in the conference committee, however.[41]

In conference committee, Reiter and the three house conferees (two Republicans and perhaps the legislature's most conservative Democrat[42]) prevailed over the two senate Democrats in dispensing with the modified "disclaimer." In its stead, the conferees offered a requirement that districts that had student handbooks must include "a statement about student rights and responsibilities" relevant to the Pledge of Allegiance. In addition, the conferees threw out the senate provision that would have allowed boards to opt out of the Pledge without going through an annual vote. One of the senate Democrat conferees refused to sign the report, and senate Democrats briefly flirted with the idea of rejecting the conference committee report and requesting that a new conference committee be appointed. But in the end, the conference committee amendments were accepted by a 39 to 11 vote. Each of the eleven "no" votes were cast by Democrats, liberal Democrats overwhelmingly. These eleven Democrats had an average score of 12 percent on a scorecard kept by the conservative Taxpayers League of Minnesota—Reiter, in contrast, had a score of 88 percent. In fact, the Taxpayers League even scored a vote in favor of the Pledge as a "taxpayer friendly" vote.[43]

After Ventura's veto, the legislature went through a similar partisan dance the following year before producing a bill for Governor Pawlenty to sign. But the partisan dynamics had been changed by the 2002 election. Republicans had not only won the governorship handily but had seen their narrow control of the house swell to an overwhelming thirty-seat margin. They also shaved a seat off of the Democrats' majority in the state senate, and the entire nation watched as former vice president Walter Mondale spectacularly failed to hang on to Paul Wellstone's U.S. Senate seat. In the house, demoralized Democrats were in no mood to oppose the Pledge of Allegiance, and the bill sailed through. Democrats in the senate, however, were not done wrangling. First, Democrats tried offering their own Pledge bill, which was similar to the one that the senate had passed the previous year, but it was narrowly rejected by the Education Committee. Having seen the Democratic bill defeated, the committee then tabled Reiter's bill, which was essentially identical to the measure Ventura had vetoed. A livid Reiter asked the full senate to discharge her bill from committee, but her request was voted down 32 to 26, again on a party-line vote. Reiter's appeal, however, seemed to spur the Democrats into action. At the committee hearing, the chair had anticipated "revisiting this issue *at some point*," but immediately after Reiter's extraordinary appeal to the whole chamber and only a week after the committee's original hearing, the committee reversed course, approving an amended version of the Democratic bill that altered what the Pledge leader would tell students. Rather than remind students that those who did not participate should "not be considered unpatriotic," the leader was to instruct students that they "should respect the right to make that choice" not to participate. At this point both sides seemed resigned to the bill, and it passed the senate on a voice vote.

However, just at the moment the Democratic senators seemed to have finally reconciled themselves to the Pledge, house Republicans decided to engage in a little partisan mischief, tacking on a partisan proposal to abolish a controversial program called Profile of Learning, which established high school graduation standards that many conservative Republicans felt took control of the curriculum away from local schools (not something that seemed to bother them with the Pledge or the flag etiquette requirement that accompanied it), were politically biased, and neglected "the basics" in favor of fuzzy, new-fangled educational ideas like critical thinking and collaborative learning. In the end, the Pledge bill that went to Governor Pawlenty was shorn of the extraneous Profile of Learning repeal tacked on by house Republicans. It was also stripped of the senate provisions that would have allowed school boards to opt out without an annual vote and would have required the Pledge leader to tell students about their right to opt out at the beginning of each year.[44]

When the governor signed the Pledge bill on May 27, 2003 (at a middle school in front of 150 sixth-grade students), the Pledge of Allegiance, for the first time in the state's history, became the law in all Minnesota schools.[45] In a slap at Ventura, Pawlenty commented that even if you couldn't "legislate patriotism . . . you sure can educate children on what makes our country great." When Kierlin had first proposed the idea two and a half years before, he had hoped the Pledge would bring Minnesotans together. Others shared this hope. In testimony before the Education Committee in February 2003, citizen Joy Kopp likened the Pledge of Allegiance to the Gettysburg Address or a well-known hymn. The Pledge, she explained to the committee, "helps to build a sense of community among us." A fourth grader who appeared before the committee in support of Reiter's bill expressed the same view—that "the pledge unites us." A casual observer, looking at the final floor vote in both houses—58 to 5 in the senate and 117 to 12 in the house—might see this as vindication of these hopes. But that view is misleading, the overwhelming margins of passage disguising the intense partisan contestation that marked every step of the bill's two-and-a-half-year journey through the legislative process. Nor is Minnesota unique. Repeatedly over the last decade and a half, in state after state, the Pledge has been pushed by one political party, has been resisted by the other, and has fostered partisan bitterness and ill will.[46]

Testing the Legal Limits

Minnesota's Pledge law, despite the intense partisan jockeying that surrounded it, is among the more relaxed of the newly enacted state regulations. It requires the Pledge to be said only once a week, does not apply to private schools, allows public school districts to opt out with an annual vote, and requires districts to include information about the rights of students. Even Reiter's original version of the bill was relatively tame in that it never attempted to deny that students had a right not to say the Pledge and required that the Pledge be said only on a weekly rather than a daily basis. In other states, Republicans sometimes proposed far more stringent restrictions that essentially ignored the Supreme Court's holding in *Barnette*.

In Virginia, for instance, in January 2001, veteran Republican state senator Warren Barry introduced (together with three cosponsors, all Republicans) a bill to require that all students recite the Pledge of Allegiance. Students who refused to recite the Pledge were to be suspended from school until they agreed to recite the Pledge with their class. An exception was granted to those students who had religious objections. To be exempted from reciting the Pledge, the student was required to present the principal with a "written objection . . . signed by an ecclesiastical officer of his religion" or "a document from an ecclesiastical officer of the relevant religion describing the tenet of the religion on which the student bases the religious objection." But even students who received a religious exemption would be required to stand respectfully at their desks while the class was reciting the words of the Pledge.[47]

Barry felt that such a law was necessary because young people lacked a proper respect for the American flag and for their country. When visiting some Virginia public schools—he was there to observe how the schools were implementing the "minute of silence" requirement that he had successfully pushed through the legislature the year before—Barry was shocked to find some students "fooling around" during the Pledge. "These kids," the sixty-seven-year-old former Marine officer lamented, "have no understanding of what the American flag symbolizes. If they refuse to salute the flag, I think they belong elsewhere." Another Republican state legislator agreed with Barry: "Anything we can do to have a resurgence of patriotism and fidelity to values is a good thing. . . . If you're offended by the pledge, you probably ought to move." The Republican governor also signaled his support for Barry's mandatory Pledge law, the need for which, he believed, was a sorry "comment on the culture of the country."[48]

The American Civil Liberties Union immediately promised to challenge the bill in court, and even the state's Republican attorney general indicated that he could not successfully defend the bill as written. Barry reluctantly allowed the bill to be rewritten by the attorney general's office so as to allow students to opt out of the Pledge if they or their parents objected on either "religious or philosophical grounds." The permission slip from priest or pastor was no longer necessary. Moreover, nonparticipating students were no longer to be compelled to stand but would be allowed to sit quietly during the Pledge. According to the attorney general's office, students would, however, be required to explain their objections to school authorities. Although disappointed that the bill had been "watered down," Barry was satisfied that the modified bill, as interpreted by the attorney general, would still mean that students could not opt out of the Pledge just because they "don't feel like it," a response he claims he received from many students when he had asked them why they didn't say the Pledge. "What I'd really like to do," he admitted to one reporter, "is have [those who refuse to say the Pledge] all go to Marine Corps boot camp for 10 weeks." The

Senate Committee on Health and Education (of which Barry was chair) passed the revised bill with three dissenting votes, each cast by a Democrat. After an emotional (and partisan) debate, the senate passed Barry's bill by a 27 to 9 vote, and again each of the dissenters was a Democrat.[49]

In the house, however, Barry ran into unexpected trouble from an alliance of what Barry characterized as "libertarians and liberals." The House Education Committee removed the mandatory suspensions for students who failed to abide by the law. Instead the house committee decided to leave punishment up to the local school district. The decision enraged Barry, who told the committee to withdraw the bill before storming out of the room. Barry charged that the bill had been "neutered" by a bunch of "spineless pinkos" who had "nibbled away on that bill to the point where it doesn't mean anything." His colleagues, he fumed, were only looking for a way to take a patriotic stand without actually changing behavior in the schools.[50] Barry quickly reconsidered, but worse was to come on the house floor, where members accepted an amendment that allowed students to opt out of the Pledge without having to give a reason. In Barry's view, the house had now "totally emasculated" his bill, and he vowed to restore its teeth in conference committee. Those who voted for the amendments, he said, lacked "patriotic backbone." In the end, though, the final bill hammered out by the conference committee ended up far closer to the house version than to Barry's, allowing students to opt out if they or their parents objected "on religious, philosophical, or other grounds" and leaving punishment and enforcement in the hands of local school boards.[51]

The bill eventually signed into law in Virginia in March 2001 ended up looking a lot like mandatory Pledge laws in many other states. Some states, however, have enacted laws, especially after September 11, that have creatively pushed the limits of what is legally allowable. Among the most stringent of these new laws was one enacted in Pennsylvania at the end of 2002. The law mandated the display of an American flag (at least three feet in length) in all public and private school classrooms and required students in both public and private schools to recite the Pledge of Allegiance or sing the national anthem each morning. The law allowed students to opt out of reciting the Pledge of Allegiance if the student had religious or personal objections, but school officials were required to notify parents that their child was refusing to pledge allegiance to the flag. No distinctions were drawn by age—high school kids of seventeen and eighteen, as well as preschool children of three or four years of age, were all required to salute the flag every day. The law did provide an exemption for private schools when compliance would violate the religious tenets of the school. Originally the bill had also required all schools to offer a period of silent prayer or meditation at the beginning of each day, but this was stripped from the bill by the Senate Education Committee.

The sponsor of the measure was Republican Allan Egolf, a sixty-five-year-old retired U.S. Air Force colonel. Egolf explained that he had introduced the bill after being notified by some veterans groups that a number of schools did not have students recite the Pledge of Allegiance and some classrooms did not even have a flag to salute. Current state law required only that each *school* display a flag and allowed schools to choose between conducting the Pledge of Allegiance daily or devoting at least one class period per week to "affirming and developing allegiance and respect for the Flag of the United States of America, and for the promoting of a clear understanding of our American way of life." The latter provision, Egolf and his fellow veterans believed, created a loophole by which schools avoided having to recite the Pledge of Allegiance. Schools, Egolf lamented, were "getting away from teaching about what our country stands for, what our founders did, and why we have the country we have. . . . We've heard people say—especially prior to 9/11—that we shouldn't say that we're different or we're proud to be Americans [because] it sounds like we think we're better than other countries. Well, in fact, our form of government *is* better." Egolf insisted that the new law was not "mandating patriotism." Instead, he explained, "we're mandating that students have the opportunity to learn; then it's up to the individual what they want to do from there—whether they agree with it or disagree with it."[52]

Egolf had been in the Pennsylvania state house since 1992, and during his six terms had secured a reputation as among the most socially conservative legislators in either house, both of which have been controlled by Republicans since 1994. Among Egolf's previous legislative initiatives were a failed attempt to cut off all funding for state universities that provided benefits to the domestic partners of faculty who were gay or lesbian and a successful effort to enact the Sanctity of Marriage Act, which stated that marriage must be between a man and a woman. He has also pushed for legislation that would withdraw state funding for public libraries that refused to install Internet filters on all library computers. Egolf's Pledge bill was introduced long before September 11, but it was only after the terrorist attacks that the bill began to attract substantial public attention and political support. The Ninth Circuit Court of Appeals' decision in June 2002 added further fuel to the fire.[53]

In the senate, the bill passed without a single dissenting vote, and in the house only sixteen representatives (all but one a Democrat) dared to oppose the measure. However, before the new law could go into effect it was challenged in court by the ACLU. The lawsuit was filed on behalf of several plaintiffs, including a number of private nonreligious schools, a teacher from one of these schools, and a parent from another, as well as a sophomore at a public high school in the suburbs of Philadelphia. The suit challenged the parental notification provision on the grounds that it attempted to intimidate students to make it less likely they would exercise their First Amendment right not to recite the Pledge. It also challenged the law on the grounds that it infringed on the liberty of nonreligious private schools and the parents who had chosen to send their students to those schools. More broadly, the ACLU argued that the new law was "an infringement of [a school's] core mission—to turn out students who can think for themselves. . . . Here, the state is telling them what they must say and do with regard to patriotism."[54]

In July 2003, a federal judge agreed with the ACLU that requiring schools to notify parents when children were exercising their constitutional rights violated students' First Amendment right of free expression. Judge Robert Kelly said the law was an effort to circumvent *Barnette*, which barred the state from requiring students to recite the Pledge of Allegiance. The school district's letter home, Kelly wrote, "would chill the speech of certain students who would involuntarily recite the Pledge or Anthem rather than have a notice sent to their parents." Indeed, by examining Egolf's own explanation of the act on the house floor, Kelly argued that there was evidence that the drafters of the bill intended the act "to chill speech by providing a disincentive to opting out." But whatever the intentions of the bill's authors, Judge Kelly found that the law clearly provided "a disincentive for students to opt out of reciting the Pledge or the Anthem and thus it coerces students into reciting a state sponsored message."[55]

The judge also held that the law, as applied to private schools, unconstitutionally infringed upon parents' liberty to provide for their children's education and private schools' right to freedom of expressive association. If the Boy Scouts have the right to exclude gays from their organization, as the U.S. Supreme Court held in 1999, then surely the state could not compel private schools to recite the Pledge of Allegiance or salute the flag on a daily basis. Kelly conceded that the state has a compelling interest in teaching patriotism and civics but maintained that a bill mandating that the Pledge of Allegiance be recited every morning was not narrowly tailored to serve that purpose. Pennsylvania, the judge pointed out, already had a law requiring that private schools either recite the Pledge of Allegiance daily or devote at least one period a week to "affirming and developing allegiance to and respect for the Flag of the United

States of America, and for the promoting of a clear understanding of our American way of life." The old law, the judge held, achieved the same state purpose with far less infringement of the constitutionally protected rights of parents and private schools.[56]

Colorado also pushed the legal limits of mandatory patriotism in the wake of September 11. When the legislature opened in January 2002, Republican minority leader John Andrews (whose other bills have included the posting of the Ten Commandments in all public schools) introduced two bills designed to ensure that the patriotism on exhibit since September 11 would be "more than a passing fad or a fashion." The first bill mandated that every public school offer "an age-appropriate unit on patriotism." The second bill required that every public school teacher and student in the public schools, from kindergarten through high school, must begin the day by reciting the Pledge of Allegiance. No exceptions were permitted. "If our public schools aren't about teaching the love of country," Andrews asked, "what are they about at all?" Andrews's rhetoric basked in the glow of patriotic unity. "We all bled together, wept together and then rallied together after Sept. 11. . . . We must not lose sight that there is something that makes us one country." Barely disguised beneath the rhetoric, however, was bare-knuckled partisanship.[57]

Republicans controlled the house and the governorship and were itching to regain control of the state senate, which they had lost in November 2000 for the first time in forty years. The Democratic senate majority rested on the slimmest of margins: eighteen Democrats and seventeen Republicans. Andrews's Pledge bill, plainly unconstitutional on its face, was referred by the Democratic leadership to the Judiciary Committee, where it was promptly killed on a party-line vote, four to three. On the morning the committee was scheduled to take up the bill, Andrews took the highly unusual step of moving to bypass the committee and have the bill voted on directly by the entire senate. The procedural vote to "blast" the bill out of committee failed on another party-line vote, eighteen to seventeen. A few days later, with identical results, Andrews attempted to use the same bypass procedure on his bill mandating patriotism classes. Democrats were infuriated by Andrews's parliamentary maneuvers, seeing them as a transparent partisan ploy to force Democrats to cast procedural floor votes that could be portrayed in the upcoming campaign as votes against the Pledge of Allegiance and patriotism in schools. Democrats' fears were confirmed when constituents in each of the eighteen Democratic districts received recorded telephone messages informing them that their senator had voted against the Pledge and against promoting patriotism in schools.[58]

In an attempt to insulate Democrats from the charge of being unpatriotic, Ken Gordon, chair of the Senate Judiciary Committee, had begun the hearing by having everyone in the room recite the Pledge. Gordon cautioned Republicans not to use the committee Democrats' votes on the mandatory Pledge law as "a measure of a person's patriotism." To do so, he said, would be "demagoguery of the worst sort." Andrews responded by posting on a Republican website the news that "Democrats in the Judiciary Committee killed the [Pledge] bill 4–3 with Chairman Ken Gordon, D-Denver, implying patriotism is demagoguery." Gordon promptly took to the senate floor, accusing Andrews of having lied about what he had said. Rancor and nastiness prevailed. Andrews apologized for the misleading statement on the website, but Republicans continued to press the patriotic advantage. After senate Democrats killed Andrews's bill, house Republicans promptly introduced a mandatory Pledge bill of their own, though this one did include an exception for those who objected on religious grounds; before passage the bill was amended to include an exception for foreign students as well. For good measure, the house Republicans also added the Pledge of Allegiance to their daily order of business.[59]

The day after the House Committee on State, Veterans, and Military Affairs approved the mandatory Pledge law, Andrews and the senate president Stan Matsunaka sparred publicly in the *Denver Post* about the wisdom of a mandatory Pledge law. Matsunaka assailed Republican "exploitation artists" who were engaging in "political grandstanding" and "blatantly partisan attempts to paint one party as more patriotic than another." Matsunaka deplored the "rush to politicize patriotism" that had been "brought on by a need to posture in advance of next year's elections." Andrews responded by reeling off a string of patriotic bills that the Democrats had killed or gutted in the first sixty days of the session (including tax breaks for those on active military duty), bills that he said were necessary to combat terrorism and teach our children why America should be "respected and protected." Democrats, he said, were not unpatriotic, but their sense of patriotism was anemic and threatened "the nation's very survival." "Their ambivalence about standards, their distaste for consequences, their burden of self-doubt and their mantra of tolerance yield a far less confident definition of patriotism than the one in Webster's: 'The love of one's country, the devotion to its welfare, the passion that inspires one to its service.'"[60]

The session ended without a Pledge bill, but Republicans—aided by the Ninth Circuit's controversial decision to invalidate the "under God" clause—continued to try to keep the Pledge alive as a campaign issue. A four-day special session in July, called by the governor to deal with the problems of drought and wildfires in the state as well as a court ruling on capital punishment, was seized upon by a Republican leader, Marilyn Musgrave, as an opportunity to introduce a resolution honoring the Pledge of Allegiance and its authors. (In the just-completed regular session, Musgrave had been the chief senate sponsor of the house bill to require all students and teachers to recite the Pledge of Allegiance, as well as the sponsor of a bill to make active duty military wages exempt from state income taxes.) Democrats tabled the resolution. A month before the general election, the *Rocky Mountain News* published a "Voter Guide" that profiled state legislative candidates across the state and posed to each of the candidates fourteen yes/no public-policy questions, ranging from the death penalty to whether more dams should be built in Colorado. The final question on the list posed to every candidate was "Should the Pledge of Allegiance be required in Colorado classrooms?" In November the Democrats narrowly lost control of the senate, giving the Republicans unified control of the government once again. The senate Republicans selected as their new leader none other than John Andrews, the individual in the state who was probably most closely identified with the Pledge of Allegiance issue. Musgrave, the other Republican who had publicly positioned herself as a defender of the Pledge, defeated Senate president Matsunaka in a hotly contested race for an open seat in Congress.[61]

Now in control of the senate, house, and governorship, the Republicans renewed their fight to require every student and teacher to recite the Pledge of Allegiance, with exceptions only for those with religious objections and for those who were not American citizens. The Republican leadership in the senate referred the Pledge bill not to the Judiciary Committee, where senate Democrats had sent the bill, nor to the Education Committee, where it might have been logically expected to go. Instead the senate leadership (following the lead of the house leadership) referred it to the Committee on State Veterans and Military Affairs, where it could be expected to receive a more friendly hearing, with fewer constitutional objections likely to be raised as well as less concern about violating the autonomy of school districts. Both house and senate committees approved the bill with little discussion (it took each committee ten minutes to approve the bill) and without any amendments. Again the only dissenting votes were cast by Democrats. On the house floor, the debate was passionate, with Democrats deriding the bill, in the words of one, as "bumper-sticker patriotism." One Republican, concerned that by compelling students to recite certain words the law was "desecrating the very pledge you are forcing them to take," joined thirteen Democrats in voting against the bill. In the senate, three Republicans and four Democrats defected from their party caucus's positions. Before the bill's final passage, opponents did manage to amend it to allow a student to be excused if the parent or guardian objected on any grounds. A student who was a citizen and did not have a parent's note, however, could not be excused unless their objections were religiously based. And teachers were exempt only if they had religious objections or were not citizens. As soon as the governor signed the bill, the legal challenges began.[62]

The American Civil Liberties Union, which had been the sole group to testify on the bill when it was in committee, immediately filed suit in federal court on behalf of three students and six teachers who contended that requiring them to say the Pledge violated their free speech rights. It took a federal judge only three days to block implementation of the law, ruling that Colorado's law clearly infringed on the First Amendment rights of students and teachers. "It doesn't matter whether you're a teacher, a student, a citizen, an administrator or anyone else," declared the judge. "It is beyond the power of the state or of government to compel the recitation of the Pledge of Allegiance." Senate president John Andrews was livid, insisting that the judge's ruling "insults the patriotism of most Coloradans. It is a judge attempting to make the law with sociology instead of applying the law and the Constitution." Republican governor Bill Owens expressed similar outrage, declaring that "the court's action is dramatically out of step with the desires and practices of most Coloradans who value and respect the Pledge of Allegiance." Both predicted the decision would be quickly overturned and "this simple and common-sense law" would be upheld. But a week later, the governor abruptly changed his tune, announcing that the state would not appeal the ruling. Instead the legislature would revise the bill to meet the judge's constitutional concerns. The following session, the legislature did exactly that, altering the bill so that it no longer applied to teachers and required only that schools give students the "opportunity" to say the Pledge.[63]

A Symbol in the Culture Wars

Today, at least thirty-five states have state laws requiring the Pledge of Allegiance in public schools. Roughly a quarter of these states—Arkansas, Colorado, Connecticut, Minnesota, Missouri, New Hampshire, Pennsylvania, Tennessee, and Texas—enacted their laws within two years of September 11, 2001. Moreover, September 11 spurred a number of other states to strengthen existing Pledge requirements, often, as in the case of Illinois and Utah, by requiring the Pledge of Allegiance not only for elementary school students but for high school students as well. Even where no change was mandated by the legislature, local school boards and schools often, on their own initiative, responded to September 11 by instituting a daily Pledge.[64]

The focus on the Pledge of Allegiance in the immediate aftermath of the terrorist attacks of September 11, 2001, was in many ways part of a spontaneous, bottom-up surge of patriotic feeling. Reciting the Pledge of Allegiance was one of the ways that Americans expressed solidarity with the victims of the attacks and affirmed their shared national identity. Many reports suggested that students now attached new meaning to the familiar words. According to an observer at one high school, "the eye-rolling and groans during the morning Pledge of Allegiance are gone." It was not only in schools that the Pledge took on renewed meaning and visibility. Across the country, in vigils, church services, sporting events, and even block parties, Americans recited the Pledge of Allegiance in the days following September 11. In Springfield, Massachusetts, for instance, on the day after September 11, several hundred Christians, Jews, and Muslims gathered for "an interfaith prayer vigil" that closed with a recitation of the Pledge of Allegiance. At Plymouth Rock, another few hundred people held an evening vigil that again featured a recitation of the Pledge of Allegiance. In New York City, steelworkers used their morning break to go outside and recite the Pledge of Allegiance before a huge twelve-by-eighteen-foot flag that had been draped over the building. Church services in Fayetteville, Georgia, at the First Baptist Church began with the Pledge of Allegiance, followed by "a video montage of the horrific scenes . . . overlaid with the question, 'What will God's people do now?'" At the Miss America Pageant, held ten days after September 11, host Tony Danza began the telecast by leading a "flag-waving, sellout crowd" of almost fourteen thousand people in reciting the Pledge of Allegiance. The enthusiasm for the Pledge was genuine and heartfelt, expressing national unity and a shared sense of purpose.[65]

The Pledge, in these contexts, clearly did express the idea of an indivisible nation. But the Pledge has also often been employed in cynical and divisive ways by politicians who have used it to mobilize political support and to portray opponents as insufficiently patriotic. The Pledge has been seized on by Republicans particularly as a means of linking themselves symbolically to the common people and portraying themselves as more in touch with the values of the average American than are liberal Democrats. Used in this way, the Pledge becomes less an expression of national unity than a sign of a sharply polarized political elite. Invoking the Pledge of Allegiance becomes a way of fighting the culture wars by other means and of dividing, not uniting, the nation. [66]

It should come as no surprise then that when George W. Bush launched his first big political advertisements of his 2004 presidential campaign, the Pledge of Allegiance was a featured image in one of those ads. A picture of the American flag fluttering amid the ruins of the World Trade Center was followed quickly by a man raising an American flag atop a flagpole and schoolchildren scampering to school and then an image of a classroom of children, hands over hearts, saying the Pledge of Allegiance. The ads provoked outrage among many for the attempt to use the tragedy of September 11 for political purposes. But the effort to use the Pledge of Allegiance for partisan advantage did not even draw comment. It seemed normal. The partisan Pledge of Allegiance, ushered in by Reagan and George W. Bush's father, had become a routine feature of a polarized American polity.[67]

CONCLUSION: PLEDGING ALLEGIANCE
IN A LIBERAL SOCIETY

Michael Newdow's appearance before the United States Supreme Court focused media attention on the Pledge of Allegiance, most of it centered, not surprisingly, around the "under God" clause. But for some observers, the oral arguments prompted deeper reflections on the place of the Pledge in American society. One such reflection came in a letter to the editor from an Oskaloosa, Kansas, woman by the name of Cynthia Annett, a coordinator of an exchange program between students from Haskell Indian Nations University in Lawrence, Kansas, and a university in Siberia. Annett reported that her Russian colleagues in Siberia were "shocked" by what they read about the Pledge—not shocked that the Pledge had been amended in the 1950s to differentiate the United States from the godless Communists but "stunned that, in America, we required a loyalty oath of our children." How was it, they demanded to know, that "an open democracy like the United States could have such a repressive institution." Annett had no answers for them. The Pledge had become so "ubiquitous in our nation's schools that most people don't even think about it at all, let alone think about it as a forced loyalty oath recited by minors."[1]

One need not accept the description of the Pledge as a "forced loyalty oath"—at least not after the Supreme Court's ruling in *West Virginia v. Barnette*—to be both puzzled and troubled by the place of the Pledge in American society. Puzzled, because democracies generally do not require their schoolchildren to pledge allegiance to the nation on a daily or even regular basis. Troubled because the rote recitation of loyalty to a nation is something we generally associate more with authoritarian regimes than liberal democracies. Why is the United States different? And should we be as troubled by it as Ms. Annett evidently is?

Testing Loyalty

Francis Bellamy chose his words carefully. Writing the Pledge, he later said, was "arduous mental labor," but not the first six words. They came effortlessly: "I pledge allegiance to my flag." The word "allegiance," Bellamy explained, "was the great word of the Civil War period." He knew that word would "still [be] familiar from Civil War memories" since it "had been used as a test of loyalty."[2]

Loyalty tests were ubiquitous during the Civil War. Across the North, those suspected of disloyalty were arrested and imprisoned. However, the government did not have the time to investigate each and every individual arrested, nor did it have the resources to detain all of those who might have uttered a disloyal or critical word of the administration. And so the government often allowed political prisoners to be released upon taking what was widely called "the oath of allegiance."[3] In early 1862, Lincoln ordered that rebel prisoners of war should also be granted their freedom if they were willing to take a loyalty oath swearing allegiance to the Union and the Constitution. At the end of the following year, the loyalty oath program was expanded when Lincoln issued a sweeping proclamation of amnesty that enabled Southerners who had aided the rebellion (with important exceptions, including officials of the "so-called confederate government" and high ranking military officers) to participate in the reconstitution of "loyal State governments" so long as they swore allegiance to the Union.[4]

For Lincoln, loyalty oaths were an instrument of policy—a means of reducing prison crowding, promoting desertion by Confederate soldiers, and, most important, winning the hearts and minds of Southerners. The oath of allegiance was linked, in Lincoln's mind at least, to a policy of mercy and forgiveness. Swear future allegiance to the Union and your past sins (provided they were not too great) could be forgiven. The loyalty oath, Lincoln explained, embodied "the Christian principle of forgiveness on terms of repentance."[5] Perhaps that is an association that the idea of an "oath of allegiance" still had for Bellamy and some others in the North, but for many others, particularly those who hailed from the South, the loyalty oath brought back memories not of Lincoln's mercy but of Northern tyranny and Republican malevolence.

Although in spirit Lincoln's policy may have been humane, its implementation was often arbitrary and cruel. The authority to decide who would be permitted to take the oath of allegiance was generally vested in prison authorities and military officials, who interpreted the executive order as they saw fit. The superintendent of a military prison in Washington, D.C., for instance, threatened prisoners of war with hanging if they did not take the oath. Other officials never offered Confederate prisoners a chance to take the oath.[6] Moreover, for most Southerners at least, mention of Civil War–era loyalty tests would likely have brought to mind not Lincoln's loyalty oaths but the so-called ironclad loyalty oath pressed upon the South by "Radical Republicans" during the Civil War and Reconstruction.

Lincoln's loyalty oaths were aimed at winning the war and reuniting North and South, but the Radical Republicans in Congress had a very different aim in mind. Their goal was to use loyalty oaths to exclude and punish those who sided with the South. Lincoln's oath required only that individuals swear their future devotion to the Union, but the ironclad oath required individuals to attest to their past loyalty as well. Only those who could swear that they had "never voluntarily borne arms against the United States" or given "aid, countenance, council or encouragement" to the Confederate army could hold federal office, elected or appointed.[7] Among Southerners, the loyalty oath became one of the most reviled symbols of the subjugation of the South by the North, an association that was still very much alive in 1892 when Bellamy penned the Pledge. Perhaps that helps explain why for decades the Pledge of Allegiance was embraced far more enthusiastically in the North than in the South.

Bellamy has left no record explaining why he chose to call it a "*pledge* of allegiance" rather than the more common term "*oath* of allegiance." John Baer speculates that perhaps the term's "uncomfortable memories for citizens of the former confederate states" may have explained Bellamy's choice of words. Baer also suggests that perhaps the word "pledge" resonated with Bellamy because of his involvement in the prohibition movement, which featured a widely known "temperance pledge." Or perhaps, as biographer Margarette Miller explains, Bellamy simply thought that the term "pledge" was a "better school word" than the "swear" language ("I, _____, do solemnly swear") used in the typical oath of allegiance.[8]

Certainly, Bellamy recognized that a unique feature of the Pledge of Allegiance was that it was aimed at children rather than at adults. Loyalty oaths arrived on American shores with the earliest settlers, but children had never been asked to take such oaths. King James required all adults who emigrated to Virginia and New England to swear an oath of allegiance to the Crown, and one of the Puritans' first actions upon establishing a colony in the New World was to establish their own loyalty oath. Indeed, Harold Hyman reports that the first item printed on the first colonial printing press was a loyalty oath.[9] The Framers rejected religious test oaths on the English model, whereby Catholics and other religious dissenters were excluded from Parliament, but the Founders wrote into the Constitution the requirement that all state and federal officers "shall be bound by Oath or Affirmation to support this Constitution." But neither the Founders nor the British Crown dreamed of requiring such an oath of children. Not even during the Civil War, with the nation wracked with fears about disloyalty, was there ever a proposal to have children take an oath of allegiance.

The Pledge of Allegiance, of course, is in certain respects quite unlike the loyalty oaths of the past. Loyalty oaths have typically been linked with the granting and withholding of some benefit, whether political office, voting rights, or sometimes even landholding rights.[10] Loyalty oaths make the rights of citizenship contingent upon expressions of allegiance to the state. Bellamy never envisioned linking citizenship rights to reciting the Pledge of Allegiance, though, as we have seen, the Pledge subsequently did become linked to the right to attend public schools, thereby becoming, as Justices Hugo Black and William Douglas pointed out in *West Virginia v. Barnette*, "a form of test oath."[11] However, so long as the Pledge is voluntary, and state-conferred benefits do not hinge on compliance, then the Pledge is fundamentally different from the forced loyalty oaths of the nation's past (and present).

The Pledge of Allegiance also differs from the loyalty oaths of past and present in that the Pledge, in schools at least, is a daily or weekly ritual. Loyalty oaths, in contrast, are typically not something an individual repeats. Prisoners of war who declared their loyalty to the Union during the Civil War were not asked to swear that loyalty on a regular basis. Once was generally enough. Today, those who become American citizens must swear the naturalization oath but once. So, too, for those assuming office. Newly elected federal officials take the oath to support the Constitution when they assume the office, but they are not asked to repeat that declaration of loyalty for the duration of their term.

But if the Pledge of Allegiance today is distinguishable from a forced loyalty oath, its continued persistence in the United States remains a puzzle. Why does the United States, alone among Western democracies, insist on having schoolchildren across the country recite a pledge of allegiance? Why does a nation that prides itself on its individualism and personal freedom have schoolchildren (and legislators) begin their day by publicly affirming their loyalty to the nation-state? Why does arguably the world's most liberal nation continue the sort of practice that is most commonly employed by the earth's most repressive regimes?

The Myth of the Civic Nation

The history of the Pledge of Allegiance, from its inception, has mirrored the history of American anxieties. The schoolhouse flag movement and the creation of the Pledge of Allegiance stemmed in large part from anxiety about the threat that new immigrants posed to the American way of life. The addition of "under God" to the Pledge in 1954 emerged out of an anxiety about the threat of Soviet Communism. For over a century, those who have been most fearful about threats to American national identity have often been most insistent on the importance of patriotic rituals like the Pledge of Allegiance. Illustrative is the California man, who wrote in the immediate wake of September 11, 2001. "It is the time to put the Pledge of Allegiance back into our schools! We have opened our doors to so many foreign people. Let them realize which . . . country they are in or leave."[12] But to say that the Pledge of Allegiance emerged out of or is sustained by anxieties about American identity does not answer the question of why Americans are so anxious about such things. Americans are presumably no more psychologically anxious or neurotic than the people of other nations. So why do Americans so often exhibit high anxiety about their national identity?

One answer is that American national identity is unlike national identity in most other countries. American national identity, as political scientist Samuel Huntington has argued, is rooted in shared political ideas, whereas "for most peoples, national identity is the product of a long process of historical evolution involving common ancestors, common experiences, common ethnic background, common language, common culture, and usually common religion."[13] According to this view, the United States is a nation founded on and held together by a rational commitment to political ideas and principles, whereas other nations are held together by pre-rational blood ties and inherited customs. One is born German or Japanese but one learns to become an American.

This was certainly Bellamy's own view. "This American kind of patriotism," Bellamy reflected in 1923,

> is quite different from the patriotism of the European nations. Over there, patriotism is in the blood. It is inherited from a dozen centuries of ancestors of the same race, temperament, tradition and language. It doesn't reason about itself. It is instinctive, ready to act on the drop of a hat. But the American variety of patriotism is more of a directly traceable product. In this conglomerate country we have very little of the inherited instinct. Outside of our dwindling Colonial stock, American ancestry is from many races and languages. Consequently the composite patriotism of our masses is mostly the result of a definite education, and its exercise is a matter of reasoning.[14]

Eight decades later, Representative Scott Jensen, sponsor of Wisconsin's 2001 Pledge law, used similar reasoning to explain why the Pledge of Allegiance was needed in the United States:

> Our nation is unique. Unlike other nations, U.S. citizenship is not based on ethnic or geographic factors, and patriotism isn't allegiance to people of the same skin color or bloodline. In the United States, patriotism is allegiance to an idea and principles of government. We have a unique responsibility to inculcate a knowledge, love and respect of those ideas in our youth.[15]

In the view of both Bellamy and Jensen, since the nation is not knit together by common traditions, language, religion, or race, the state must take steps, starting with the public schools, to make good Americans. Liberal principles paradoxically require a paternal government.

The idea-based nature of American identity perhaps does explain some key aspects of the peculiar ritual of the Pledge of Allegiance. Certainly the final six words of the Pledge of Allegiance—"with liberty and justice for all"—are a capsule expression of the American creed. In writing the Pledge, Bellamy self-consciously strove to provide not just an expression of allegiance but the *reasons* for allegiance, the ideals for which the flag and nation stood. The absence of such reasons was, in Bellamy's view, a primary reason why the Balch salute was inadequate as an expression of allegiance. Moreover, so long as those final six words are understood to be aspirational rather than descriptive, they are words by which citizens can judge rather than merely justify a nation's actions. The Pledge might therefore be said to mirror the paradoxical nature of American identity in that it invites citizens to pledge allegiance not just to a particular nation but to a set of liberal political principles that provide a standard for criticizing that same nation.[16]

On the other hand, this understanding of the Pledge of Allegiance is not altogether satisfying either. To begin with, it is not true that the United States is the only nation in which national identity is based on political ideas and principles of governance. Indeed civic nationalism was arguably first achieved not in the United States but in Great Britain, "a nation-state composed of four nations—the Irish, the Scots, the Welsh, and the English—united by a civic rather than an ethnic definition of belonging." In their classic study *The Civic Culture*, Gabriel Almond and Sidney Verba found that in 1959 about half of the British survey respondents volunteered political ideals or institutions as among the things about their country that they were "most proud of." France and Canada also have national identities that are grounded in important ways in shared attachment to political principles. Indeed, if Michael Ignatieff is to be believed, "most Western nation-states now define their nationhood in terms of common citizenship and not by common ethnicity." In none of these Western nation-states, however, has a civic definition of nationality translated into the ritual of a daily flag salute or pledge of allegiance in schools.[17]

Moreover, it is certainly not true that national identity in the United States is based solely or even mostly on freely chosen political ideals. Most Americans are in fact born and not made. They are Americans not because of what they believe or what they have pledged to believe, but because they are born (and/or live) in a particular geographic place. In that respect, American nationality and citizenship is not unlike nationality and citizenship in most of the rest of the world. For the overwhelming majority of Americans, their national identity is not something they consciously adopt, but something they are born into and take for granted, much like their race, religion, and family. The idea that patriotism is categorically different in the United States than elsewhere is a myth—political scientist Bernard Yack calls it "the myth of the civic nation."[18]

But myths have consequences. Although American national identity is not as distinctive as is often claimed, the belief that America is exceptional powerfully shapes the nation's politics and culture. American exceptionalism is a source of national pride but at the same time a source of national anxiety. In particular, the belief that the United States cannot count on the potent, pre-rational cohesive power of blood ties fuels fears that the nation's political institutions may be subverted by aliens and radicals, which in turn produces anxious calls for the government to promote patriotism.

Illustrative were the sentiments expressed by Mississippi's state superintendent of public education, who in 1891 was asked to speak to the annual meeting of the National Education Association on the subject of "Teaching Patriotism." J. R. Preston began from the premise that "not one . . . of the strongest cohesive forces of a nationality" was present in the United States. Unlike Europe, America lacked "common sympathies, identity of race and descent, the same language, the same religion, identity of political antecedents." Although the nation was connected through commerce, that bond appealed "to no higher motive than self-interest" and so could not be counted on to foster "a true spirit of nationality." Only through teaching patriotism in the public schools, Preston stressed, could the nation make up for the lack of common culture, ethnicity, and race. The public schools, he concluded, "are the great fusing furnace" and "from the plastic stream of American childhood they must mould [*sic*] American patriots."[19]

Preston's speech—in which he frets over a range of "grave political and social evils" facing the nation, including "an overflow of immigrants"[20]—perfectly encapsulates the connection between ethnic and racial anxieties on the one hand and the liberal creed on the other. Bellamy's own comment about "our dwindling Colonial stock" also hints at the ethnic and racial anxieties that, as we saw in chapter two, underlay his understanding of American national identity and patriotism. Proud assertion of liberal principles coexists side-by-side with racial and ethnic anxieties; confidence about the transforming and beneficent power of American institutions and ideals goes hand-in-hand with deep forebodings about the dangers posed by the subversive "other." The nation's liberal dreams are not separable from its racial and ethnic nightmares. The liberal hope invites the illiberal fear, and the Pledge of Allegiance embodies both.

A Chosen People

Viewing the Pledge of Allegiance as simply an expression of a civic national identity or the American Creed is rendered even more problematic by the two words added in 1954: "under God." The Supreme Court might decide the words only signify a "ceremonial deism," but that is certainly not what those who added the words intended them to mean. They intended the words "under God" to convey that America is a religious nation unlike the Communist nations. Nor does the concept of ceremonial deism capture how millions of Americans understand those words—not the millions who feel excluded by a reference to a monotheistic God and not the millions more who believe that the Pledge expresses their conviction that America is in fact a nation under God.

Certainly the president of the United States does not think the words are simply ceremonial deism. Speaking at a school in Nashville, Tennessee, in September 2002, George W. Bush explained that the thirty-one words of the Pledge "help define our country." In a single sentence, Bush continued, "we affirm our form of government, our belief in human dignity, our unity as a people, *and our reliance on Providence.*" Our "enemies," the president pointed out, "hate the words" of the Pledge of Allegiance. In fact those enemies "want to erase them," which is why "we're determined to stand for these words, and live them out in our lives."[21] For the president of the United States the words "under God" are as meaningful as the final six words, "with liberty and justice for all." Both define what it means to be an American.

A letter sent by the Bush White House to those writing the president regarding the Ninth Circuit's decision amplified Bush's understanding of the meaning of the "under God" clause. The letter, issued over Bush's signature, reiterated the president's belief that the Pledge helped "define our Nation" and that the Pledge affirmed "our reliance on God." Going further still, Bush opined that "when we pledge allegiance to One Nation under God, our citizens participate in an important American tradition of humbly seeking the wisdom and blessing of Divine Providence." In closing, the president expressed his hope that we would always "live by that same trust" in God and that "the Almighty [would] continue to watch over the United States of America."[22]

The close of Bush's letter echoed remarks he made the week after the Ninth Circuit's ruling in a July 4 speech in the town of Ripley, West Virginia. The president's Independence Day address began with the crowd reciting the Pledge of Allegiance and, according to news accounts, "shouting out" the words "under God." Bush defiantly promised that "no authority of government can ever prevent an American from pledging allegiance to this one nation under God." Our freedom, Bush explained, was "granted to each one of us by Almighty God." Americans, the president continued, "know that our country did not come about by chance." America was a special place of freedom, a nation that "bears the hopes of the world." And yet Americans have always known, "from the day of our founding," that "America's own great hope has never been in ourselves alone" but in our faith in God. America had been a beacon of liberty because God had faithfully "watch[ed] over the United States of America."[23]

Bush's rhetoric suggesting that Americans were God's chosen people is, of course, hardly original. Eighty years before, President Woodrow Wilson expressed the same belief—"that God planted in us the vision of liberty" and "that we are chosen . . . to show the way to the nations of the world how they walk in the paths of liberty." Almost thirty years before entering the presidency, Ronald Reagan confessed that he believed "that God in shedding his grace on this country has always in this divine scheme of things kept an eye on our land and guided it as a promised land." As president, at a swearing-in ceremony for new citizens, Reagan reiterated this view. "It's long been my belief," Reagan explained (after joining the new citizens in reciting the Pledge of Allegiance), "that America is a chosen land, placed by some Divine Providence here between the two oceans to be sought out and found only by those with a special yearning for freedom." America's divine mission is twofold: to serve as a haven of liberty, a promised land, but also to extend light into the darkness, to redeem the world.[24]

In the hands of Bush, Reagan, and Wilson, religious national identity is fused with civic national identity. What God plants in Americans is a universal ideal, "the vision of liberty," just as the peculiar genius of the Anglo-Saxon race, in the minds of Francis Bellamy and Josiah Strong, was a love of liberty. To those who believe in America's divine mission, there is no conflict between a nation knit together by universal values and a nation selected by God to nurture or spread those values. According to this reading, "under God" in the post-1954 Pledge of Allegiance is not an empty ceremonial deism but rather a profound expression of what sociologist Robert Bellah famously termed America's "civil religion."[25]

But the concept of "civil religion" obscures the very real conflict between a religious conception of American national identity and a secular, civic conception of national identity. This conflict was revealed in perhaps its baldest form in comments made in August 1987 by Vice President (and presidential hopeful) George H. W. Bush in response to a question from the atheist Rob Sherman, who the following year would file a lawsuit in federal court challenging the constitutionality of the "under God" clause in the Pledge of Allegiance. Sherman, who was reporting for an atheist news organization, asked the vice president whether he intended to reach out to atheist citizens in the coming presidential campaign. Bush's response: "I don't know that Atheists should be considered as citizens, nor should they be considered patriots. This is one nation under God." Bush's answer underscores the ways in which a religious conception of national identity excludes those who do not share that religious belief, just as surely as a racial or ethnic conception of national identity excludes those not of that race or ethnicity. Little wonder that the Pledge's declaration that the United States is "one nation under God" appears to atheists to be logically akin to the statement that the United States is "one nation under white males"—historically accurate perhaps, but exclusionary nonetheless.[26]

If the idea of America as a civic nation is largely myth, the idea of America as God's chosen people is pure fantasy. These two ideas provide the underpinnings of the belief in American exceptionalism, though in truth there is little that is exceptional about believing that God favors one's own nation. That particular delusion is one that, sadly, afflicts many peoples of the world. In his recent book, *Chosen Peoples*, Anthony Smith has documented the many ways in which the Old Testament idea of a chosen people has shaped the national identities of a wide range of peoples.[27] And, of course, the idea that God is on one's side is not even peculiar to the Judeo-Christian tradition, as even the most cursory survey of Islamic rhetoric indicates.[28] We are no more a nation under God than is Rwanda or Romania. Yet the myths persist, shaping who we are for good and for ill.

The Paradox of the Pledge

Striving to explain why he wanted every public school student and teacher to recite the Pledge of Allegiance daily, Colorado Springs Republican Doug Lamborn told his state house colleagues: "I think America is special, and the Pledge of Allegiance points that out." The Pledge of Allegiance highlights American exceptionalism because what makes America special is that it is a nation committed to "liberty and justice for all" and that it is a nation "under God." Belief in American exceptionalism saves the Pledge of Allegiance from being just another nationalistic loyalty oath of the kind that authoritarian regimes across the globe have so often favored. One pledges oneself not just to the nation and certainly not to the nation's leaders but rather to the ideals for which the nation stands.[29]

Both the civic identity and religious identity expressed in the Pledge of Allegiance can be used to judge America and judge it harshly. God and justice are external standards one can use to find a nation's actions wanting. Acknowledging that God is watching over and judging a nation can lead to national humility and even repentance. That is the spirit in which Thomas Jefferson famously reflected upon the injustice of slavery: "I tremble for my country when I reflect that God is just; and that his justice cannot sleep forever." Given the impossibility of ever achieving true justice or liberty, one can imagine, as Samuel

Huntington feared, that these ideals would be a perpetual indictment of existing policies and institutions. And one might also hope that pursuit of these
ideals might spur us to become a better, more just nation.

But the historical record reveals that the Pledge has largely not been used
to promote national self-criticism or to mobilize movements for social justice.
It was created to mark a monumental celebration of American accomplish-
ments, the World's Columbian Exposition in Chicago, and, ever since, the
meaning of the Pledge of Allegiance has remained almost entirely celebratory.
Whether "with liberty and justice for all" is viewed as a descriptive or aspirational statement, the words are generally interpreted as an affirmation of the
greatness of the United States, the peculiar repository of the world's universal
values. Every day, young people across the nation are pressured, if not coerced,
not only to affirm allegiance to America but to attest to American exceptionalism, to affirm Lamborn's contention that "America is special."

There are few nations of any significance that have not been buoyed by the
belief that they are special. And given the economic abundance, political sta-
bility, democratic freedoms, and military power that have characterized much
of the history of the United States, it is perhaps not surprising that a belief in
American exceptionalism has flourished. Preference easily slides over into pride,
and pride can just as easily become arrogance.[30] Celebrating one's own nation
is achieved by denigrating other nations. The United States is portrayed, as Dinesh D'Souza does, as "an oasis of goodness in a desert of cynicism and barbarism." America's "shining city on the hill" (to use one of President Reagan's
favorite images) presupposes a darkness into which America can shine its liberating light.[31]

Nationalism the world over has its dangers. But in the United States, those
dangers often take a distinctive form because the myth of the civic nation allows us to believe that our nationalism is unlike that of other nations. We have
good, idealistic patriotism; they have bad, ethnic nationalism. Our values are
universalistic; theirs are chauvinistic and parochial. The myth of the civic nation—"a mixture of self-congratulation and wishful thinking," says Yack—encourages us to fool ourselves into believing that our motives are different, that
they are pure and unsullied by base national interest. And it is a short step from
this belief to the assumption that we can be trusted to do what is right and rational. We easily lull ourselves into believing that American interests and
human rights are one and the same thing, and that what is good for America
is good for the world. Over a century and a half ago, Herman Melville expressed
the conceit this way: "We Americans are the peculiar, chosen people—the Is-

rael of our time; we bear the ark of the liberties of the world. . . . [T]he political Messiah . . . has come in us, if we would but give utterance to his promptings. And let us always remember that with ourselves, almost for the first time in the history of earth, national selfishness is unbounded philanthropy; for we cannot do a good to America, but we give alms to the world." These are the myths that invite the nation down the path to empire—an idealistic empire perhaps, but an empire nonetheless.[32]

If the twin myths of the civic nation and the chosen people tempt the United States to act as the messianic savior of the world or, more modestly, to pose as a righteous beacon of liberty, the myths also foster intense national anxiety. For the darkness always threatens to envelop the shining city and extinguish the light. As political scientist Hugh Heclo writes, "the very fact of its exceptional mission meant that America was continually endangered."[33] It meant, too, that what was at stake was massive, the price of failure incalculable. If the United States was, as Lincoln said, "the last, best hope on earth," then the failure of the United States was the world's failure. Destruction or subversion of the United States meant extinguishing the light forever. Little wonder that those most boastful of America's greatness have so often also been the ones wracked with anxieties about America's future and its identity.

The paradox of the Pledge of Allegiance is that it expresses both the conceit and the anxieties, the confidence and the fears. On the one hand, the Pledge reflects a profound faith in the transformative and liberating power of American ideas. Immigrants need not be excluded if they can be remade. The markers of citizenship are not race or ethnicity but adherence to the central tenets of a creedal orthodoxy. Recite the words of the Pledge and one can be Americanized. Bellamy believed that the truths of the nation's creed expressed in the Pledge were self-evident: "Their truth is so palpable that it is undebatable. To say it is to see it. To feel it is to be governed by it."[34] And there is an undeniable power to the Pledge, especially the magnificent final two words—a nation committed to liberty and justice not just for whites, or for men, or for the rich and powerful, but *for all*, or at least for all Americans.

Yet there are unmistakable strains of national insecurity and anxiety embedded in the history of the Pledge of Allegiance as well. Why, after all, should faith in the enduring power of American ideas and institutions manifest itself in a requirement that children affirm publicly and daily their fealty to those ideas and institutions? Would the culturally confident need the continual expression of the visible signs of inner faith? If America is a great nation, and if the truths of its ideas and institutions are self-evidently obvious, then why the need for daily expressions of allegiance? The Pledge ritual seems better suited to an insecure nation than a confident one, to a nation worried about change and fearful of the commitment of its young people and its newcomers. Backers of the Pledge are often cast as true patriots, but it is arguably those who would dispense with a daily Pledge who are the ones who harbor the greatest faith in the enduring power and strength of American institutions and American ideas. Perhaps that is the true paradox of the Pledge of Allegiance.

Notes

Preface

1. Janet Davies, "Outcry Surprises 9th Circuit Judge," *Statesman Journal* (Salem, Ore.), June 28, 2002, 1A, 3A. *Newdow v. U.S. Congress* 292 F.3d 597 (2002).

2. *Congressional Record–House*, June 27, 2002, H4125. *Congressional Record–Senate*, June 26, 2002, S6102. The author of the House resolution was James Sensenbrenner, a Wisconsin Republican. The three opposing votes were all by Democrats. Eleven Democrats were also recorded as present but not voting.

3. "Rep. Pitts Blasts San Francisco Pledge Ruling," News from Congressman Joe Pitts, June 26, 2002 (http://www.house.gov/pitts/press/releases/020626r-pledgeruling .htm). P. J. Reilly, "Pitt Stands Up for Pledge on Capitol Steps," *Intelligencer Journal* (Lancaster, Pa.), June 27, 2002, A4. *Congressional Record–Senate*, June 26, 2002, S6103, S6102. "Lawmakers Blast Pledge Ruling," CNN.com, June 27, 2002, at http://www.cnn.com/2002/LAW/06/26/pledge.allegiance. Doug Erickson, "'Under God' in Pledge Ruled Unconstitutional," *Wisconsin State Journal (Madison)*, June 27, 2002, A1.

4. Howard Fineman, "One Nation, Under . . . Who?" *Newsweek*, July 8, 2002, pp. 23–24. *Statesman Journal* (Salem, Ore.), July 1, 2002, 5C, and July 5, 2002, 8C.

5. "Transcript: Bush, Putin Pledge a United Front against Terrorism," White House, Office of the Press Secretary, Calgary, Canada, June 27, 2002, available at http://usembassy.state.gov/tokyo/wwwhec0652.html. "Court Rules That 'God' in Pledge Violates Constitution; Decision Draws Outrage," *St. Louis Post-Dispatch*, June 27, 2002, A1. Dori Meinert, "Congress Backs the Pledge," Copley News Service, June 27, 2002. "[Missouri] Congressional Delegation Reacts to Pledge of Allegiance Decision," Associated Press State and Local Wire, June 26, 2002. "[Kansas] Congressional Delegation Reacts to Pledge of Allegiance Decision," Associated Press State and Local Wire, June 27, 2002.

6. Louis Hartz's famous formulation was "no feudalism, no socialism." See *The Liberal Tradition in America* (New York: Harcourt Brace, 1955).

7. Uday Singh Mehta, *The Anxiety of Freedom: Imagination and Individuality in Locke's Political Thought* (Ithaca: Cornell University Press, 1992).

8. *Washington Post*, March 22, 2001, T9.

1. Creating the Pledge

1. The questions can be found at http://www.ins.usdoj.gov/graphics/services /natz/100q.pdf.

2. Extract from an 1890 speech by Richard Edwards, Illinois State Superintendent of Public Instruction, in George W. Gue, *Our Country's Flag* (Davenport, Iowa: Egbert, Fidlar, and Chambers, 1890), 154.

3. Scot M. Guenter, *The American Flag, 1777–1924* (Rutherford, N.J.: Fairleigh Dickinson University Press, 1990), 36, 57, 69–73. George T. Balch, *Methods of Teaching Patriotism in the Public Schools* (New York: D. Van Nostrand, 1890), 61. The 1880 text quoted by Guenter (on page 69) is from George Henry Preble, *History of the Flag of the United States of America, and of the Naval and Yacht-Club Signals, Seals, and Arms, and Principal National Songs of the United States, with a Chronicle of the Symbols, Standards, Banners, and Flags of Ancient and Modern Nations,* 2d ed. rev. (Boston: A. Williams, 1880).

4. Balch, *Methods of Teaching Patriotism,* 61–62.

5. Ibid., 61.

6. Guenter, *American Flag,* 104–5. Balch, *Methods of Teaching Patriotism,* xi, 27. Stuart McConnell, *Glorious Contentment: The Grand Army of the Republic, 1865–1900* (Chapel Hill: University of North Carolina Press, 1992), 20. "Origin of Flag Presentation to Educational Institutions," in *Ceremony of Flag Presentation to Columbia University of the City of New York, May Second, 1896, and May Seventh, 1898, by Lafayette Post No. 140, Department of New York, Grand Army of the Republic* (privately printed by Lafayette Post, 1899), 105–7. Homer was particularly impressed by its effect upon "the children of foreign parentage whose home education did not tend in that direction" (105).

7. Guenter, *American Flag,* 105. *Journal of the Twenty-Third Annual Session of the National Encampment,* Grand Army of the Republic, Milwaukee, Wis., August 28, 29, 30, 1889 (St. Louis, Mo.: A. Whipple, 1889), 41. Wallace Evan Davies, *Patriotism on Parade: The Story of Veterans' and Hereditary Organizations in America, 1783–1900* (Cambridge, Mass.: Harvard University Press, 1955), 219. Mary R. Dearing, *Veterans in Politics: The Story of the G.A.R.* (Baton Rouge: Louisiana State University Press, 1952), 405. McConnell, *Glorious Contentment,* 228.

8. Davies, *Patriotism on Parade,* 219. Dearing, *Veterans in Politics,* 472. McConnell, *Glorious Contentment,* 228.

9. Cecilia Elizabeth O'Leary, *To Die For: The Paradox of American Patriotism* (Princeton, N.J.: Princeton University Press, 1999), 155–56. Frank Luther Mott, *A History of American Magazines, 1850–1865* (Cambridge, Mass.: Harvard University Press, 1938), 268. The schoolhouse flag movement and the Columbus Day Celebration also proved good business for the *Companion.* By June 1893, when the *Companion* issued its special World's Fair issue, the number of subscribers had reached 560,000 ("Our World's Fair Number," *Youth's Companion,* June 22, 1893, reprinted in Louise Harris, *The Flag over the Schoolhouse* [Providence, R.I.: C. A. Stephens Collection, 1971], 88).

10. Mott, *History of American Magazines,* 266–68. C. A. Stephens, *Stories of My Home Folks* (Boston: Perry Mason Company, 1926), 9. Harris, *Flag over the Schoolhouse,* 13. See also Louise Harris, *"None but the Best"* (Providence, R.I.: C.A. Stephens Collection, 1966).

11. Harris, *Flag over the Schoolhouse*, 20–21. Harris, *None but the Best*, 132.

12. "Teaching Patriotism," *Youth's Companion* 62 (1889): 429. The person who first drew attention to this article was Scot Guenter in his fine book *The American Flag* (page 121); see also Morris G. Sica, "The School Flag Movement: Origin and Influence," *Social Education* (October 1990): 381. Louise Harris, despite her exhaustive search for material in the *Companion* relating to the schoolhouse flag movement, somehow managed to overlook this article. As Guenter recognized, the article contradicts Harris's insistence that the *Youth's Companion* was the original source of the schoolhouse flag movement.

13. Stephens, *Stories of My Home Folks*, 9; see also 8. This line is repeated, in fact plagiarized, by Margarette Miller in *I Pledge Allegiance* (Boston: Christopher Publishing, 1946), 90. Similar testimony of Ford's close oversight is offered by Harris, who reports that "every story, article, item, current event, advertisement, and whatever that was printed in *The Companion* passed through the hands of Daniel Sharp Ford for his approval" (Harris, *Flag over the Schoolhouse*, 37; see also Harris, *None but the Best*, 22).

14. See Stephens, *Stories of My Home Folks*, 3, 12.

15. Harris, *Flag over the Schoolhouse*, 15. Louise Harris states that Upham did not become the head of the premium department until 1886, but she seems to be in error, perhaps confusing it with the date Ford made his nephew a business partner, which was 1886. John W. Baer, in *The Pledge of Allegiance: A Centennial History, 1892–1992* (Annapolis, Md.: J. W. Baer, 1992), 19, following Harris, makes the same mistake. But the Upham genealogy, published in 1892 and written with the help of both James Upham and his father, indicates that James Upham "took charge of an important department" upon his arrival at the firm (F. K. Upham, *The Descendants of John Upham of Massachusetts* [Albany, N.Y.: Joel Munsell's Son's, 1892], 385–86). Francis Bellamy's biographer, Margarette S. Miller, in *Twenty-Three Words* (Portsmouth, Va.: Printcraft Press, 1976), 73, has Upham taking charge of the premium department upon his arrival at the *Youth's Companion* in 1872.

16. Upham did enlist in the Home Guard in his hometown of Fairfax, situated in a remote part of northern Vermont, far from the fighting. Upham turned eighteen on December 27, 1863, but did not join the Union army, even though the army was desperate for recruits and the war had well over a year still to run. The conscription law passed in the spring of 1863 did not affect Upham since the age of conscription was twenty; it was legal, however, to enlist at age eighteen. Margarette Miller obscures Upham's choice not to serve in the Union army, writing only that "the sons of suitable age were soon at the front. The war spirit was manifested everywhere; and Upham, then in his teens, enlisted as a member of the Home Guard" (Miller, *Twenty-Three Words*, 73).

17. Francis Bellamy, "The Story of the Pledge of Allegiance to the Flag," 6, Francis Bellamy Papers, Rare Books and Special Collections, Rush Rhees Library, University of Rochester, Rochester, N.Y. (hereafter cited as Bellamy Papers). See also Miller, *Twenty-Three Words*, 75; James B. Upham, "The School House Flag," *State Journal* (Topeka, Kans.), July 23, 1892, p. 8; and Mary Yerger Raymond, "And So

America Was Rediscovered 400 Years Later," *Tampa Daily Times*, December 19, 1925, 7C.

18. Harris, *Flag over the Schoolhouse*, 17–18. Guenter, *American Flag*, 18. Balch reprinted the winning essay from New York in a long footnote in *Methods of Teaching Patriotism* (78–80).

19. "Have You Raised a Flag over Your School-House?" *Youth's Companion*, December 25, 1890, in Harris, *Flag over the Schoolhouse*, 34. "Who Originated Columbus School Day?" *School Journal* (November 12, 1892), 436. "Exposition Legislation," Interactive Guide to the World's Columbian Exposition, Chicago, Illinois, May–October 1893; available at ⟨http://users.vnet.net/schulman/Columbian/columbian .html#LEGISLATION⟩. Raymond, "And So America Was Rediscovered." See also Bellamy, "Story of the Pledge," 8, Bellamy Papers.

20. Harris, *Flag over the Schoolhouse*, 31, 34, 41. "Who Originated Columbus School Day?" 436. Bellamy, "Story of the Pledge," 7, Bellamy Papers. See also Guenter, *American Flag*, 125.

21. "Is Your School to Celebrate?" *Youth's Companion*, May 26, 1892, and "Raise the Schoolhouse Flag," *Youth's Companion*, January 14, 1892, reprinted in Harris, *Flag over the Schoolhouse*, 51, 48.

22. Miller, *Twenty-Three Words*, 43, 46, 53–55. It was Ford, Bellamy told the church elders, who had urged him to "show in my preaching how the Bible was full, from lid to lid, of sympathy with the poor and their cause; and that the Savior was emphatically the poor man's friend" (Bellamy to the Committee on Christian Work of the Social Union, January 1, 1891, in Miller, *Twenty-Three Words*, 55).

23. Miller, *Twenty-Three Words*, 53, 55, 58–59.

24. Ibid., 9, 14, 23.

25. After the Civil War, the Reverend Upham left the presidency of the New Hampton Institute to become editor of the *Watchman and Reflector*, an important Boston-based journal of Baptist opinion, which at that time was co-owned by none other than his brother-in-law, Daniel Sharp Ford. In his late sixties, he again went to work for Ford as the *Youth's Companion's* "health editor," a post he held for at least a decade (Upham, *Descendants of John Upham*, 201). Upham described his brother-in-law as "a layman in Boston, who by his wealth, example, counsel and large ideas of Christian stewardship, has done perhaps as much as any one in that city to stir the churches to active enterprise in their work" (170).

26. Upham, *Descendants of John Upham*, 169. James Upham, *A Sketch of the Life and Character of Dea. Joshua Upham of Salem, Mass* (Boston: N.p., 1885), 28. In fact, so earnest was this wish that Joshua Upham sent his son to college so that the son could be the minister that the father had not been. As Reverend Upham tells the tale, "in the earlier part of [Joshua's] Christian life, his mind was much exercised with the thought that it was his duty to preach the gospel," but he felt inhibited by his relative lack of education. Joshua reconciled himself to his situation by deciding that it was God's will that this work should be left to the son, and so, recalled the Reverend Upham, "on my birth, I was consecrated to the Lord for that purpose, and in due time sent to college with that end in view" (25).

27. Miller, *Twenty-Three Words*, 54. "Studies in Social Christianity," *The Dawn*, September 15, 1889, 5.

28. Miller, *Twenty-Three Words*, 12, 15, 73. Charles E. Fairman, "James B. Upham, the Founder of Flag Day," *Historical Bulletin* 8 (June 1906): 159–63. John Albert Scott, *Rome, N.Y.: A Short History* (Rome, N.Y.: Rome Historical Society, 1983).

29. Miller, *Twenty-Three Words*, vi; see also 1–2. Upham, *Descendants of John Upham*, 48, 53, 71. Bellamy's and Upham's interest in their ancestors was typical of men of their generation, background, and social class. This obsession with genealogy prompted a Vermont University professor, in 1886, to scathingly remark that "the American of the present day . . . would rather know who was his grandfather in the year 1600, than to know who will be the next president" (Barbara Miller Solomon, *Ancestors and Immigrants: A Changing New England Tradition* [Chicago: University of Chicago Press, 1956], 60). Historian Michael Kammen also reminds us that "we must recall just how obsessed people of this generation really were with genealogy" (*Mystic Chords of Memory: The Transformation of Tradition in American Culture* [New York: Vintage, 1993], 249). See also Davis, *Patriotism on Parade*, 47–49.

30. David Hackett Fischer, *Albion's Seed: Four British Folkways in America* (New York: Oxford University Press, 1989), 16. Arthur E. Morgan, *Edward Bellamy* (New York: Columbia University Press, 1944), 13–14. Miller, *Twenty-Three Words*, 2–3. Upham, *Descendants of John Upham*, 33–50, 386.

31. Ernest Lee Tuveson, *Redeemer Nation: The Idea of America's Millennial Role* (Chicago: University of Chicago Press, 1968), 59. "The Joseph Bellamy House: The Great Awakening in New England," available at http://www.cr.nps.gov/nr/twhp /wwwlps/lessons/85bellamy/85bellamy.htm. See also http://www.cr.nps.gov/nr/twhp /wwwlps/lessons/85bellamy/85facts2.htm; and Mark Valeri, *Law and Providence in Joseph Bellamy's New England: The Origins of the New Divinity in Revolutionary America* (New York: Oxford University Press, 1994).

32. Miller, *Twenty-Three Words*, 1, 5.

33. Hubert Howe Bancroft, *The Book of the Fair* (Chicago: Bancroft Company, 1893), 921, available at http://columbus.gl.iit.edu/bookfair/ch26.html#921. Miller, *Twenty-Three Words*, 76–77. Miller, *I Pledge Allegiance*, 87–89. According to Margarette Miller, Ford told Bellamy: "Of course, you are to work under James [Upham] and do nothing without his consent" (Miller, *I Pledge Allegiance*, 90). Bellamy also wrote Ford detailed progress reports of what he had done and was planning to do. See, for instance, Bellamy to Daniel Sharp Ford, April 18, 1892 (there are two separate letters for this date, one of five pages, and the other of six pages), June 10, 1892, and June 27, 1892, Bellamy Papers.

34. Miller, *I Pledge Allegiance*, 91–92. Francis Bellamy, "Affidavit Concerning the True Origin [of the] Pledge of Allegiance to the Flag," August 13, 1923, 1–2, Bellamy Papers.

35. Miller, *Twenty-Three Words*, 80, 83, 100. Guenter, *American Flag*, 129. "For Thirteen Millions: A Columbian Celebration for the Public Schools," *Boston Herald*, March 31, 1892, 5. Bellamy to Ford, April 12, 1892 (first letter), Bellamy to Ford, April 12, 1892 (second letter), 3–4, and Bellamy, "Story of the Pledge," 10, Bellamy

Papers. See also Bellamy, "Affidavit," 2–3, and Bellamy's form letter, "To the Super-intendent of Schools," September 10, 1892, Bellamy Papers.

36. Bellamy to Ford, April 18, 1892 (second letter), 4–6, Bellamy Papers. "A Lesson in Patriotism: General Palmer Talks about the National Columbian Public School Celebration of October 12th, Albany, N.Y., May __ 1892," Bellamy Papers. Miller, *I Pledge Allegiance*, 103–5. In his effort to secure Ford's support for the Washington, D.C., venture, Bellamy also told his boss that it "would in the end give the Companion really magnificent advertising" (April 18, 1892 [second letter], 6, Bellamy Papers).

37. Bellamy, "Interview with President Harrison," Bellamy Papers. On the funding of the 1889 centennial, see Kammen, *Mystic Chords of Memory*, 445.

38. Harrison followed through on his promise, sending Bellamy a supportive though hardly gushing letter of support within a fortnight: "I am very much pleased with the idea. Properly conducted such exercises will be instructive to the pupils, and will excite in every village in the land an interest in this great anniversary" (May 23, 1892, reproduced in Miller, *Twenty-Three Words*, 102).

39. Karen Orren, "Benjamin Harrison," in *The Reader's Companion to the American Presidency*, ed. Alan Brinkley and Davis Dye (New York: Houghton Mifflin, 2000), 269. Francis Bellamy, "The Pledge of Allegiance to the Flag," *Stone and Webster Journal* 43 (October 1928): 469. Bellamy, "Interview with President Harrison," Bellamy Papers. Raymond, "And So America Was Rediscovered." Bellamy also gave another account in which he delivered the boastful retort about congressional approval to Lodge but not to the president. See Bellamy, "Story of the Pledge," 11, Bellamy Papers.

40. Miller, *Twenty-Three Words*, 97. Raymond, "And So America Was Rediscovered." The final congressional resolution did not actually pass both houses of Congress until late June, held up in part because of a dispute over whether the date of celebration should be October 12 or 21. More alarming for Bellamy, by mid-July there still had been no presidential proclamation. An anxious Bellamy returned to the nation's capital to try to expedite the matter. Finding that the president's order to issue the proclamation had been sent to the State Department, Bellamy called on the Secretary of State to urge him to issue the proclamation quickly. The secretary, though initially affronted by Bellamy's boldness, ended up inviting Bellamy to draft the proclamation. A surprised Bellamy seized the opportunity. "Let the national flag," he wrote, "float over every schoolhouse in the country and the exercises be such as shall impress upon our youth the patriotic duties of American citizenship." The presidential proclamation was issued later that same evening, and from that moment, Bellamy later wrote, he knew that the school celebration was "bound to go." These events are related in Bellamy, "Story of the Pledge," 12, Bellamy Papers; Bellamy, "The Pledge of Allegiance to the Flag," 470; and Miller, *Twenty-Three Words*, 111–12.

41. Miller, *Twenty-Three Words*, 292–93.

42. Bellamy to Ford, April 18, 1892 (second letter), 1–3, and Francis Bellamy to President Benjamin Harrison, May 12, 1892, Bellamy Papers. There is no mention of the religious exercise in the letter to President Harrison.

43. Bellamy to Harrison, May 12, 1892, and Bellamy to Ford, April 18, 1892 [second letter], 3, Bellamy Papers. Bellamy explained to Ford that the purpose of providing an afternoon program was that, "unless we are keenly alert, the Public School idea will frequently be ignored in the Citizen's Celebration [of Columbus day], and Hamlet will be left out of Hamlet. Therefore we must prepare a Citizen's Program in which the School idea shall be the dominant feature, and in which delegations of pupils can take certain part" (2–3).

44. Bellamy to Ford, June 7, 1892, Bellamy Papers. Miller, *Twenty-Three Words*, 108–10. Harris, *Flag over the Schoolhouse*, 62–63. Harris, *None but the Best*, 101.

45. Bellamy to Ford, June 7, 1892, 2–3, Bellamy Papers. Miller, *Twenty-Three Words*, 109. Miller, *I Pledge Allegiance*, 138–39. "National School Celebration of Columbus Day, The Official Programme," reprinted in Harris, *Flag over the Schoolhouse*, 66. Bellamy's authorship of the address was no secret, however. In Newton, Massachusetts, Bellamy was a guest of honor at the morning ceremonies held in the town's high school and was publicly honored as the author of the address. See *Newton Graphic*, October 28, 1892, p. 2, and *Newton Journal*, October 28, 1892, p. 2.

46. Miller, *Twenty-Three Words*, 119, 320. George T. Balch, *A Patriotic Primer for the Little Citizen*, rev. ed. (Indianapolis: Levey Bros., 1898), 16. Bellamy, "Affidavit," 4, 7–8, Bellamy to Mrs. Lue Stuart Wadsworth, July 12, 1923, and Bellamy, "Story of the Pledge," 7, Bellamy Papers.

47. Miller, *Twenty-Three Words*, 120. Raymond, "And So America Was Rediscovered." Bellamy, "Affidavit," 4–5, Bellamy, "Story of the Pledge," 13, and Bellamy to Mrs. Lue Stuart Wadsworth, Bellamy Papers.

48. Miller, *Twenty-Three Words*, 122–23. Miller, *I Pledge Allegiance*, 151. Bellamy, "Story of the Pledge," 15–16, Bellamy Papers. Raymond, "And So America Was Rediscovered." Bellamy, "Affidavit," 4–5, Bellamy Papers. In the program, the salute remained anonymous, attributed neither to Bellamy nor to the *Youth's Companion*. The decision was Ford's, who thought there was already quite enough of the *Companion* in the program. See Bellamy's "Affidavit," 7, Bellamy Papers, and Miller, *Twenty-Three Words*, 123.

49. "National School Celebration of Columbus Day: The Official Programme," *Youth's Companion*, September 8, 1892, reprinted in Harris, *Flag over the Schoolhouse*, 64–68.

50. Ibid., 66–68. See also Bellamy to Ford, April 18, 1892 (second letter), 1–3, Bellamy Papers.

51. A survey of the nation's superintendents of education that was carried out by Bellamy's committee a few weeks before the celebration found that about 120,000 public schools in the country—over half of the nation's public schools—were planning to participate in the celebration (Miller, *Twenty-Three Words*, 130–31). Miller was of the opinion that this number probably underestimated the number of schools participating, although she allowed that "it is reasonable enough to realize that in all probability many villages and towns took no part in the programme" (171). After the day of celebration, however, the *Youth's Companion* reported that "the schools were few which did not celebrate" and estimated that "the flag was raised and saluted by

hundred of thousands of schools" ("Columbus Day," November 17, 1892, in Harris, *Flag over the Schoolhouse*, 80). My own survey of newspapers suggests that at least in the larger towns and cities the participation of public schools was, if not universal, extraordinarily widespread. Even where there were no parades and little if anything in the way of civic celebration (for instance in Washington, D.C., and Augusta, Georgia), the morning patriotic exercises were apparently carried out in the public schools. See, for instance, the reports in the Atlanta *Constitution*, October 22, 1892.

52. The *Milwaukee Sentinel*, for instance, reported that the exercises followed by the Lutheran parochial schools of Milwaukee were the same as those in the public schools, except for "the singing of the 'Te Deum Laudamas'" (October 22 , 1892, p. 7).

53. *New York Times*, October 11, 1892, p. 2. *National Tribune*, October 27, 1892, p. 12.

54. *Malden Evening News*, October 22, 1892, p. 2. Bellamy had long been aware that Roman Catholics had very different ideas about the meaning of Columbus Day. For instance, in July 1892, he told the secretary of state that it was important that the president's proclamation "be so worded that [it] would not cast any reflection upon the Romanists who were planning to give to the Columbian anniversary a Roman Catholic color" (Bellamy, "The Pledge of Allegiance to the Flag," 470).

55. *Indianapolis Sentinel*, October 22, 1892, p. 4. A similar message was preached at a morning mass at St. Mary's Cathedral in San Francisco: "We, as Catholics, feel a great pride in this celebration for America was discovered in Catholic days and by a great son of the church. The newly discovered continent was colonized largely by Catholics and they have at all times been prominent factors in this great nation" (*San Francisco Examiner*, October 22, 1892, p. 3).

56. Press reports were almost uniformly enthusiastic about the program and the day of celebration. One exception was the *Kansas City Star* (October 22, 1892, p. 4), which acerbically opined: "Now that the dedication ceremonies are done and that the Columbus jubilee is over, some friend of the Columbus family should go to the courts and get out an injunction to prevent the use of the distinguished explorer's name by any man, woman, or child for one year. Only this or some similar proceeding will keep the memory of the hero green. Already the cavalcade tramping around his ashes has made the thought of Columbus an unsightly one. A little more straining of public tolerance and the name Columbus will become a nuisance and an abomination in the sight of the Lord. Let the Columbian badges be put away and preserved in the family Bible; let the Columbian odes and poetry be soaked in brine. Let Isabella, the trump queen of diamonds, and Ferdinand, the brunette king who didn't count as much as a red ten-spot, be shuffled in the deck. Let there be a new deal. Give Balboa or Magellan or Coronado or Captain Kid or Paul Boyton a show."

57. "Columbus Day," *Youth's Companion*, November 17, 1892, in Harris, *Flag over the Schoolhouse*, 80. Among the many clues to Bellamy's authorship of this editorial is the concluding paragraph, which suggests that while October 21 was a day "in which Columbus was honored it was America that was celebrated," phrasing that echoes not only the theme but the language of the address he delivered in Malden. The reference to the school system being "under God" was also language Bellamy used in his Malden address.

2. The Meaning of the Pledge

1. Bill Martin and Michael Sampson, *I Pledge Allegiance* (Cambridge, Mass.: Candlewick Press, 2002). See also June Swanson, *I Pledge Allegiance,* 2d ed. (Minneapolis: Carolrhoda Books, 2002), esp. 17–23.

2. Mary Yerger Raymond, "And So America Was Rediscovered 400 Years Later," *Tampa Daily Times,* December 19, 1925, 7C. Francis Bellamy, "The Pledge of Allegiance to the Flag," *Stone and Webster Journal* 43 (October 1928): 471. In a similar vein, Bellamy described the Columbus Day celebration as an "attempt to retain the fine, loyal ideals that had been handed down to us by our fathers" (Raymond, "And So America Was Rediscovered").

3. Peter Dreier and Dick Flacks, "Patriotism's Secret History," *Nation,* June 3, 2002, 40. See also John W. Baer, *The Pledge of Allegiance: A Centennial History, 1892–1992* (Annapolis, Md.: J. W. Baer, 1992); and Sidney Blumenthal, *Pledging Allegiance: The Last Campaign of the Cold War* (New York: Harper, 1990), 263.

4. Franklin Rosemont, "Bellamy's Radicalism Reclaimed," in *Looking Backward, 1988–1888,* ed. Sylvia E. Bowman (Amherst: University of Massachusetts Press, 1988), 154. Richard J. Ellis, *The Dark Side of the Left: Illiberal Egalitarianism in America* (Lawrence: University Press of Kansas, 1998), 46.

5. "Postscript," to Edward Bellamy, *Looking Backward: 2000–1887* (New York: Penguin, 1982), 232. John C. Cort, *Christian Socialism: An Informal History* (Maryknoll, N.Y.: Orbis Books, 1988), 223. Arthur E. Morgan, *Edward Bellamy* (New York: Columbia University Press, 1944), 249–50. Arthur Lipow, *Authoritarian Socialism in America: Edward Bellamy and the Nationalist Movement* (Berkeley: University of California Press, 1982), 123. Margarette S. Miller, *Twenty-Three Words* (Portsmouth, Va.: Printcraft Press, 1976), 51.

6. Morgan, *Edward Bellamy,* 248, 254. Lipow, *Authoritarian Socialism in America,* 85. John L. Thomas, *Alternative America: Henry George, Edward Bellamy, Henry Demarest Lloyd, and the Adversary Tradition* (Cambridge, Mass.: Harvard University Press, 1983), 249. In 1890, Bliss wrote in the *Dawn* that "the greatest fault of *Looking Backward* [is] that it uses a somewhat military phraseology and a somewhat regimented conception of society" (Cort, *Christian Socialism,* 234). Francis Bellamy also distanced himself from "military socialism" in "The Tyranny of All the People," *Arena* 4 (July 1891): 180–91.

7. Miller, *Twenty-Three Words,* 48. James Dombrowski, *The Early Days of Christian Socialism in America* (New York: Columbia University Press, 1936), 99. See also Everett W. MacNair, *Edward Bellamy and the Nationalist Movement, 1889–1894* (Milwaukee: Fitzgerald Co., 1957), 60.

8. "Studies in Social Christianity," *The Dawn,* September 15, 1889, 5, 7. Miller, *Twenty-Three Words,* 54. Francis Bellamy, "Aims and Methods," *The Dawn,* August 15, 1889, 7. Francis Bellamy, "Educational Department," *The Dawn,* May 1890, 44. "The Yesterday of Labor," *The Dawn,* November 15, 1889, 7 (authorship of this tract is attributed to Bellamy in *The Dawn,* October 1891). The outline of the first course of study presented by the committee was: "I. A Digest of 'Looking Backward,' by the

Author; II. The Yesterday of Labor, or the Rule of Might; III. The To-day of Labor, or Something Still Wrong; IV. The To-morrow of Labor, or What can be Done; V. The Subject Reviewed in the Light of the Bible." The topics for the second course were: "I. The Competitive System; II. Co-operation and Profit Sharing; III. The Land Question; IV. Socialism vs. Anarchy; and V. Christian Socialism" ("Studies in Social Christianity," *The Dawn,* September 15, 1889, 6).

9. Francis Bellamy, "Aims and Methods," *The Dawn,* August 15, 1889, 7. See also "What Play for Individuality under Socialism?" a paper given at several venues in the early 1890s. It is available in the Francis Bellamy Papers, Rare Books and Special Collections, Rush Rhees Library, University of Rochester, Rochester, N.Y. (hereafter cited as Bellamy Papers).

10. Morgan, *Edward Bellamy,* 249, and also 251. "The Yesterday of Labor," *The Dawn,* November 15, 1889, 7. On the conservatism of much of the Nationalist movement, see Lipow, *Authoritarian Socialism in America;* on its exclusivity and elitism see the 1889 article by Cyrus Field Willard, as quoted in Lipow, *Authoritarian Socialism in America,* 127. Contrast Willard's elitism with the concluding sentences of a paper by Francis Bellamy on "Municipal Government," read first in November 1890 at an annual meeting of the Baptist Congress and published six months later in the *Dawn*: "But before all, after all, under all, trust the people. Trust them with an undismayed, invincible trust. Make the people trustworthy by putting more trust in them" (*The Dawn,* May 1, 1891, 7).

11. Bellamy to Mrs. Lue Stuart Wadsworth, July 12, 1923, Bellamy Papers. Bellamy, "The Story of the Pledge of Allegiance to the Flag," 14, Bellamy Papers. See also Francis Bellamy, "Affidavit Concerning the True Origin [of the] Pledge of Allegiance to the Flag," August 13, 1923, 5, Bellamy Papers; and Cecilia Elizabeth O'Leary's *To Die For: The Paradox of American Patriotism* (Princeton, N.J.: Princeton University Press, 1999), 161.

12. Bellamy's address, which first appeared in the official program published in the *Youth's Companion,* September 8, 1892, 446, is conveniently reprinted in Miller, *Twenty-Three Words,* 116–18.

13. By December 1890, Bellamy is no longer listed as a vice president of the Society of Christian Socialists, though Bliss did publish Bellamy's talk on "Municipal Government" in May 1891. Bellamy's last writing done specifically for the *Dawn* was a regular column he wrote as editor of the magazine's "Educational Department," which appeared in the summer of 1890. Miller suggests that Bellamy's enthusiasm for Christian socialism began to dim as he became immersed in Upham's patriotic work at the *Companion;* see Miller, *Twenty-Three Words,* 84, as well as 75–76, 78. Certainly by 1896, as editor of the *Illustrated American,* Bellamy's views had become thoroughly conventional and stridently anti-Populist. He strongly opposed William Jennings Bryan in 1896, accusing him of being a "wicked deceiver of the people," in "Mr. Bryan, What Do You Mean?" *Illustrated American,* August 1, 1896, 166 (see also Miller, *Twenty-Three Words,* 177), and of having "unfurled the Red Flag" (September 26, 1896, 418). He praised the safely conservative National (Gold) Democratic ticket of John Palmer and Simon Buckner ("Democracy's New Birth," October 27,

1896, 518), as well as William McKinley, as "goodly giants" (September 19, 1896, 387). After McKinley's election, Bellamy sang the praises of the "strong and sane Americanism" of the administration's policy. Particularly pleasing to Bellamy was that McKinley had shown through his policies that "the imperial instincts of the race will not be thwarted under his hand" (August 28, 1897, 259).

14. Francis Bellamy, "Americanism in the Public Schools," in National Education Association, *Journal of Proceedings and Addresses: Session of the Year 1892 Held at Saratoga Springs, New York* (New York: National Education Association, 1893), 61–67. The speech was widely reported in the press. The entire speech was reprinted verbatim, for instance, in the *Boston Evening Transcript,* July 16, 1892.

15. Bellamy, "Americanism in the Public Schools," 61–63.

16. Ibid., 62–64; emphasis added. See also "A Patriotic Election," *Youth's Companion* (1892): 95; and Margarette Miller, *I Pledge Allegiance* (Boston: Christopher Publishing, 1946), 124–25.

17. "Mr. Bellamy's Lecture: The Spirit of Americanism—Perils from Immigration—Liberty, Equality, and Fraternity in Relation to the New American Idea," *Portland Daily Press,* January 13, 1893. Available in Bellamy Papers.

18. Ibid. "Americanism of the Future: Interesting Lecture in the Woman's Literary Union Course by Francis Bellamy." The latter newspaper account of this talk is available in the Bellamy Papers, but the name of the newspaper is not identified in the clipping. Miller quotes extensively from this speech *(Twenty-Three Words,* 132–33) but leaves out altogether Bellamy's discussion of immigration.

19. *Illustrated American,* August 28, 1897, 258. See also John W. Baer, *The Pledge of Allegiance: A Centennial History, 1892–1992* (Annapolis, Md.: J. W. Baer, 1992), 51–52. Cecilia Elizabeth O'Leary's *To Die For: The Paradox of American Patriotism* (Princeton, N.J.: Princeton University Press, 1999) is an excellent book and highly attentive to the racial and ethnic anxieties lurking behind American patriotism. But even she, perhaps misled by Bellamy's socialist sympathies, ignored this aspect of Bellamy's thought. O'Leary wrote: "The optimism of patriots like Bellamy, who thought the United States would be enriched by the new immigrants, was paralleled by an intolerant brand of flag-waving patriotism that would later develop into a full-blown nativism and anticommunism" (178). But Bellamy's own writings plainly contradict this characterization of his view of immigrants and cast doubt upon our ability to clearly separate out the optimistic, good patriots and the nativistic, bad patriots.

20. Desmond King, *Making Americans: Immigration, Race, and the Origins of the Diverse Democracy* (Cambridge, Mass.: Harvard University Press, 2000), 51, 293. Kate Holladay Claghorn, "The Changing Character of Immigration," *World's Work,* Vol. 1, 1900–1901. Available online at http://www.history.ohio-state.edu/projects /immigration/CharacterofImmigration/CharacterImmigration.htm.

21. John Higham, *Strangers in The Land: Patterns of American Nativism, 1860–1925* (New York: Atheneum, 1975; orig. pub. 1955), 95–96. O'Leary, *To Die For,* 62. "Report of Committee on Systematic Plan of Teaching the Lessons of Loyalty to Our Country and One Flag," Boston, Mass., August 17, 1892, in *Journal of the Twenty-Sixth National Encampment, Grand Army of the Republic,* Washington, D.C., Sep-

tember 21 and 22, 1892 (Albany, N.Y.: S.H. Wentworth Publisher, 1892), 82. King, *Making Americans,* 52. John A. Garraty, *Henry Cabot Lodge: A Biography* (New York: Knopf, 1953), 101. See also the speeches delivered by Frederic Taylor and Charles Emory Smith (with Colonel George Balch in the audience), which were printed in the *New York Times,* November 26, 1892, p. 5.

22. In the pages of the *Atlantic Monthly,* Walker had eviscerated Edward Bellamy and the Nationalist movement, pronouncing as "palpable robbery" Bellamy's scheme by which "one who produces twice as much as another shall yet have no more" (259). He vigorously defended competition, noting that it was "survival of the fittest" that had "developed man from purely animal conditions into the capacity for civilization" (261). The true remedy, Walker believed, was not less competition but more (262). "Perfect competition," he concluded, "would result in absolute justice" (262). The article, "Mr. Bellamy and the New Nationalist Party," *Atlantic Monthly* (1890), 248–63, is available online at http://cdl.library.cornell.edu/cgi-bin/moa/moa-cgi?notisid =ABK2934-0065-41.

23. Higham, *Strangers in the Land,* 38, 48–49, 101. Seymour Martin Lipset and Earl Raab, *The Politics of Unreason: Right-Wing Extremism in America, 1790–1970* (New York: Harper and Row, 1970), 79.

24. That same year saw the birth of his daughter, Anna Louise Strong, portrayed by Diane Keaton in the 1981 movie *Reds.*

25. Josiah Strong, *Our Country: Its Possible Future and Its Present Crisis* (New York: Baker and Taylor, 1885), 105–6, 119, 123–24. Except where otherwise noted, the quotations from *Our Country* are from the 1885 edition.

26. Ibid., 30, 43–46.

27. The year before Strong wrote, the American Catholic hierarchy had decreed "that a parochial school must be erected near each Catholic church and that parents must send their children to Catholic schools unless they were released from that obligation by the local bishop" (Thomas J. Schlereth, *Victorian America: Transformations in Everyday Life, 1876–1915* [New York: Harper, 1991], 246). In 1890, according to historian David Tyack, "only about 8 percent of the 676,000 Catholic students attended public schools" ("School for Citizens: The Politics of Civic Education from 1790 to 1990," in *E Pluribus Unum,* ed. Gary Gerstle and John Mollenkopf [New York: Russell Sage, 2001], 342). For further evidence of Protestant anxieties about parochial schools during this period, see the 1889 commencement speech by Colonel Schoonmaker, a member of the New Jersey State Board of Education, who advocated a constitutional amendment outlawing parochial schools (*New York Times,* June 29, 1889, p. 1).

28. The quotations in this paragraph are drawn from the revised 1891 edition, using the pagination of the 1963 Harvard University Press edition, edited by Jurgen Herbst. The 1891 edition added a chapter on the perils facing the public schools and elaborated substantially on the perils posed by "Romanism." Quotations are from pages 75, 79–80, 87, 89–90.

29. Strong, *Our Country,* 161, 175, 178.

30. Ibid., 171–72.

31. Louise Harris, *Flag over the Schoolhouse* (Providence, R.I.: C.A. Stephens Collection, 1971), 96–98. Also on the select list was *Civil Government in the United States* by John Fiske, who shortly thereafter became the first president of the Immigration Restriction League, founded in 1894. On Fiske's role as a "popularizer of the Anglo-Saxon legend," see Barbara Miller Solomon, *Ancestors and Immigrants: A Changing New England Tradition* (Chicago: University of Chicago Press, 1956), esp. 62–69.

32. "Our Mixed Population," *Youth's Companion* (November 10, 1892): 596.

33. Higham, *Strangers in the Land,* 18, 21.

34. Ibid., 54–55. Bellamy, "Interview with President Harrison," Bellamy Papers. In his speech to the National Education Association in July 1892, Bellamy quoted this part of his interview with President Harrison ("Americanism in the Public Schools," 63).

35. Gwendolyn Mink, *Old Labor and New Immigrants in American Political Development: Union, Party, and the State, 1875–1920* (Ithaca, N.Y.: Cornell University Press, 1986), 48. Selma Berrol, "Public Schools and Immigrants: The New York City Experience," in *American Education and the European Immigrant: 1840–1940,* ed. Bernard J. Weiss (Urbana: University of Illinois Press, 1982), 35. The 1874 Compulsory Education Act required that "all parents and those who have the care of children shall instruct them, or cause them to be instructed, in spelling, reading, writing, English grammar, geography and arithmetic. And every parent, guardian or other person having control and charge of any child between the ages of eight and fourteen years shall cause such child to attend some public or private day school at least fourteen weeks in each year." Laws of the State of New York, 1874, p. 532, available online at http://www.washingtonpolicycenter.org/Misc/PBNovelloMiscCompulsion.html.

36. Michael Kammen, *Mystic Chords of Memory: The Transformation of Tradition in American Culture* (New York: Vintage, 1993), 233, 239. "America for Americans—Dr. Parkhurst Would Have Immigrants Discard Their Prejudices," *New York Times,* January 9, 1888, p. 3. On Parkhurst, see Warren Sloan, *Battle for the Soul of New York: Tammany Hall, Police Corruption, Vice, and Reverend Charles Parkhurst* (New York: Cooper Square Press, 2002).

37. George T. Balch, *Methods of Teaching Patriotism in the Public Schools* (New York: D. Van Nostrand, 1890), vi–vii, xxvi, xxix–xxx, xxxiii, xxxv. Balch's lecture is what prompted the critical editorial ("Teaching Patriotism") in the *Youth's Companion* discussed in the previous chapter.

38. Ibid., 12, 23, 25–26. At the close of the book, Balch offers a more expansive conception of American patriotism and citizenship. The patriotic activities centered around the American flag, he explained, aimed to cultivate "in the heart of every pupil, not only . . . the minor virtues of punctuality, order, neatness, cheerfulness of temper, obedience, truthfulness and studiousness, but . . . those higher and nobler traits of character, generosity, integrity, firmness, humanity, magnanimity, intrepidity and loyalty, of which true patriotism is the sum and crown; and so insensibly to the child, elevate its thoughts and gradually lead its mind, through the constant use and continuous training of the highest and best attributes of its nature, to a profound appreciation of what it means to love one's country" (109).

39. Ibid., 34–35. George T. Balch, *A Patriotic Primer for the Little Citizen,* rev. ed. (Indianapolis: Levey Bros., 1898), 16.

40. Balch, *Methods of Teaching Patriotism,* viii. In *Methods,* Balch echoes approvingly an earlier 1855 report of the then newly formed Society, which stated that "the greatest danger that can threaten a country like ours is from the existence of an ignorant, debased, permanently poor class in the great cities. It is still more threatening if this class be of foreign birth, and of different habits from those of our own people. The members of it come at length to form a separate population. They embody the lowest passions and most thriftless habits of the community" (xxiii).

41. Ibid., 70–71, ix.

42. Ibid., 38, 78, 103, 73.

43. It seems likely that in a number of schools the children used the ordinary military salute rather than Upham's variant. The *New York Daily Tribune,* for instance, reported that schoolchildren said the pledge "with their hands to their heads, in military fashion" (October 21, 1892, p. 3). Similarly, the *Boston Evening Transcript* noted that "the pupils, facing the flag, gave, in unison, the military salute and reverently said, 'I pledge allegiance'" (October 22, 1892, p. 8). There is no mention in either of these press reports of children extending their arms toward the flag.

44. James B. Upham, "The School House Flag," *State Journal* (Topeka, Kans.), July 23, 1892, p. 8. Bellamy, "Story of the Pledge," 5–6, 15–16, Bellamy Papers. "The Schoolhouse Flag," *Youth's Companion* (July 3, 1891): 376. The article by Upham in the *State Journal* is taken virtually verbatim from the *Companion* article published a year earlier. It seems highly likely therefore that Upham wrote the 1891 *Companion* article. The last quotation about the values represented by the flag appears in the *Companion* article but was dropped from the *State Journal* article.

45. Balch, *Methods of Teaching Patriotism,* 44. Bellamy's evening address in Malden, October 21, 1892, as reported in *Malden Evening News,* October 22, 1892, p. 2.

46. James Parton, "The Grand Army of the Republic," *Youth's Companion* (1891): 307. Thomas, *Alternative America,* 245. George M. Fredrickson, *The Inner Civil War: Northern Intellectuals and the Crisis of the Union* (New York: Harper and Row, 1965), 227. In *Looking Backward,* Dr. Leete tells Julian West: "We even are able to sympathize with the declaration of some of the professional soldiers of your age that occasional wars with their appeals, however false, to the generous and self-devoting passions, were absolutely necessary to prevent your society otherwise so utterly sordid and selfish in its ideals, from dissolving into absolute putrescence" (Fredrickson, *Inner Civil War,* 228). On intellectuals' search for "the moral equivalent of war" during this period, see Fredrickson, *Inner Civil War,* chapter fourteen.

47. "Columbus Day," *Youth's Companion,* November 17, 1892, in Harris, *Flag over the Schoolhouse,* 80. *New York World,* October 11, 1892, p. 1. *New York Times,* October 11, 1892, p. 2. *Malden Evening News,* October 22, 1892, p. 2. See also *Atlanta Constitution,* October 22, 1892, p. 3. The idea of schools as "the army of the future" was taken a further step by the Grand Army of the Republic, which began to push for making military instruction a part of the regular curriculum of public schools. See Mary R. Dearing, *Veterans in Politics: The Story of the G.A.R.* (Baton Rouge: Louisiana

State University Press, 1952), 476–81. Boston and New York City were leaders in this effort (477). By 1895, twenty thousand students in New York regularly practiced military drilling in public schools (479–80). At least one state, Arizona, passed a law requiring military instruction in schools (480). The *New York Tribune* welcomed the trend because learning military drills at an early age would enable the children "to become if need be, good soldiers in later life" (477). Surveying the movement's successes in the mid-1890s, a GAR commander declared that "this new experiment is especially gratifying at this period, when disorganizing doctrines are disseminated so insidiously. . . . A force conservative of the safeguards of the social organization is thus built up among the youth, from whom these enemies might otherwise draw a swarm of dangerous recruits" (479).

48. Robert H. Wiebe, *The Search for Order, 1877–1920* (New York: Hill and Wang, 1967).

49. Bellamy characterized Upham as "a practical dreamer" ("Story of the Pledge," 7, Bellamy Papers) and elsewhere as an "idealist, whose dreams were distinguished by the hardheaded practicality necessary to make them a reality" (Raymond, "And So America Was Rediscovered").

50. Bellamy, "Story of the Pledge," 6, Bellamy Papers. Raymond, "And So America Was Rediscovered." Stuart McConnell, *Glorious Contentment: The Grand Army of the Republic, 1865–1900* (Chapel Hill: University of North Carolina Press, 1992), xv. See also Miller, *Twenty-Three Words*, 73. This backward-looking nostalgia for the old Americanism is also evident in Bellamy's speeches from this period. See, for instance, "Mr. Bellamy's Lecture: The Spirit of Americanism—Perils from Immigration—Liberty, Equality, and Fraternity in Relation to the New American Idea," Bellamy Papers.

51. Baer, *Pledge of Allegiance*, 22–23. There is a picture of Upham in the uniform of a Knight Templar in Miller, *Twenty-Three Words*, 70. Paul Upham confirms that there was "a strong family tradition" in the Upham family of reaching the highest ranks within the Masonic order (e-mail communication with the author, March 4, 2003). Bellamy was also a Mason, although Masonry did not appear to play the central role in Bellamy's life that it evidently did in Upham's.

52. Lynn Dumenil, *Freemasonry and American Culture, 1880–1930* (Princeton, N.J.: Princeton University Press, 1984), 16, 54, 240n27. "Origin of the Knights Templar" on the Frequently Asked Questions page of the website of The Grand Encampment of Knights Templar (http://www.knightstemplar.org/freqaq.html#origin). On the late-nineteenth-century romance with the chivalric age, see T. J. Jackson Lears, *No Place of Grace: Antimodernism and the Transformation of American Culture, 1880–1920* (New York: Pantheon, 1981), chapter three.

53. Dumenil, *Freemasonry and American Culture*, 94–95, 97.

54. Bellamy, "Story of the Pledge," 6, Bellamy Papers.

55. Upham, "School House Flag," 8. See also "The Schoolhouse Flag," *Youth's Companion* (July 2, 1891): 376.

56. The "divine mission" phrase was from a speech Upham delivered at a flag-raising ceremony at the Navesink Lighthouse in New Jersey in April 1893. The spot was selected because this was the first sight of land for vessels entering the harbor of New

York. Upham presented the mammoth flag, which was a gift of the Lyceum League, a debating society of young people organized by Upham in 1891. Upon raising the flag, those in attendance saluted the flag and recited Bellamy's Pledge of Allegiance. Upham's short speech is given verbatim in Miller, *Twenty-Three Words*, 135.

3. Spreading the Pledge

1. Francis Bellamy, "Affidavit Concerning the True Origin [of the] Pledge of Allegiance to the Flag," August 13, 1923, 6, Francis Bellamy Papers, Rare Books and Special Collections, Rush Rhees Library, University of Rochester, Rochester, N.Y. (hereafter cited as Bellamy Papers). Francis Bellamy, "The Story of the Pledge of Allegiance to the Flag," 16, Bellamy Papers. Francis Bellamy, "The Pledge of Allegiance to the Flag," *Stone and Webster Journal* 43 (October 1928): 471.

2. Scot M. Guenter, *The American Flag, 1777–1924* (Rutherford, N.J.: Fairleigh Dickinson University Press, 1990), 124. Merle Curti, *The Roots of American Loyalty* (New York: Columbia University Press, 1946), 190–91.

3. Mary R. Dearing, *Veterans in Politics: The Story of the G.A.R.* (Baton Rouge: Louisiana State University Press, 1952), 474–75. The Woman's Relief Corps' list of seven states—Michigan, Pennsylvania, Illinois, Connecticut, Montana, Iowa, and South Dakota—does not include North Dakota or New Jersey, which, according to Curti, had passed such laws in 1890. By 1895, according to the Grand Army of the Republic, the flag flew "over 17,988 of the 26,588 public schools within the twenty-one Grand Army departments" (Dearing, *Veterans in Politics,* 472).

4. According to the *Youth's Companion,* these were New Hampshire, Massachusetts, Rhode Island, Connecticut, New York, New Jersey, Pennsylvania, Ohio, Michigan, Illinois, Wisconsin, North Dakota, Washington, Wyoming, Idaho, New Mexico, Arizona, and Oklahoma ("School Flag Laws," *Youth's Companion,* July 27, 1905, in Louise Harris, *The Flag over the Schoolhouse* [Providence, R.I.: C.A. Stephens Collection, 1971], 161); the latter three were still territories in 1905. Three of the seven states listed by the WRC in 1895—Montana, Iowa, and South Dakota—are not on the *Youth's Companion* list. Jesse Flanders counted seventeen states and territories with mandatory flag laws in 1903, including Montana and Delaware but not Pennsylvania, Oklahoma, or New Mexico (Jesse Knowlton Flanders, *Legislative Control of the Elementary Curriculum* [New York: Teachers College, Columbia University, 1925], 8–9).

5. Flanders, *Legislative Control of the Elementary Curriculum,* 8–10. According to Flanders's count, the states adding a mandatory flag display law between 1903 and 1913 were California, Iowa, Kansas, Maine, Nevada, New Mexico, Oklahoma, Oregon, Pennsylvania, South Dakota, Utah, and Vermont. Cecilia Elizabeth O'Leary, in *To Die For: The Paradox of American Patriotism* (Princeton, N.J.: Princeton University Press, 1999), 230, reports that twenty-three states had mandatory flag display laws by 1913, but her only cited source is Flanders, so it is unclear how she arrived at this lower figure.

6. Flanders, *Legislative Control of the Elementary Curriculum,* 12. David R. Manwaring, *Render unto Caesar: The Flag-Salute Controversy* (Chicago: University of Chicago Press, 1962), 3. The statute was subsequently amended to include also "instruction in [the flag's] correct use and display"—dropped was the requirement that the salute be at the opening of each school day. See William G. Fennell and Edward J. Friedlander, *Compulsory Flag Salute in Schools, a Survey of the Statutes and an Examination of Their Constitutionality* (New York: Committee on Academic Freedom, American Civil Liberties Union, 1936), 4. This survey is also in the ACLU Archives on microfilm reel 129.

7. Charles R. Skinner, ed., *Manual of Patriotism: For Use in the Public Schools of the State of New York* (1904), xv–xvi, 47. The manual was first published in 1900.

8. "Patriotism by Manual," *Nation,* December 6, 1900, 439–40.

9. George T. Balch, *Methods of Teaching Patriotism in the Public Schools* (New York: D. Van Nostrand, 1890), 64, 20.

10. Manwaring, *Render unto Caesar,* 3. According to Flanders, the Arizona and Kansas statutes were "expressed in the same language" as the New York statute. The Rhode Island law differed in requiring the commissioner of education to print a program "providing for a uniform salute to the flag to be used daily during the session of the school" (Flanders, *Legislative Control of the Elementary Curriculum,* 12).

11. Wallace Evan Davies, *Patriotism on Parade: The Story of Veterans' and Hereditary Organizations in America, 1783–1900* (Cambridge, Mass.: Harvard University Press, 1955), 243. Flanders, *Legislative Control of the Elementary Curriculum,* 49–57.

12. Skinner, ed., *Manual of Patriotism,* 35.

13. *Acme Haversack,* "History of the Patriotic Salutes to the Flag," *McEvoy Magazine for School and Home* (June 1908), 250. This item was originally published in *Acme Haversack of Patriotism and Song,* published in March 1895. See Margarette S. Miller, *Twenty-Three Words* (Portsmouth, Va.: Printcraft Press, 1976), 142–43. In the 1890s New York's Baron de Hirsch Fund Schools, which were established to help newly arrived Jewish immigrant children from Russia and Eastern Europe learn English, employed a declaration of "Allegiance to the Flag" that bore no resemblance to either the Bellamy pledge or the Balch salute. The pledge of allegiance recited by these children read: "Flag of our Republic, inspirer of battle, guardian of our homes, whose Stars and Stripes stand for bravery, purity, truth, and union, we hail thee! We, the children of many lands, who find rest under thy folds, do pledge our lives, our hearts, and our sacred honor to love and protect thee, our country, and the American people forever." See *New York Times,* July 3, 1897, p. 12; and July 4, 1893, p. 8.

14. Morris G. Sica, "The School Flag Movement: Origin and Influence," *Social Education* (October 1990): 381. Dearing, *Veterans in Politics,* 474.

15. Appendix in Miller, *Twenty-Three Words* (no pagination).

16. Dearing, *Veterans in Politics,* 475. Miller, *Twenty-Three Words,* 369. Harris, *Flag over the Schoolhouse,* 177. Manwaring, *Render unto Caesar,* 7. Stanley Coben, "A Study in Nativism: The American Red Scare, 1919–1920," *Political Science Quarterly* (March 1964): 71. Evidently unaware of the history of the Balch salute, Manwaring mistakenly assumes that the VFW motto was the basis of the Balch salute. However, the

VFW was not organized nationally until 1913, long after the creation of the Balch salute. See Bessie Louise Pierce, *Citizens' Organizations and the Civic Training of Youth* (New York: Charles Scribner's Sons, 1933), 52.

17. According to a booklet produced by the *Companion* around 1918, "from time to time . . . versions of the Pledge have appeared with the word 'country' substituted for 'Republic' or with the word 'American' inserted before 'flag,' but the alterations never have gained widespread popularity or have long survived" (Miller, *Twenty-Three Words*, 368).

18. Washington County Flag Salute Case (*Murray Estep v. School District of Canonsburg*), ACLU Archives (1937), reel 141, vol. 958. More faithful to Balch's original was the wording used ("We give our heads and our hearts to God and country; one country, one language, one flag") at Honolulu's Royal School, in which the Balch salute was recited in a weekly flag ceremony into the 1930s. See Vern Hinkley, "A Teacher Who Molded New Americans," *New York Times*, April 19, 1931, p. 82.

19. Appendix in Miller, *Twenty-Three Words* (no pagination).

20. The one exception that I have found is in the December 22, 1892, issue in which the *Companion* promoted observance of Washington's Birthday by calling for "every public school in America [to] observe the day and salute the flag" (Harris, *Flag over the Schoolhouse*, 82).

21. Ibid., 111–13, 116, 135–44.

22. "How It Came About," *Youth's Companion*, January 28, 1904, in Harris, *Flag over the Schoolhouse*, 148–49.

23. Miller, *Twenty-Three Words*, 135.

24. Ibid., 170–74.

25. Personal reminiscence by Francis Russell, in Nat Brandt, "To the Flag," *American Heritage* 22 (June 1971): 74.

26. The *Companion* document is reprinted in Miller, *Twenty-Three Words*, 367–69. The dispute can be followed in the works of Margarette Miller, who takes Bellamy's side, and Louise Harris, who takes Upham's side. One of the great, and hitherto unacknowledged, ironies of this authorship controversy is that Miller, who dedicated her life to demonstrating that Bellamy was the rightful author of the Pledge of Allegiance, plagiarized substantial chunks of her 1946 book *I Pledge Allegiance* (Boston: Christopher Publishing, 1946). Nearly the whole of chapter ten (from pages 52 to 55) is taken almost word for word from Charles Fairman's 1906 eulogy of James Upham, and the opening paragraph of chapter seventeen is taken verbatim from an 1892 article, "Who Originated Columbus School Day?" published in the *School Journal* (November 12, 1892). Both items appear in Miller's bibliography, but otherwise there is no indication in the text that these sections borrow from, let alone plagiarize from, these sources. Moreover, sometimes the plagiarized material is from sources that do not show up in the bibliography and are not mentioned in the book. For instance, a long parenthetical paragraph on pages 151–52 is taken word for word from the 1941 edition of James Moss's *The Flag of the United States* (at pages 108–9). Determining the precise extent of the plagiarism would require access to the papers of Margarette Miller, which are vigilantly guarded by Frank P. Di Berardino.

27. Alvin Owsley, national commander of the American Legion, quoted in *New York Times,* June 15, 1923, A4. "Report of the National Americanism Commission," in *Proceedings of the Sixth National Convention of the American Legion, St. Paul, Minnesota, September 15–19, 1924* (Washington, D.C.: Government Printing Office, 1925), 127. See also Scot M. Guenter, *The American Flag, 1777–1924* (Rutherford, N.J.: Fairleigh Dickinson University Press, 1990), 175.

28. National Flag Conference, Auspices of the National American Commission, The American Legion, Memorial Continental Hall, Washington, D.C., June 14–15, 1923, p. 4. *New York Times,* June 15, 1923, p. 4. The first quotation is in the transcript of Harding's speech printed in the *Times* but is not in the transcript kept by the National Flag Conference.

29. National Flag Conference, 76–77, 183. "Report of the National Americanism Commission," 121. See also National Flag Conference, 177–79, 224, 229, 260–62. Another core objective of the Legion's Americanism Commission was restriction of immigration. It lobbied Congress to exclude "all aliens for a period of five years" ("Report of the National Americanism Commission," 120–21).

30. The language of the army's Flag Circular was read to the delegates at the outset of the conference by Captain George Chandler of the U.S. Army. See National Flag Conference, 9–19, quotations at 11. Gridley Adams was the only delegate to object to the time allotted to the committee. A matter of such great importance, he complained, "should hardly be a matter of hasty action. . . . There are matters which ought to be looked up. There are many sources from which we ought to obtain information as to the meaning of this or that element of the flag and how those elements . . . should be recognized and used." Adams suggested that the committee should be given two months to work out the rules of the code (National Flag Conference, 79–80).

31. National Flag Conference, 18, 296–97.

32. Ibid., 297–98.

33. Ibid., 292. On two separate occasions on the opening day, the convention heeded a call from the floor to recite the Pledge of Allegiance (78, 103).

34. National Flag Conference, 118. Mrs. Weyman was not an official delegate at the conference, and thus there is no record of her first name or her affiliation. Given that the meeting was held in the meeting hall of the Daughters of the American Revolution, she may have been a member of the DAR. Certainly we know there were a large number of women in attendance who were not delegates. By one estimate, four-fifths of those who attended the conference were women, whereas men outnumbered women among the invited delegates by about two to one (page 90).

35. Gridley Adams, *So Proudly We Hail . . . !* (United States Flag Foundation, 1953), 43, emphasis in original. For this attribution, one has to rely largely on Adams's own claims about his role in the change to the Pledge, for there is no transcript or notes of the committee deliberations. Adams often tended to exaggerate his own exploits. For instance, in his self-published book *So Proudly We Hail!* he described himself (on the copyright page) as "author [of] the *present* form of the Pledge of Allegiance." Although Adams is not the most reliable witness, there does not seem any reason to

doubt his claim that he was the driving force on the committee behind the alteration of the words of the Pledge of Allegiance.

36. *New York Times*, June 14, 1945, p. 18.

37. E. J. Kahn, Jr., "Profiles: Three Cheers for the Blue, White, and Red," *New Yorker* (July 5, 1952), 37. Gridley Adams, "United States Flag Foundation: Its Origin and Buildup, 1920–1955," 1–2, New York Public Library. Adams recalled that "when the regular meeting opened for discussion American Legionnaire Powell called the roll, and then he asked 'Is Mr. Gridley Adams present?' I was unaffiliated and sat in the very last row. When I responded 'Here!' those 72 faces in front turned to see 'that guy with whom we have been contending,' and the war Dept's Flag expert [Captain Chandler] came back to shake my hand (others seemingly shook their fists) and thanked me for the bringing about the Conference because of my sketches in Briggs's cartoon."

38. *New York Times*, May 19, 1938, A20; and February 25, 1952, A20. By my count, the *New York Times* alone published thirty-two letters to the editor by Adams, the first in 1913 and the last in 1957.

39. Adams, "United States Flag Foundation," 2. Kahn, "Profiles," 38.

40. For the 1924 flag code, see Garland W. Powell, *"Service": For God and Country* (Indianapolis: Cornelius Printing, 1924), 45–56, quotations at 54. The 1924 flag code also attempted to make it clearer that the salutes for men and women during a parade or during the raising or lowering of the flag were parallel. To do this, the revised code indicated that "when not in uniform, men should remove the headdress with the right hand and hold it at the left shoulder, *the hand being over the heart*" (53, emphasis added).

41. Kahn, "Profiles," 38.

42. Gridley Adams was also one of the most fervent backers of Upham in the authorship controversy. Adams claimed to have "received many letters" from James Upham, and he claimed that Upham told him that the idea for the Pledge of Allegiance was his and not Bellamy's (*New York Times*, June 14, 1945, p. 18). Bellamy, in Adams's view, was "more or less taking dictation from Upham" (Kahn, "Profiles," 38).

43. "Tampan, Author of Pledge to Flag, Protests against Proposal to 'Mangle' It," *Tampa Morning Tribune*, April 16, 1929, p. 2. See also Miller, *Twenty-Three Words*, 296.

44. Francis Bellamy, "A New Plan for Counter-Attack on the Nation's Internal Foes: How to Mobilize the Masses to Support Primary American Doctrines," May 1, 1923, 1, Bellamy Papers.

45. Ibid., 2–3, emphasis in original.

46. Ibid., 10–11, emphasis in original.

47. Ibid., 12–13.

48. Ibid., 17–18, 30–31.

49. Ibid., 23–25.

50. Ibid., 21–22.

51. Ibid., 5–17.

52. Although no other state statutes at this time went as far as the state of Washington's, there were plenty of local regulations that were every bit as severe. As early as 1897, for instance, a local board of education in southern California enacted a rule

that all students must salute the flag and that any school official failing to enforce the rule "shall be deemed disloyal and shall be at once dismissed." A student who refused to salute the flag would be removed from school and only allowed to return if the parent submitted a written "pledge of obedience." Moreover, the student who wished to be readmitted was required to "first deliver to his or her teacher a written apology for such disloyalty, and a pledge to thereafter comply with this rule" (Wallace Evan Davies, *Patriotism on Parade: The Story of Veterans' and Hereditary Organizations in America, 1783–1900* [Cambridge, Mass.: Harvard University Press, 1955], 220).

53. Washington SB 93, Chapter 90, Section 4, Laws of 1919. The statutory amendment also included a provision requiring the flag to be flown "upon or near" every public school. District officials were required to acquire a new flag when the existing flag had become "tattered, torn, or faded." Failure to comply carried with it the same penalties as a failure to administer the Pledge of Allegiance.

54. For one example of the dire consequences predicted by the press, see "The Real Motive behind the Strike Proposal," *Tacoma News Tribune*, February 1, 1919, p. 1, in which the editors warn that "the radical leaders propose to punish every person in the city . . . , make the city go without food, light or heat, tear down present institutions and cause untold misery and suffering. . . . [E]veryone will suffer. No one will escape." For more on the strike see the informative webpage of the Seattle General Strike Project coordinated by University of Washington professor James Gregory. It is available at http://faculty.washington.edu/gregoryj/strike/. The Strong editorial is quoted in part in Robert L. Friedheim, "The Seattle General Strike of 1919," *Pacific Northwest Quarterly* (July 1961): 81–98, which is available through the Seattle General Strike Project. It can also be accessed directly at http://www.tpl.lib.wa.us/cgi-win/fulltcgi .exe/General_Strike_of_1919%7Clabor/genstrik.19.

55. Robert K. Murray, *Red Scare: A Study in National Hysteria, 1919–1920* (Minneapolis: University of Minnesota Press, 1955), 63. *Seattle Star*, February 5, 1919, reprinted as an advertisement in *Seattle Post-Intelligencer*, February 6, 1919, p. 11. See also John Higham, *Strangers in the Land: Patterns of American Nativism, 1860–1925* (New York: Atheneum, 1975; orig. pub. 1955), 226–27.

56. Sharon Boswell and Lorraine McConaghy, "Strike! Labor Unites for Rights," *Seattle Times*, March 31, 1996, at http://seattletimes.nwsource.com/centennial /march/labor.html. Murray, *Red Scare*, 61–63. *Seattle Post-Intelligencer*, February 6, 1919, p. 1. The unions strategically exempted from the strike certain essential services like garbage pickup and milk delivery (Murray, *Red Scare*, 61).

57. Murray, *Red Scare*, 64.

58. "Curb I.W.W. and Alien Agitators," *Seattle Times*, February 9, 1919, p. 15. "Teaching Foreign Languages in Schools Prohibited in Bill before State House," *Bellingham Herald*, February 5, 1919, p. 1.

59. "Teachers Must Show Patriotism," *Seattle Times*, February 11, 1919, p. 9. "To Purify Schools," *Seattle Times*, February 4, 1919, p. 14.

60. "Teaching Americans," *Seattle Post-Intelligencer*, January 20, 1919, p. 6.

61. "Notes of the Legislature: Senate Bars Red Flag," *Washington Standard* (Olympia), February 28, 1919, p. 1.

62. "Divided Allegiance," *Seattle Post-Intelligencer,* February 12, 1919, p. 6.

63. "Restricting Immigration," *Seattle Post-Intelligencer,* January 7, 1919, p. 6.

64. Manwaring reported that passage of the statute "was apparently in reaction to the IWW disorders in Centralia" (*Render unto Caesar,* 3). The problem with this chronology is that the violent confrontations in Centralia occurred in November 1919, nearly eight months after the bill became law.

65. There was a substantial debate in the senate on a few provisions of SB 93, principally a controversial proposal to lengthen the term of school directors from three to five years ("State Fights on School Measure," *Olympian,* February 6, 1919, p. 1; "Bill Changing School Code Is Passed by Senate," *Seattle Post-Intelligencer,* February 6, 1919, p. 9). When the acting governor signed the bill, the *Seattle Times* devoted five lines to the bill, mentioning only that the bill eliminated compulsory vaccination ("Bill Signed by Governor," *Seattle Times,* March 12, 1919, p. 8).

66. In the end, the house finally won out, managing to amend the section so that a penalty could be levied only if the refusal or neglect was "willful."

67. Coben, "A Study in Nativism," 65–67. Higham, *Strangers in the Land,* 226.

68. Coben, "A Study in Nativism," 52; see also 70. Robert Justin Goldstein, ed., *Desecrating the American Flag: Key Documents of the Controversy from the Civil War to 1995* (Syracuse, N.Y.: Syracuse University Press, 1996), 59–60; see also 56–57. In 1920 the Montana man's case reached a federal judge who poured scorn on the court that had convicted and sentenced the man, quoting George Bernard Shaw to the effect that during the war the courts in the United States "were stark, staring, raving mad." However, the judge let the verdict and the sentence stand since neither the law nor the sentence was unconstitutional. Only the governor's power of pardon could rectify the injustice, concluded the federal judge. The case is *Ex parte Starr* (1920) 263 F. 145.

69. *New York Times,* June 15, 1923, p. 4.

70. "Calls on Columbia to Oust Prof. Hayes," January 17, 1927, *New York Times,* p. 19; and "Prof. Hayes Derides Patriotic 'Cults,'" *New York Times,* January 16, 1927, p. 26. Both articles are available as clippings in the ACLU Archives, reel 50, vol. 317. The professor in question was Carlton Hayes, a well-known historian of modern European history and nationalism, who would later be appointed ambassador to Spain by President Franklin Roosevelt.

71. Bessie Louise Pierce, *Citizens' Organizations and the Civic Training of Youth* (New York: Charles Scribner's Sons, 1933), 49. "Freedom of Speech," April 1927, ACLU Archives, reel 50, vol. 317. "Legion Report Asks Investigation," *Daily Local News* (West Chester, Pa.), April 18, 1927, ACLU Archives, reel 50, vol. 317.

72. Pierce, *Citizens' Organizations,* 35.

73. David Tyack, Thomas James, and Aaron Benavot, *Law and the Shaping of Public Education, 1785–1954* (Madison: University of Wisconsin Press, 1987), 169–71, 174. J. K. Flanders, "Lawmakers Encroach upon the Schoolmen," *New York Times,* September 6, 1925, p. 14. See also Flanders, *Legislative Control.*

74. Appendix to the report on the Flag Salute compiled by William G. Fennell and Edward J. Friedlander, ACLU Archives, reel 129, vol. 872. Those ten states (and the date of adoption) were New York (1898), Rhode Island (1901), Arizona (1903),

Kansas (1907), Nebraska (1917), Maryland (1918), Washington (1919), Delaware (1925), New Jersey (1932), Massachusetts (1935).

75. "Court Row Looms in Girl's Refusal to Salute Flag," *Atlanta Journal,* October 14, 1936, ACLU Archives, reel 128, vol. 867. "Flag Salute Is Ordered," *New York Times,* November 1, 1935, p. 23.

76. "Pledge Flag with Curtis," *New York Times,* February 5, 1930, p. 11. "Smith Proclaims Flag Week in State," *New York Times,* June 7, 1925, p. 20.

77. *New York Times,* September 13, 1936, IV:9.

4. Making the Pledge Safe for Democracy

1. "The Flag as Fetish," *The Independent,* January 15, 1903, in Robert Justin Goldstein, ed., *Desecrating the American Flag: Key Documents of the Controversy from the Civil War to 1995* (Syracuse, N.Y.: Syracuse University Press, 1996), 67. "Flag Day," *Harper's Weekly,* June 25, 1898, quoted in Margarette S. Miller, *Twenty-Three Words* (Portsmouth, Va.: Printcraft Press, 1976), 264. "Training in Patriotism," *Nation,* August 2, 1906, 92. Merle Curti, *The Roots of American Loyalty* (New York: Columbia University Press, 1946), 200. "Flag Salute," *Grand Army Record* (November 1895), 86, quoted in Wallace Evan Davies, *Patriotism on Parade: The Story of Veterans' and Hereditary Organizations in America, 1783–1900* (Cambridge, Mass.: Harvard University Press, 1955), 220.

2. *New York Times,* September 14, 1911, p. 2; and September 15, 1911, pp. 4, 8.

3. Ibid., October 8, 1912, p. 1; and October 9, 1912, p. 12.

4. Ibid., October 10, 1912, p. 9; October 11, 1912, p. 10; and November 9, 1912, p. 7.

5. Ibid., November 11, 1912, p. 10; and November 2, 1912, p. 8.

6. Ibid., November 6, 1912, p. 14.

7. *Mother Earth,* July 1916, in Goldstein, *Desecrating the American Flag,* 68. Cecilia Elizabeth O'Leary, *To Die For: The Paradox of American Patriotism* (Princeton, N.J.: Princeton University Press, 1999), 231.

8. David R. Manwaring, *Render unto Casear: The Flag-Salute Controversy* (Chicago: University of Chicago Press, 1962), 11.

9. Ibid., 11–12. *Troyer v. State* 29 Ohio Dec. 168 (1918), quotation at 171.

10. Manwaring, *Render unto Caesar,* 11–12. The quotation is from a letter from Nevin Bender to Roger Baldwin, June 29, 1929, ACLU Archives, reel 61, vol. 357, "Delaware." See also "Mennonite Children in Delaware Excluded from School," ACLU Archives (1929), reel 61, vol. 356.

11. Manwaring, *Render unto Caesar,* 12–13. *New York Times,* March 1, 1926, p. 34. "That's That," *Denver Post,* April 27, 1926, in ACLU Archives, reel 44, vol. 297. Although there was no state law requiring the Pledge, there was a statute empowering the state superintendent of public schools "to provide the necessary instruction and information that all teachers . . . may teach the pupils therein the proper respect of the flag of the United States, to honor and properly salute the Flag when passing in

parade and to properly use the Flag in decorating and displaying." The county superintendent ruled that under this clause "it is necessary for teachers to insist on the pupils saluting the flag, for how else can they be taught the 'proper manner' of so doing?" Clearly, then, the county superintendent ruled, the Denver school board "had the legal right to make a rule demanding that all children must salute the flag" (Alice B. McCormack to Olive Yahrah, February 17, 1926, ACLU Archives, reel 44, vol. 299).

12. Manwaring, *Render unto Caesar,* 13. "The Flag, the Boy, the Law," ACLU Archives (1926), reel 44, vol. 298. "To the Common People Who Think," *Elijiah Voice* (October 1925); American Civil Liberties Union press release, August 29, 1926; and "In the Matter of the Welfare of Russell Tremain," J-926, In the Superior Court of the State of Washington in and for the County of Whatcom, all in ACLU Archives, reel 44, vol. 298.

13. "In the Matter of the Welfare of Russell Tremain," J-926, In the Superior Court of the State of Washington in and for the County of Whatcom, ACLU Archives, reel 44, vol. 298.

14. "A Religious Fanatic," ACLU Archives, reel 44, vol. 298. J. W. Tremain to Roger Baldwin, August 6, 1926, ACLU Archives, reel 44, vol. 299. "Parents Get Tremain Boy, Court Rules," ACLU Archives, reel 50, vol. 317. Manwaring, *Render unto Caesar,* 14. In its press release dated August 29, 1926, the ACLU emphasized the sect's opposition to the "idolatrous act" of saluting the flag, but the Elijiah Voice Society, in its literature, emphasized not idolatry but their objections to militarism and "the war spirit." The idolatry emphasis of the ACLU presumably fit more neatly into the religious freedom argument that the civil liberties organization wanted to make and conveniently avoided the Elijiah Voice Society's more politically contentious critique of the connection between patriotism and militarism.

15. "Prof. Hayes Derides Patriotic 'Cults,'" *New York Times,* January 16, 1927, p. 26, in ACLU Archives, reel 50, vol. 317. "The Flag, the Boy, the Law," ACLU Archives, reel 44, vol. 298. On the early role of the Grand Army of the Republic in promoting military drilling in schools, see O'Leary, *To Die For,* 181–85. See also the various articles on military training in schools in the ACLU file, "Militarism in Schools," ACLU Archives (1930), reel 71, vol. 381.

16. Manwaring, *Render unto Caesar,* 15. "Mother and Son Would Go to Jail Rather Than Sacrifice Religious Belief," *Oklahoma Leader,* January 13, 1928, ACLU Archives, reel 54, vol. 337, "Oklahoma." Karl Pretsheld to Forrest Bailey, ACLU Archives, reel 54, vol. 337, "Oklahoma."

17. Bessie Louise Pierce, *Citizens' Organizations and the Civic Training of Youth* (New York: Charles Scribner's Sons, 1933), 107. *Hardwicke v. Board of School Trustees* (1921) 54 Cal. App. 696, quotation at 711–12. See also Manwaring, *Render unto Caesar,* 8, 15. *Hardwicke* involved the case of two children who were expelled from school because the parents would not consent to have their children participate in certain dances "wherein the children were required to dance with partners of the opposite sex with their arms clasped around or about the shoulders of their dance partner." These dances were a required part of the curriculum, and the district attorney sought to draw an analogy between dancing and the Pledge of Allegiance refusal in neighboring

Solano County. The court, which found in favor of the parents with religious objections to dancing, declared (for the reasons given in the quotation in the text) that no analogy could be drawn between the two cases.

18. "Girl Flag Rebel Yields, Carries It," ACLU Archives, reel 50, vol. 317.

19. "Young Pioneer Is Suspended from School Here for Doubting History Teacher and Not Signing 'Pledge,'" *Daily Worker,* December 8, 1926, p. 2, in ACLU Archives, reel 44, vol. 298, "Academic Freedom: Illinois." On the Young Pioneers of America, see Paul C. Mishler, *Raising Reds: The Young Pioneers, Radical Summer Camps, and Communist Political Culture in the United States* (New York: Columbia University Press, 1999).

20. Manwaring, *Render unto Caesar,* 66. *New York Times,* October 20, 1935, p. 37. Letter to Rev. R. E. Miller, June 25, 1929, ACLU Archives, reel 61, vol. 357.

21. Manwaring, *Render unto Caesar,* 26–27, 30.

22. Ibid., 30–31; Shawn Francis Peters, *Judging Jehovah's Witnesses: Religious Persecution and the Dawn of the Rights Revolution* (Lawrence: University Press of Kansas, 2000), 24–25.

23. William G. Fennel and Edward J. Friedlander, *Compulsory Flag Salute in Schools* (New York: Committee on Academic Freedom, American Civil Liberties Union, 1936), 3–4. *New York Times,* May 14, 1935, p. 42. Later in the same session, the legislature also passed a law requiring every Massachusetts teacher to take a loyalty oath, which was much resented by educators across the state. One wit told a cheering audience of educators: "I am for a compulsory oath . . . an oath to require every teacher every day to swear at the societies who brought about this oath." The group that had spearheaded the new law was the American Legion. See "6,000 Teachers War on Bay State Oath," *New York Times,* October 19, 1935, p. 34.

24. Although the law was new, the practice of saying the Pledge of Allegiance in Massachusetts schools was not. As the court pointed out, for many years Lynn had a rule requiring the flag salute and Pledge of Allegiance to "be given in every school at least once a week and at such other times as occasion may warrant." In fact Carleton Nicholls had, without objection, saluted the flag and recited the Pledge of Allegiance in his two previous years at the school. *Nicholls v. Lynn* (1937) 297 Mass. 65, quotation at 66.

25. Manwaring, *Render unto Caesar,* 31. *Nicholls v. Lynn* (1937) 297 Mass. 65, quotation at 66. *New York Times,* October 1, 1935, p. 9. The name is spelled "Nicholls" in the court records, but in contemporary press reports the name is generally spelled "Nichols" (see *New York Times,* October 9, 1935, p. 25; and October 10, 1935, p. 27). For simplicity's sake I have followed the spelling in the court records.

26. Manwaring, *Render unto Caesar,* 31. Peters, *Judging Jehovah's Witnesses,* 27. *New York Times,* October 6, 1935, II:6.

27. *New York Times,* October 9, 1935, p. 35.

28. Ibid., October 9, 1935, p. 35; and October 10, 1935, p. 27.

29. "Compulsory Flag Saluting and Its Results," ACLU Archives (1937), reel 141, vol. 958. "Children of Several States Expelled from School for Refusing on Religious Grounds to Salute the Flag," January 3, 1936, in ACLU Archives (1936), reel 129,

vol. 872. *New York Times,* November 14, 1935, p. 24. See also Manwaring, *Render unto Caesar,* 56.

30. "Children of Several States Expelled from School for Refusing on Religious Grounds to Salute the Flag." "Compulsory Flag Saluting and Its Results." Manwaring, *Render unto Caesar,* 77.

31. "Compulsory Flag Saluting and Its Results."

32. Ibid. "67 Women, 80 Men Seized," *Pittsburgh Sun-Telegraph,* May 25, 1936, ACLU Archives, reel 128, vol. 869.

33. "Compulsory Flag Saluting and Its Results." See also Manwaring, *Render unto Caesar,* 63.

34. *Nicholls v. Lynn* (1937) 7 N.E.2d 577, quotation at 580.

35. *Hering v. State Board of Education* (1937) 189 A. 629.

36. *Leoles v. Landers* (1937) 192 S.E. 218, quotation at 222.

37. *Bleich v. Board of Public Instruction* (1938) 190 So. 815, quotation at 816. Several of the Florida justices evidently had second thoughts. For when the state's attorney general petitioned for a rehearing of the case, two justices voted to grant the rehearing. As one of them explained, "That we can find no support in Scripture for such religious belief, or conception, does not warrant our condemnation of the reasoning of one whose construction of some part of the Bible may lead him to entertain convictions of that sort. The most profound Bible students the world has ever known have disagreed amongst themselves as to the construction to be given to many passages of Scripture and this difference of opinion amongst the learned has led, and is still leading to the organization of various denominations and to the following of various creeds. The punishment of expulsion from public school is an unusual and severe punishment. It not only affects the child to whom it is administered but it destroys the usefulness of that child as a citizen and thereby deprives the public of the benefit of the best available citizenship in that child. It will have its effect upon the offspring in the future generation springing from that child; and, as has been suggested by the Attorney General, it affords the vehicle by which a designing parent may frustrate the provisions of law requiring school attendance of children within certain designated ages. It occurs to me that in the interest of preserving American ideals, and especially that of religious freedom, ... we should not by law require one to affirmatively engage in an act, not essential to the public welfare or the support of the government, which he or she conscientiously believes to be contrary to his or her religious tenets, and thereby make of such person a martyr to his or her religious faith. The salute of the flag is, after all, a physical demonstration of respect, and nothing more. Certainly, there can be no logical reason why some alternative expression of respect and loyalty cannot be substituted for those whose religious tenets, faith or beliefs precludes their indulgence in a physical salute and thereby satisfy the demands of patriotism and at the same time respect the religious views of the individual" (817–18).

38. Manwaring, *Render unto Caesar,* 67, 71. *Gabrielli v. Knickerbocker* (1938) 82 P.2d 391. *People of the State of New York v. Sandstrom* (1939) 18 N.E.2d 840, quotations at 842–44. Grace Sandstrom's refusal induced a local pastor to deliver a sermon on "Would Jesus Salute the Flag?" The Reverend David Sloatman assured his congre-

gation, which included the entire local school board and the principal of Grace's school, that Jesus would have saluted the flag, for "Jesus was an exemplary citizen" who "taught submission to authority." In the Epistles, for instance, "Christians are exhorted to be law-abiding citizens even when they suffer injustice from the state" and "in I Peter we are told: 'Submit to every human institution for the Lord's sake, whether to the Emperor as supreme, or to governors as men sent by him for the punishment of evil-doers or for the praise of them that do well.'" And then, without a hint of irony and untroubled by the inconsistency, Sloatman concluded that "we may well believe that Jesus would salute a flag that stands for freedom of speech and liberty of conscience" ("Pastor Urges Salute of Flag," November 5, 1937, ACLU Archives, reel 128, vol. 876, "Academic Freedom, 2, Sandstrom case").

39. *People of the State of New York v. Sandstrom* (1939) 18 N.E.2d 840, quotations at 845–47. Transcript of Testimony, November 5, 1937, at Justice Court, Brookhaven, Suffolk County, New York, a copy of which is in the ACLU Archives, reel 141, vol. 958. The pages of the transcript are not numbered.

40. Relevant biographical information about Gobitas and his family can be found in chapter one of Peters, *Judging Jehovah's Witnesses*. The family's surname was misspelled as "Gobitis" throughout the various court challenges.

41. Manwaring, *Render unto Caesar,* 76–77, 82–83. Peters, *Judging Jehovah's Witnesses,* 27, 37–38.

42. Manwaring, *Render unto Caesar,* 91. Peters, *Judging Jehovah's Witnesses,* 39. *Gobitis v. Minersville* (1937) 21 F. Supp. 581, quotations at 584–85. The following year Maris was elevated to the U.S. Court of Appeals for the 3d District, where he served for the next twenty years.

43. Manwaring, *Render unto Caesar,* 93.

44. Ibid., 97–98. *Gobitis v. Minersville School District* (1938) 24 F. Supp. 271, quotation at 274.

45. Manwaring, *Render unto Caesar,* 106–7.

46. Peters, *Judging Jehovah's Witnesses,* 46.

47. *Minersville School District v. Gobitis* (1939) 108 F.2d 683, quotation at 683n3. Peters, *Judging Jehovah's Witnesses,* 47. The cases in which the U.S. Supreme Court had refused to overturn lower court rulings on the flag salute were *Leoles v. Landers* (1937) 302 U.S. 656; *Hering v. State Board of Education* (1938) 303 U.S. 624; *Johnson v. Deerfield* (1939) 306 U.S. 621 and (1939) 307 U.S. 650; and *Gabrielli v. Knickerbocker* (1939) 306 U.S. 621.

48. Peters, *Judging Jehovah's Witnesses,* 54–55. *Minersville School District v. Gobitis* (1940) 310 U.S. 586, quotations at 595, 597.

49. Peters, *Judging Jehovah's Witnesses,* 55, 57. Manwaring, *Render unto Caesar,* 136–37. *Minersville School District v. Gobitis* (1940) 310 U.S. 586, quotation at 598.

50. Peters, *Judging Jehovah's Witnesses,* 65–66.

51. Manwaring, *Render unto Caesar,* 143–44. *Minersville School District v. Gobitis* (1940) 310 U.S. 586, quotations at 598, 601–7.

52. Peters, *Judging Jehovah's Witnesses,* 67–69. Manwaring, *Render unto Caesar,* 153–54.

53. Peters, *Judging Jehovah's Witnesses,* 71.

54. Ibid., 90–92.

55. Ibid., 86–87. Manwaring, *Render unto Caesar*, 165.

56. Manwaring, *Render unto Caesar*, 175–76. Peters, *Judging Jehovah's Witnesses*, 84, 108–9, 111, 116.

57. Peters, *Judging Jehovah's Witnesses*, 82.

58. Ibid., 96–98.

59. On December 11, 1941, just a few days after the bombing of Pearl Harbor, the Mount Baker School District in Deming, Washington, took advantage of the state attorney general's revised opinion to issue a resolution requiring the flag salute and Pledge of Allegiance. In justifying the resolution, the district noted that "certain patrons" in the schools had "an attitude that is outstandingly disloyal towards the government of the United States" (ACLU Archives, reel 210, vol. 2428, "Academic Freedom, Washington, 5, Knight Expulsion"). Moreover, the resolution continued, these patrons had presented their "arguments pertaining to religious liberty in a very unbiblical way." The school district accepted that the Bible is "recognized as the highest authority" but insisted that the Bible teaches a specific obedience and respect of organized government to wit—

> Romans: Chapter 13, Verses 1–7
> I Peter: Chapter 2, Verses 13–17
> Proverbs: Chapter 8, Verses 15–16
> John: Chapter 19, Verse 11
> Daniel: Chapter 2, Verse 2
> Ecclesiastes: Chapter 8, Verse 8
> Matthew: Chapter 22, Verses 17–21.

The Jehovah's Witnesses were not only disloyal but false prophets.

60. Peters, *Judging Jehovah's Witnesses*, 165. Manwaring, *Render unto Caesar*, 167–75, 187–88. The anti-Witness violence was most prevalent in Texas, home to about one-quarter of the recorded incidents between 1940 and 1943.

61. *Jones v. Opelika* (1942) 316 U.S. 584, quotation at 624. Peters, *Judging Jehovah's Witnesses*, 65, 237–38.

62. *Bolling v. Superior Court* (1943) 133 P.2d 803, quotations at 806, 809. *State v. Smith* (1942) 127 P.2d 518, quotation at 522.

63. Manwaring, *Render unto Caesar*, 208–9. *Barnette v. West Virginia State Board of Education* 47 F. Supp. 251, quotation at 255. The resolution and whereas clauses are contained in footnote 2 in *West Virginia State Board of Education v. Barnette* 319 U.S. 624 (1943).

64. The Court had already, at the beginning of May, reversed itself on the issue of licensing and taxes after rehearing the same case they had decided less than a year before. The reversal was made possible by the appointment of Rutledge to replace James Byrnes, who had left the Court for a post in the Roosevelt administration. See Peters, *Judging Jehovah's Witnesses*, 241–42.

65. Ibid., 238–39.

66. *West Virginia State Board of Education v. Barnette* 319 U.S. 624 (1943), quotations at 640–42.

67. Ibid., quotations at 646–47.

68. Peters, *Judging Jehovah's Witnesses,* 258. Manwaring, *Render unto Caesar,* 239.

69. "Schools Here Try 'Nazi-Type' Salute," *New York Times,* March 9, 1937, p. 25.

70. "City Schools to Keep Old Salute to Flag," *New York Times,* March 10, 1937, p. 25.

71. *West Virginia State Board of Education v. Barnette* 319 U.S. 624 (1943), 627n3. "Flag Salute Like Nazis' Revised by Jersey School," *New York Times,* September 20, 1939, p. 3. "Army Salute for Children," *New York Times,* October 3, 1941, p. 18. "West Virginia Banishes 'Nazi' Salute in Schools," *New York Times,* February 2, 1942, p. 17. See also "Wants Flag Salute Changed," *New York Times,* September 8, 1940, p. 22; and "New Flag Salute Ruled," *New York Times,* October 16, 1940, p. 10.

72. James A. Moss, *The Flag of the United States: Its History and Symbolism* (Washington, D.C.: United States Flag Association, 1941, 3d ed.), 108. "D.A.R. Backs Hand Salute," *New York Times,* October 18, 1941, p. 21. See also the letter from the executive secretary of the United States Flag Association to the chairman of the Senate Judiciary Committee "vigorously protest[ing]" the proposed change to the Pledge. The association's executive secretary warned that the change would produce "great confusion and necessitate the re-educating of the entire nation at a time when the American people should uphold well-established customs and traditions "(Eleanor Austin to Frederick Van Nuys, December 3, 1942, in Bill File, HJR 359, National Archives, Washington, D.C.). Copies of the letter were sent to each member of the Senate Judiciary Committee.

73. *New York Times,* July 5, 1941, pp. 1, 6. *Rocky Mountain News,* July 5, 1941, p. 1.

74. Discussion, such as it was, took place in a subcommittee of the House Judiciary Committee on March 26, 1942. See the Bill File for HJR 288, National Archives, Washington, D.C. The American Legion and VFW are identified as the source of the bill in "A Statement of Hon. Sam Hobbs," included in the Bill File. Hobbs, an Alabama Democrat, sponsored the resolution. A modified resolution was reintroduced shortly thereafter by Hobbs as HJR 303. The original HJR 288 made no mention of the Pledge of Allegiance, which may have been one reason HJR 303 replaced HJR 288. According to the executive secretary of the United States Flag Association, the USFA's "President General, Dr. William Tyler Page, was instrumental in having Section 7 giving the Pledge of Allegiance and the manner of rendering included in H.J. Res. 303" (Eleanor Austin to Honorable Charles McLaughlin [chairman of the House Judiciary Committee], December 4, 1942, in Bill File, HJR 359, National Archives, Washington, D.C.).

75. Gridley Adams, "United States Flag Foundation: Its Origin and Buildup, 1920–1955," 5, New York Public Library. E. J. Kahn, Jr., "Profiles: Three Cheers for the Blue, White, and Red," *New Yorker* (July 5, 1952), 38–39. After the passage of the December law, Adams was given (at Adams's request) the pen with which FDR signed the act of Congress into law, a pen Adams later offered to return when the White House displayed an American flag below the president's desk at FDR's last inaugural.

76. Gridley Adams, *So Proudly We Hail . . . !* (United States Flag Foundation, 1953), 40. Adams writes that "*we* told the story of the 'Lincoln hand-over-the-heart' salute" (emphasis added), but it is unclear to whom the "we" refers. Since elsewhere he is

quite free with the "I" pronoun and not at all shy about trumpeting his many contributions to the flag code and flag usage, it seems possible that it may have been another person who actually related the Lincoln story to Representative Hobbs. He implies that he deserves credit for the change in a letter to the editor in the *New York Times*: "And through my efforts, the Federal Flag Code was amended in December, 1942. The changes included doing away with the meaningless 'extended arm' salute when public school pupils recite the pledge, and substituting the Lincoln 'hand-over-the-heart' salute" (June 14, 1945, p. 18).

77. Gridley Adams, letter to the editor, *New York Times*, June 14, 1945, p. 18.

78. Adams refers to the hand-over-the-heart salute as "the Lincoln salute for civilians" in a compilation of flag rules he wrote for the *New York World Telegram*, which was published on June 13, 1942, ten days before Congress approved Public Law 623. A condensed form of the piece was published in the *Reader's Digest* 41 (August 1942), 113, under the title "Honor Your Flag, Written for the NEA Service." Adams recommended that "all persons not in uniform salute a passing or a stationary Flag by holding the right hand over the heart. If out of doors, men should remove the hat and hold it in [the] right hand over the heart—the Lincoln salute for civilians." Adams's prescriptions generally followed the 1924 Flag Code. Public Law 623, enacted by Congress on June 22, followed the 1924 Flag Code closely, but departed from it in specifying that "men without hats merely stand at attention." (The 1924 Flag Code had failed to make any provision for men without hats, evidently assuming that no man would be without his hat.) The revised flag code in Public Law 829 was altered to advise that men without hats should also place their right hand over their hearts. The only category of person in Public Law 829 that was now to "stand at attention" without placing hand over heart was noncitizens or, in the language of the new law, "aliens." Neither the flag code of 1924 nor Public Law 623 had made any separate provisions for aliens.

79. In 1945, as World War II ground to a close, Congress gave "official recognition" to the Pledge of Allegiance (*New York Times*, June 14, 1945, p. 18).

5. A Nation under God

1. Linda A. Moore, "Pledge Writer's Kin Want Justice for All Amid 'God' Furor," *Commercial Appeal* (Memphis, Tenn.), June 28, 2002, A1. Sally Wright, letter to the editor, *New York Times*, July 14, 2002, IV:14.

2. "National School Celebration of Columbus Day: The Official Programme," *Youth's Companion*, September 8, 1892. Reprinted in Louise Harris, *The Flag over the Schoolhouse* (Providence, R.I.: C.A. Stephens Collection, 1971), 64–68. On "America" as a "national hymn," see Scot M. Guenter, *The American Flag, 1777–1924* (Rutherford, N.J.: Fairleigh Dickinson University Press, 1990), 131.

3. *Youth's Companion* (September 8, 1892): 446. *Malden Evening News*, Oct. 22, 1892, p. 2, emphasis added. The "under God" phrase is also used in "Columbus Day," *Youth's Companion*, November 17, 1892, in Harris, *Flag over the Schoolhouse*, 80. Although unsigned, the "Columbus Day" article was likely written by Bellamy.

4. George T. Balch, *A Patriotic Primer for the Little Citizen,* rev. ed. (Indianapolis: Levey Bros., 1898), 15–16.

5. Bellamy letter, dated July 23, 1923, in Margarette S. Miller, *Twenty-Three Words* (Portsmouth, Va.: Printcraft Press, 1976), 320. See also Francis Bellamy, "A New Plan for Counter-Attack on the Nation's Internal Foes: How to Mobilize the Masses to Support Primary American Doctrines," May 1, 1923, 12; and Francis Bellamy, "Affidavit Concerning the True Origin [of the] Pledge of Allegiance to the Flag," August 13, 1923, 4, in Bellamy Papers.

6. Bellamy, "A New Plan," 10, 22–23.

7. George T. Balch, *Methods of Teaching Patriotism in the Public Schools* (New York: D. Van Nostrand, 1890), 22. Josiah Strong, *Our Country: Its Possible Future and Its Present Crisis,* ed. Jurgen Herbst (Cambridge, Mass.: Harvard University Press, 1963, orig. pub. 1891), 93, 97, 215. Strong embraced "the entire separation of Church and State" but rejected that this principle required a divorce of government and religion. Those who advocated a secular state, Strong argued, "fail to distinguish . . . between *church* and *religion.*" For Strong, it was self-evident that "religious readings in the public schools" did not violate the principle of separation of church and state. For government in the United States, Strong emphasized, "is, and always has been, religious" (97). The protestations of Francis Bellamy's great-grandchildren notwithstanding, Bellamy almost certainly would have embraced Strong's understanding of what was (and was not) entailed in the principle of the separation of church and state.

8. *Holy Trinity v. United States* 143 U.S. 457 (1892), quotation at 471. *United States v. McIntosh* 283 U.S. 605 (1931), quotation at 625. The 1948 case was *McCollum v. Board of Education* 333 U.S. 203 (1948). The key cases from the early 1960s are *Engel v. Vitale* 370 U.S. 421 (1962) and *School District of Abington Township v. Schempp* 374 U.S. 203 (1963). Although the phrase "under God" is hardly foreign to the spirit of the original Pledge of Allegiance, the dispersion of the Pledge throughout the nation may have been helped by the omission of any reference to God. For while prayer in public schools was not uncommon in the late nineteenth century, public schools became more self-consciously secular in the twentieth century. Schools could adopt Bellamy's godless pledge without fear that they would be accused of violating the separation of church and state. Interestingly, the Balch salute, which in its original form invoked God, was modified in the early twentieth century so that the most commonly recited form of that salute no longer included a reference to God.

9. The phrase "under God" is not in the only extant draft of the Gettysburg Address that is in Lincoln's hand and that was, without question, written before delivery of the speech, the so-called "Nicolay text." Some believe that this draft was the text Lincoln read from at Gettysburg, in which case Lincoln must have improvised the words when speaking. Gary Wills, however, demonstrates persuasively that it is unlikely that this draft was the delivery text (*Lincoln at Gettysburg: The Words That Remade America* [New York: Simon and Schuster, 1992], 193–95).

10. The only two uses of the phrase "under God" in the *Messages and Papers of the Presidents* are by John Adams and Lincoln's secretary of the navy, Gideon Welles. Adams and Welles both referred not to a nation under God but to an individual being under God. Adams declared: "To enable me to maintain this declaration I rely, under

God, with entire confidence on the firm and enlightened support of the National Leg-islature and upon the virtue and patriotism of my fellow-citizens" (Special Session Message, May 16, 1797, *Messages and Papers of the Presidents, John Adams*, 1:229). In a similar vein, Welles, speaking after Lincoln's death, said: "To him [Lincoln] our grat-itude was justly due, for to him, under God, more than to any other person, we are indebted for the successful vindication of the integrity of the Union and the mainte-nance of the power of the Republic" (Announcement to the Navy, *Messages and Pa-pers of the Presidents, Abraham Lincoln*, 5:3489).

11. Herbert Hoover, Inaugural Address, March 4, 1929, *Public Papers of the Presi-dents of the United States, Herbert Hoover*, 1.

12. In the letter, Roosevelt wrote: "My prayer shall ever be that this Nation, under God, may vindicate through all coming time the sanctity of the right of all within our borders to the free exercise of religion according to the dictates of conscience" (Let-ter to Michael Williams on Religious Tolerance, March 30, 1937, *The Presidential Pa-pers of Franklin D. Roosevelt* [Item 49 on the American Freedom Library CD-ROM, Western Standard Publishing Company, 1997]). On the post–Pearl Harbor uses of "under God," see Fireside Chat, December 9, 1941; Fireside Chat, October 12, 1942; State of the Union Address, January 11, 1944; and Address to Congress on the Yalta Conference, March 1, 1945; as well as Greeting to Yank Magazine on the Publica-tion of Its First Issue, May 28, 1942; and Proclamation 2542 Proclaiming April 6 as Army Day, March 20, 1942.

13. St. Patrick's Day Address in New York City, March 17, 1948, 189; Radio Re-marks in Independence on Election Eve, November 1, 1948, 940; Address in Casper, Wyoming, May 9, 1950, 326; Radio and Television Address to the American People on the Situation in Korea, July 19, 1950, 541; Address in Philadelphia at the Dedi-cation of the Chapel of the Four Chaplains, February 3, 1951, 139; all in the *Public Papers of the Presidents of the United States, Harry S. Truman*. The currency of the "under God" expression during Truman's second term can also be gleaned from a large banner hung at a December 1950 meeting of the National Council of Churches. Di-rectly above a large cross, the banner declared in bold lettering: "This Nation Under God." A picture of the banner is contained in Martin E. Marty, *Modern American Re-ligion: Under God, Indivisible, 1941–1960* (Chicago: University of Chicago Press, 1996), 272.

14. *New York Times*, July 12, 1952, p. 4. Remarks Broadcast as Part of the Ameri-can Legion "Back to God" Program, February 7, 1954, *Public Papers of the Presidents of the United States, Dwight D. Eisenhower*, 244. Eisenhower's remarks were delivered on the same date that the Reverend George Docherty delivered his sermon recom-mending that "under God" be included in the pledge. That sermon and its import are discussed below.

15. Will Herberg, *Protestant-Catholic-Jew: An Essay in American Religious Sociology* (Garden City, N.Y.: Doubleday, 1955), 64, 69. See also Marty, *Modern American Re-ligion*, chapter seventeen. The constitutional amendment, which was sponsored by Senator Ralph Flanders, a Republican from Vermont, received a hearing before the Senate Judiciary Subcommittee on Constitutional Amendments, but the chair of the

subcommittee, William Langer, was the only elected official who bothered to show up. See Mark Silk, *Spiritual Politics: Religion and America since World War II* (New York: Simon and Schuster, 1988), 99–100. The wording of Flanders's resolution is given in the *New York Times*, May 23, 1954, p. 30.

16. Richard M. Fried, *The Russians Are Coming! The Russians Are Coming! Pageantry and Patriotism in Cold-War America* (New York: Oxford University Press, 1988), 96–97. Silk, *Spiritual Politics*, 100. Jon G. Murray, "A Pledge Too Far," *American Atheist* 30 (November 1988): 17, 21. Benson's proposal that cabinet meetings begin with a prayer induced Eisenhower to circulate a questionnaire in which he asked the members of the cabinet whether they would prefer to begin meetings with a prayer, have no prayer, or have a silent prayer. The latter option prevailed. One aide remembers a meeting in which partway through the meeting, Eisenhower realized he had forgotten the prayer, and blurted out, "Jesus Christ, we forgot the silent prayer" (correspondence with Fred Greenstein, July 15, 2003).

17. Marty, *Modern American Religion*, 355.

18. Herbert Hoover, "The Voice of World Experience," Address before the American Newspaper Publishers Association, Waldorf Astoria, New York City, April 27, 1950, quoted in Marty, *Modern American Religion*, 301. Silk, *Spiritual Politics*, 44.

19. On the development of the idea of a "Judeo-Christian" tradition as an alternative to the idea of a Christian nation or civilization, see Silk, *Spiritual Politics*, chapter two.

20. Speech to Freedoms Foundation in New York, December 24, 1952, as quoted in Silk, *Spiritual Politics*, 44. Remarks Recorded for the "Back-to-God" Program of the American Legion, February 20, 1955, 274, and Message to the National Co-Chairmen, Commission on Religious Organizations, National Conference of Christians and Jews, July 9, 1953, 489–90, both in *Public Papers of the Presidents of the United States, Dwight D. Eisenhower*.

21. "God's Country," *Time*, May 4, 1953, 57–58. Petition of Plywacki, No. 12393, United States District Court for the District of Hawaii 115 F. Supp. 613 (October 23, 1953). See also Petition of Plywacki 107 F. Supp. 593 (October 17, 1952); and *Plywacki v. United States* 205 F.2d 423 (June 26, 1953).

22. *Zorach v. Clauson* 343 U.S. 306 (1952), quotation at 313.

23. Silk, *Spiritual Politics*, 92, 94.

24. Christopher J. Kauffman, *Patriotism and Fraternalism in the Knights of Columbus: A History of the Fourth Degree* (New York: Herder and Herder, 2001), 2. Bessie Louise Pierce, *Citizens' Organizations and the Civic Training of Youth* (New York: Charles Scribner's Sons, 1933), 130.

25. On the evolution of the Knights of Columbus, see Christopher J. Kauffman, *Faith and Fraternalism: The History of the Knights of Columbus, 1882–1982* (New York: Harper and Row, 1982).

26. Hart offered this account of events in a letter written on the day Eisenhower signed the "under God" clause into law. The letter appeared in the July 1954 edition of the Knights' magazine *Columbia* and was entered into the *Congressional Record* by Louis Rabaut on July 13, 1954; see *Congressional Record–Appendix*, A5037–38. This

is also the account in Kauffman, *Faith and Fraternalism*, 385, which is based on Hart's narrative of events (478n37). The Knights of Columbus distributed a leaflet, "How the words 'UNDER GOD' came to be added to the Pledge of Allegiance to the Flag," which mirrors the account by Hart and Kauffman. It also notes that in October 1954 the National Executive Committee of the American Legion approved a resolution acknowledging the Knights' role in having initiated the idea of adding "under God" to the Pledge of Allegiance. The Knights' role in the process was also acknowledged in an August 6, 1954, letter from Eisenhower to Hart.

27. The National Fraternal Congress resolution was adopted at the September 1952 annual meeting, and a number of state Fraternal Congresses followed the lead of the national organization. For instance, on February 12, 1953, the New York Fraternal Congress approved the "under God" proposal recommended by the national body and sent a copy of the resolution to the entire New York delegation urging congressional adoption. The resolution was entered in the *Congressional Record* on March 25, 1953, by Republican Congressman Edmund Radwan (A1494).

28. Extension of Remarks by Louis C. Rabaut, April 21, 1953, *Congressional Record–Appendix*, A2063. *Congressional Record*, May 5, 1954, 6077–78. See also the *Congressional Record*, August 20, 1954, 15828–29. Rabaut recounts the origins of the resolution in the *Congressional Record*, June 7, 1954, 7758. Mahoney is identified as the letter writer in Rep. Francis Dorn's comments in the *Congressional Record*, June 7, 1954, 7765; Rabaut's remarks of July 13, 1954, in the *Congressional Record–Appendix*, A5038; as well as in Clayton Knowles, "Big Issue in D.C.: The Oath of Allegiance," *New York Times*, May 23, 1954, E7. Rabaut's original resolution followed the punctuation in the Gettysburg Address in including a comma after "one Nation," but that comma was later excised by the House Judiciary Committee (*Congressional Record*, June 7, 1954, 7766).

29. The survey of 1,602 people was conducted by Gallup between March 28 and April 2, 1953. The precise wording of the question was: "It has been suggested that the words, 'under God,' should be added to the Oath of Allegiance to the flag so that it would read: 'I pledge allegiance to the flag of the United States of America and to the Republic for which it stands, one nation under God, indivisible, with liberty and justice for all.' Would you favor or oppose this change?" Regionally, the strongest support for the "under God" clause lay in the South (74 percent) and Rocky Mountain region (81.5 percent), and the weakest support came from the Pacific region (63 percent). Those who had been to college also tended to be somewhat less supportive (65 percent) than the rest of the population. In addition, older people tended to be more enthusiastic about the clause—about three-fourths of those over sixty supported the change, while only two-thirds of those between the ages of eighteen and twenty-nine favored altering the Pledge. However, there was no major demographic group that came close to opposing the addition of "under God" to the Pledge of Allegiance.

30. The second "under God" resolution to be introduced in Congress (on January 6, 1954) was done at the request of a local American Legion chapter in upstate New York. The resolution's sponsor was New York representative John Pillion, a Presby-

terian and Republican. See the congressman's remarks included in the *Congressional Record*, June 2, 1954, 7590–91.

31. Silk, *Spiritual Politics*, 95–96. The quotation from Hart is from a letter by Hart that was entered into the *Congressional Record*, July 13, 1954, A5038.

32. *Congressional Record*, June 7, 1954, 7763. Kenneth Dale, "Put God in Flag Pledge, Pastor Urges," *Washington Post*, February 8, 1954, p. 12.

33. "War on 'Secularized . . . Society,'" an excerpt from Docherty's sermon accompanying Bill Broadway's profile ("How 'Under God' Got into the Pledge") of Docherty in the *Washington Post Weekly*, July 15–21, 2002, p. 30.

34. Ibid.

35. Ibid. Oakman's account of the origins of his resolution is in the *Congressional Record–House*, June 7, 1954, 7759. Ferguson's comments are in the *Congressional Record–Senate*, February 10, 1954, 1600. Both the Oakman and Ferguson resolutions proposed the wording "one nation indivisible, under God." The wording of Ferguson's resolution was subsequently changed by the Senate Judiciary committee to "one nation under God, indivisible."

36. The list of eighteen resolutions, with the name of the congressional sponsor and the date introduced, was included as an attachment to a letter that Rabaut sent Eisenhower on June 9, 1954, and is available in the White House Records Office, Bill File, June 14, 1954, HJR 243 to amend Pledge of Allegiance, Eisenhower Library, Abilene, Kansas. Seventeen resolutions were introduced by House members, ten of whom were Catholics. The lone resolution on the Senate side was introduced by a Presbyterian. Information about the religious affiliations of members was derived from J. Michael Sharp, ed., *Directory of Congressional Voting Scores and Interest Group Ratings*, 2d ed. (Washington, D.C.: Congressional Quarterly, 1997), and supplemented with information from the *Current Biography Yearbook* and *Who's Who in America*.

37. *Congressional Record*, February 12, 1954, 1700.

38. Ibid., February 18, 1954, 2008–9. See also Bolton's comments in ibid. on June 7, 1954, 7757–58. Although Bolton's resolution was not the one acted on by the House, it was the first resolution to contain the identical wording and punctuation of the bill eventually signed into law.

39. According to one account, Paramount "recorded portions of the event for a newsreel that ran in movie theaters for weeks afterward" (Broadway, "How 'Under God' Got into the Pledge," July 15–21, 2002, p. 30).

40. Silk, *Spiritual Politics*, 97. In a letter informing Homer Ferguson of the committee's action, Chairman William Langer said only that the committee decided that the bill "appeared unwarranted on the basis of the information available to the Committee" (William Langer to Homer Ferguson, April 6, 1954, Bill File for S.J. Res. 126, 83d Congress, Records of the Senate Judiciary Committee [Record Group 46], National Archives and Records Administration, Washington, D.C.). That the committee had concerns about the separation of church and state is suggested by Ferguson's reply, dated April 26, in which he emphasized to Langer that "the addition of these words to the Pledge would, in no sense constitute any violation of the first

amendment" (Ferguson to Langer, April 26, 1954, Bill File for S.J. Res. 126, 83d Congress, Records of the Senate Judiciary Committee [Record Group 46], National Archives and Records Administration, Washington, D.C.). In a previous letter to Langer, Ferguson had gone out of his way to emphasize that the resolution was not a violation of the First Amendment. Ferguson wrote: "Adoption of this resolution would in no way run contrary to the provisions of the first amendment to the Constitution. This is not an act establishing a religion. A distinction exists between the church as an institution and a belief in the sovereignty of God. The phrase 'under God' recognizes only the guidance of God in our national affairs. It does nothing to establish a religion. Neither will this resolution violate the right of any person to disbelieve in God or reject the existence of God. The recognition of God in the pledge of allegiance to the flag of our Nation does not compel any individual to make a positive affirmation in the existence of God in whom one does not believe" (Ferguson to Langer, March 10, 1954, Bill File for S.J. Res. 126, 83d Congress, Records of the Senate Judiciary Committee [Record Group 46], National Archives and Records Administration, Washington, D.C.).

Ferguson's March 10 letter was included in the committee report as containing "the most cogent and compelling reasons for the passage of the resolution" (*Congressional Record,* May 10, 1954, 6231; the committee report is also available in the Eisenhower Library). The House Judiciary Committee's report on HJR 243, dated May 28, 1954, drew upon and elaborated Ferguson's contention that the amendment to the Pledge did not violate the First Amendment. See the Committee Report No. 1693, House of Representatives, 83d Congress, 2d session. The House committee report and the Senate committee report are available in the White House Records Office, Bill File, Box 22, Eisenhower Library. Rabaut also devoted substantial attention to rebutting concerns about "conflicts between the [under God] measure . . . and traditional American principles of church-state relationships as embodied in the letter and spirit of the first amendment to the Constitution." See "Does the Addition of the Phrase 'Under God' to the Pledge of Allegiance to the Flag Endanger the First Amendment?" *Congressional Record–Appendix,* April 1, 1954, A2527.

41. Congressman Barratt O'Hara, quoted in *Congressional Record,* June 7, 1954, 7761. Senator Alexander Wiley, quoted in *Congressional Record,* May 4, 1954, 5915. See also remarks by Rep. Wolverton, *Congressional Record,* June 7, 1954, 7762. The mail became a prominent part of the media coverage of the issue. The *New York Times* reported that Congress was being "flooded with mail" pressing adoption of the "under God" clause (May 23, 1954, E7), and *Newsweek* observed that "thousands of letters poured in daily" (May 31, 1954, 25). The Hearst editorial stated: "It seems to us that in times like these when Godless communism is the greatest peril this Nation faces, it becomes more necessary than ever to avow our faith in God and to affirm the recognition that the core of our strength comes from Him" (*Congressional Record,* May 4, 1954, 5915).

42. Rabaut provides a narrative of events in the *Congressional Record,* June 7, 1954, 7758. On the same day, Rep. Oakman opined that the Senate Judiciary Committee was "doubtless spurred on by" the action of the House committee (*Congressional*

Record, June 7, 1954, 7762). A letter from the Legislative Reference Service was included in the House Judiciary Committee report (Report No. 1693), a copy of which is in the White House Records Office, Bill File, June 14, 1954, HJR 243 to amend Pledge of Allegiance, Eisenhower Library. Ferguson's explanation of the resolution is in the *Congressional Record,* May 11, 1954, 6348.

43. At the same time, Warren Upham was assuring people that his cousin James B. Upham (who the Upham family still insisted was the real author of the Pledge) would have welcomed the change to the Pledge of Allegiance. Religion, he noted, was "deeply rooted in the Upham family." The only reason the words "under God" were not inserted in the original Pledge, the cousin insisted, was that "it was written during a period when devoutness was taken for granted." Because "pagan philosophies have been introduced by the Soviet Union," his patriotic cousin would have "wholeheartedly" agreed that the Pledge should be altered by "reaffirming belief in God." Warren Upham's remarks appear in an article by Shirley Munroe Mullen, titled "'Under God' Would Help Combat Pagan Influences," which appeared in a Malden newspaper on May 13, 1954. It was entered into the *Congressional Record* by Rep. Angier Goodwin (*Congressional Record–Appendix,* June 1, 1954, A4066–67).

44. *Congressional Record,* June 7, 1954, 7760–61.

45. Ibid., 7759.

46. Ibid. The plea to waive "pride of authorship" came from Rep. Oakman. The day's debate extends from pages 7757 through 7766.

47. Ibid., June 8, 1954, 7833. See also Rep. Oakman's comments praising Ferguson in ibid., June 10, 1954, 7989.

48. Louis Rabaut to Mr. President, June 9, 1954; Homer H. Gruenther to Gerald D. Morgan and Bernard M. Shanley, June 9, 1954; Alberta to Governor, June 10, 1954; White House Records Office, Bill File, June 14, 1954, HJR 243 to amend Pledge of Allegiance, Eisenhower Library. Rabaut's letter was also printed in the *Congressional Record,* June 9, 1954, 7935.

49. Thomas E. Stephens to Gerald D. Morgan, June 10, 1954, White House Central Files, Official File, OF 102-C-2 Pledge of Allegiance, Eisenhower Library.

50. *Congressional Record,* June 22, 1954, 8617. The event was covered in the *New York Times,* June 15, 1954, p. 31.

51. Statement by the President upon Signing Bill to Include the Words "Under God" in the Pledge to the Flag, June 14, 1954, *Public Papers of the Presidents of the United States, Dwight D. Eisenhower,* 563. The presidential statement was reprinted in its entirety the next morning in the *New York Times,* June 15, 1954, p. 31.

52. *New York Times,* January 4, 1956, p. 12.

53. Ibid., May 23, 1954, p. 30. The Unitarian Ministers Association communicated their views to the chairman of the House Judiciary Committee, Chauncey Reed, in a letter dated June 1, 1954. John MacKinnon to Chauncey Reed, June 1, 1954, in Bill File for HJR 243, 83d Congress, Box 1114, 9E2/21/12/3, National Archives.

54. Adams's letter of May 25, 1954, was entered into the *Congressional Record* (May 27, 1954, A3916) by Rep. Multer, who found the letter "most apropos." Adams decided to write to Multer because the congressman had recently spoken out against

Senator Flanders's constitutional amendment, which declared that the nation "devoutly recognizes the authority and law of Jesus Christ." Adams also wrote letters to the chairmen of the Senate and House Judiciary Committees, protesting against the bill as a violation of the separation of church and state. Adams emphasized that his protest stemmed not from any bias against religion but rather from his commitment to the Constitution. He warned that adding these words "will alienate thousands of Citizens from ever 'Pledging allegiance to the Republic for which it stands'" (May 23, 1954, Bill File for HJR 243, 83d Congress, Box 1114, 9E2/21/12/3, National Archives).

55. *New York Times,* June 18, 1954, p. 22; June 23, 1954, p. 26; June 30, 1954, p. 26; July 8, 1954, p. 22; and July 17, 1954, p. 12.

56. *New York Times,* August 20, 1956, p. 8. *Time,* July 12, 1954, p. 68.

57. Kauffman, *Faith and Fraternalism,* 386. The letter from Eisenhower is dated August 6, 1954.

58. *New York Times,* August 15, 1956, p. 14; and September 25, 1957, p. 14.

59. *Lewis v. Allen* (1957) 159 N.Y.S.2d 807, quotations at 812.

60. Ibid., quotations at 813.

61. *New York Times,* November 27, 1964, p. 34. *Lewis v. Allen* 200 N.E.2d 767 (1964); *Lewis v. Allen* 11 A.D. 2d 447 (1960). See also *New York Times,* December 3, 1960, p. 20.

62. *New York Times,* June 20, 1963, p. 20; April 10, 1964, p. 16; September 14, 1964; and February 16, 1965, p. 33. In 1977, Murray was quoted in the *New York Times* as referring to the Bible as an "idiotic book" (July 28, 1977, A15). Two revealing biographies of Madalyn Murray O'Hair have recently been published: Bryan F. Le Beau, *The Atheist: Madalyn Murray O'Hair* (New York: New York University Press, 2003), and Ted Dracos, *Ungodly: The Passions, Torments, and Murder of Atheist Madalyn Murray O'Hair* (New York: Free Press, 2003).

63. *Engel v. Vitale* (1963) 370 U.S. 421, quotation at 435n21. *School District of Abington Township v. Schempp* (1963) 374 U.S. 203, quotations at 303–4; Goldberg quotes Black's footnote at 307.

64. *Smith v. Denny* (1968) 280 F. Supp. 651; *Smith v. Denny* (1969) 417 F.2d 614. *Sherman v. Community Consolidated School District* (1989) 714 F. Supp. 932; *Sherman v. Community Consolidated School District* (1991) 758 F. Supp. 1244; *Sherman v. Community Consolidated School District* (1992) 980 F.2d 437; *Sherman v. Community Consolidated School District* (1993) 508 U.S. 950.

65. Bob Norman, "One Nation, Divisible under God," *New Times* (Broward–Palm Beach, Florida), September 30, 1999. *Newdow v. U.S.* (2000) 207 F.3d 662. *Newdow v. Congress* (2000) U.S. Dist. (May 25, 2000) Lexis 22367. *Newdow v. Congress* (2000) U.S. Dist. Lexis 22366. Newdow has had no success in two other legal challenges he has mounted against the injection of religion into public life. The first is a suit Newdow brought against taxpayer-funded chaplains in Congress, and the second is a suit against clergy-led prayer at presidential inaugurations. In the latter case, decided on February 24, 2004, a three-judge panel of the Ninth Circuit Court of Appeals brushed aside his case as "futile," and argued that Newdow lacked standing to

sue since he did not suffer "a sufficiently concrete and specific injury" from the prayer (*Newdow v. Bush* 89 Fed. Appx. 624). In the former case, decided on March 24, 2004, a district judge granted Newdow "taxpayer standing" but rejected his claim that taxpayer-funded chaplains in Congress violated the establishment clause (*Newdow v. Eagen* 309 F. Supp. 2d 29).

66. Norman, "One Nation, Divisible under God." Tony Mauro, "Newdow at Odds with Allies," *Legal Times,* November 10, 2003, 10.

67. Mauro, "Newdow at Odds with Allies." Tony Mauro, "Justices Take on High-Profile First Amendment Cases," Special to the First Amendment Center Online, October 15, 2003, at http://www.firstamendmentcenter.org/analysis.aspx?id=12074. Mark Silk, "Under Whatever," *Religion in the News,* Fall 2003, vol. 6, no. 3, online at http://www.trincoll.edu/depts/csrpl/RINVol6No3/From%20the%20Editor603.htm.

68. *Newdow v. U.S. Congress* (2002) 292 F. 3d 597, quotations at 605–6. See also *Lemon v. Kurtzman* (1971) 403 U.S. 602; *Lynch v. Donnelly* (1984) 465 U.S. 668; and *Lee v. Weisman* (1992) 505 U.S. 577, as well as *County of Allegheny v. ACLU* (1989) 492 U.S. 573; and *Santa Fe Independent School District v. Doe* (2000) 5530 U.S. 290.

69. *Newdow v. U.S. Congress* (2002) 292 F. 3d 597, quotations at 607, 609–10.

70. Ibid., quotations at 613, 615.

71. *Newdow v. U.S. Congress* (2002) 328 F.3d 466.

72. *Lee v. Weisman* (1992) 505 U.S. 577, quotations at 590, 592.

73. *Elk Grove Unified School District v. Michael A. Newdow* (2004) 124 S. Ct. 2301, quotations at 2327, 2330. *Lee v. Weisman* (1992) 505 U.S. 577, quotation at 632. Ever the judicial radical masquerading in conservative robes, Thomas was not content to undo *Lee v. Weisman* but wanted also to remake establishment clause jurisprudence dating back at least a half century. According to Thomas, the establishment clause should apply only to the federal government, not to states and localities, so although the federal government cannot establish a religion, state and local governments are free to do so. See *Elk Grove Unified School District v. Michael A. Newdow* (2004), at 2330–31.

74. *Elk Grove Unified School District v. Michael A. Newdow* (2004), quotations at 2319–20. The government's contention that "under God" is best understood as a descriptive phrase is ironic in view of the fact that—as we shall see in chapter six—public school officials have often argued that students protesting the phrase "liberty and justice for all" are misguided because the phrase is not to be understood as a descriptive claim but rather as an aspiration.

75. Oral Argument before the Supreme Court of the United States, in *Elk Grove Unified School District v. Michael A. Newdow,* Washington, D.C., March 24, 2004, Alderson Reporting Company, 28–30, 33–34; available at http://www.supremecourtus.gov/oral_arguments/argument_transcripts/02-1624.pdf. *Elk Grove Unified School District v. Michael A. Newdow* (2004) 124 S. Ct. 2301, at 2320.

76. *Elk Grove Unified School District v. Michael A. Newdow* (2004) 124 S. Ct. 2301, quotation at 2321.

77. Ibid., 2321–22.

78. Ibid., 2322–23. *Lynch v. Donnelly* (1984) 465 U.S. 668, quotation at 716. O'Connor does not explain how having "under God" in the Pledge of Allegiance solemnizes the flag salute. Was Bellamy's original Pledge lacking in solemnity? Certainly nobody who proposed adding the words "under God" to the Pledge argued that it would make the Pledge or flag salute more solemn, nor did they argue that the Pledge sans God lacked solemnity.

79. *Elk Grove Unified School District v. Michael A. Newdow* (2004) 124 S. Ct. 2301, quotations at 2324. In oral argument, the government's lawyer, Theodore Olson, counted fourteen Supreme Court justices who had agreed in various judicial dicta that the reference to "under God" in the Pledge of Allegiance was not unconstitutional (Oral Argument, 16).

80. Brief Amicus Curiae of Buddhist Temples, Centers and Organizations Representing over 300,000 Buddhist Americans in Support of Respondents, February 12, 2004. Links to this and the other friend of the court briefs are conveniently available at The Pew Forum on Religion and Public Life's "Pledge of Allegiance Resources" webpage: http://pewforum.org/religion-schools/pledge/.

81. *Elk Grove Unified School District v. Michael A. Newdow* (2004) 124 S. Ct. 2301, quotation at 2325. O'Connor's declaration about how the Pledge is understood ignored empirical evidence presented in several briefs that contradict her claim. The brief by the Americans United for Separation of Church and State and the ACLU, for instance, points to a 1967 study by two social scientists that surveyed first graders and found that "the questionnaire responses showed that a number of second-grade children believed the pledge of allegiance was a prayer to God." The study found that most first-graders did not understand many of the words in the Pledge of Allegiance, and "insofar as they form an understanding of its meaning, they focus on terms that are recognizable to them, such as God" (Amicus Curia Brief of Americans United for Separation of Church and State, American Civil Liberties Union, and Americans for Religious Liberty in Support of Affirmance, 13–14). Less directly relevant but still suggestive is a 1994 national survey, which found that 71 percent of respondents believed that "In God We Trust" endorsed a belief in God, and 53 percent said it endorsed religion over atheism (Amicus Curia Brief of the Freedom from Religion Foundation, Inc., in Support of the Rev. Dr. Michael A. Newdow, Respondent, A4).

82. *Elk Grove Unified School District v. Michael A. Newdow* (2004) 124 S. Ct. 2301, quotations at 2312. The majority was made up of five judges (Stevens, Kennedy, David Souter, Ruth Bader Ginsburg, and Stephen Breyer). Justice Scalia recused himself from the case after Newdow had objected that a speech that Scalia gave in January 2003 disqualified him from being an impartial judge in the pending case. In the ten-minute speech, given at a celebration of religious freedom cosponsored by the Knights of Columbus and the Knights Templar, Scalia criticized the last forty years of Supreme Court establishment jurisprudence, specifically noting that past Supreme Court rulings had given the Ninth Circuit Court "some plausible support" for its conclusion that the Pledge of Allegiance was unconstitutional. Correctly interpreted, Scalia explained, the Constitution forbids government from favoring one religion over another but does not require the government "to be neutral between religiousness and

nonreligiousness." Judicial efforts to drive religion out of the public sphere were "contrary to our whole tradition, to 'in God we trust' on the coins, to [presidential] Thanksgiving proclamations, to [congressional] chaplains, to tax exemption for places of worship, which has always existed in America." See Jacqueline L. Salmon, "Scalia Defends Public Expression of Faith," *Washington Post*, January 13, 2003, B3; "Scalia Decries Rulings on Church-State Separation," *The Record* (Bergen County, N.J.), January 13, 2003, A10.

83. *Newdow v. U.S. Congress* (2002) 292 F. 3d 597, at 602. *Elk Grove Unified School District v. Michael A. Newdow* (2004) 124 S. Ct. 2301, at 2307–8.

84. *Elk Grove Unified School District v. Michael A. Newdow* (2004) 124 S. Ct. 2301, at 2307, 2310. *Newdow v. U.S. Congress* (2002) 313 F.3d 500, at 503.

6. Protesting the Pledge

1. *New York Times*, May 19, 1988, B12.

2. E. J. Dionne, "Let's Be Upfront about 'Under God,'" *Pittsburgh Post-Gazette*, June 28, 2002, A19. E. J. Dionne, "Dukakis Is Termed Extreme Liberal," *New York Times*, May 20, 1988, II:5.

3. *New York Times*, September 26, 1957, A13.

4. *West Virginia State Board of Education v. Barnette* (1943) 319 U.S. 624, quotations at 642–43.

5. *New York Times*, May 18, 1963, p. 13; December 19, 1963, p. 35; and January 25, 1966, p. 34. *Holden v. Board of Education* (1966) 46 N.J. 281. Local posts of the American Legion and the Veterans of Foreign Wars weighed in by supporting a proposal to suspend welfare payments to those who refused to salute the flag. See "Compulsory U.S. Flag Salute Urged for Relief Recipients," *New York Times*, June 22, 1963.

6. *New York Times*, February 1, 1964, A25; April 15, 1964, A41; and April 16, 1964, A39.

7. Ibid., March 4, 1969, A7; and June 27, 1971, A63.

8. Ibid., October 25, 1969, p. 35; and October 28, 1969, p. 22. The superintendent's ruling is quoted in *Frain v. Baron* (1969) 307 F. Supp. 27, at 30.

9. *Frain v. Baron*, quotations at 30. The "blacks are oppressed" quotation is from a profile of Mary Frain in the *New York Times*, January 31, 1970, p. 33. The case of the junior high school girls got extensive press coverage; see, for example, *New York Times*, October 8, 1969, p. 35; October 10, 1969, p. 96; November 1, 1969, p. 35; as well as the profile on January 31, 1970, p. 33.

10. *Frain v. Baron*, quotations at 32–33. *Tinker v. Des Moines Independent Community School District* (393 U.S. 503) was decided in February 1969, ten months before Judge Judd issued his December ruling. What the record in *Frain* did show, however, is that there was a contagion associated with the actions. After the judge had issued a temporary restraining order in October, approximately fifty students at the junior high school chose to sit silently on "one or more occasions" over the next month during the Pledge of Allegiance. There is evidence, too, that refusals spread at the

Queens high school, for the following school year principal Louis Schuker was back in the news for allegedly harassing a number of students who were choosing to sit during the Pledge of Allegiance. The threats of reprisal and punishments were serious enough that the threatened students again sought the help of the ACLU, which induced Judd to threaten the principal with contempt charges if he did not desist in harassing the students (*Frain v. Baron* at 30; *New York Times,* December 16, 1970, A32).

11. *New York Times,* January 26, 1970, A1; and February 5, 1970, A38.

12. The *Times* editorial is January 29, 1970, p. 36. The quotation from the state superintendent of schools is in the *New York Times,* January 26, 1970, p. 1. Press reports that the Pledge is often not said in classrooms can be found in *New York Times,* October 8, 1969, p. 35; and January 26, 1970, p. 44. The state department of education directive is reported in the *New York Times,* January 31, 1970, p. 33.

13. *New York Times,* June 24, 1970, p. 59. *In re Bielenberg* 9 Ed.Dept.Rep. 196 (1970), quotations at 198–99. Nyquist found that while the *Barnette* decision "includes broad language, the Courts have consistently referred to it as being 'based on the First Amendment's guarantee of religious freedom'" (197). Nyquist also mentions *Tinker* but distinguishes Bielenberg's case from *Tinker* on the implausible grounds that whereas wearing black armbands "did not concern speech or action that intrudes upon the work of the school or the rights of other students" (197–98), refusing to stand for the Pledge of Allegiance does intrude on the work of the school and the rights of other students.

14. *New York Times,* December 6, 1970, A49; *Look,* December 1, 1970, p. 21; and *New York Times,* December 9, 1970, A55. See also *Fort Lauderdale News,* December 28, 1970, B1. Seven years earlier, a Pennsylvania representative, James G. Fulton, introduced a resolution in Congress to amend the last clause of the Pledge of Allegiance to read "with liberty, equality of opportunity and equal justice under law for all" ("Rights Clause Proposed in Pledge of Allegiance," *New York Times,* August 29, 1963, p. 12).

15. *New York Times,* July 12, 1970, p. 35. The case was *Richards v. Board of Education* 70-C-625 (E.D.N.Y. 1969).

16. *Goetz v. Ansell* (1973) 477 F.2d 636, quotations at 637–38. The decision was reported in the *New York Times,* April 20, 1973, p. 37.

17. *New York Times,* June 28, 1977, A35; and August 17, 1977, B3.

18. Ibid., August 17, 1977, A1; and June 28, 1977, A35.

19. Ibid., June 28, 1977, p. 35; August 17, 1977, B3; February 19, 1978, p. 33; and October 16, 1977, XI:6. *Lipp v. Morris* (1978) 579 F.2d 834.

20. *Banks v. Board of Public Instruction* (1970) 314 F. Supp. 285, quotations at 294–96.

21. *Tinker v. Des Moines Independent School District* 393 U.S. 503, quotation at 506.

22. Bob Shemeligian, "I Would Prefer Not To," *Las Vegas Mercury,* July 11, 2002. Meinhold phone interview with author, July 28, 2003. *New York Times,* March 12, 1966, A3.

23. *New York Times,* September 7, 1968, A19.

24. Ibid., April 23, 1969, A37. *Russo v. Central School District* (1972) 469 F.2d 623, quotations at 625–26.

25. *Russo v. Central School District*, at 632–33. The school board reversed course once again in mid-May, requiring that students who refused to recite the Pledge must stand in "respectful silence," exactly what Russo had been doing since the beginning of the school year. Nonetheless the school board, at a June meeting, agreed to fire her (627). The 1924 civilian flag code read: "Civilian adults will always show full respect to the Flag, when the pledge is being given, by merely standing at attention, men removing the headdress" (Garland W. Powell, *"Service": For God and Country* [Indianapolis: Cornelius Printing, 1924], 54).

26. *Russo v. Central School District*, quotations at 631–33.

27. *New York Times*, February 18, 1974, p. 28. Russo was profiled in the *New Yorker* in 1973, in Daniel Lang, "A Reporter At Large: Love of Country," July 30, 1973, 35–48.

28. *Hanover v. Northrup* (1970) 325 F. Supp. 170, at 170–71. Leonard Stevens, "Do We Need a New Pledge of Allegiance," *Look*, December 1, 1970, 19. *New York Times*, February 23, 1970, A24.

29. *New York Times*, February 23, 1970, A24. *Hanover v. Northrup*, quotations at 172–73.

30. *Fort Lauderdale News*, December 8, 1970, B1; December 9, 1970, B1; December 10, 1970, B1; December 11, 1970, B1; December 14, 1970, B3; December 18, 1970, B1; December 28, 1970, B1; and January 8, 1970, B1. *New York Times*, December 27, 1970, p. 41; and February 28, 1971, p. 95.

31. *New York Times*, May 31, 1970, p. 40.

32. From the Statement of Belief by August L. Lundquist, included as an appendix to the majority's opinion in *State v. Lundquist* (1971) 262 Md. 534, at 555–56.

33. *State v. Lundquist*, quotations at 541, 551. See also *New York Times*, May 21, 1970, A40; and September 5, 1970, A19.

34. *State v. Lundquist*, quotations at 565, 567–68.

35. It is true that in the fall semester of 1977 a Chicago kindergarten teacher, Joethelia Palmer, was fired for refusing "to teach any subjects having to do with love of country, the flag or other patriotic matters in the prescribed curriculum." Palmer, a Jehovah's Witness, immediately challenged her dismissal, citing not only *Barnette* but also *Russo* and *Hanover*, but lost in federal district court and in the court of appeals. The district judge made it clear that *Russo* and *Hanover* did not apply to Palmer's case because the school board had demonstrated that Palmer had not only refused to lead the Pledge of Allegiance but had "also refused to teach certain patriotic songs and conduct holiday activities." And that sort of "curricular nonconformity" was not protected, even if refusing to participate in the Pledge was. The judge allowed that the refusal to lead the Pledge of Allegiance may have played "a substantial part" in the teacher's dismissal, but the judge found that the teacher's failure to follow the prescribed curriculum, and the demonstrated disruption that refusal caused to the education of the five year olds in her charge, meant that the school board "would have reached the same conclusion in the absence of *the protected activity*" (*Palmer v. Board*

of Education [1979] 466 F. Supp. 600, quotations at 604; emphasis added). The appeals court, too, focused not on the Pledge of Allegiance but on the teacher's refusal to teach the prescribed curriculum, particularly patriotic holidays like Lincoln's Birthday (*Palmer v. Board of Education* [1979] 603 F.2d 1271, at 1274). Neither opinion rejected the reasoning in *Russo* and *Hanover* that refusing to recite the Pledge was a constitutionally protected activity, so long as it did not disrupt the classroom or unreasonably interfere with student learning.

36. Opinions of the Justices to the Governor, Supreme Judicial Court of Massachusetts (1977) 372 Mass. 874. Dukakis was not the first governor to have been stuck by the legislature with the choice of signing into law a clearly unconstitutional flag salute statute or vetoing it and being made to seem unpatriotic. In 1950, only seven years after *Barnette*, both houses of the New York state legislature unanimously passed a bill that would have made daily recital of the Pledge compulsory for all the state's public schoolchildren. Republican governor Thomas Dewey vetoed the bill, explaining that "patriotism is aroused in the voluntary devotion of its citizens and not in their being compelled by law to manifest respect for its institutions by daily rituals" (*New York Times*, April 9, 1950, A63). Dewey's veto was welcomed by the state department of education and the state school board, both of which had opposed the bill, but it brought the governor bitter criticism from many, including from Gridley Adams, who deplored the governor's veto at a time when enemies are "sow[ing] the seeds of hate for the U.S.A" (Gridley Adams, *So Proudly We Hail . . . !* [United States Flag Foundation, 1953], 44). A law requiring a daily salute surfaced again in New York in 1955, and it was again vetoed, this time by Democratic governor Averell Harriman, who worried that a daily pledge would become "habitual" and "lose the dignity and patriotic fervor which it is entitled to engender" (*New York Times*, April 30, 1955, A19). The following year Harriman did sign a bill that required the state education commissioner to establish a program for a pledge of allegiance to the flag. Previous law only required a salute to the flag. See *New York Times*, March 25, 1956, A47.

37. Opinions of the Justices to the Governor, Supreme Judicial Court of Massachusetts (1977) 372 Mass. 874.

38. Ibid., quotations at 876, 878–79.

39. Useful portraits of both judges can be found in the memorials available on the webpage of the Supreme Judicial Court of Massachusetts, Office of Reporter of Decisions (1804–Present), at http://www.massreports.com/directory/memorials.htm. The first quotation is taken from a comment by Quirico quoted in a 2000 memorial tribute to the justice. The other quotations are from the decision written by the two judges in Opinions of the Justices to the Governor, Supreme Judicial Court of Massachusetts (1977) 372 Mass. 874, quotations at 881. In reaching their conclusion, the two dissenters had to strain mightily in their construction of the statute. The sixth sentence of the 1935 law had prescribed that "failure for a period of two consecutive weeks by a teacher to salute the flag and recite said pledge as aforesaid, or to cause the pupils under his charge so to do, shall be punished for every such period by a fine of not more than five dollars," and the new fourth sentence of the 1977 law left this

penalty provision unchanged. The judges maintained that, since the new language in the 1977 bill did not speak of teachers "causing" their pupils to do anything and also did not mention the flag salute but only the Pledge of Allegiance, the sentence imposing a punishment should essentially be ignored: "It should then be read to impose no fine on teachers either for 'failure . . . to salute the flag and recite said pledge as aforesaid,' or for failure to 'cause' pupils to do anything." Perhaps not quite persuaded by their own logic, the judges added that "a further amendment to strike the two quoted clauses from the sixth sentence would of course make this reading clearer." It is questionable whether the justices' creative interpretations of this statute embodied the philosophy of judicial restraint that both championed.

40. Indeed, this was precisely the conclusion that a federal court of appeals reached in 1992 when considering the Illinois statute. The court concluded: "If it means 'all pupils' then it is blatantly unconstitutional; if it means 'willing pupils' then the most severe constitutional problem dissolves. When resolving statutory ambiguities, the Supreme Court of Illinois adopts readings that save rather than destroy state laws. . . . Given *Barnette*, which long predated enactment of this statute, it makes far more sense to interpolate 'by willing pupils' than 'by all pupils.' School administrators and teachers satisfy the 'shall' requirement by leading the Pledge and ensuring that at least some pupils recite. Leading the Pledge is not optional, . . . but participating is. This makes sense of the statute without imputing a flagrantly unconstitutional act to the State of Illinois" (*Sherman v. Community Consolidated School District* [1992] 980 F.2d 437; quotation at 442).

41. A poll conducted May 23–26, 1991, by Gallup found that 78 percent of the people surveyed agreed that "school children should be required to pledge allegiance to the flag in all US schools." Only 2 percent did not have an opinion on the question, and the remaining 20 percent disagreed.

42. Steven V. Roberts, "Bush Intensifies Debate on Pledge, Asking Why It So Upsets Dukakis," *New York Times*, August 25, 1988, A1. Bill Peterson, "Bush Fans Rhetorical Six-Gun in Texas," *Washington Post*, August 26, 1988, A6.

7. One Nation . . . Indivisible?

1. Steven V. Roberts, "Bush Intensifies Debate on Pledge, Asking Why It So Upsets Dukakis," *New York Times*, August 25, 1988, A1.

2. Remarks to the National Catholic Education Association in Chicago, Illinois, April 15, 1982, 467; Remarks at a White House Ceremony in Observance of National Day of Prayer, May 6, 1982, 574; Message to the Congress Transmitting a Proposed Constitutional Amendment on Prayer in School, May 17, 1982, 647; and Radio Address to the Nation on Prayer, September 18, 1982, 1182, all in *Public Papers of the Presidents of the United States, Ronald Reagan.*

3. Radio Address to the Nation on Prayer in Schools, February 25, 1984, 262; Remarks at an Ecumenical Prayer Breakfast in Dallas, Texas, August 23, 1984, 1166–68,

in *Public Papers of the Presidents of the United States, Ronald Reagan*. See also Remarks to the Student Congress on Evangelism, July 28, 1988, in *Public Papers of the Presidents of the United States, Ronald Reagan*, 989–93.

4. Remarks on Receiving the Department of Education Report on Improving Education, May 20, 1987, 546; Remarks at the Annual Convention of the American Federation of Teachers in Los Angeles, California, July 5, 1983, 1012, in *Public Papers of the Presidents of the United States, Ronald Reagan*.

5. Michael Norman, "President Visits Jersey to Help Rep. Fenwick," *New York Times*, September 18, 1982, A26. Remarks at the Swearing-In Ceremony for New United States Citizens in White House Station, New Jersey, September 17, 1982, 1179; Remarks at Naturalization Ceremonies for New United States Citizens in Detroit, Michigan, October 1, 1984, 1394; and Remarks at a Reagan-Bush Rally in Brownsville, Texas, October 2, 1984, 1414, all in *Public Papers of the Presidents of the United States, Ronald Reagan*. See also Remarks and a Question-and-Answer Session at St. Agatha High School in Detroit, Michigan, October 10, 1984, in *Public Papers of the Presidents of the United States, Ronald Reagan*, 1481.

6. Remarks during a White House Ceremony Commemorating Flag Day, June 14, 1983, 858; Remarks at a Flag Day Ceremony in Baltimore, Maryland, June 14, 1985, 769; Radio Address to the Nation on Flag Day and Father's Day, June 14, 1986, 771; Radio Address to the Nation on International Trade, June 13, 1987, 641; and Remarks at the Bicentennial Celebration of the United States Constitution, September 16, 1987, 1049, all in *Public Papers of the Presidents of the United States, Ronald Reagan*.

7. Remarks at a Republican Campaign Rally in Mesquite, Texas, November 5, 1988, 1464; Remarks at a Republican Party Rally in Cape Girardeau, Missouri, September 14, 1988, 1166; and Remarks at a Fundraising Brunch for Senatorial Candidate Susan Engeleiter in Milwaukee, Wisconsin, November 2, 1988, 1432, all in *Public Papers of the Presidents of the United States, Ronald Reagan*. These partisan uses of the Pledge were repeated in Remarks at a Republican Party Campaign Fundraiser in St. Louis, Missouri, September 14, 1988, 1168; Remarks at a Republican Party Rally in Waco, Texas, September 22, 1988, 1197; Remarks at a Columbus Day Dinner in West Orange, New Jersey, October 12, 1988, 1326; Remarks at a Republican Campaign Rally in Columbus, Ohio, October 19, 1988, 1348; and Remarks at a Republican Campaign Rally in San Bernardino, California, November 1, 1988, 1426, all in *Public Papers of the Presidents of the United States, Ronald Reagan*. Other partisan uses of the Pledge by Reagan during the 1988 presidential campaign can be found in Remarks at a White House Briefing for Conservative Political Leaders, July 5, 1988, 923; Remarks to Reagan Administration Political Appointees, August 12, 1988, 1066; Remarks at a Fundraiser for Representative Robert J. Lagomarsino in Santa Barbara, California, August 27, 1988, 1112; Remarks at the Republican Governors Club Dinner, October 4, 1988, 1281; Remarks at a Republican Campaign Rally in Bowling Green, Kentucky, October 21, 1988, 1365, 1368; Remarks at a Fundraising Luncheon for Senatorial Candidate Alan Keyes in Baltimore, Maryland, October 26, 1988, 1386; Remarks at a Republican Campaign Rally in Fullerton, California, November 1, 1988, 1420, 1422; Remarks at a Republican Campaign Rally in Voorhees,

New Jersey, November 4, 1988, 1452; Remarks at a Republican Campaign Rally in Mount Clements, Michigan, November 5, 1988, 1459; and Remarks at a Republican Campaign Rally in Long Beach, California, November 7, 1988, 1473, all in *Public Papers of the Presidents of the United States, Ronald Reagan.*

8. A centerpiece of Dumont's unsuccessful campaign against Hughes was a comment by a then-unknown history professor, Eugene Genovese, who declared in an April teach-in at Rutgers that he "welcome[d] . . . the impending Vietcong victory in Vietnam." Dumont angrily demanded that the state fire the tenured Genovese, a call that was echoed by former Vice President Richard Nixon when he came to the state to campaign for Dumont. Nixon explained that "when it comes between American boys defending freedom of speech and Professor Genovese's rights to use that freedom, I'm for American boys every time" (*New York Times,* October 25, 1965, A31). Dumont agreed that "anyone who defends the right of a college professor on the public payroll is way off base. You don't keep your constitutional rights alive by losing wars" (*New York Times,* October 28, 1965, p. 39). Hughes, however, citing academic freedom, refused to intervene, and ended up winning the governor's race by the largest margin in state history. In addition, the Democrats took control of both houses of the state legislature for the first time since 1913 (*New York Times,* November 3, A1). See also Arnold Beichman, "Study in Academic Freedom," *New York Times Magazine,* December 19, 1965, pp. 14, 69.

9. *New York Times,* October 19, 1965, A30; and July 31, 1965, A18. Dukakis also likened Bush's focus on the Pledge to Senator McCarthy's anti-Communist witch hunt. See Ben Bradlee, Jr., "Dukakis Likens Bush Attacks to McCarthyism," *Boston Globe,* September 10, 1988, A1.

10. It was at the 1984 Republican National Convention in Dallas, Texas, that a demonstrator was arrested for burning an American flag, an arrest that would eventually culminate in the U.S. Supreme Court's controversial decision in 1989 to protect flag-burning as symbolic speech.

11. "Rule Is Rejected on Saluting Flag," *New York Times,* April 12, 1984, A23. Victoria Benning, "Brookline Settles Longtime Battle," *Boston Globe,* June 5, 1992, p. 18.

12. *New York Times,* May 5, 1971, A28. *New York Times,* September 9, 1984, A55. The details of Lynch's ruling are laid out in the *Tribune* (Oakland, Calif.), May 10, 1984, A1.

13. Susan Chira, "One Pledge Is Put Aside by Assembly," *New York Times,* February 15, 1983, B2. Luther F. Bliven, "Assembly Rejects Daily Pledge to Flag," *Post-Standard* (Syracuse, N.Y.), February 18, 1987, A6. Elizabeth Wasserman, "To Pledge or Not to Pledge," *Post-Standard* (Syracuse, N.Y.), March 31, 1987, B1.

14. "Foundation of Patriotism," *Post-Standard* (Syracuse, N.Y.), March 10, 1987, A7. Gus Bliven, "Pledge Is Now a 'Good Idea,'" *Post-Standard* (Syracuse, N.Y.), June 5, 1987, A12. "Pledge: Didn't Require Two Hours of Debate by Lawmakers," *Post-Standard* (Syracuse, N.Y.), June 13, 1987, editorial page.

15. The entire paragraph from the 1992 platform reads: "Just as spiritual principles—our moral compass—help guide public policy, learning must have a moral basis. America must remain neutral toward particular religions, but we must not remain neutral toward religion itself or the values religion supports. Mindful of our

country's Judeo-Christian heritage and rich religious pluralism, we support the right of students to engage in voluntary prayer in schools and the right of the community to do so at commencements or other occasions. We will strongly enforce the law guaranteeing equal access to school facilities. We also advocate recitation of the Pledge of Allegiance in schools as a reminder of the principles that sustain us as one Nation under God."

16. *Congressional Record,* June 15, 1954, 8198.

17. Tom Kenworthy, "House Skirmishes over Pledge of Allegiance," *Washington Post,* September 10, 1988, A10. Tom Kenworthy, "Pledge Makes House Debut; A Long Run Appears Likely," *Washington Post,* September 14, 1988, A10.

18. Glenn R. Simpson, "'Sieg Heil' Gonzalez Says about Pledging Allegiance," *Roll Call,* June 28, 1993. Gonzalez's comments in full were: "In fact, nothing is sadder than to see the herd instinct in taking the Pledge of Allegiance here in the House of Representatives. What is that pledge? That pledge was not around until just three decades, three and a half, four decades ago. Here we are, we have taken an oath, and that oath is to the Constitution, not to the flag. The flag is a symbol. Here we are, like a good little herd, reminiscent of the Hitlerian period: 'Sieg Heil, Sieg Heil.' That sounds terrible, and maybe it sounds like it is erratic, but that is the way I feel and think. It is sad when we forget that the main oath is the main thing. That oath is to uphold and protect the Constitution against all enemies, domestic and foreign."

19. A month after introducing the resolution, Smith left the Republican party for the U.S. Taxpayers party, determined to seek the presidential nomination of the latter. Several months later, Smith returned to the Republican fold. In 2002, he was beaten in a Republican primary election by John Sununu, son of George H. W. Bush's chief of staff.

20. John Nichols, "Democrats Learn to Win," *The State of Politics* 20 (April 22, 1999), available at http://www.shepherd-express.com/shepherd/20/17/news_and _views/the_state_of_politics.html.

21. Luke Timmerman, "Pledge Feud, Mailing Campaign Prompt Legislative Aide to Quit," *Capital Times* (Madison, Wis.), November 20, 1999, A1. Luke Timmerman, "Clash over the Pledge; Supervisors' Silence Makes Others See Red," *Capital Times* (Madison, Wis.), July 14, 1999, A1.

22. David Blaska, "To Say or Not to Say?" *Wisconsin State Journal* (Madison), August 28, 1999, A7. "Wiganowsky's Political Pledge," *Capital Times* (Madison, Wis.), July 23, 1999, A12. Marv Balousek, "Supervisor's Letter Elicits Reaction; Pledge of Allegiance Flap Pleases GOP," *Wisconsin State Journal* (Madison), November 20, 1999, B1. Timmerman, "Pledge Feud, Mailing Campaign."

23. Timmerman, "Pledge Feud, Mailing Campaign." Kevin Murphy, "Official Who Refuses to Say Pledge Quits Job as Aide," *Milwaukee Journal Sentinel,* November 24, 1999, p. 2. Matt Pommer, "Veterans Panel Hopeful Grilled," February 21, 2002, *Capital Times* (Madison, Wis.), A2.

24. Anita Clark, "Incumbent Seeks 5th Term for District 35," *Wisconsin State Journal* (Madison), February 7, 2000, B3. If political aspirants were reluctant to criticize

Heiliger, the press showed no such reticence. See, in particular, two hard-hitting editorials ("Don Heiliger's Cruel Politics," November 23, 1999, A10, and "Don Heiliger's Extreme Views Smack of McCarthyism," March 22, 2000, A7) in Madison's *Capital Times*.

25. The survey of Oregon city councils was carried out in the winter of 2003–4 by the author with the assistance of Alexis Walker.

26. The survey of state legislatures was carried out in the spring of 2004 by the author with the help of Alexis Walker. The state legislatures that indicated that they did not recite the Pledge of Allegiance on a daily or weekly basis were the Nebraska legislature, the house in Hawaii and Texas, and the senate in Hawaii, Kansas, Maryland, North Carolina, North Dakota, Oklahoma, Texas, Virginia, Washington, and West Virginia. The North Carolina legislature, however, does say the Pledge of Allegiance at the opening of the legislative session and on special occasions such as Flag Day, Memorial Day, and July 4. There is no state in which the senate says the Pledge and the house does not, and in the great majority of states the practice of reciting the Pledge began on the house side and was later copied by the senate.

27. Quotation from Mark Singer, "I Pledge Allegiance, " *New Yorker* (November 26, 2001), 54. Republicans controlled the assembly the entire time between 1995 and 2002. Democrats controlled the state senate during this period for all but two years (1997–1998).

28. The first quotation is taken from Representative Jensen's webpage at http://www.legis.state.wi.us/assembly/asm98/news/updates/032803.htm. The subsequent quotations are from Scott R. Jensen, "Patriotism Begins at a Young Age," *Wisconsin State Journal* (Madison), September 17, 2001, A10.

29. Sarah Wyatt, "Schools Drafting Policies for Saying Pledge Every Day," Associated Press State and Local Wire, September 28, 2001. Reports varied greatly on student reactions to the new law. At one Madison high school the Pledge was read over the public address system by the student council president, and the principal reported that "not many kids participated" in saying the Pledge. Another high school chose to play the national anthem in the student center, and only about 15 of the school's 140 students showed up. Doug Erickson, "Pledge, Anthem Under Way in the Madison Schools," *Wisconsin State Journal* (Madison), October 2, 2001, D1.

30. Erickson, "Pledge, Anthem Under Way in the Madison Schools."

31. Ibid. Singer, "I Pledge Allegiance," 56. One of the dissenters, a law professor at the University of Madison, explained her opposition: "I voted against the motion on the playing of the national anthem because I believed that the mere playing of the anthem in every classroom would not give either viewpoint its due respect. . . . It would not create a respectful atmosphere in which students could sing the national anthem and it would not allow students who object not to participate" (Kathyrn Kingsbury, "Board Restores Pledge," *Capital Times* [Madison, Wis.], October 16, 2001, A1). She favored instead having a separate location, like a cafeteria or auditorium, where those who wished to recite the Pledge or sing the anthem could do so, while those who did not wish to could remain in another place such as the classroom. The proposal

was defeated because it was "too time-consuming and cumbersome" (Singer, "I Pledge Allegiance," 57).

32. Doug Erickson, "Pledge Policy Angers Residents," *Wisconsin State Journal* (Madison), October 10, 2001, A1. Dennis Chaptman, "Madison Schools' Pledge Ban Sparks Fury," *Milwaukee Journal Sentinel*, October 9, 2001, A1. Singer, "I Pledge Allegiance," 57. "Tourism Officials Fear Pledge Fallout," *Capital Times* (Madison, Wis.), October 12, 2001, D1. The precise wording of the board resolution was the following: "Instruct the superintendent to instruct the principals to play the national anthem without words (an instrumental version) over the public address system, or any other mechanical reproduction using whatever technology is available, at a point in time the administrative team deems appropriate during the school day" (Kingsbury, "Board Restores Pledge").

33. Singer, "I Pledge Allegiance," 57–58. See also the accounts in Kingsbury, "Board Restores Pledge"; Doug Erickson, "Voluntary Participation Emphasized," *Wisconsin State Journal* (Madison), October 17, 2001 A1; and Annie Laura Gaylor, "Pledge Furor Provokes Pledge Patriotism," available online at http://www.ffrf.org/fttoday/nov01/pledge.html.

34. Mike Leon, "Right-Wing Assault on Madison Progressives Misfires," April 4, 2002, available at http://www.counterpunch.org/leonmadison.html. Singer, "I Pledge Allegiance," 58. Matt Pommer, "Whose Fortunes Will Rise on Pledge Issue?" *Capital Times* (Madison, Wis.), October 22, 2001, A2.

35. Leon, "Right-Wing Assault." See also Dennis Chaptman, "Recall over Pledge of Allegiance Fails," *Milwaukee Journal Sentinel*, December 13, 2001, B2; John Nichols, "Recall Leaders Misunderstand Madison," *Capital Times* (Madison, Wis.), December 18, 2001, A6; Doug Erickson, "Pledge Issue Not Dominating School Board Races," *Wisconsin State Journal* (Madison), February 3, 2002, A1; Doug Erickson, "Keys Elected President of School Board," *Wisconsin State Journal* (Madison), April 23, 2002, B1; and Editorial, "For Bill Keys and Freedom," *Capital Times* (Madison, Wis.), April 1, 2003, A8.

36. Anthony Lonetree, "Governor Indicates He'll Veto Pledge Bill," *Star Tribune* (Minneapolis), May 21, 2002, A8. "Text of Ventura Veto Message of Pledge of Allegiance Bill," Associated Press State and Local Wire, May 22, 2002.

37. The poll results are reported in James Walsh, "Plenty of Allegiance to the Pledge," *Star Tribune* (Minneapolis), May 5, 2003, B1. Examples of praise for Ventura's veto are George Hesselberg, "Ventura Hits Right Note on Pledge," *Wisconsin State Journal* (Madison), June 4, 2002, D1; and an editorial, "Pledge of Allegiance: Ventura Veto Defensible on Principle," *Star Tribune* (Minneapolis), May 25, 2002, A22.

38. *Session Weekly* (Minnesota House of Representatives, Public Information Office), April 20, 2001, 7, available at http://www.house.leg.state.mn.us/hinfo/swkly/2001-02/sw1601.pdf.

39. Tom Scheck, "Pledge Requirement Passes Senate," Minnesota Public Radio, News, April 25, 2002, available at http://news.mpr.org/features/200204/25_scheckt_pledge/. "Senator Fischbach Announces Flag Appreciation Act," Press Release, Sep-

tember 18, 2001, available at http://www.michellefischbach.org/press_releases /2001/flagact091801.htm.

40. State of Minnesota, Journal of the Senate, Eighty-Second Legislature, March 12, 2002, 5292–94, available at http://www.senate.leg.state.mn.us/journals/2001-2002 /31202082.pdf. John Welsh, "Sponsor Delays Vote on Requiring Pledge," *Pioneer Press*, March 13, 2002, newspaper cutting provided to the author by the office of state senator Mady Reiter, February 10, 2004. Reiter refers to the provision as a "disclaimer," in Anthony Lonetree, "Senate Panel Revives Pledge Bill," *Star Tribune* (Minneapolis), February 20, 2003, B5.

41. State of Minnesota, Journal of the Senate, Eighty-Second Legislature, April 25, 2002, 6312, available at http://www.senate.leg.state.mn.us/journals/2001-2002 /42502102.pdf.

42. As of 2002, Paul Marquart had earned a 50 percent lifetime score from the Taxpayers League of Minnesota. Only one house or senate Democrat had a higher lifetime score—Representative Mark Thompson at 56 percent—and he was defeated in November 2002 by his Republican opponent.

43. Minnesota, Journal of the Senate, Eighty-Second Legislature, May 17, 2002, 6862–63, at http://www.senate.leg.state.mn.us/journals/2001-2002/51702114.pdf. The Taxpayers League scorecard is available at http://www.taxpayersleague.org /2002_scorecard/list.php?typ=senate. The roll call on the vote is available at http://www.senate.leg.state.mn.us/journals/2001-2002/51702114.pdf. In 2003 Reiter scored a perfect 100 percent, earning her the moniker of "Taxpayers Best Friend" and lifting her lifetime score to 92 percent.

44. Anthony Lonetree, "Legislators Revive Debate over Pledge," *Star Tribune* (Minneapolis), February 14, 2003, B1; emphasis added. Anthony Lonetree, "Senate Panel Revives Pledge Bill," *Star Tribune* (Minneapolis), February 20, 2003, B5. Anthony Lonetree and Mark Brunswick, "Pledge Bill Sails through the Senate without a Flap," *Star Tribune* (Minneapolis), March 14, 2003, B2. Anthony Lonetree, "House Approves Pledge Bill—with Anti-Profile Kicker," *Star Tribune* (Minneapolis), March 25, 2003, B5. Anthony Lonetree, "Pledge Is In, Profile Is Out," *Star Tribune* (Minneapolis), May 18, 2003, B1.

45. Brian Bakst, "Last Mile Proves Long for Legislators," Associated Press State and Local Wire, May 28, 2003.

46. James Walsh, "Plenty of Allegiance to the Pledge," *Star Tribune* (Minneapolis), May 5, 2003, B1. Anthony Lonetree, "Legislators Revive Debate over Pledge," *Star Tribune* (Minneapolis), February 14, 2003, B1.

47. Virginia state law, prior to Barry's bill, recommended but did not require schools to recite the Pledge. The progress of his bill (SB 1331) through the legislative process is documented in the Legislative Information System of the Virginia General Assembly at http://leg1.state.va.us/cgi-bin/legp504.exe?ses=011 &typ=bil&val=sb1331.

48. Christina A. Samuels, "School Day to Begin with Pledge—or Not," *Washington Post*, August 23, 2001, T3. Lisa Rein, "A Call for Mandatory Pledge in Schools," *Washington Post*, January 25, 2001, A1.

49. Emily Wax and Lisa Rein, "Va. Senate Panel Passes Pledge Bill," *Washington Post,* January 26, 2001, B1. Stephen Dinan, "Committee OKs 'Pledge' Exemption," *Washington Times,* January 26, 2001, C4. Marc Fisher, "Lawmakers Can't Mandate Patriotism," *Washington Post,* January 30, 2001, B1. Stephen Dinan, "Senate Oks Pledge for Public Schools," *Washington Times,* January 31, 2001, C1. Samuels, "School Day to Begin With Pledge—or Not."

50. Stephen Dinan, "Riled Barry Wants Pledge Bill Killed," *Washington Times,* February 15, 2001, C1. Lisa Rein, "Va. Senator Drops Bill to Require Pledge," *Washington Post,* February 15, 2001, B1. Barry's "spineless pinko" jab was at least less offensive than his 1993 reference to gay people in the military as "fags in the foxhole" (Lisa Rein, "Maverick Va. Senator Pledged to Impolicy," *Washington Post,* February 22, 2001, B1).

51. Rein, "Maverick Va. Senator Pledged to Impolicy." Stephen Dinan, "'Emasculated' Pledge Bill Gains Passage in House," *Washington Times,* February 22, 2001, C1. Bizarrely, Barry suggested that in removing "all language relative to religious and philosophical objection," the house committee had made the bill "unconstitutional."

52. Ryan Robinson, "Mandating the Pledge," *Lancaster New Era* (Lancaster, Pa.), November 14, 2002, A1. Jim Brown, "PA Legislation Requires Schools Allow Pledge, Nat'l Anthem," November 21, 2002, available at http://headlines.agapepress.org/archive/11/212002e.asp. Dan Hardy, "Indivisible in Pa.? Not exactly," *Philadelphia Inquirer,* February 7, 2003, available at http://www.philly.com/mld/philly/news/5124933.htm.

53. The bill was originally introduced on June 15, 1999, as House Bill 1673 but never made it out of the Education Committee. During the following session, on February 8, 2001, Egolf reintroduced the bill as House Bill 592, and this time it was referred to the Veterans Affairs and Emergency Preparedness Committee, where it fared better. During the summer the bill was then put into the Rules Committee, which reported it out two weeks after September 11, 2001. E-mail communication with Teri Root, Secretary to Rep. Egolf, January 29, 2004.

54. Hardy, "Indivisible in Pa.? Not exactly."

55. *Circle School v. Phillips* (2003) 270 F. Supp. 2d 616, quotations at 624, 626.

56. Ibid., esp. 626–29, quotation at 627.

57. "Englewood Representative Introduces Flag Bill," Associated Press State and Local Wire, January 25, 2002. Steven K. Paulson, "Democrats Kill Requirement for Pledge of Allegiance," Associated Press State and Local Wire, February 5, 2002. John Sanko, "Patriotism Bill Up in Air," *Rocky Mountain News* (Denver), February 8, 2002, A20. The texts of SB136 and SB149 can be found in the "Prior Session Information" section of the Colorado state legislative website at http://www.leg.state.co.us/. Andrews, who was a speechwriter for Nixon and a Reagan appointee, is profiled in John J. Sanko, "Andrews Rises from Political Dead," *Rocky Mountain News* (Denver), November 8, 2002, A24.

58. Arthur Kane, "GOP Tries End Run on Bills," *Denver Post,* February 13, 2002, A18.

59. John Sanko, "Pledge Mandate Fails to Fly," *Rocky Mountain News* (Denver), February 6, 2002, A14. Arthur Kane, "Patriotism Bill Stirs Ire in Senate," *Denver Post,* February 27, 2002, A17.

60. Stan Matsunaka, "Do We Need Bills on Patriotism? NO: Love of Country Comes from Within," *Denver Post,* March 8, 2002, B7. John Andrews, "Do We Need Bills on Patriotism? YES: It Goes Far beyond Political Flag-Waving," *Denver Post,* March 8, 2002, B7.

61. Voter Guide, *Rocky Mountain News* (Denver), October 12, 2002, special pull-out section. On Musgrave, see Coleman Cornelius, "The Fight in the 4th District: State Senators Face Off for Chance to Represent Far-Flung Area," *Denver Post,* October 7, 2002, A10.

62. John J. Sanko, "Senate Supports Daily Pledge," *Rocky Mountain News* (Denver), May 7, 2003, A17. "House Approves Bill Requiring Pledge of Allegiance," Associated Press State and Local Wire, May 1, 2003. The vote on the house floor is recorded in the House Journal, May 1, 2003, p. 2197, and the vote on the senate floor is recorded in the Senate Journal, May 7, 2003, p. 1545. These votes, as well as the progress of HB 1368 through the relevant committees, can be accessed via the "Prior Session Information" section of the Colorado state legislative website at http://www.leg.state.co.us/. A Utah law signed into law in March 2003 also required a note from a parent or guardian for a student to be excused from saying the Pledge of Allegiance.

63. Karen Abbott, "Pledge Law Hits Barrier," *Rocky Mountain News* (Denver), August 16, 2003, A4. Julie Martinez, "Accord on Pledge Nears Approval," *Denver Post,* February 24, 2004, A1. See also Karen Abbott, "Backing Off on Pledge," *Rocky Mountain News* (Denver), August 23, 2003, A4. Some Colorado high school students reacted by protesting the new law. In Grand Junction, Colorado, for instance, three students gave the raised arm "Nazi salute" during the Pledge of Allegiance to protest what they regarded as an "unjust" and "fascist" law. The community was thrown into a tizzy, some fretting about the students' lack of patriotism, others complaining about the students' anti-Semitism, or at least lack of sensitivity. The school superintendent responded with a directive instructing schools to expel any student who made "offensive ges tures," including the "Nazi salute," during the Pledge. See Jim Spencer, "Pledge Protest a Harsh Lesson in Civil Liberties," *Denver Post,* October 26, 2003, A29.

64. This trend, of course, predated September 11, 2001. Between June 1999 and September 11, 2001, five states (Alaska, Florida, Nevada, Utah, and Virginia) established a mandatory Pledge requirement. Moreover, a number of states that secured a Pledge requirement after September 11, 2001, could point to legislative efforts in preceding sessions to enact a daily or weekly Pledge of Allegiance in schools. The data in this paragraph are derived largely from studies conducted by Jennifer Piscatelli of the Education Commission of the States. The data are available on the ECS website at http://www.ecs.org/.

65. Andrea Jones, "Young See Strange, New World," *Atlanta Journal-Constitution,* September 16, 2001, F5. Robert O'Neill, "Religious Leaders Unite to Lead Multi-

faith Prayer Service," Associated Press State and Local Wire, September 13, 2001. "America Attacked," *Patriot Ledger* (Quincy, Mass.), September 15, 2001, p. 3. Paul Riede, "Hundreds Buy Flags to Display Solidarity," *Post-Standard* (Syracuse, N.Y.), September 14, 2001, A1. Jim Auchmutey, "Turning to God," *Atlanta Journal-Constitution*, September 17, 2001, C1. John Curran, "Miss Oregon Katie Harman Wins Miss America Crown," Associated Press State and Local Wire, September 22, 2001.

66. Although the Pledge of Allegiance has almost exclusively been used by conservative Republicans to discomfort liberal Democrats, there has been at least one case of the Pledge of Allegiance being put to political use by the left. In 1998, Ralph Nader wrote to the CEOs of the nation's one hundred largest corporations, requesting that they begin their annual shareholders' meetings by leading the company in reciting the Pledge of Allegiance. About half of the companies to which he wrote did not reply; of the half that did reply, only one—Federated Department Stores—welcomed the suggestion. The rest of the responses were unenthusiastic. Some wrote only that it would not be a productive use of company time, but others took the bait, explaining that it was inappropriate for a global company with many international employees and shareholders to ask for a pledge of allegiance to the United States flag. Kodak explained that it needed to "maintain a global perspective to compete effectively in a global economy," and Motorola derided the "political and nationalistic overtones" of the Pledge. Nader then mailed off copies of the corporate responses to several well-placed columnists, at least two of whom wrote scathing indictments of the corporations' refusal to say the Pledge. See Patrick Buchanan, "Patriotism in the Boardroom," *New York Post*, July 1, 1998, 25; and Jeff Jacoby, "Fortune 100 Patriotism," *Austin American-Statesman* (Texas), August 1, 1998, A13.

67. The advertisement was entitled "Tested," and can be viewed online at http://www.georgewbush.com/tvads/.

Conclusion: Pledging Allegiance in a Liberal Society

1. Cynthia Annett, "Forced Loyalty," *Lawrence Journal-World* (Kansas), March 31, 2004. My thanks to Fred Woodward for bringing this letter to my attention.

2. Francis Bellamy, "Affidavit Concerning the True Origin [of the] Pledge of Allegiance to the Flag," August 13, 1923, 4–5, in Francis Bellamy Papers, Rare Books and Special Collections, Rush Rhees Library, University of Rochester, Rochester, N.Y. (hereafter cited as Bellamy Papers). Francis Bellamy, "The Story of the Pledge of Allegiance to the Flag," 14, Bellamy Papers.

3. Ward Hill Lamon to C. J. Faulkner, October 24, 1861, as quoted in Harold M. Hyman, *To Try Men's Souls: Loyalty Tests in American History* (Berkeley: University of California Press, 1960), 144.

4. Hyman, *To Try Men's Souls*, 201, 206. Lincoln, "Proclamation of Amnesty and Reconstruction," December 8, 1863, in Roy P. Basler, ed., *The Collected Works of Abraham Lincoln* (New Brunswick, N.J.: Rutgers University Press, 1953), 7:54.

5. Hyman, *To Try Men's Souls*, 188.

6. Ibid., 201–2.

7. Ibid., 188. The language of the original 1862 ironclad oath can be found in *Ex Parte Garland* (1867) 71 U.S. 333.

8. John W. Baer, *The Pledge of Allegiance: A Centennial History, 1892–1992* (Annapolis, Md.: J. W. Baer, 1992), 48. Margarette S. Miller, *Twenty-Three Words* (Portsmouth, Va.: Printcraft Press, 1976), 121.

9. Hyman, *To Try Men's Souls*, 5–7, 11, 15. The Puritan oath included a declaration that one would not "plot or practice any evil against [the government], or consent to any that shall do so; but will timely discover and reveal the same to lawfull authority now here established" (15).

10. For an early instance of landholding rights being made contingent on taking a loyalty oath, see Hyman, *To Try Men's Souls*, 26.

11. *West Virginia State Board of Education v. Barnette* (1943) 319 U.S. 624, quotation at 644.

12. John Moisan, Letter to the Editor, *Daily News of Los Angeles*, October 18, 2001, N16.

13. Samuel P. Huntington, *American Politics: The Promise of Disharmony* (Cambridge, Mass.: Harvard University Press, 1981), 23. For Huntington's own anxieties about American national identity, see his recent book *Who Are We? The Challenges to America's National Identity* (New York: Simon and Schuster, 2004). According to Huntington, immigration, multiculturalism, globalization, and cosmopolitanism so "battered" American national identity, that "by 2000, America was, in many respects, less a nation than it had been for a century" (4–5). Huntington frets that "ideology is a weak glue to hold together people otherwise lacking racial, ethnic, and cultural sources of community" (12). To survive as a nation, Huntington argues, Americans must try to "reinvigorate" their core "Anglo-Protestant culture." This, he explains, "would mean a recommitment to America as a deeply religious and primarily Christian country, encompassing several religious minorities, adhering to Anglo-Protestant values, speaking English, [and] maintaining its European cultural heritage" (20, 59).

14. Francis Bellamy, "A New Plan for Counter-Attack on the Nation's Internal Foes: How to Mobilize the Masses to Support Primary American Doctrines," May 1, 1923, 6, Bellamy Papers.

15. Scott R. Jensen, "Patriotism Begins at a Young Age," *Wisconsin State Journal* (Madison), September 17, 2001, A10.

16. Huntington emphasizes this paradox of American national identity in *American Politics*.

17. Michael Ignatieff, *Blood and Belonging: Journeys into the New Nationalism* (New York: Noonday Press, 1993), 6–7. Ignatieff acknowledges that Germany is a "prominent exception" (7). Gabriel A. Almond and Sidney Verba, *The Civic Culture: Political Attitudes and Democracy in Five Nations* (Boston: Little, Brown, 1965), 64. On Great Britain as the first civic nation, see Liah Greenfeld, *Nationalism: Five Roads to Modernity* (Cambridge, Mass.: Harvard University Press, 1992), chapter one. On Canada and France as "civic nations," see Bernard Yack, "The Myth of the Civic Nation," *Critical Review* 10 (spring 1996): 193–211.

18. Yack, "The Myth of the Civic Nation." See also Anthony W. Marx, *Faith in Nation: Exclusionary Origins of Nationalism* (New York: Oxford University Press, 2003), who argues that we "have to finally abandon the image of a Western 'civic' founding distinct from illiberal nationalism elsewhere" (ix).

19. J. R. Preston, State Superintendent of Public Instruction, Jackson, Mississippi, "Teaching Patriotism," in National Education Association, *Journal of Proceedings and Addresses* (New York, 1891), 103, 110. Preston's speech to the NEA is also quoted in Cecilia Elizabeth O'Leary, *To Die For: The Paradox of American Patriotism* (Princeton, N.J.: Princeton University Press, 1999), 175, 179, though in the text she attributes the "fusing furnace" quotation simply to a "teacher."

20. Preston, "Teaching Patriotism," 102–3.

21. "Remarks by the President on Teaching American History and Civic Education," East Literature Magnet School, Nashville, Tennessee, September 17, 2002; emphasis added. The president's remarks are available at http://www.whitehouse.gov /news/releases/2002/09/20020917-7.html.

22. George W. Bush to Mitsuo Murashige and Associates, November 13, 2002, printed as an appendix in the friend of the court brief submitted in *Elk Grove Unified v. Newdow* by the Americans United for Separation of Church and State, American Civil Liberties Union, and Americans for Religious Liberty. The brief can be accessed at http://pewforum.org/religion-schools/pledge/docs/AmericansUnited.pdf. The letter to Murashige, a Hawaiian Buddhist leader, was in response to a September letter conveying Buddhist support for the Ninth Circuit Court ruling.

23. George Bush, "President Honors Veterans at West Virginia Fourth of July Celebration," Ripley, West Virginia, July 4, 2000. The speech is available at http://www .whitehouse.gov/news/releases/2002/07/20020704-3.html. The account of the reciting of the Pledge of Allegiance is from Dana Milbank, "Believe It or Not, Bush Celebrates 4th in Ripley," originally published in the *Washington Post* and available at http://www.post-gazette.com/nation/20020705bushfourth0705p4.asp. Bush's comments in the Ripley speech were reproduced in a weekly radio address to a national audience two days later.

24. Walter A. McDougall, *Promised Land, Crusader State: The American Encounter with the World since 1776* (Boston: Houghton Mifflin, 1997), 136. Hugh Heclo, "Reagan and the American Public Philosophy," in W. Elliot Brownlee and Hugh Davis Graham, eds., *The Reagan Presidency: Pragmatic Conservatism and Its Legacies* (Lawrence: University Press of Kansas, 2003), 3. Ronald Reagan, "Remarks at the Swearing-In Ceremony for New United States Citizens in White House Station, New Jersey," September 17, 1982, in *Public Papers of the Presidents of the United States, Ronald Reagan*, 1178. The speech is also available at http://www.reagan.utexas.edu /resource/speeches/1982/91782d.htm.

25. Robert N. Bellah, "Civil Religion in America," *Daedalus* (winter 1967): 1–21. Robert N. Bellah, *The Broken Covenant: American Civil Religion in Time of Trial* (New York: Seabury Press, 1975).

26. "Can George Bush, with Impunity, State That Atheists Should Not Be Considered Either Citizens or Patriots?" at http://www.positiveatheism.org/writ/ghwbush

.htm. Bush's statement probably would not have drawn objections from the 68 percent of Americans polled in 1992 who said that a belief in God was "very important" or "extremely important" for "a true American" (Huntington, *Who Are We?* 87).

27. Anthony D. Smith, *Chosen Peoples: Sacred Sources of National Identity* (New York: Oxford University Press, 2003).

28. For instance, Hamas leader Abd al-Aziz Rantissi, responding to news that the United States had vetoed a United Nations Security Council resolution condemning the Israeli assassination of his predecessor, insisted that America had "declared war against God. Sharon declared war against God and God declared war against America, Bush and Sharon. . . . The war of God continues against them, and I can see the victory coming up from the land of Palestine by the hand of Hamas" ("Hamas Leader: Bush Is Enemy of God, Islam," MSNBC News Service, March 28, 2004, at http://www.msnbc.msn.com/id/4575552/). Less than a month later the Israeli government assassinated Rantissi as well.

29. John Sanko, "Senate Supports Daily Pledge," *Rocky Mountain News* (Denver), May 7, 2003, A17.

30. On "the easy step from preference to pride," see John H. Schaar, "The Case for Covenanted Patriotism," in *Patriotism,* ed. Igor Primoratz (New York: Humanity Books, 2002), 244.

31. Dinesh D'Souza, *What's So Great about America* (2002), as quoted in Rogers M. Smith, *Stories of Peoplehood: The Politics and Morals of Political Membership* (New York: Cambridge University Press, 2003), 192. The point about the "shining city" is made in Heclo, "Reagan and the American Public Philosophy," 24. The phrase "city on the hill" is, of course, from John Winthrop. The word "shining" was not a part of Winthrop's original, although Reagan (and others) frequently attributed the entire phrase to Winthrop. See, for instance, Reagan's "farewell address," available at http://www.reaganfoundation.org/reagan/speeches/farewell.asp. The "shining" part reflects the Sermon on the Mount, where Jesus said, "You are the light of the world. A city set on a hill cannot be hid. Nor do men light a lamp and put it under a bushel, but on a stand, and it gives light to all in the house. Let your light so shine before men, that they may see your good works and give glory to your Father who is in heaven" (Matthew 5:14–16).

32. Yack, "Myth of the Civic Nation," 196. Herman Melville, *White-Jacket* (1850), as quoted in Ernest Lee Tuveson, *Redeemer Nation: The Idea of America's Millennial Role* (Chicago: University of Chicago Press, 1968), 157. See also the relevant and perceptive comments by Peter Beinart in "All Too Human," *New Republic,* May 24, 2004, 8.

33. Heclo, "Reagan and the American Public Philosophy," 24.

34. Bellamy, "A New Plan," 16.

Index

ACLU. *See* American Civil Liberties Union

Adams, Gridley
   Dewey's flag salute veto criticized, 266n36
   and the flag conferences, 65–67, 241nn30,35, 242n37
   and flag etiquette, 66–67, 117–18
   hand-over-the heart salute backed by, 119–20, 251n76, 252n78
   opinionated nature of, 66–67, 242n38
   on the power of repetition, 80
   role of, in amending Pledge, 65–66, 241n35
   "under God" clause opposed, 138, 259n54
   on the United Nations, 66
   Upham backed in authorship dispute, 242n42

Adams, John, 174, 253n10

AFT. *See* American Federation of Teachers

Alaska, 186–87, 275n64

Aliens and the flag salute, 82–84, 191. *See also* Immigrants, anxiety about; Immigrants and immigration

Almond, Gabriel, 215

"America" ("My Country, 'tis of Thee"), 20, 122, 140

American Civil Liberties Union (ACLU)
   American Legion contacted by, to discuss anti-Witness violence, 107
   American Legion's warning against, 77
   Colorado Pledge law challenged, 206
   and the *Newdow* case, 143
   Pennsylvania Pledge law challenged, 202
   Pledge refusals defended by, 86–88, 92–93, 98, 100, 102, 161–62, 246n14,
      264n10 (see also *Gobitis* case; Jehovah's Witnesses)
   "under God" clause challenged, 141
   Virginia Pledge bill challenged, 199

American Federation of Teachers (AFT), 164, 176

American Flag Manufacturing Company, 55

American Jewish Congress (AJC), 143

American Legion
   Americanization program supported by, 77–78
   "Back to God" program, 125–26
   and the flag code, 58, 63, 116, 118, 251n74 (*see also* National Flag Conferences)
   and immigration, 241n29
   loyalty oath backed by, 247n23
   Pledge legislation supported by, xiii, 129, 195
   and Pledge refusal by Meinhold, 164
   radicalism combated by, 77
   suspension of welfare payments to protesters urged by, 263n5
   "under God" clause supported by, 132, 136, 137, 256n30
   violence against Jehovah's Witnesses perpetrated by, 106–7

American national identity, 213–16, 277n13
   dangers of nationalism, 220–21
   exceptionalism of, 216–21, 279n31
   faith and, 127–29, 131, 216–21, 278nn23,24,26

American Protection Association, 34

Americans United for Separation of Church and State (AU), 143

American Youth's Association, 14

Andrews, John, 203–4, 206

Anglo-Saxon race, 22, 35–37, 124. *See also*
   American national identity; Immigrants, anxiety about

Annett, Cynthia, 209

Anxieties, underlying the Pledge, xi–xiv, 213,
   221–22. *See also* Communism, anxiety
   about; Immigrants, anxiety about; Materialism, anxiety about; Radicals, anxiety about; Socialism, anxiety about

Argentina, 37

Arizona
   flag salute statutes, 54, 78, 239n10,
      244n74
   legislature, Pledge recitation by, 186
   military instruction in schools, 237n47
   school flag display laws, 238n4

Arkansas, 206

Ashcroft, John, xi

Atheists
   addition of "under God" clause opposed,
      131
   citizenship and patriotism questioned,
      218–19, 278n26
   Docherty's contempt for, 132
   Madalyn Murray O'Hair, 141, 260n62
   "under God" clause challenged, 141–42,
      147, 158 (*see also* Newdow, Michael)

Baer, John, xix, 211

Balch, George
   Civil War nostalgia, 4
   compulsory patriotism, opposed by, 53
   death of, 56
   immigrants, anxiety about, 4, 38–43, 49
   materialism, anxiety about, 43–44, 49
   on New York City flag displays, 3–4
   and the schoolhouse flag movement, 6,
      38–43, 44–45
   on teaching patriotism, 40–41, 53,
      235nn37,38, 236n40

Balch salute
   physical, 41, 42(illus.), 44
   verbal, 18, 54–56, 123, 214, 240n18

Ball, Isabel, 65

Banks, Andrew, 162

Banning, Sandra, 150–51. *See also* Newdow,
   Michael

Barnes, Wilson K., 169–70

Barnette case (*West Virginia v. Barnette*),
   110–15, 155, 212
   interpretation and application, 156, 158,
      167, 169–71
   legal limits tested, 198–206

Barry, Warren, xii, 198–200

Bartlett, Julian, 139

Bates, Leroy, 167–68

Bellah, Robert, 218

Bellamy, David and Lucy Ann, 10–11

Bellamy, Edward
   "An Echo of Antietam," 45–46
   Looking Backward, 26–28, 231n6,
      236n46
   Walker's criticism of, 234n22

Bellamy, Francis, 2(illus.)
   on American versus European
      patriotism, 214
   on Anglo-Saxons, virtues of, 22
   on Balch's salute, 18, 123, 214
   changes to Pledge opposed by, 68, 121
   Christian socialism of, 9, 11, 27–29,
      231n6, 232n13
   Columbian celebration planning/public-
      ity, 10, 14–17, 45, 227n33,
      228nn36–40
   Columbian celebration program
      design/execution, 17–23, 29, 46,
      50–51, 122–23, 229nn43–45, 230n54
   death of, 79
   egalitarian commitments of, 9, 25–31,
      232n10
   Ford's relationship with, 9–10, 226n22,
      227n33
   genealogy, interest in family, 12–13,
      227n29
   goals in writing Pledge, 25, 28–29, 50,
      210–12, 221, 231n2
   hired by *Youth's Companion,* 9–10, 47
   historical obscurity of, 1

immigrants, anxiety about, 13, 30–33, 49, 68, 216, 233n19
as Mason, 237n51
materialism, anxiety about, 13, 31, 49
as minister at Boston's Bethany Baptist Church, 9
Pledge authored by, 1–2, 3(illus.), 18–19, 25, 210, 229n48
Pledge history written by, 57
radicals/subversives, anxiety about, 68–71, 232n13
on religion and government, 121–23, 253n7
religious upbringing of, 9–11
"under God" clause opposed by son of, 135
Upham's relationship with, 10, 18–19, 50, 227n33
on Upham, 237n49
See also Pledge of Allegiance; Youth's Companion
Bellamy, Joseph, 13
Bemis, Edward, 34
Benen, Steve, 143
Benson, Ezra Taft, 126, 255n16
Berkeley, California, 180
Bible
city on a hill image in, 279n31
Pledge refusals based on reading of, 89, 96–98, 248n37
public school use of, banned, 124, 140
"under God" in the King James Bible preface, 124
used to uphold Pledge, 248n38, 250n59
Biddle, Francis, 108
Bielenberg, In re, 159, 264n13
Bielenberg, Kristina, 159
Black, Hugo, 109, 141, 155, 212
Bleich v. Board of Public Instruction, 96–97, 248n37
Bliss, W. D. P., 27, 28, 231n6, 232n13
Bolton, Oliver, 134, 137, 257n38
Bond, Kit, xi
Bonney, Charles, 13–14
Bookstein, Isadore, 140

Boston, 57, 237n47
Boy Scouts, 63, 69, 115, 202
Brachna, Stanley, 93–94
Braucher, Robert, 171–72, 266n39
Breckenridge, William Campbell Preston, 18
Brennan, William, 141–42, 148
Briggs, Clare, 66
Brown, Theron, 18
Brown, W. P., 87–88
Bryan, William Jennings, 232n13
Buddhists, 147, 149, 278n22
Bush, George H. W.
atheists' citizenship questioned by, 218, 278n26
1988 presidential campaign of, 26, 153–54, 172–73, 174, 177–78, 181–82, 269n9
and September 11 memorial service, 187, 188(illus.)
Bush, George W., x–xi, 187, 188(illus.), 189(illus.), 208, 217–18
Byrd, Robert, x

California
conflict over Pledge in Berkeley, 180
flag salute (1942), 59(illus.), 62(illus.)
flag salute laws, 242n52
Pledge cases in, 89, 97, 246n17
school flag display laws, 238n5
state assembly, Pledge recitation by, 186
"under God" clause challenged in, 141–43 (see also Newdow, Michael)
Carter, Jimmy, 187
Catholics
and anti-Catholicism, xiii, 35, 123
Communism opposed by, xiii, 130
and the national Columbus Day celebration, 21–22, 230nn54,55
parochial schools of, 22, 35, 123, 234n27
"under God" clause supported by, 130–34, 136, 257n36
See also Knights of Columbus
Ceremonial deism, 140–42, 148–49, 217–18, 260n65. See also Religion and government

Chambers, Whitaker, 129
Chambers Elementary School (Cleveland), 176
Chicago, 85, 90
Children's Aid Society, 40
Christianity. *See* Christian socialism; Religion and government; Religious belief(s); "Under God" clause; *and specific denominations*
Christian socialism, 27–29, 226n22, 231n8, 232n13
Church and state, separation of. *See* Religion and government; "Under God" clause
Churches, 70–71, 123, 128. *See also* Religion and government; Religious belief(s); *and specific religious groups*
Citizenship
    atheists' citizenship questioned, 218, 278n26
    Balch on behaviors of good citizenship, 41, 235n38
    naturalization ceremonies, 1, 176–77, 212
    schools required to teach, 77–79 (*see also* Public schools)
    See also Patriotism
Civic nation, myth of, 213–16
Civil religion, 218
Civil War
    Balch served in, 4
    flag display spurred by, 3
    loyalty oaths of, 210–12
    nostalgia for, xiii, 4, 23, 45–46, 49
    Upham's role in, 7, 225n16
    veterans' role in flag raising ceremonies, 4–5, 20
    See also Grand Army of the Republic
Cleveland, Grover, 15
Clinton, Bill, 187, 188(illus.)
Coercion test, 144, 145–46
Cold War. *See* Communism, anxiety about
Colorado
    flag salute and patriotism statutes, 203–6, 245n11, 275nn62,63
    Pledge refusals, 86, 245n11

"Columbia's Banner" (Proctor), 18, 20
Columbus, Christopher. *See* National Columbian Public School Celebration
Columbus Day, first celebration of. *See* National Columbian Public School Celebration
Communism, anxiety about, xiii–xiv
    Bellamy's, 68–71
    Catholics', 130
    Dumont's mandatory Pledge proposal and, 178
    state flag salute statutes and, 75–80
    "under God" phrase and, 125, 127–37, 259n43 (*see also* "Under God" clause)
    in Washington state, 71–75, 243nn53–56, 244nn64–66
    See also Radicals, anxiety about; Socialism, anxiety about
Communists, salute refusals by, 90
Compulsory Education Act (1874), 39, 235n35
Congress, U.S.
    chaplains, 260n65
    and the Columbian celebration, 16–17, 228n40
    immigration law, 34
    Pledge recitation by, 182–84
    reaction to Ninth Circuit *Newdow* ruling, ix–xi
    recognition of God, 126
    salute and flag etiquette codified, 113, 116–20, 251nn74–76, 252nn77–79
    "under God" clause added, 130–37, 255n26, 256nn27–30, 257nn35–40, 258nn41,42, 259nn43–46
Connecticut, 78, 166–67, 238nn3,4
Constitution, U.S.
    Bicentennial celebrations, 177
    First Amendment protections, 111–12, 140, 145–46, 148, 170, 206, 261n73
    Flanders's Christian amendment to, 126, 254n15, 259n54
    George H. W. Bush's ignorance about authors of, 174

oath of support required of state/federal
    officers, 212
schools required to teach, 78
See also Pledge of Allegiance, laws requir-
    ing; Religion and government; "Under
    God" clause; and specific cases
Coolidge, Calvin, 88
Curtis, Charles, 79

Danza, Tony, 207
Darte, George, 77
Daschle, Tom, ix
Daughters of the American Revolution
    (DAR), 54, 63, 116, 129, 241n34
Davies, Wallace, 54
Davis, Dwight, 63
Delaware, 78, 86, 238n4, 245n74
Denver, Colorado, 86
Denver Post, 86
Desegregation, flag salute refusal in protest
    of, 154
Des Moines Register, 105
Dewey, Thomas, 266n36
Di Berardino, Frank P., xviii–xix, 240n26
Docherty, George MacPherson, 132–34,
    254n14, 257n39
Dorgan, Byron, x
Douglas, William, 109, 155, 212
Dreier, Peter, 26
D'Souza, Dinesh, 220
Dukakis, Michael
    1988 presidential campaign, 26, 153–54,
        172–73, 177–78, 269n9
    Pledge bill vetoed by, 26, 153, 170–73, 179
Dumenil, Lynn, 48
Dumont, Wayne, 178, 269n8

Eaves, Hubert, 85
"Echo of Antietam, An" (E. Bellamy),
    45–46
Egolf, Allan, 201, 274n53
Eisenhower, Dwight
    and Docherty's sermon, 132, 133,
        254n14

inadvertent desecration of flag by, 67
    on religion as basis of American govern-
        ment, 125–28, 134, 255n16
    and the "under God" clause, 136–37, 139
Elijiah Voice Society, 86–88, 246n14
Elk Grove v. Newdow. See Newdow case
Endorsement test, 144, 147–49
English-only instruction, 78
Establishment clause. See Constitution,
    U.S.; Religion and government;
    "Under God" clause
European national identities, 214–15

Ferguson, Homer, 133–37, 257nn35,40
Fernandez, Ferdinand, 145
First Nationalist Club of Boston, 27–28
Fiske, John, 235n31
Flacks, Dick, 26
Flag, American
    desecration, 67, 82, 269n10
    history, 2–3
    in homes, 117–18
    National Flag Conferences, 58, 62–67,
        241nn29–34
    respect for, 26, 58, 62, 76, 79, 82 (see also
        Flag code; Flag etiquette)
    salute laws (see Flag salute laws; Manda-
        tory Pledge rules/laws)
    salutes (see Flag salutes, physical; Flag
        salutes, spoken; Pledge of Allegiance)
    school flags (see School flag display laws;
        Schoolhouse flag movement)
    Upham on symbolism of, 44, 236n44
Flag code
    Congress adopts, 116–17, 165, 251n74
    Congress amends, 117–20, 251nn75,76,
        252n78
    origins of, 63–65, 119–20, 165, 242n40,
        252n78, 265n25 (see also National
        Flag Conferences)
    See also Flag etiquette
Flag Day (June 14), 52, 111, 177
Flag display laws. See School flag display
    laws

Flag etiquette
  federally codified, 114, 116–20
  Gridley Adams and, 66–67, 117–18
  male versus female, 58, 64–65, 242n40
  military, 58, 64, 67, 241n30
  See also Flag code; Flag salutes, physical
Flag salute laws
  Balch's opposition, 53
  constitutionality, 90–91, 95–96, 103–5,
    111–12
  in the early twentieth century, 54, 58,
    239n10
  New York state (1898), 52–53, 54, 239n6
  penalties for noncompliance, 72, 242n52,
    243n53
  perceived need for, 51, 190
  Washington state (1919), 71–75,
    242n52, 243n53, 244nn64–66
  between World War I and World War II,
    78–79, 91–92, 245n11
  See also Pledge of Allegiance, laws re-
    quiring; *and specific states*
Flag salute refusals, 82–85. *See also* Pledge
  of Allegiance, refusals
Flag salutes, physical
  Balch salute, 18, 41, 42(illus.)
  early diversity of, 58, 59–62(illus.)
  hand-over-heart salute, 62(illus.),
    67, 119–20, 119(illus.), 251n76,
    252nn77,78
  hybrid salute, 19–20, 59(illus.)
  male versus female, 58, 64–65, 242n40
  military-style, 19, 41, 44, 61(illus.), 115,
    118(illus.), 236n43
  National Flag Conferences and, 58,
    64–65, 67
  Nazi salute used in protest, 275n63
  raised-arm salute, 19, 20, 44, 60(illus.),
    67, 91, 114(illus.), 116–20
  removal of hat during, 58, 64–65, 67,
    119(illus.), 242n40, 252n78
Flag salutes, spoken
  Balch salute, 18, 54, 55–56, 123, 214,
    240n18

Bellamy pledge (*see* Pledge of Allegiance)
  early diversity of, 54–56, 58, 239n13
Flanders, Jesse, 238nn3–5
Flanders amendment (Ralph Flanders),
    126, 254n15, 259n54
Florida
  mandatory Pledge law, 275n64
  Pledge refusals, 96–97,162, 167–68,
    248n37
  state senate, Pledge recitation by, 186
  "under God" clause challenged in, 142
Ford, Daniel Sharp
  Bellamy mentored/hired by, 9–10,
    226n22
  and the Columbian school celebration,
    14, 17–19, 227n33, 228n36,
    229nn43,48
  editorial work, 7, 225n13
  Pledge approved by, 19
  religious principles, 122, 226nn22,25
  and "Teaching Patriotism" editorial, 7
Ford, Gerald, 187, 188(illus.)
Frain v. Baron, 157–59, 167, 263nn9,10
Frankfurter, Felix, 103–5, 109–10, 112–13.
    See also *Gobitis* case
Freedom, anxiety of, xii
Freethinkers of America, 140–41
Frizzell, Mrs. J. W., 64

GAR. *See* Grand Army of the Republic
Genealogy, 12–13, 227n29
Genovese, Eugene, 269n8
George, Ruth, 94
Georgia, 79, 94, 96, 187
Gettysburg Address, 124, 126, 140, 142,
    253n9, 256n28
Gingrich, Newt, 153
Girl Scouts, 69, 115
Giuliani, Rudy, 187, 189(illus.)
Gobitas, Walter and Lilian (daughter), 99,
    106. See also *Gobitis* case
Gobitis case *(Minersville School District v.
  Gobitis),* 99–105, 109–13,
    249nn40,42,47

aftermath, 105–10
misspelling of family's name in court cases, 249n40
Goetz, Theodore, 160–61
Goldberg, Arthur, 141
Goldman, Emma, 84–85
Goldstein, Herbert, 77
Gompers, Samuel, 67
Gonzales, Henry, 183, 270n18
Goodwin, Alfred, ix–x, 144–46, 152. See also *Newdow* case
Gordon, Ken, 204
Grand Army of the Republic (GAR)
and the Columbian school celebration, 15, 17, 45
flag salute ceremonies recommended, 55–56, 129
immigrants, anxieties about, 33
and military instruction in schools, 236n47
and the schoolhouse flag movement, xiii, 4–5, 44–45
Grassley, Charles, x
Great Britain, civic nationalism in, 215
Guenter, Scot, xix, 225n12

Halleck, Charlie, 136
Hanover, Nancy, 166–67
Hansen, Ole, 73
Harding, Warren, 62, 69
Harper's Weekly, 82
Harris, Louise, xix, 225nn12,13,15
Harrison, Benjamin, 8, 15–16, 38, 228n38
Hart, Luke, 130–32, 139, 255n26
Hartz, Louis, xii
Hawaii, 187, 271n26
Hayes, Carlton, 77, 244n70
Heclo, Hugh, 221
Heiliger, Don, 184–86
Hendricks, Lillian, 57
Herberg, Will, 126, 129
Hering v. State Board of Education, 249n47
Hill, David, 17
Hitler, Adolf, 102. See also Nazi Germany

Hobbs, Sam, 119, 120, 251n74, 252n76
Holidays, national, 52, 54, 78–79. *See also specific holidays*
Holloway, Mrs. Reuben Ross, 63
Holtzman, Lester, 182
Homer, Charles F., 4, 224n6
Hoover, Herbert, 125, 127
House of Representatives. *See* Congress, U.S.
Hughes, Charles Evans, 104
Hughes, Richard, 178, 269n8
Huntington, Samuel, 213, 219–20, 277n13
Hyman, Harold, 212

Idaho, 238n4
Ignatieff, Michael, 215, 277n17
Illinois
school flag display laws, 238nn3,4
school flag salute and citizenship instruction statutes, 79, 172, 207, 267n40
violence against Jehovah's Witnesses, 106
Immigrants, anxiety about
and American exceptionalism, 215–16
Balch's, 4, 38–43, 49
Bellamy's, 13, 30–33, 49, 68, 216, 233n19
Pledge amended in 1923 because of, 65–66
Pledge tied to, xi–xii, 30–43, 49
in *Our Country* (Strong), 34–37, 38
schoolhouse flag movement and, 4, 30–31, 37–43, 49
Immigrants and immigration
Americanization, 30–31, 35, 38, 216
citizenship (naturalization) ceremonies, 1, 176–77, 212
restrictions on, 34, 37, 241n29
statistics, 33, 37–39
See also Aliens and the flag salute
Industrial schools, 40, 42(illus.)
Industrial Workers of the World (IWW), 73–75
"In God We Trust" motto, 126, 131, 138, 141

Iowa, 238nn3–5
I Pledge Allegiance (Martin and Sampson), 24
I Pledge Allegiance (Miller). *See* Miller,
    Margarette

Jackson, Robert, 111–12, 155, 169. See also
    Barnette case
Jacobs, Seymour, 164
James, Edward, 92
Jefferson, Thomas, 219
Jehovah's Witnesses
    in Nazi Germany, 91, 105–6, 108
    Pledge refusals, 91–110, 247nn24,25,
        248n37, 265n35
    violence against, 93–94, 105–9, 250n60
Jehovites, 86, 245n11
Jensen, Scott, 190, 214
Jews and Judaism, 32–33, 127, 131
Johnson, Lyndon, 137, 163–64
Johnson, Timothy, xi
Jones v. Opelika, 109
Judd, Orin, 157–60, 167
Judeo-Christian philosophy versus Com-
    munism, 127–29, 132. *See also* Com-
    munism, anxiety about

Kammen, Michael, 227n29
Kansas
    flag salute laws, 54, 78, 239n10, 245n74
    Pledge refusals, 109–10
    school flag display laws, 238n5
Keating, Kenneth, 135
Kelly, Robert, 202–3
Kennedy, Anthony, 145, 146, 262n82
Kentucky, 186–87
Keys, Bill, 193
Kierlin, Bob, 194–95, 198
Kiwanis Club, 154
Klug, Scott, 193
Knights of Columbus, 56, 129–32, 139,
    181, 255n26, 256nn27,28
Knights of Labor, 34
Knights Templar (Masonic order), 47–48,
    237n51

Kopp, Joy, 198
Kuhn, Jamie, 184–86

Labor strikes, 72–75, 243nn53–56
LaHood, Ray, x
Lamborn, Doug, 219
Langer, William, 257n40
Lawrence, David, 113
Lee v. Weisman, 144–47
Lehman, Irving, 98–99
Lemon test, 144
Leoles v. Landers, 249n47
Liberal Club, 77
Limbaugh, Rush, 192
Lincoln, Abraham
    Gettysburg Address, 124, 126, 140, 142,
        253n9, 256n28
    hand-over-heart salute associated with,
        119–20, 251n76, 252n78
    and loyalty oaths, 210–11
    on United States as "last, best hope on
        earth," 221
Lipp, Deborah, 161–62
Local government, Pledge recitation by,
    179–80, 184–88
Lodge, Henry Cabot, 15–16, 33–34,
    228n39
Looking Backward (E. Bellamy), 26–27, 28,
    231n6, 236n46
Loyalty oaths, 209–13, 247n23
Lundquist, August L., 168–70

Madison, Wisconsin, 184–85, 190–93,
    271n31, 272n32
Mahoney, H. Joseph, 131, 256n28
Maine, 78, 107–8, 186, 238n5
Malden, Massachusetts, Columbus Day
    celebration, 21–22, 46, 122–23
Manual of Patriotism (Skinner), 52–54
Manwaring, David, xix, 85, 239n16
Marine Corps, xii, 199
Maris, Albert, 100–102, 249n42
Maryland, 78, 141, 168–70, 245n74,
    271n26

Masons, 47–48, 237n51

Massachusetts
   Brookline Pledge controversy, 179–80
   flag salute laws, 78, 91–93, 153–54,
      170–73, 245n74, 247n23
   Malden Columbus Day celebration,
      21–22, 46, 122–23
   Pledge refusal cases, 91–93, 95,
      247nn24,25
   post–September 11 Pledge recitations, 207
   school flag display laws, 238n4

Materialism, anxiety about, xii, 7–8, 31, 34,
      43–45, 48–49, 127, 129, 131, 134,
      137, 259n43

Matsunaka, Stan, 204–5

McCallum, Scott, 192

McCarthy, Joseph, 127

McDonagh, Peter, 162

McLaughlin, Frank, 128

"Meaning of the Four Centuries, The" (F.
      Bellamy address), 18, 20, 50, 122–23

Meinhold, Al, 163–64

Melville, Herman, 220–21

Mennonites, 85–86

Methodist Council of Bishops, 126

Methods of Teaching Patriotism in the Public
      Schools (Balch), 40–41, 42

Meyer, Agnes, 138

Michigan, 238nn3,4

Military, the
   flag etiquette in, 58, 63–64, 241n30
   flag salute modeled on salute given in,
      19, 41, 41(illus.), 43–46, 61(illus.),
      115, 118(illus.), 236nn43,46
   and the history of the Pledge, xii–xiii
   instruction in schools/colleges, 88,
      236n47
   as model for industrial organization in
      Looking Backward, 27
   officers at 1923 Flag Conference, 63–64,
      242n37
   See also Civil War; Grand Army of the
      Republic; War

Miller, Arthur, 167

Miller, Margarette
   availability of papers of, xviii–xix
   on Bellamy, 12, 227n33
   plagiarism by, 225n13, 240n26
   on public school participation in
      Columbian celebration, 229n51
   on Upham, 18–19, 225n16
   on use of "pledge" over "oath," 211–12

Minersville School District v. Gobitis. See
      Gobitis case

Minnesota, 193–98, 206, 273nn42,43

Miss America Pageant, 207

Mississippi, 187

Missouri, 187, 206

Montana, 238nn3,4

Montgomery, Sonny, 183

Moran, Jerry, xi

Morgan, Gerald, 137

Moyle, Olin, 99, 100

Multer, Abraham J., 138, 259n54

Murphy, Frank, 104, 109

Murray O'Hair, Madalyn, 141, 260n62

Musgrave, Marilyn, 205

Muslims, 155, 219, 279n28

"My Country, 'tis of Thee" ("America"), 20,
      122, 140

Nader, Ralph, 276n66

Nation (magazine), 52–53, 82

National anthem, instrumental version,
      191–92. See also "Star-Spangled
      Banner, The"

National Columbian Public School
      Celebration
   Catholics involvement in, 21–22,
      230nn54,55
   designing the program, 17–19,
      229nn43,45,48
   flag salute created for, 18–19
   official program and celebration, 19–23,
      46, 50–51, 122–23, 229n51,
      230nn52,54–57
   planning and publicity, 13–17, 45,
      227n33, 228nn36–40

National Columbian Public School
    Celebration *(continued)*
    Youth's Companion schoolhouse flag effort
    and, 8–9
National Education Association, Bellamy's
    address to, 29–31
National Flag Association, 113–15
National Flag Conferences (1923, 1924),
    58, 62–67, 116, 119–20, 241nn29–35,
    242nn37,40
National Fraternal Conference, 130,
    256n27
National identity. *See* American national
    identity; European national identities
Nationalist movement, 27, 28, 232n10,
    234n22
Nativism. *See* Immigrants, anxiety about
Navesink Lighthouse flag-raising (Sandy
    Hook, N.J.), 57, 237n56
Nazis
    Jehovah's Witnesses persecuted by, 91,
        105
    Nazi-style salute used by U.S. protestors,
        275n63
    Pledge likened to loyalty oaths used by,
        102, 113, 179, 183, 270n18
    raised-arm salute likened to salute used
        by, 91, 114(illus.), 113–17, 120, 183,
        270n18
    violence against Jehovah's Witnesses in
        United States compared to methods
        of, 108
Nebraska, 78–79, 245n74, 271n26
Nevada, 163–64, 186, 238n5, 275n64
Newdow, Michael
    custody disputes, 150–51
    other establishment clause challenges,
        260n65
    "under God" clause challenged, x,
        142–52, 209, 261nn73,74
Newdow case, ix, 142–52, 209, 261nn73,74
    reactions to Ninth Circuit ruling, ix–xi,
        217
New Hampshire, 108, 186, 206, 238n4

New Jersey
    flag salute laws, 78, 95–96, 155, 178,
        245n74, 269n8
    hand-over-heart salute, 115
    Navesink Lighthouse flag-raising, 57,
        237n56
    Pledge refusals in, 82–84, 95–96, 155
    school flag display laws, 51–52, 238nn3,4
New Mexico, 238nn4,5
New Republic (magazine), 105
New York
    flag salute laws, 52–54, 78, 156, 164,
        239n6, 244n74, 266n36
    legislature, Pledge recitation by, 180–81
    Pledge refusals by students, 90, 97–99,
        156–61, 248n38, 263nn9,10,
        264nn12–14
    Pledge refusals by teachers, 164–66,
        265n25
    school flag display laws, 238n4
    "under God" clause challenged in, 140
New York City
    Balch salute used in schools, 18, 40–41,
        42(illus.)
    Bush, Pataki, and Giuliani Pledge recita-
        tion, 187, 189(illus.)
    Columbus Day celebration (1892), 21
    flag displays before 1900, 3–4, 15–16
    flag saluted in, 42(illus.), 60–61(illus.),
        113–15
    Hirsch Fund Schools pledge of alle-
        giance, 239n13
    immigrants, 38–39
    military drilling in public schools, 237n47
    Pledge refusals in, 84–85, 156–60, 164,
        263nn9,10
New York Civil Liberties Union, 157
New York Herald Tribune, 107–8
New York Times, 83–84, 140, 158
Nicholls, Carleton, 92–93, 95, 247nn24,25
Nicholls v. Lynn, 92–93, 95, 247nn24,25
Ninth Circuit Court of Appeals, and *New-
    dow,* ix–xi, 144–46, 150–51. *See also*
    Goodwin, Alfred; *Newdow* case

Nixon, Richard, 269n8
North Carolina, 271n26
North Dakota, 51–52, 238nn3,4, 271n26
Nowinski, Peter A., 142
Nyquist, Ewald, 159, 264n13

Oakman, Charles, 133, 257n35, 258n42
O'Connor, Sandra Day, 144, 146–51. See also *Newdow* case
Ohio, 85–86, 94, 238n4
Oklahoma, 88–89, 108, 238nn4,5, 271n26
O'Leary, Cecilia Elizabeth, xix, 233n19, 238n5, 278n19
Olson, Theodore, 262n79
Oregon, 78, 186, 238n5
Our Country (Strong), xii, xv, 34–37, 38, 123–24, 253n7
Owens, Bill, 206

Palmer, A. Mitchell, 76
Palmer, Joethelia, 265n35
Palmer, John, 15, 232n13
Palmer v. Board of Education, 265n35
Parents and Teachers Association (PTA), 63, 115
Parker, John M., 76
Parkhurst, Charles H., 39
Parochial schools
    and Columbian school celebration, 22, 230n52
    Protestant anxieties about Catholic, 35, 123, 234n27
    See also Private schools
Parton, James, 45
Pataki, George, 187, 189(illus.)
Patriotism, 215
    Balch on teaching, 40–41, 53, 235nn37,38, 236n40
    Bellamy on, 29–31, 214
    Jensen on, 190, 214
    Lundquist on compulsory, 168–69
    and myth of the civic nation, 215
    Nation on, 52–53

New York *Manual of Patriotism*, 52–54, 239n6
    Pledge as embodiment of, 24–25, 79–80
    post–September 11 resurgence, 207
    Upham's nostalgic concept of, 47–49
    Ventura on voluntary nature of, 194
    and vigilantism, 76, 105–9, 244n68
    Washington state's mandating of, 71–75, 243nn53,56
    Youth's Companion editorial on teaching, 6–7
    See also Flag salute laws; Pledge of Allegiance, refusals; Schoolhouse flag movement
Pawlenty, Tim, 194, 197–98
Pennsylvania
    mandatory Pledge law, 200–203, 206, 274n53
    Pledge refusal cases, 93–94, 99–105, 249nn40,42,47 (see also *Gobitis* case)
    school flag display laws, 51, 200, 238nn3,5
Pitts, Joe, x
Pledge of Allegiance
    Adams on power of, 80
    and American exceptionalism, 213, 219–20 (see also American national identity)
    anxieties underlying, xi–xiv, 32–33, 213, 221–22 (see also Immigrants, anxiety about; Materialism, anxiety about; Radicals, anxiety about)
    authorship of, disputed, 57, 240n26, 242n42, 259n43
    Bellamy on power of, 69, 71, 80, 221
    Bellamy's goals in writing, 25, 28–29, 50, 214
    Bellamy's plan to spread, 68–71, 123
    children's books portray, 24, 26
    children's understanding of, 150, 262n81
    corporations resist, 276n66
    likened by Bellamy to Lord's Prayer, 69, 123
    local governments recite, 179–80, 184–88

Pledge of Allegiance *(continued)*
   loyalty oath compared to, 209–13, 219
   meanings attached to, 24–29 (*see* Pledge
     of Allegiance, wording of)
   National Flag Conferences (1923, 1924)
     amend, 65, 67, 241n35
   original version, 1–2, 3(illus.), 19, 28–29,
     210, 229n48
   paradoxes of, 219–22
   Reagan on, 176–77
   set to music, 137
   spread of, in first half of twentieth cen-
     tury, 50–80
   Stone's radio recitation, 116,
     117–19(illus.)
   Upham's role in creation of, 18–19
   See also National Columbian Public
     School Celebration; Schoolhouse flag
     movement
Pledge of Allegiance, laws requiring
   constitutionality, 90–91, 95–96, 103–5,
     111–12, 154–73, 202–3, 206
   legal limits tested, 198–206
   public support for, 173, 194, 267n41
   September 11 terror attacks' effect on
     spread of, 193–98, 206–7
   See also Flag salute laws; *and specific states*
Pledge of Allegiance, politicization of
   in New Jersey gubernatorial campaign
     (mid-1960s), 178
   during the early 1980s, 179–82
   in 1988 presidential campaign, 26, 151,
     153–54, 170, 172–73, 177–78,
     181–82, 269n9
   after 1988, 182–87
   Reagan and, 175–78, 179
   after September 11 attacks, 187–208
Pledge of Allegiance, refusals
   ACLU defends, 86–88, 92–93, 98, 100,
     102, 161–62, 246n14, 264n10
   Bible as basis for, 89, 96–98, 248n37
   desegregation, protest against, 154
   by Jehovah's Witnesses, 91–110,
     247nn24,25, 248n37, 265n35

   by noncitizens, 83–84, 191
   racial inequality, as protest against,
     155–63, 165–68
   religious beliefs as motive for, 85–113
   right to sit during Pledge, 156–63, 165,
     192, 263n10
   socialist and Communist, 84, 90
   students suspended/expelled for Pledge
     refusal, 82–94, 99–100, 108, 157–59,
     161, 198–200
   by teachers, 163–71, 265nn25,35,
     266n39
   Vietnam War, as opposition to, 156,
     163–64
   violence resulting from, 76, 93–94,
     105–9, 244n68, 250n60
   "with liberty and justice for all," based on
     reading of, 155–63, 165–68
   See also Flag salute, refusals; Supreme
     Court, U.S.; *and specific individuals,*
     cases, and states
Pledge of Allegiance, wording of
   "allegiance," 210–11
   "indivisible," 25, 71
   "my flag" changed to "the flag," 65–66,
     241n35
   "of America" added, 67
   original version, 1–2, 3(illus.), 19, 28–29,
     210, 229n48
   "pledge," 211–12
   "under God" (*see* "Under God" clause)
   "with liberty and justice for all," 28–29,
     71, 214, 220 (*see also* "With liberty
     and justice for all")
Plywacki, Wladyslaw, 128
Powell, Garland, 65–66, 242n37
Pratt, Francis, 14
Prayer in schools, 124, 140, 145, 175, 201
Preston, J. R., 216
Prinos, Anna and Pauline (sister), 94
Private schools
   created to avoid saying the Pledge, 86, 94
   mandatory Pledge laws applied to,
     200–202

Proctor, Edna Dean, 18. *See also* "Columbia's Banner"
PTA. *See* Parents and Teachers Association
Public schools
Americanizing immigrants, 30, 35,
38–39, 216
Balch salute used, 18, 55–56
citizenship curriculum requirements,
77–78
Columbian school celebration, 19–23,
45–46, 229n51
early-twentieth-century flag salutes,
54–56, 57, 58, 59–62(illus.), 239n13
English-only instruction, 78
flag display laws, 51–52, 185, 188–89,
200, 238nn3,5
military instruction, 88, 236n47
prayer and Bible reading in, 123–24,
140, 145, 175, 201
public support for mandatory Pledge in,
173, 194, 267n41
students suspended/expelled from, for
Pledge refusal, 82–94, 99–100, 108,
157–59, 161, 198–200
teachers dismissed for "subversive propaganda," 77
teachers' refusal to say/lead Pledge,
163–71, 265nn25,35, 266n39
teaching patriotism and citizenship, 5–6,
16, 20–21, 23, 30–31, 40–41, 46, 216
See also Flag salute laws; National
Columbian Public School Celebration; Pledge of Allegiance, refusals;
Schoolhouse flag movement
Puritan loyalty oaths, 212, 277n9

Quirico, Francis, 171–72, 266n39

Rabaut, Louis, 131, 133–34, 136–37,
256n28, 258n40
Racial inequality, Pledge refusals in protest
of, 155–63, 165–68
Radicals, anxiety about
American Legion's, 77

Bellamy's, 68–71, 232n31
National Flag Conference pervaded by,
63
Pledge shaped by, xiii, 63, 68–80, 215
state flag salute statutes as product of,
71–80, 244nn64–66
Washington state's patriotism statutes as
product of, 71–75, 243nn53–56,
244n64–66
widespread nature of, 71, 75–76, 215
See also Communism, anxiety about; Socialism, anxiety about
Rantissi, Abd al-Aziz, 279n28
Reagan, Ronald, 175–79, 218, 220,
279n31
Refusals. *See* Pledge of Allegiance, refusals
Rehnquist, William, 146–47, 150
Reiter, Mady, 195–97, 273n43
Religion and government
Bellamy's understanding of, 121–23,
253n7
before the 1950s, 123–26, 128–29,
217–18
ceremonial deism, 140–42, 148–49,
217–18, 260n65
under Eisenhower, 125–28, 255n16
establishment clause jurisprudence,
140–52, 261n73, 262n82
faith and American national identity,
127–29, 131, 216–21, 278nn23,24,26
George W. Bush's views, x–xi, 217–18
Reagan and, 175–78, 218
religion in public schools, 122–24, 140,
145, 175, 201
Republican platform (1988 and 1992),
182, 269n15
Strong's understanding of, 123–24,
253n7
See also "Under God" clause
Religious belief(s)
anxiety about materialism and self-
seeking shaped by, xii
of Bellamy, 9–11, 22, 27–28, 121–24,
226n22

Religious belief(s) *(continued)*
  Christian socialism, 27–29, 226n22,
    231n8, 232n13
  Communism lacking in, 125–29, 132, 134
  Hartz's narrative ignores, xii
  Pledge refusals motivated by, 85–113
  of Upham, 9–11, 122
  See also Religion and government;
    "Under God" clause
Republicanism, xiii
Republican Party, partisan uses of Pledge.
    See Pledge of Allegiance, politicization
    of; *and specific individuals*
Respect for the American flag, 26, 58, 62,
    76, 79, 82. *See also* Flag, American;
    Flag etiquette; Flag salutes, physical
Rhode Island, 78, 238n4, 244n74
Richards, Donald, 160
"Ritual for Teaching Patriotism in the Pub-
    lic Schools" (American Flag Manufac-
    turing Co.), 55
Roberts, Harold, 14–15, 17
Rogin, Michael, xv–xvi
Roosevelt, Franklin D.
  Frankfurter and, 103
  Gridley Adams and, 67, 251n75
  on the Pledge, 116
  "under God" phrase used by, 125,
    254n12
Roudabush, Charles E., 99–102
Rowland, John G., 182
Russell, Francis, 57
Russo, Susan, 165–66, 265n25
Russo v. Central School District, 165–66,
    265n25
Rutherford, Joseph, 91–93
Rutledge, Wiley, 111

Sandstrom, Grace, 97–99, 248n38
Sandstrom, New York v., 97–99, 248n38
San Francisco, 55
Scalia, Antonin, 262n82
School flag display laws, 51–52, 185,
    188–89, 200, 238nn3–5

Schoolhouse flag movement
  anxieties about immigrants a spur to, 4,
    30–31, 37–43, 49
  origins, 2–4, 15–16, 38–43, 47
  Pledge's origins in, 2, 18–19
  Youth's Companion and, 5–9, 23, 44, 47,
    224n9, 236n44
  See also National Columbian Public
    School Celebration; School flag
    display laws
Schools, industrial, 40, 42(illus.)
Schools, private. *See* Parochial schools;
    Private schools
Schools, public. *See* Public schools
Schuker, Louis, 157–58, 264n10
Schwartz, Milton, 143
Seattle general strike, 72–74,
    243nn53–56
Seattle Post-Intelligencer, 73–75
Sedition conviction for ridiculing flag, 76
Senate, U.S. *See* Congress, U.S.
Separation of church and state. *See*
    Constitution, U.S.; Religion and
    government; "Under God" clause
September 11 terror attacks
  Bush 2004 campaign use of images
    from, 208
  Pledge of Allegiance after, 187–98
Shapiro, Steven, 143
Sherman, John, 16–17
Sherman, Rob, 142, 218
Sloatman, David, 248n38
Smith, Anthony, 219
Smith, Bob, 184, 270n19
Socialism, anxiety about
  Bellamy's, 68–71, 232n13
  in Washington state, 71–75, 243n54,
    244n64
  See also Communism, anxiety about;
    Radicals, anxiety about
Socialist views
  Bellamy's, 25–32, 231n6, 232nn10,13,
    233n19
  Pledge refusals motivated by, 84, 90

See also Christian socialism; *Looking Backward*

"Song of Columbus Day" (Brown), 18, 18

So Proudly We Hail! (Adams), 66, 241n35

South Dakota, 238nn3–5

Starr, Ex parte, 76, 244n68

"Star-Spangled Banner, The" (Key), 62–63, 76, 191–92, 244n68

State legislatures, Pledge recitation by, 180–81, 186–87, 271n26. *See also specific states*

State v. Lundquist, 168–70

Stevens, John Paul, 150, 262n82

St. Louis Dispatch, 105

Stone, Harlan, 104–5, 109, 116, 117–19(illus.).

Strong, Anna Louise, 72

Strong, Josiah, xii, xv, 34–38, 123–24, 253n7

Styron, William, 167

Subversives, anxieties about. *See* Communism, anxiety about; Radicals, anxiety about; Socialism, anxiety about

Supreme Court, U.S.
  Barnette case, 110–15, 155, 212 (see also *Barnette* case)
  declines to hear Pledge refusal cases, 97, 166, 249n47
  declines to hear "under God" challenges, 140, 142
  Gobitis case, 102–5, 107–13
  Lee v. Weisman, 144–46
  Newdow case, 143, 146–52, 209 (see also *Newdow* case)
  school prayer and Bible reading banned by, 124, 140, 145

Teachers
  loyalty oaths for, 78, 247n23
  Pledge refusals by, 163–71, 265nn25,35, 266n39
  See also Public schools

"Teaching Patriotism" (*Youth's Companion* editorial), 6–7, 225n12, 235n37

Tennessee, 186, 206

Texas, 154, 187, 206, 271n26

Thomas, Clarence, 146, 150–51, 261n73

Thompson, Jim, 172

Tigert, John, 63

Tremain, Russell, 86–88, 246n14

Truman, Harry, 67, 125, 127, 254n13

"Under God" clause, 121–52
  anti-Communism as spur to addition of, xiii–xiv, 125, 129–37, 216, 259n43
  constitutionality debated, ix, 132–33, 138, 140–52, 257n40 (see also *Newdow* case)
  constitutional amendment possible, 143–44
  history of phrase, 122, 124–26
  meanings, 138–39, 141–42, 147–50, 216–19, 261n74, 262n78
  not in original Pledge, 121–22, 259n43
  objections to, 138–42, 149
  Pledge amended to include, 129–37, 255n26, 256nn27–30, 257nn35–40, 258nn41,42, 259nn43–46
  reactions to Ninth Circuit *Newdow* ruling, ix–xi, 217
  Reagan's use of, 175–78
  and Republican platform (1988 and 1992), 182, 269n15
  trouble adjusting to addition of, 139–40

Unitarians, "under God" clause opposed by, 138, 259n53

United Nations, 66

United States Flag Association, 79, 80, 115–16, 120, 251n72

Upham, James B.
  background and religious outlook, 7–13, 122, 225n16, 227n29
  on Balch's pledge, 123
  Bellamy assigned to work with, 10, 47
  Bellamy on, 237n49
  in Civil War, 7, 225n16
  and the Columbian school celebration, 8, 14, 18–19, 21, 23, 45, 227n33

Upham, James B. *(continued)*
  on the enduring nature of the Pledge, 50
  immigrants, anxiety about, 49
  Lyceum League revived, 36
  as Masonic Knight Templar, 47–48, 122,
    237n51
  materialism, anxiety about, 7–8, 48–49
  Navesink Lighthouse flag-raising speech,
    237n56
  and the origins of the Pledge, 18–19
  patriotic nostalgia of, 47–49
  Pledge copies printed, 56
  raised-arm salute invented by, 19–20,
    44, 115
  and the *Youth's Companion* schoolhouse
    flag effort, 7–9, 44, 49, 225n15,
    236n44
  See also *Youth's Companion*
Upham, James, Rev. (father), 11,
    226nn25,26
Upham, John (ancestor), 12–13
Upham, Joshua (grandfather), 11, 226n26
Upham, Warren (cousin), 259n43
Utah, 207, 238n5, 275nn62,64

Ventura, Jesse, 193–94
Verba, Sidney, 215
Vermont, 238n5
Veterans of Foreign Wars (VFW)
  and the federal flag code, 116, 251n74
  Lipp chided, 162
  Pledge legislation supported by, xiii, 195
  motto, 56, 239n16
  suspension of welfare payments to salute
    protesters urged, 263n5
Vietnam War, Pledge refusals in protest of,
    156, 163–64
Vigilantism, 76, 105–9, 244n68
Virginia, 198–200, 271n26, 273n47,
    275n64

Walker, Francis, 33–34, 234n22
War
  flag display stimulated by, 3

  as model for heroic sacrifice, xii–xiii, 4,
    43–46, 49
  See also Civil War; Military, the; Vietnam
    War
Ward, De Witt C., 4
Warner, William, 5
Washington (state)
  flag salute and citizenship laws, 71–75,
    78, 108–9, 242n52, 243n53,
    244nn64–66, 245n74, 250n59
  legislature, Pledge recitation by, 187,
    271n26
  Pledge refusal cases, 86–88, 246n14
  school flag display laws, 238n4
  Seattle general strike, 72–74, 243nn53–56
Washington, D.C., 59(illus.), 78, 115
Washington's Birthday, 52, 240n20
Waukau, Sarah, 184–86
Webster, Bethuel, 164
Welles, Gideon, 253n10
West Virginia, 106, 110, 115, 271n26. See
    also *Barnette* case
West Virginia v. Barnette. See *Barnette* case
Weyman, Mrs., 65, 241n34
Whalen, Frank, 114
Wheeler, Glen, 187–88
Whiting, Oscar, 84
Wieliewicz, Louis, 93
Wiganowsky, Dave, 184–86
Willard, Cyrus Field, 232n10
Wilson, Woodrow, 217–18
Wisconsin
  patriotic textbook statute, 78
  Pledge controversy in Madison, 184–86
  Pledge statute, 185, 188–93, 271n31,
    272n32
  raised-arm flag salute, 114(illus.)
  school flag display laws, 51, 185, 188–89,
    238n4
"With liberty and justice for all"
  meanings attached to, 24, 26, 28–29, 71,
    138, 147, 214, 220
  Pledge refusals based on, 155–63, 165–68
  proposed changes to, 159–60, 264n14

Women
  flag salute for, 58, 64–65, 242n40
  as National Flag Conference delegates,
    241n34
Women's Literary Union, Bellamy's address
  to, 31
Women's Relief Corps (WRC), 55–56, 65
World's Columbian Exposition, 8, 13–14.
  See also National Columbian Public
  School Celebration
World War I, 58, 84–86
World War II, Pledge refusals during,
  102–14
Wright, Jim, 183
Wyoming, 238n4

Yack, Bernard, 215, 220, 278n18
Youth's Companion (magazine), 5–6, 224n9
  Civil War nostalgia in, 45
  and the Columbian school celebration,
    13–21, 46, 50–51, 224n9, 229n48,51
  Pledge promoted by, 56, 240n20
  racial anxieties in, 37
  and the schoolhouse flag movement,
    5–9, 23, 44, 47, 224n9, 236n44
  Strong's *Our Country* promoted by,
    36–37
  Upham credited by, with authoring
    Pledge, 57, 240n26
  See also Bellamy, Francis; Ford, Daniel
    Sharp; Upham, James B.